TUNDRA

Bringing you high-quality cartoons since 1991!

(And a few low-quality ones as well.)

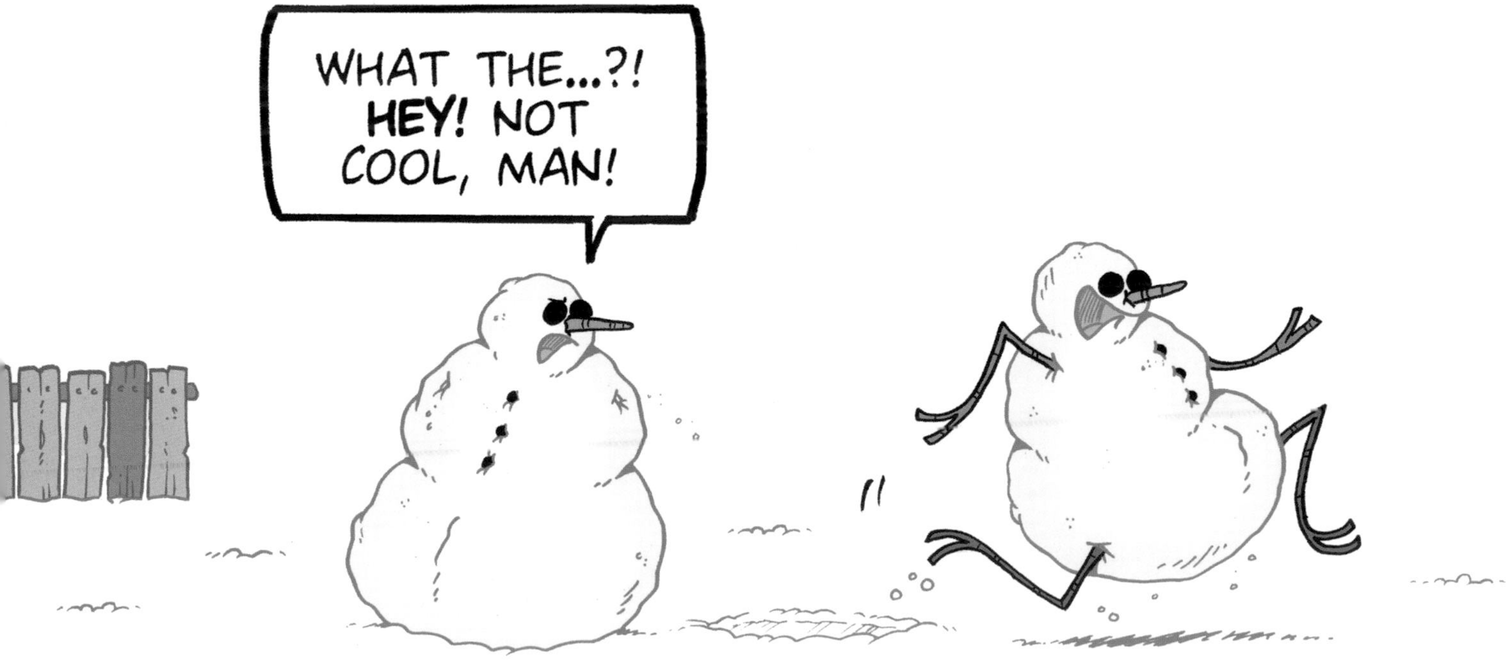
WHAT THE...?! HEY! NOT COOL, MAN!

TUNDRA

Tooth Chattering Fun

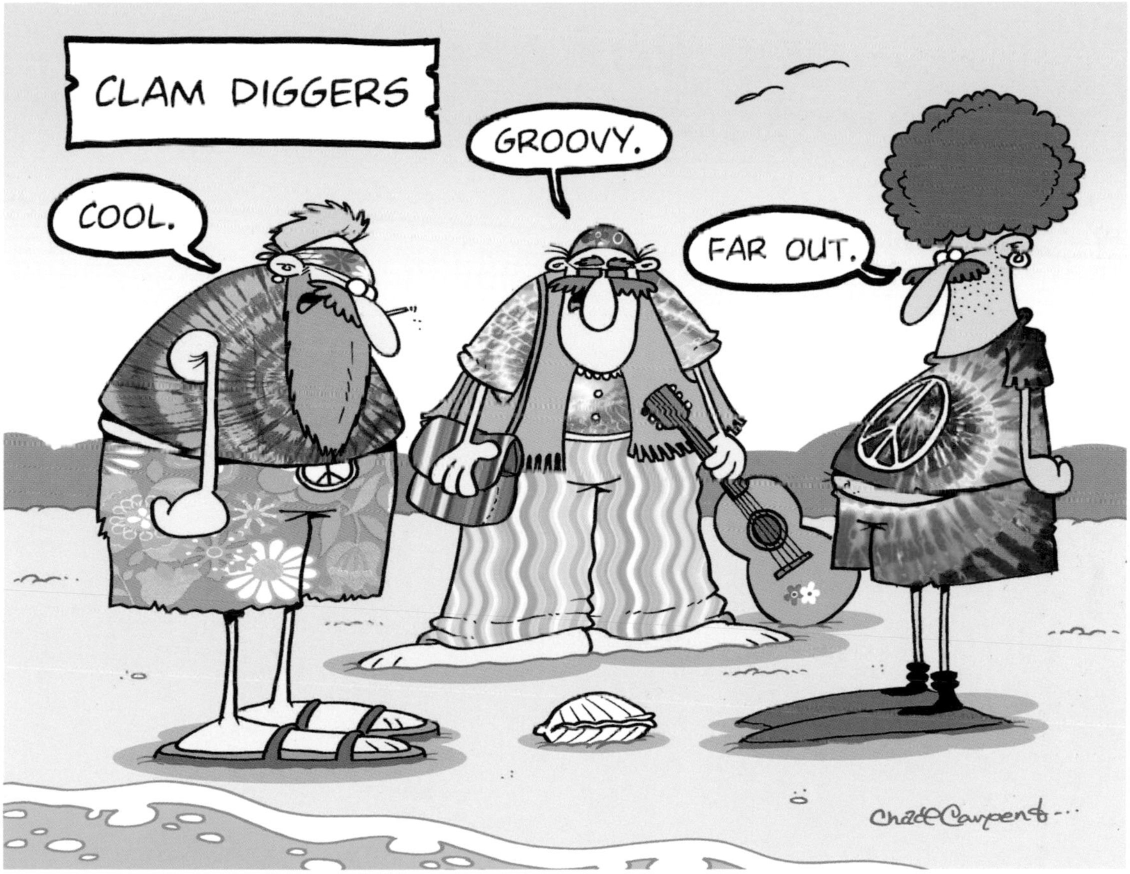

CLAM DIGGERS
COOL.
GROOVY.
FAR OUT.

TUNDRA

Tooth Chattering Fun

Colored by Karen Carpenter

PUBLISHED BY
TUNDRA & ASSOCIATES, INC.
PO BOX 871354
WASILLA, ALASKA 99687

For additional copies of this or other fine TUNDRA merchandise, please visit the Official TUNDRA website at:

www.tundracomics.com

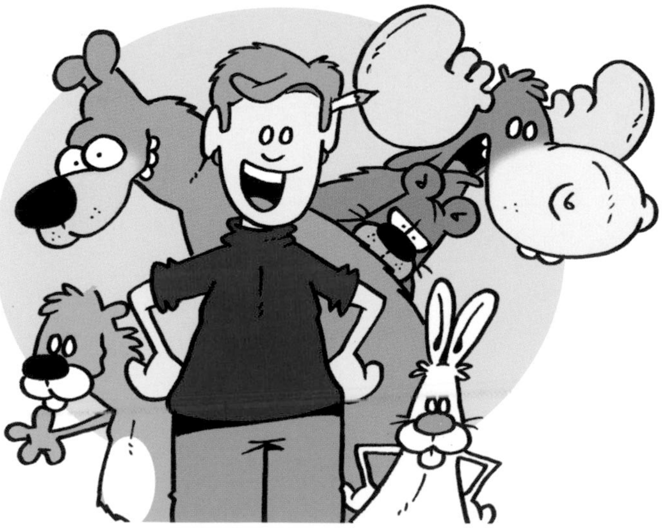

Library of Congress Control Number: 2014936573
First Printing April 2014
ISBN: 978-1-57833-981-5
Book design, Vered R. Mares, Todd Communications
Printed by Samhwa Printing Co., Ltd., Seoul, Korea, through
Alaska Print Brokers, Anchorage, Alaska

To Tyson

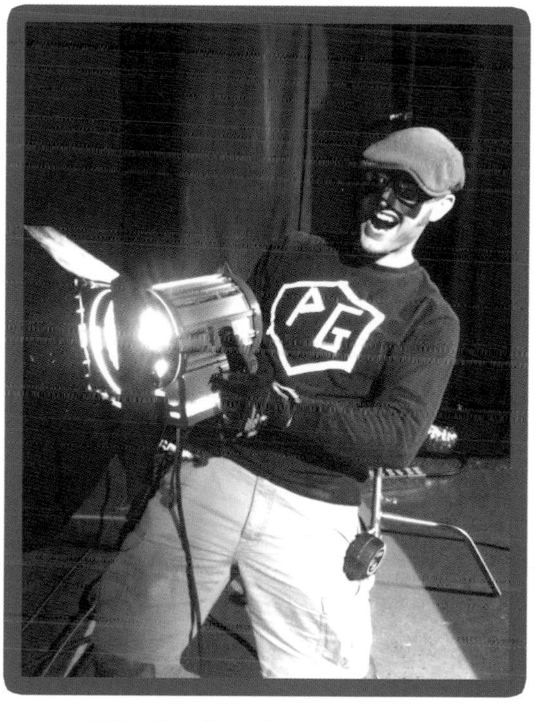
PG

My baby brother

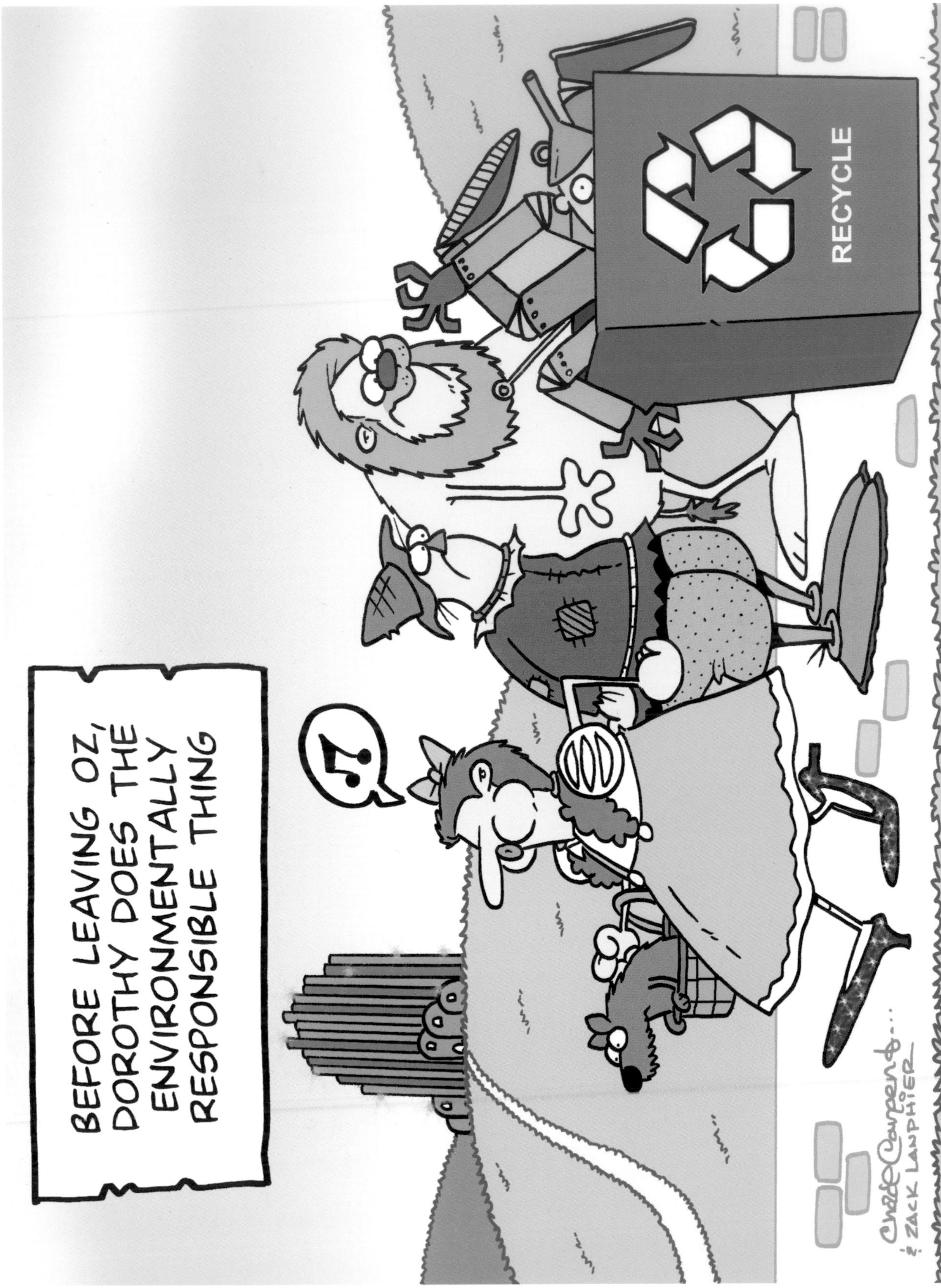
BEFORE LEAVING OZ, DOROTHY DOES THE ENVIRONMENTALLY RESPONSIBLE THING
RECYCLE
ZACK LANPHIER

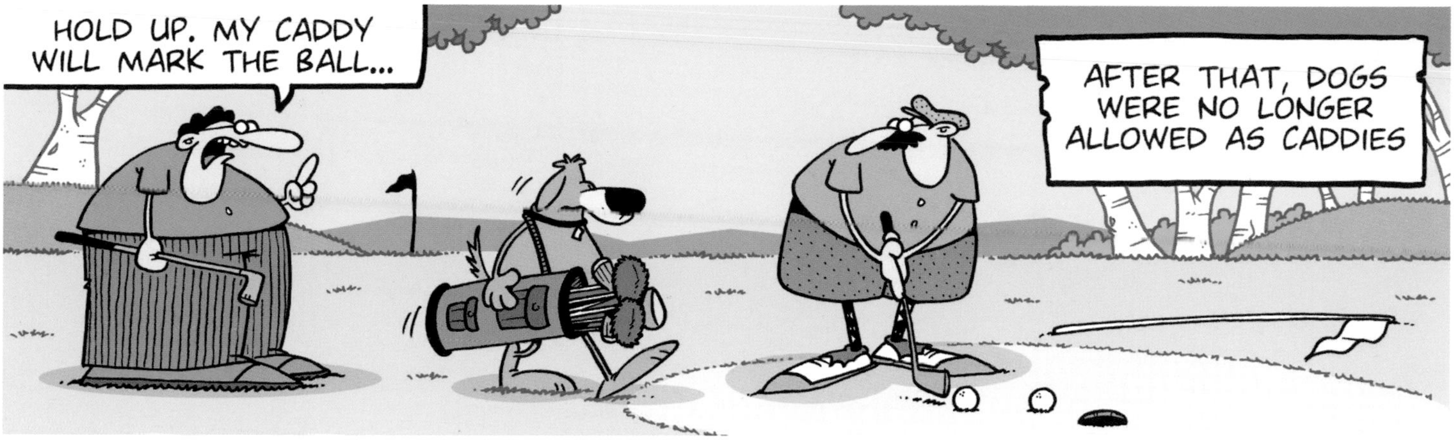
HOLD UP. MY CADDY WILL MARK THE BALL...
AFTER THAT, DOGS WERE NO LONGER ALLOWED AS CADDIES

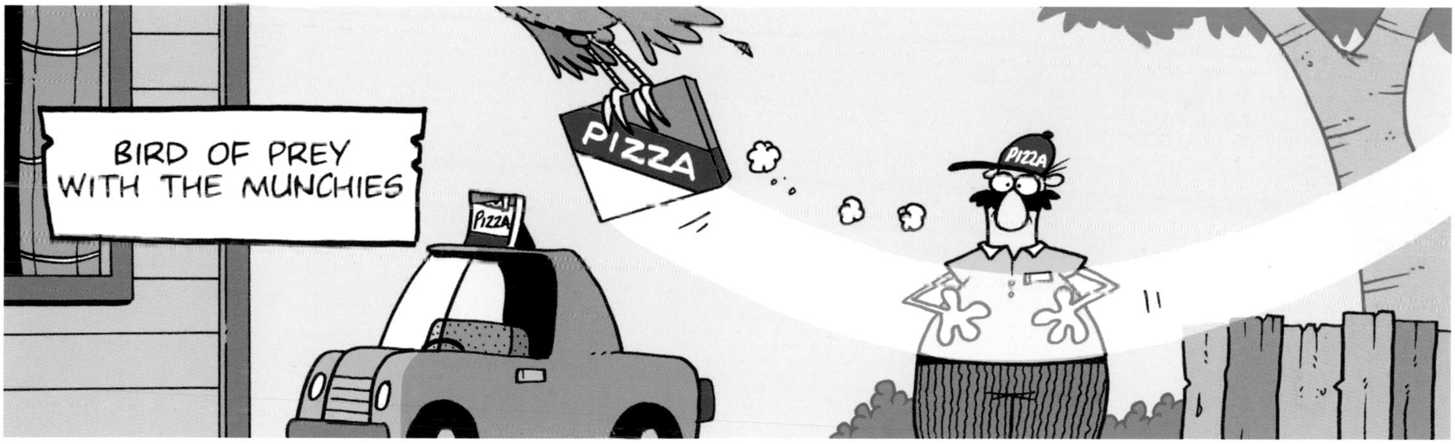
BIRD OF PREY WITH THE MUNCHIES
PIZZA
PIZZA
PIZZA

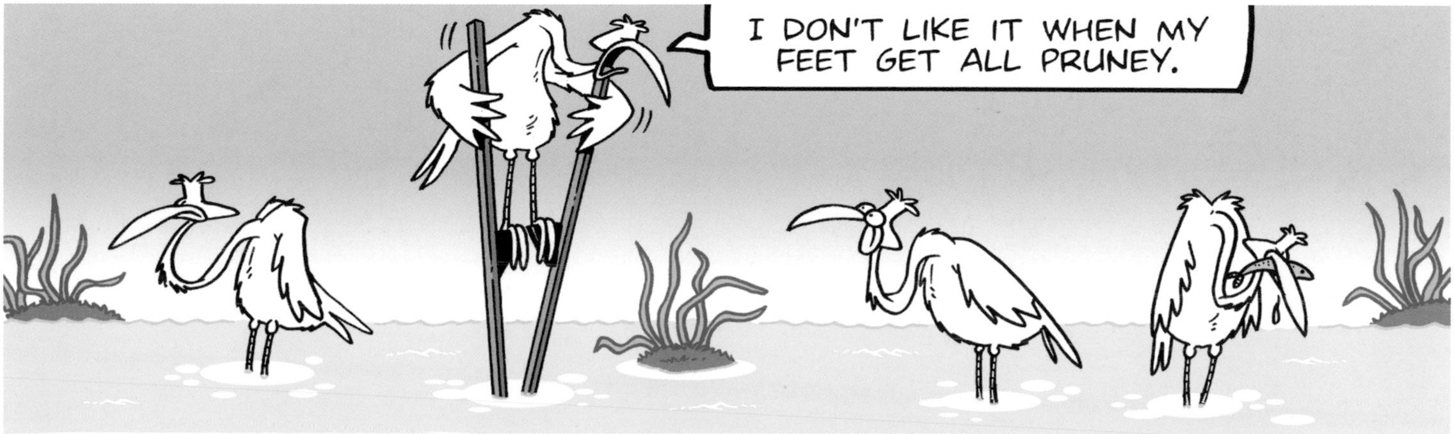
I DON'T LIKE IT WHEN MY FEET GET ALL PRUNEY.

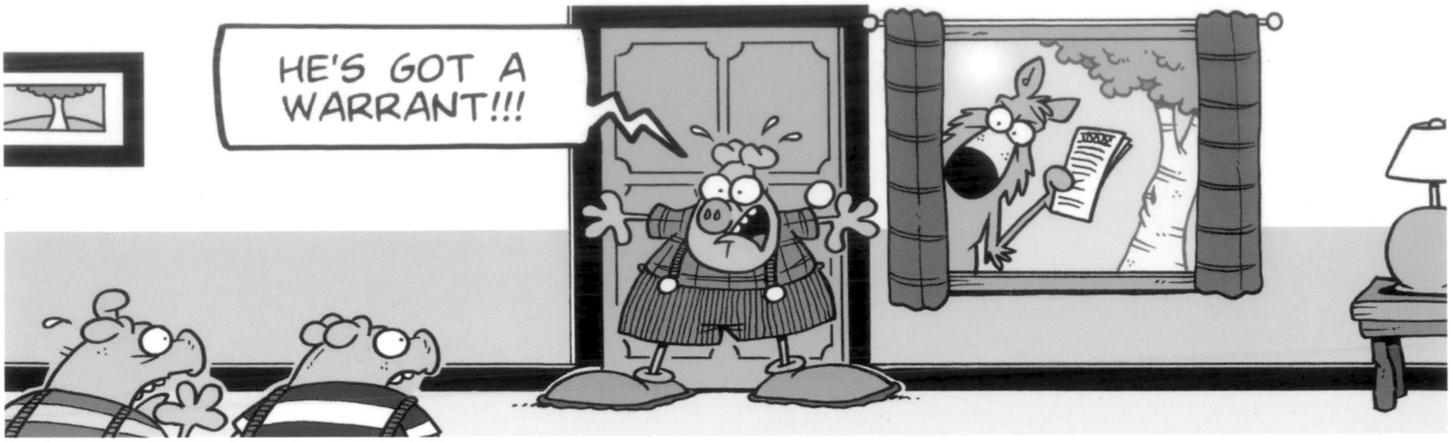
HE'S GOT A WARRANT!!!

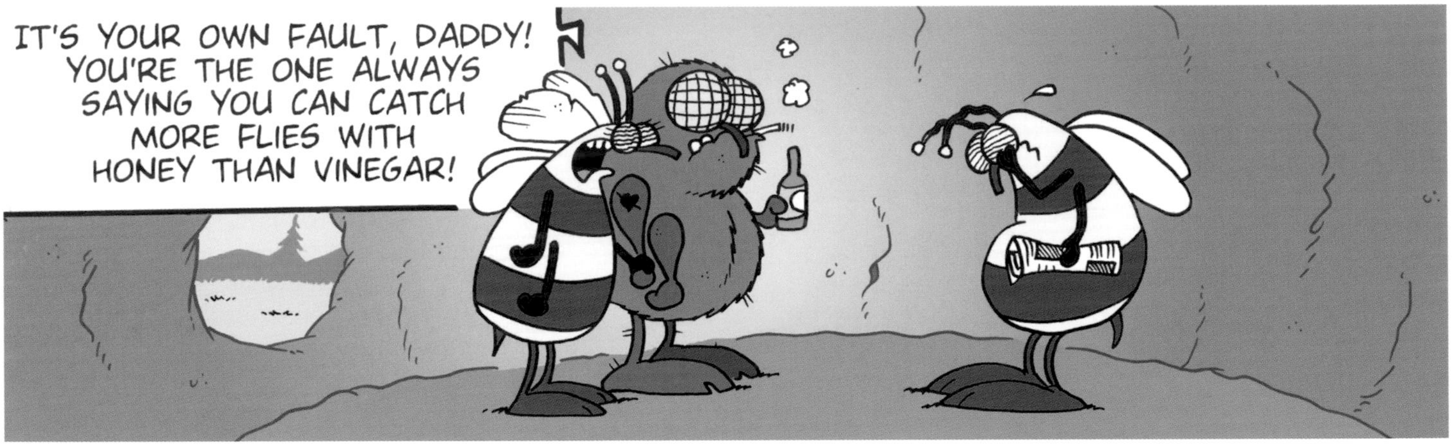
IT'S YOUR OWN FAULT, DADDY! YOU'RE THE ONE ALWAYS SAYING YOU CAN CATCH MORE FLIES WITH HONEY THAN VINEGAR!

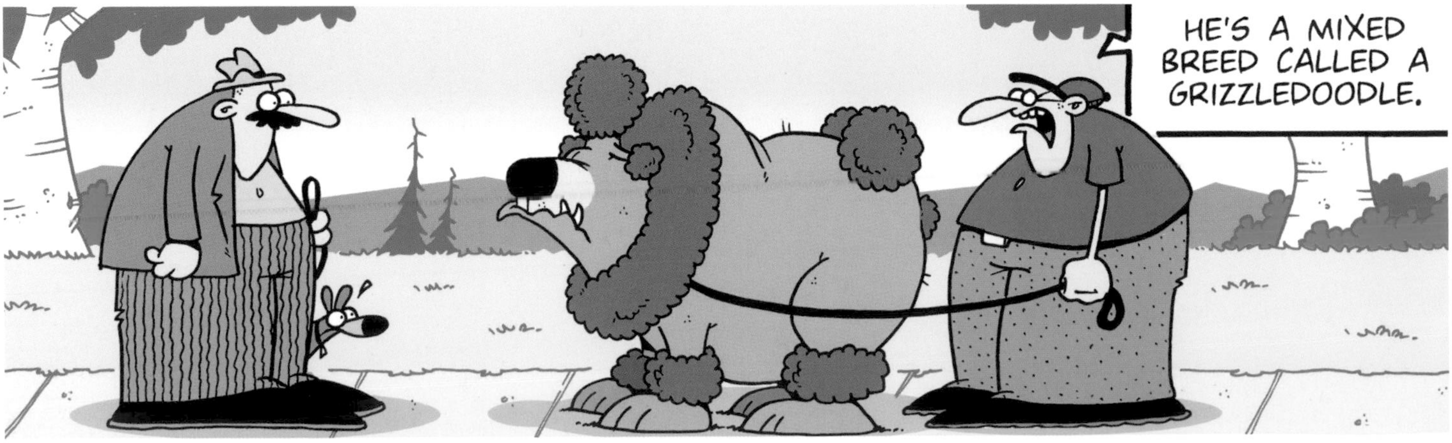
HE'S A MIXED BREED CALLED A GRIZZLEDOODLE.

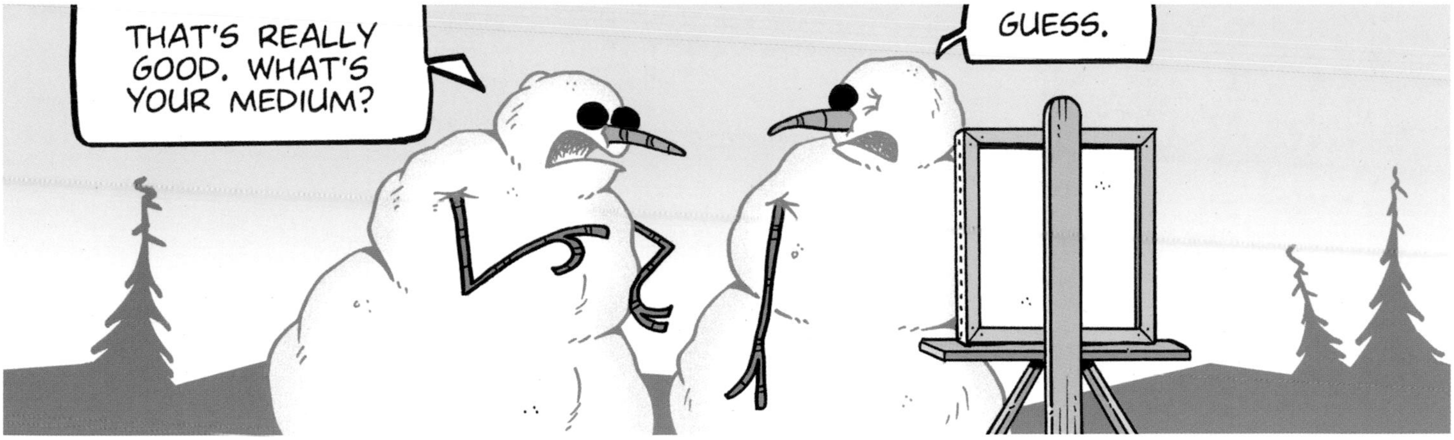
THAT'S REALLY GOOD. WHAT'S YOUR MEDIUM?
GUESS.

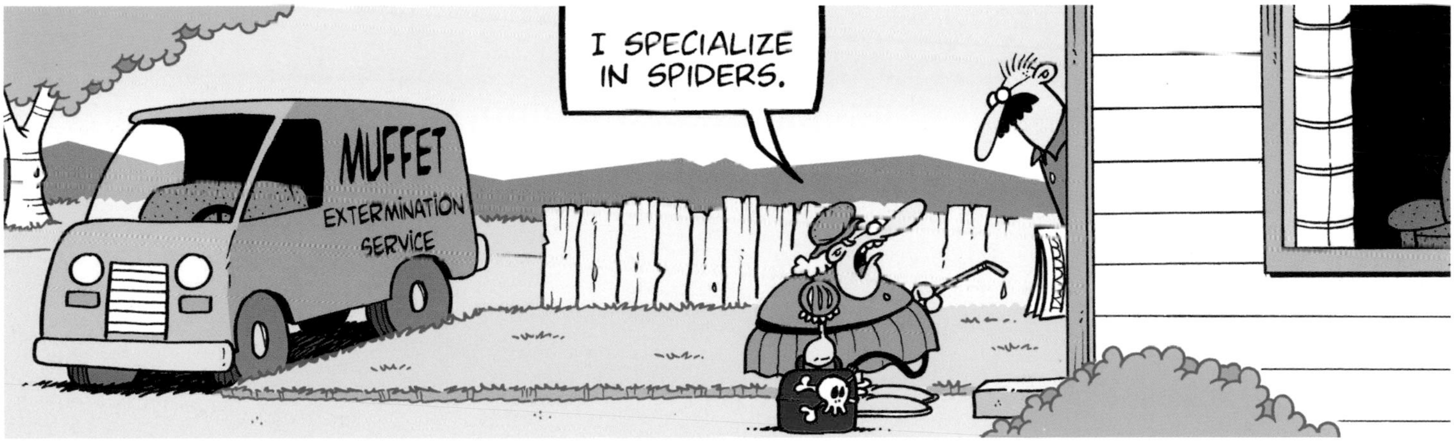
I SPECIALIZE IN SPIDERS.
MUFFET
EXTERMINATION SERVICE

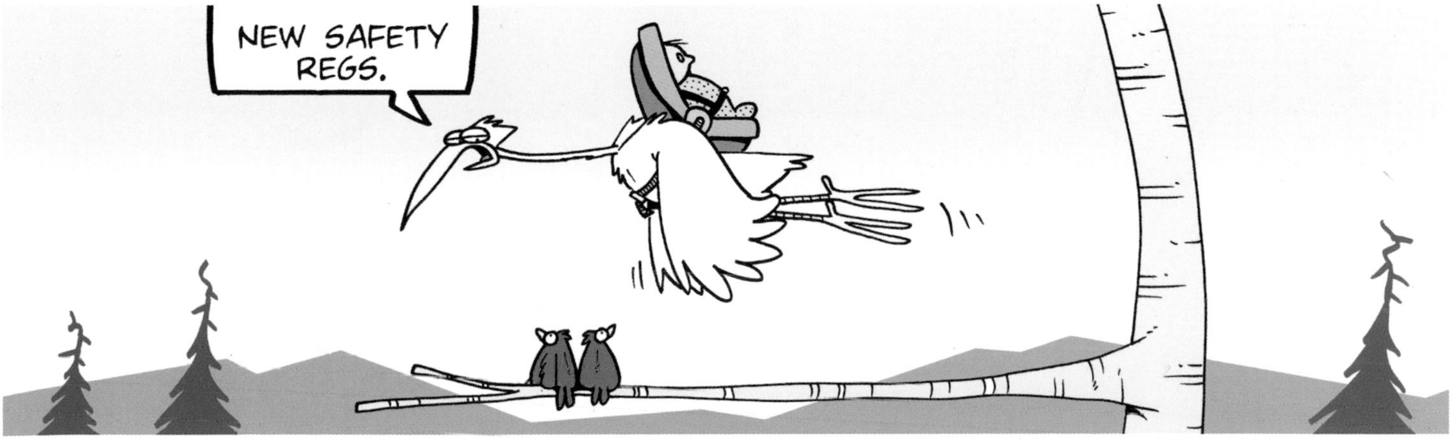
NEW SAFETY REGS.

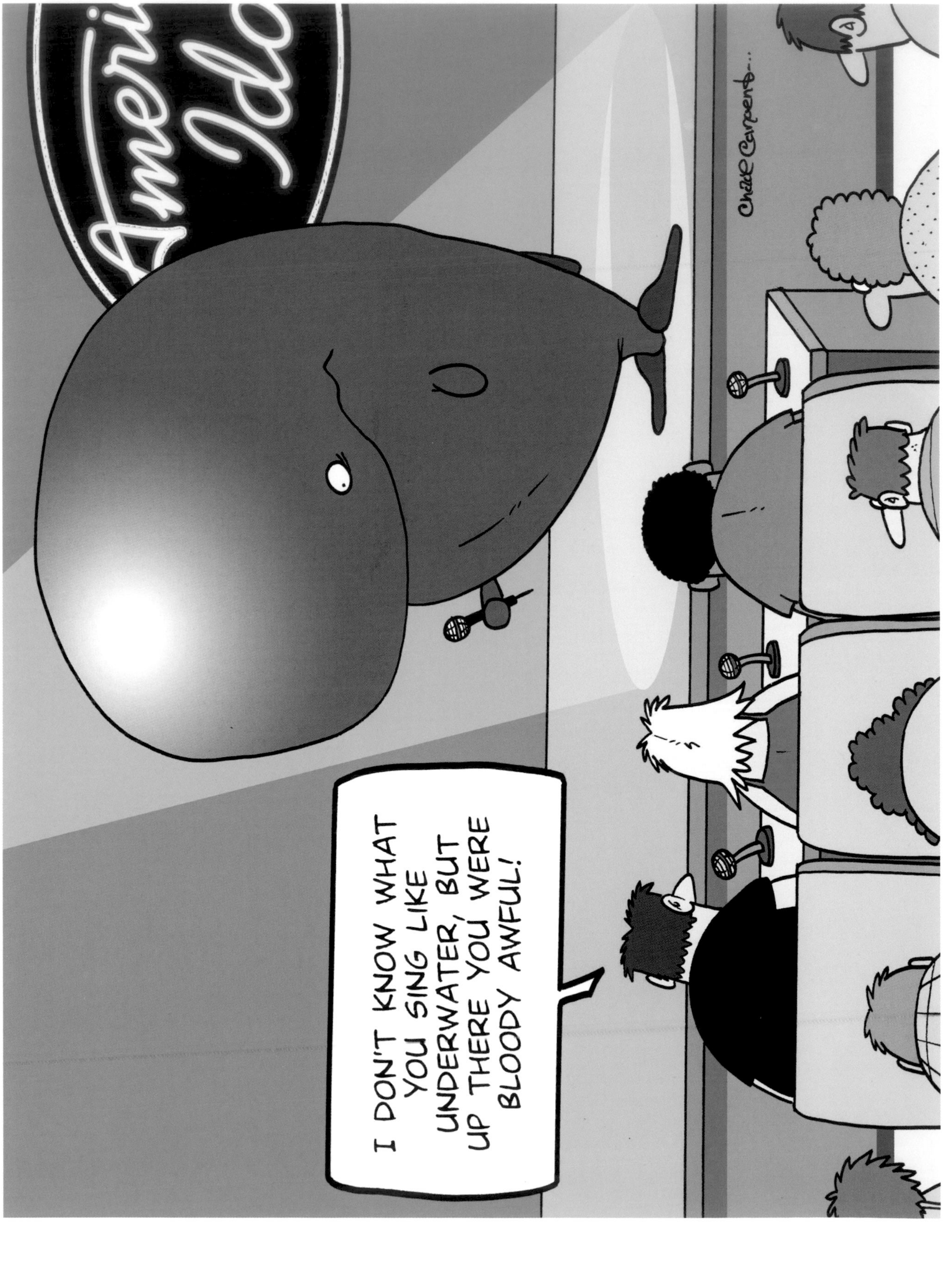
I DON'T KNOW WHAT YOU SING LIKE UNDERWATER, BUT UP THERE YOU WERE BLOODY AWFUL!

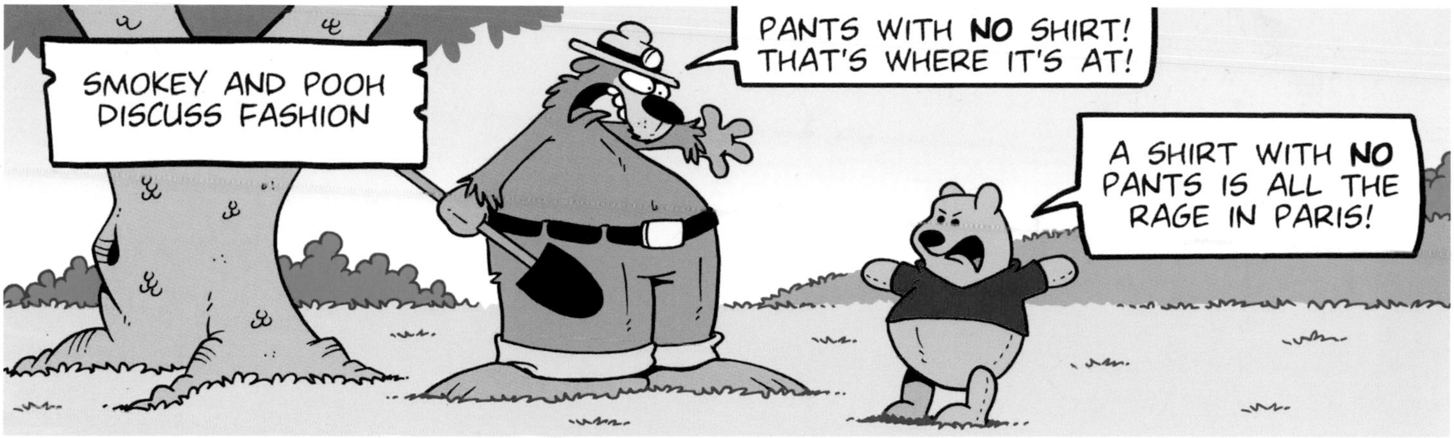
SMOKEY AND POOH DISCUSS FASHION
PANTS WITH NO SHIRT! THAT'S WHERE IT'S AT!
A SHIRT WITH NO PANTS IS ALL THE RAGE IN PARIS!

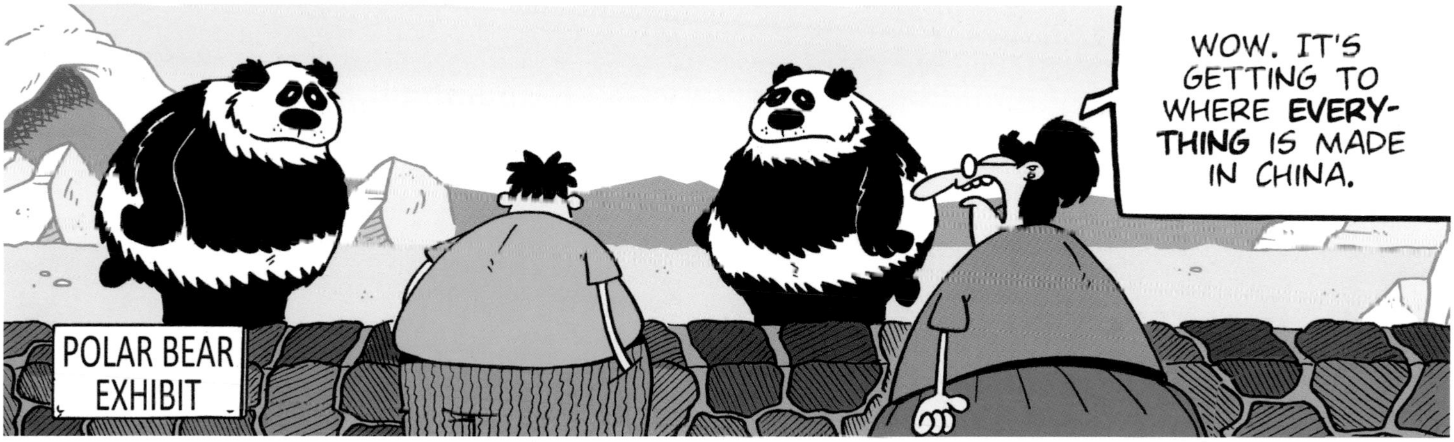
POLAR BEAR EXHIBIT
WOW. IT'S GETTING TO WHERE EVERYTHING IS MADE IN CHINA.

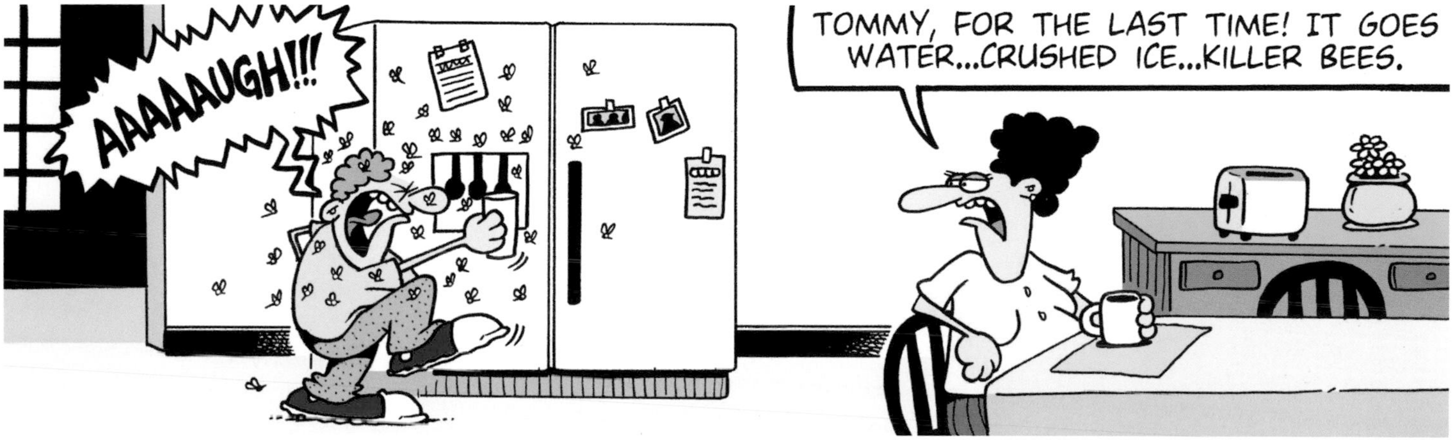
AAAAAUGH!!!
TOMMY, FOR THE LAST TIME! IT GOES WATER...CRUSHED ICE...KILLER BEES.

TUNDRA

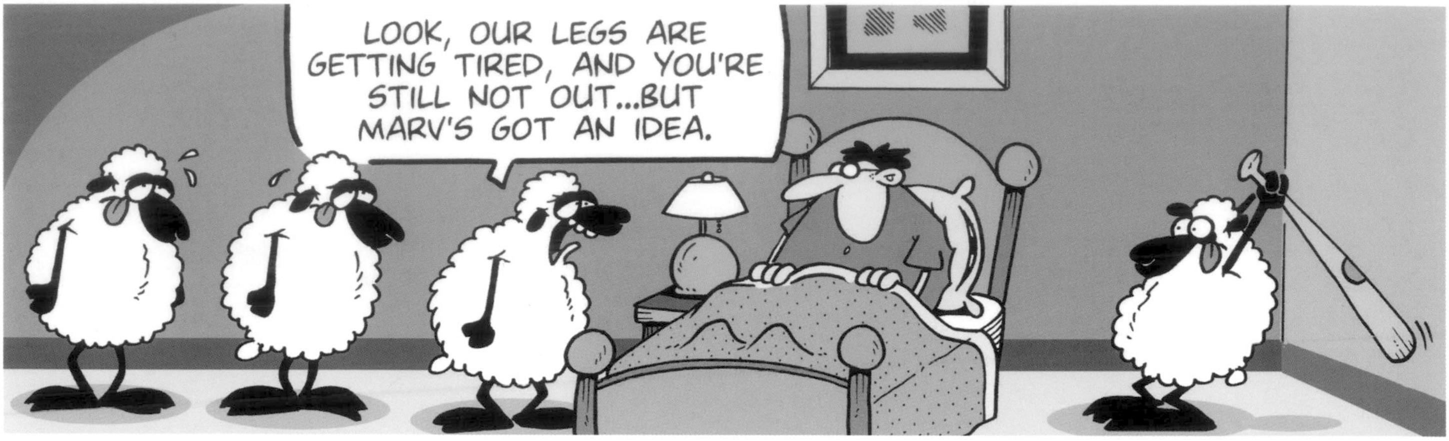
LOOK, OUR LEGS ARE GETTING TIRED, AND YOU'RE STILL NOT OUT...BUT MARV'S GOT AN IDEA.

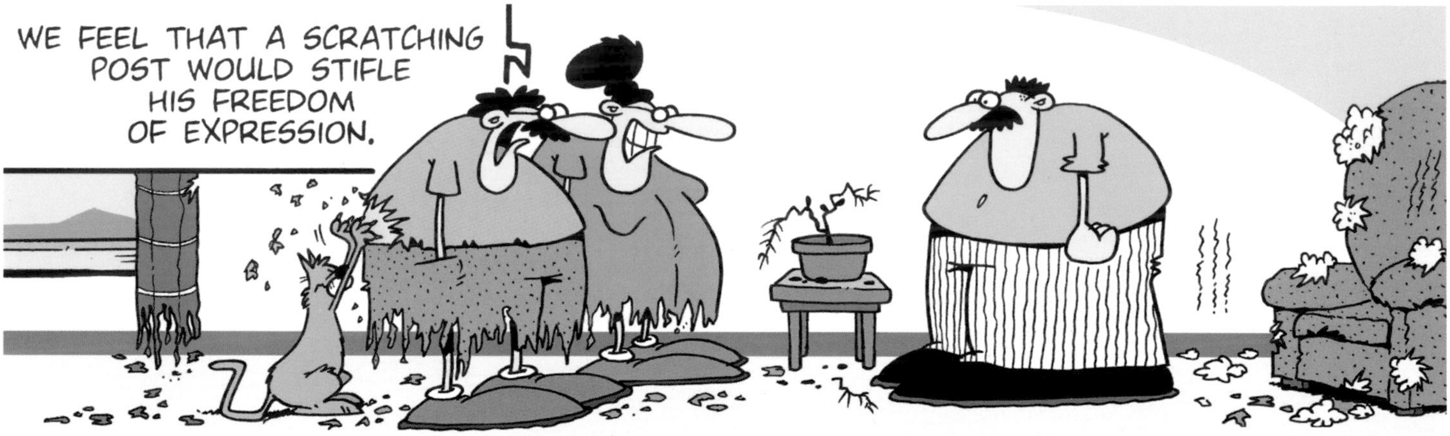
WE FEEL THAT A SCRATCHING POST WOULD STIFLE HIS FREEDOM OF EXPRESSION.

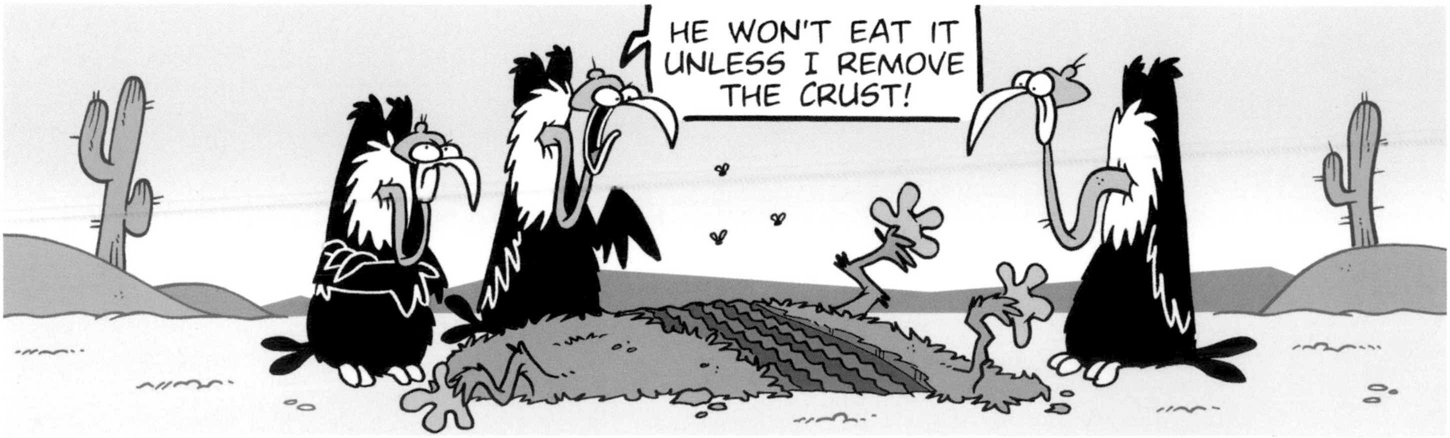
HE WON'T EAT IT UNLESS I REMOVE THE CRUST!

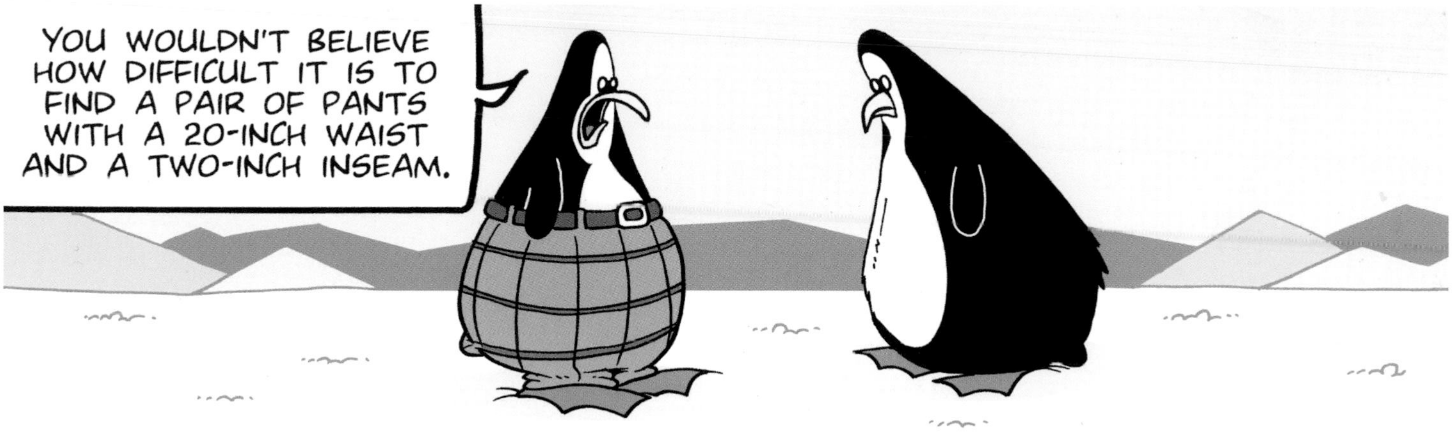
YOU WOULDN'T BELIEVE HOW DIFFICULT IT IS TO FIND A PAIR OF PANTS WITH A 20-INCH WAIST AND A TWO-INCH INSEAM.

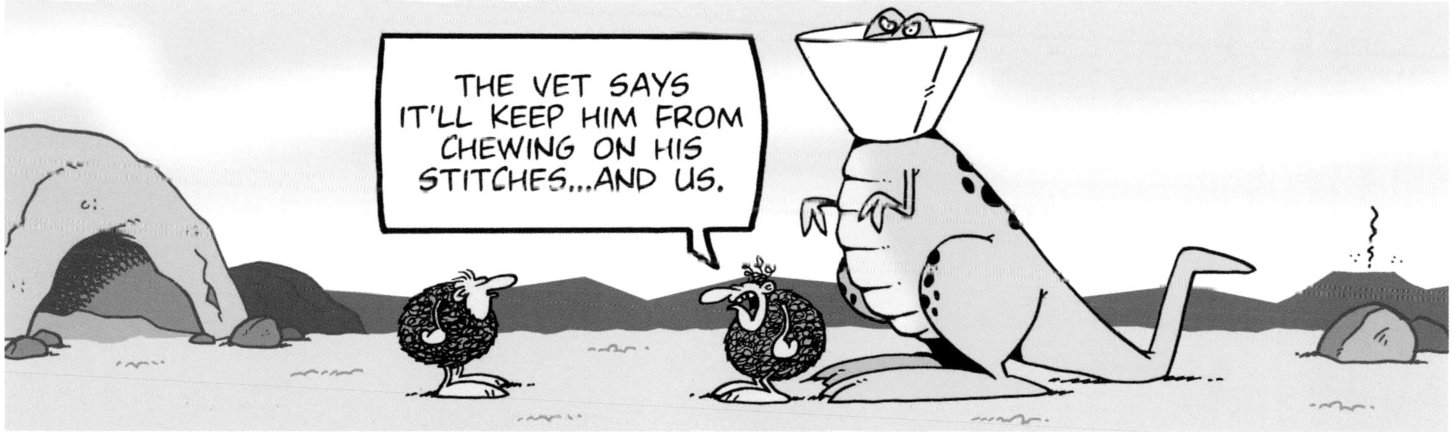
THE VET SAYS IT'LL KEEP HIM FROM CHEWING ON HIS STITCHES...AND US.

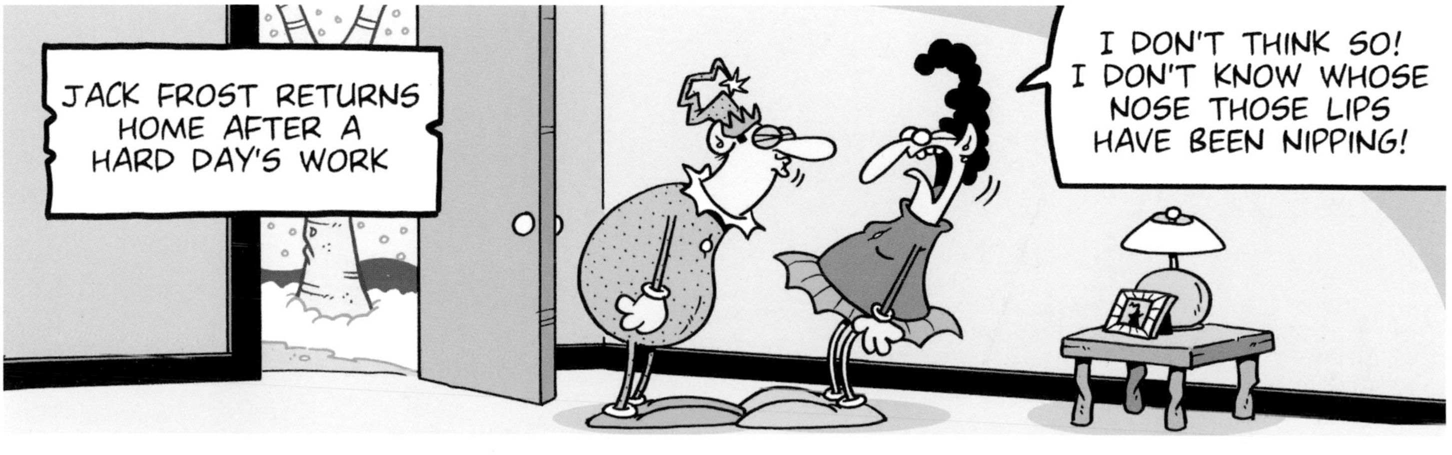
JACK FROST RETURNS HOME AFTER A HARD DAY'S WORK
I DON'T THINK SO! I DON'T KNOW WHOSE NOSE THOSE LIPS HAVE BEEN NIPPING!

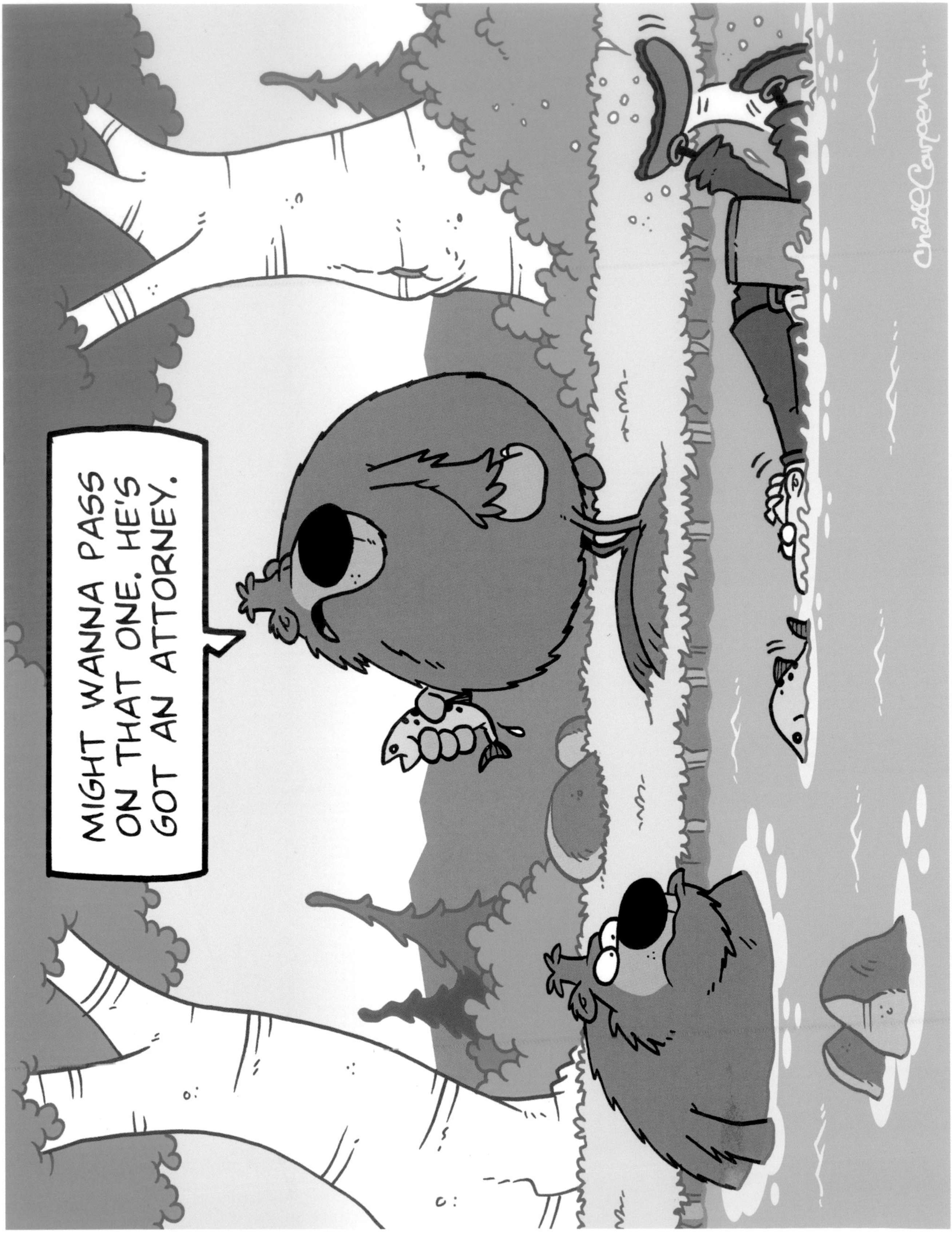
MIGHT WANNA PASS ON THAT ONE. HE'S GOT AN ATTORNEY.

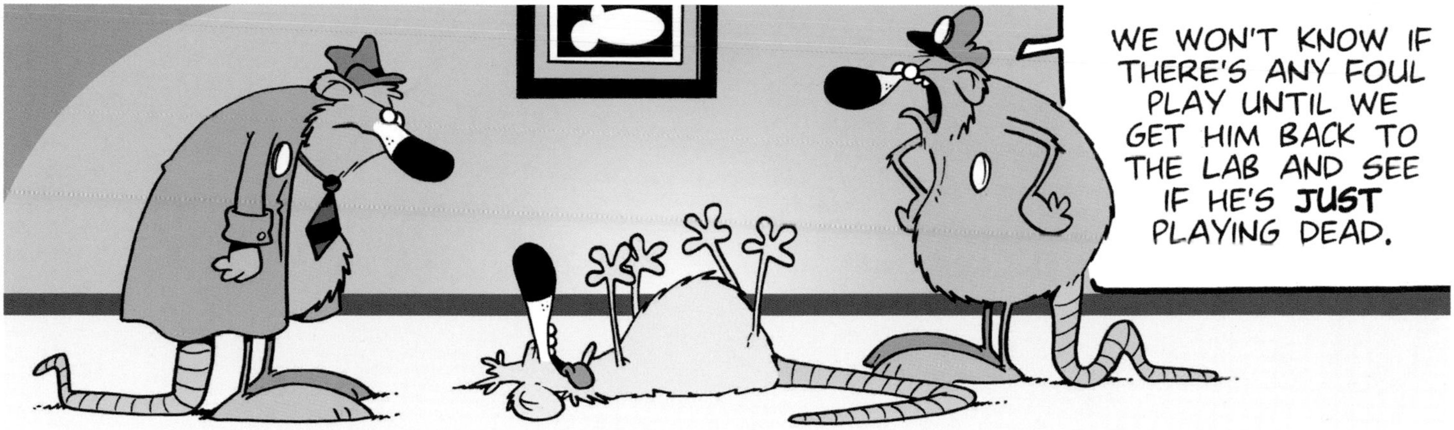
WE WON'T KNOW IF THERE'S ANY FOUL PLAY UNTIL WE GET HIM BACK TO THE LAB AND SEE IF HE'S **JUST** PLAYING DEAD.

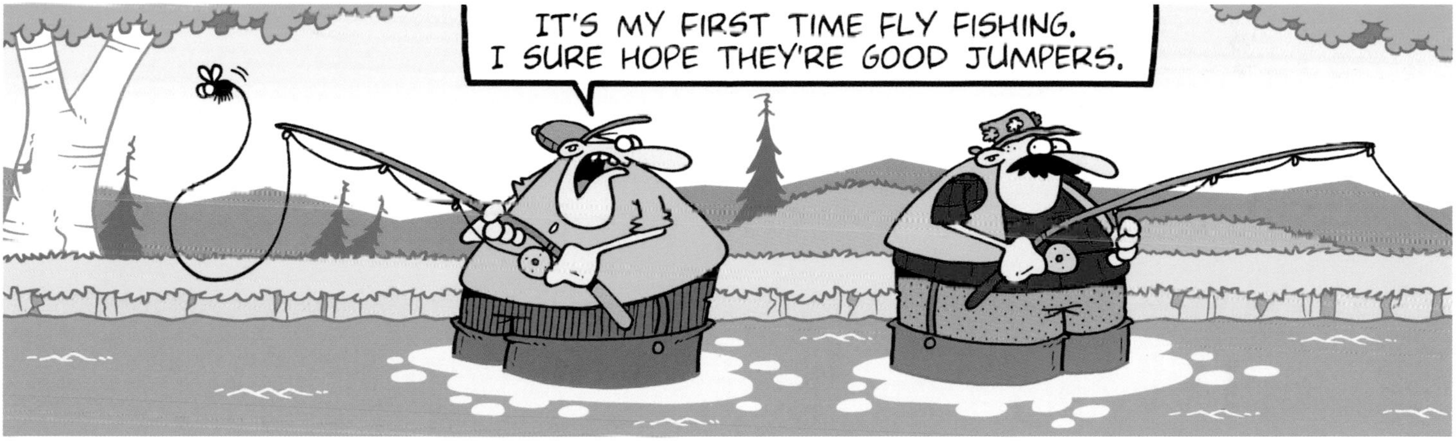
IT'S MY FIRST TIME FLY FISHING. I SURE HOPE THEY'RE GOOD JUMPERS.

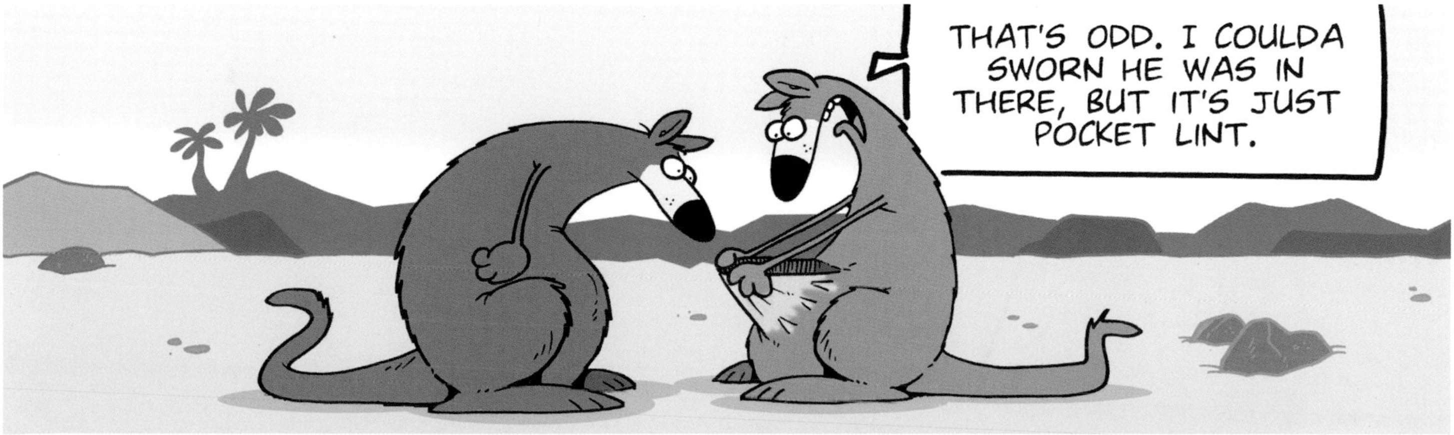
THAT'S ODD. I COULDA SWORN HE WAS IN THERE, BUT IT'S JUST POCKET LINT.

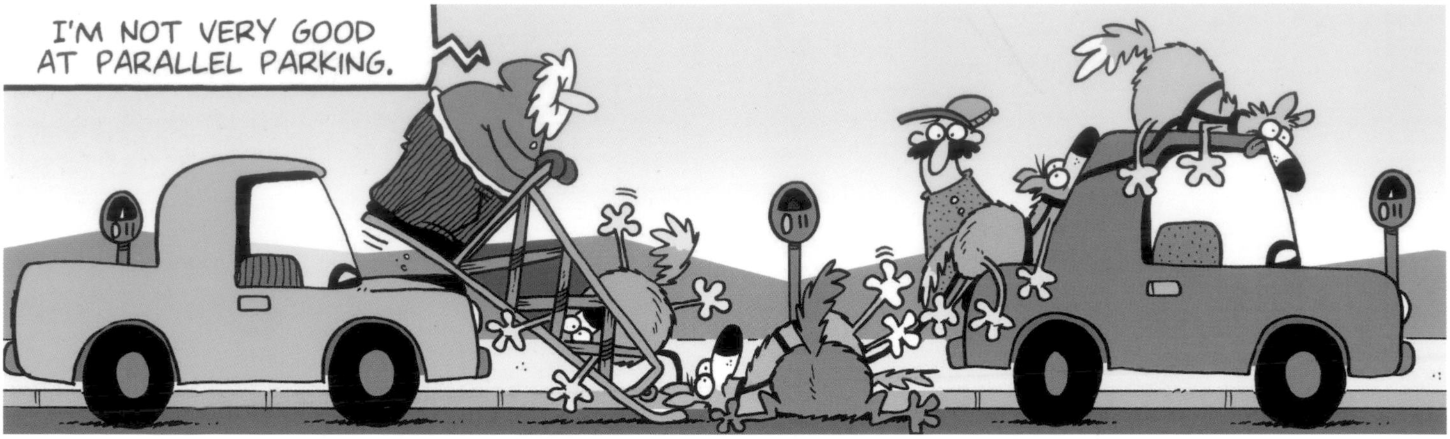
I'M NOT VERY GOOD AT PARALLEL PARKING.

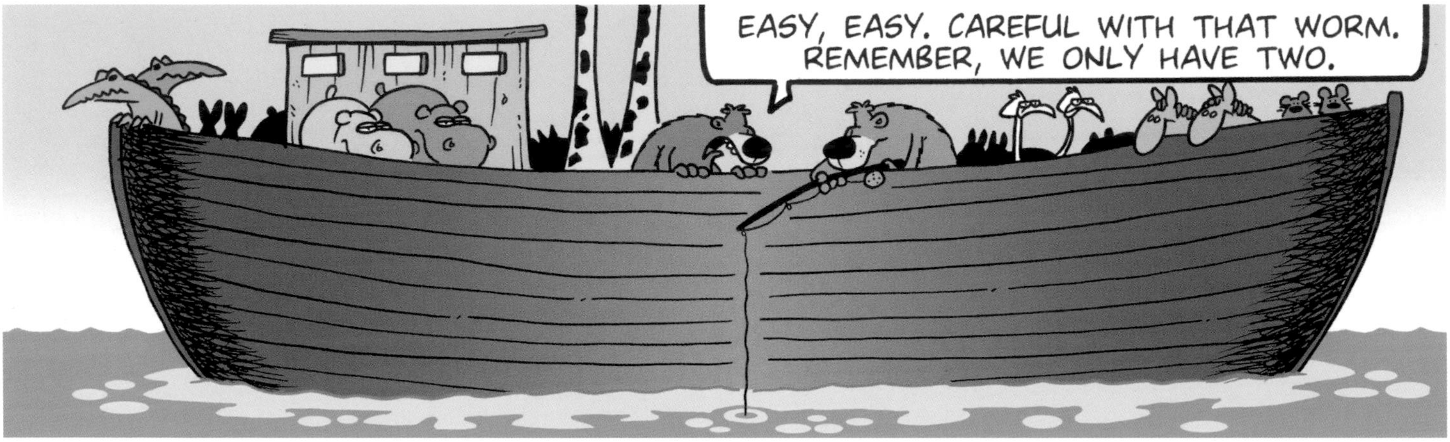
EASY, EASY. CAREFUL WITH THAT WORM. REMEMBER, WE ONLY HAVE TWO.

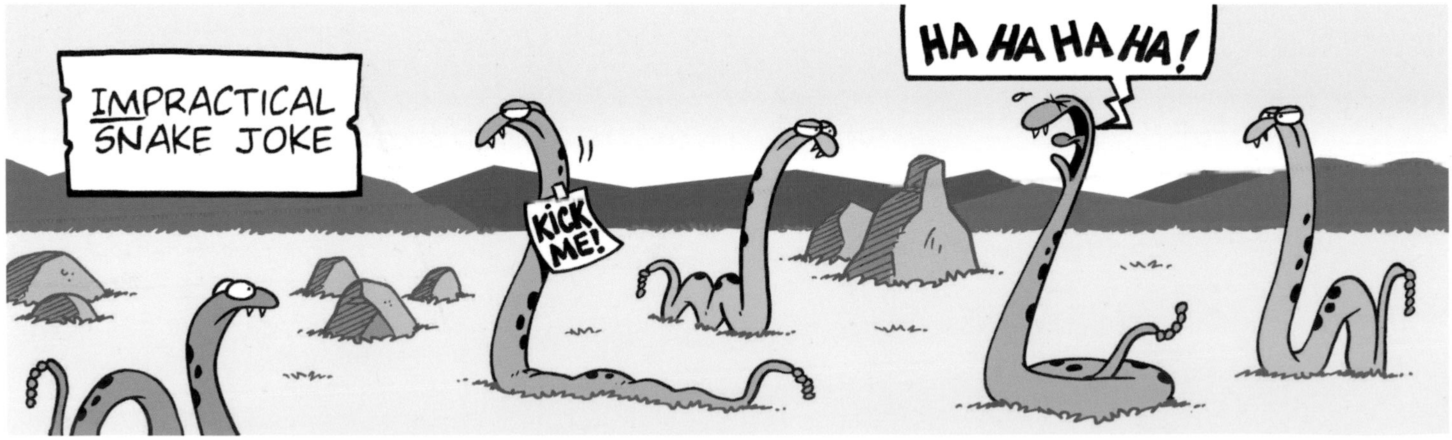
IMPRACTICAL SNAKE JOKE
HA HA HA HA!
KICK ME!

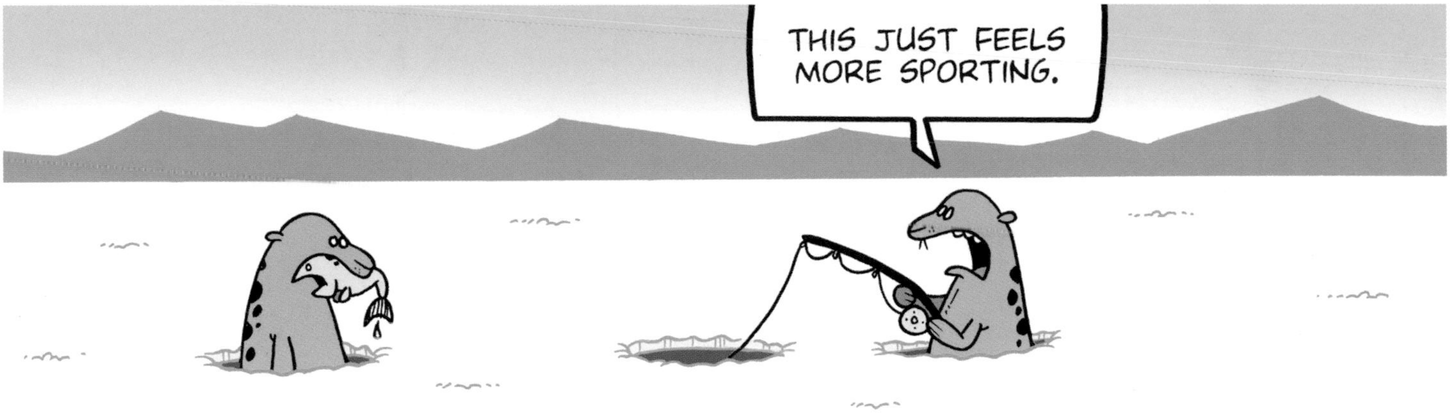
THIS JUST FEELS MORE SPORTING.

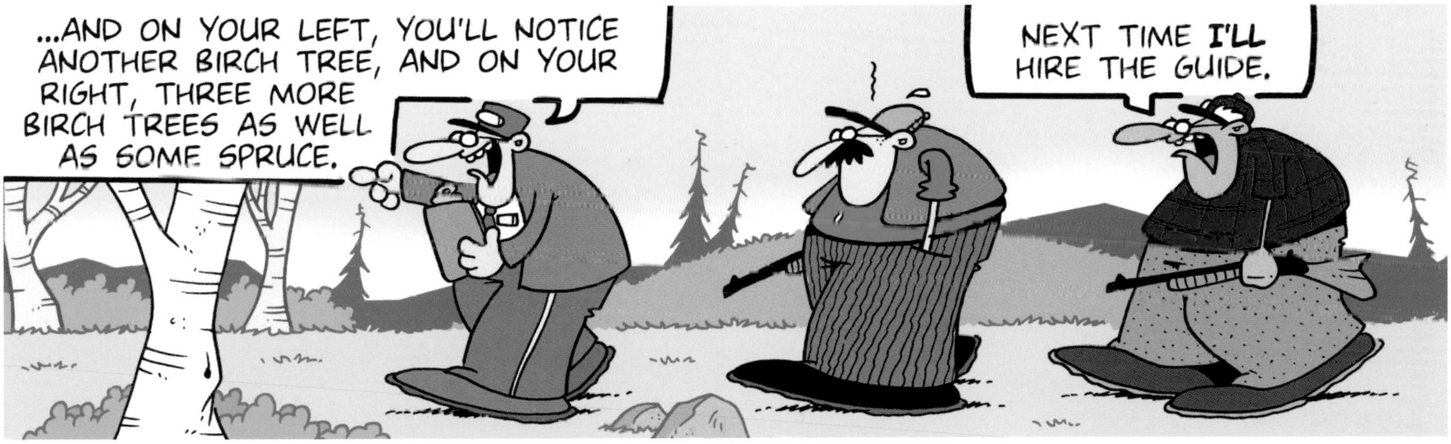
...AND ON YOUR LEFT, YOU'LL NOTICE ANOTHER BIRCH TREE, AND ON YOUR RIGHT, THREE MORE BIRCH TREES AS WELL AS SOME SPRUCE.
NEXT TIME **I'LL** HIRE THE GUIDE.

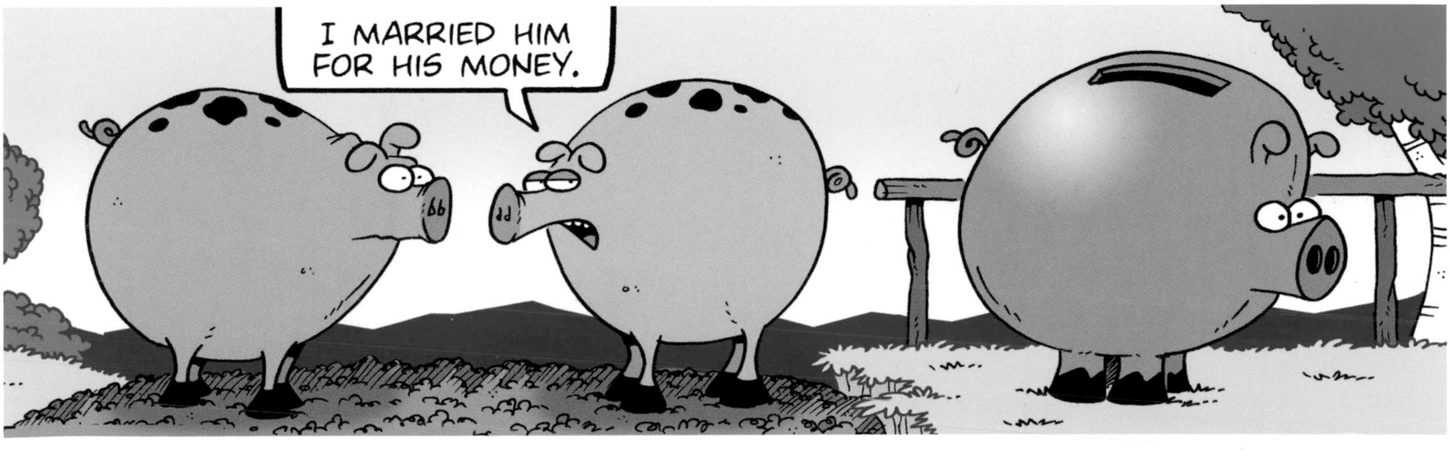
I MARRIED HIM FOR HIS MONEY.

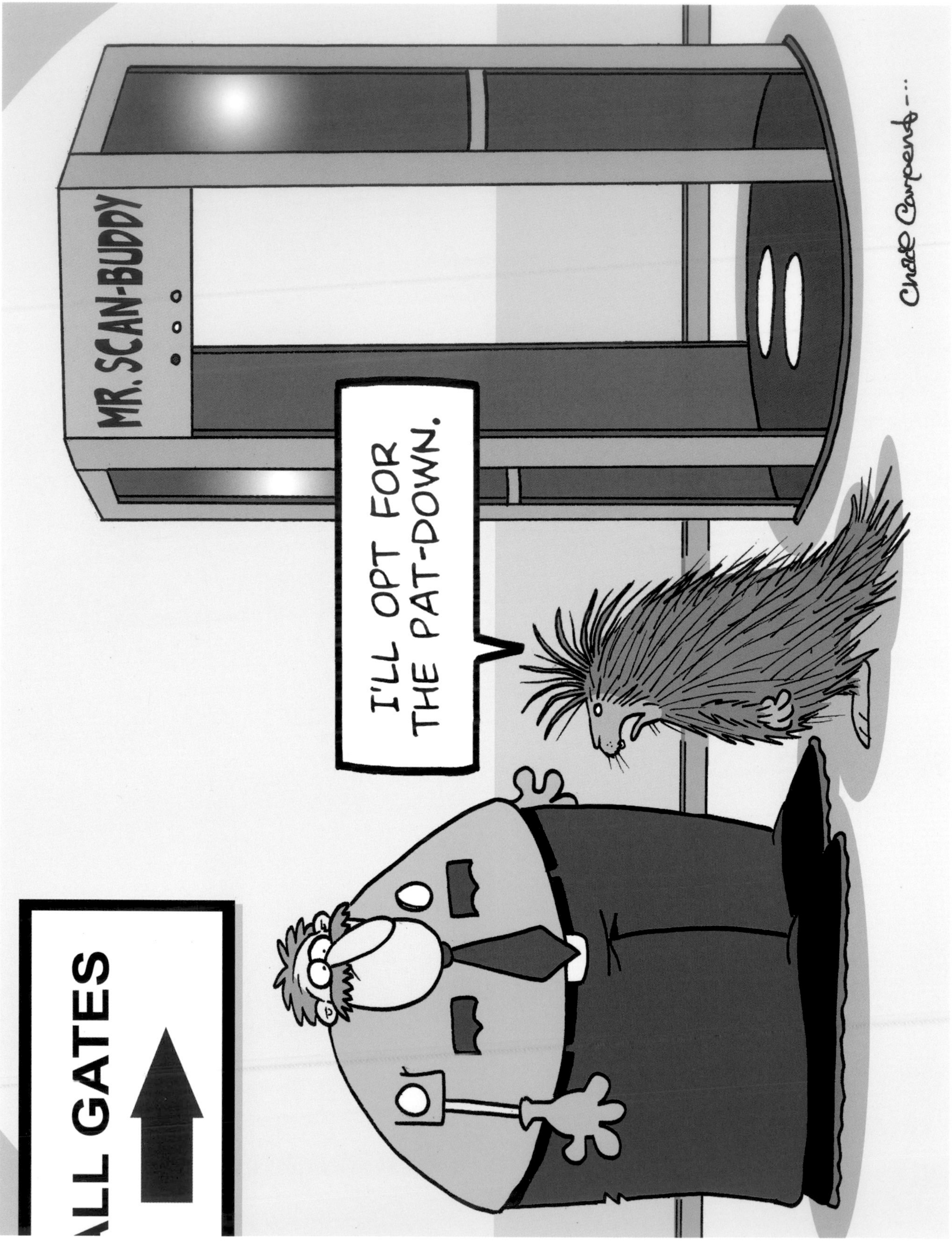
ALL GATES
I'LL OPT FOR THE PAT-DOWN.
MR. SCAN-BUDDY

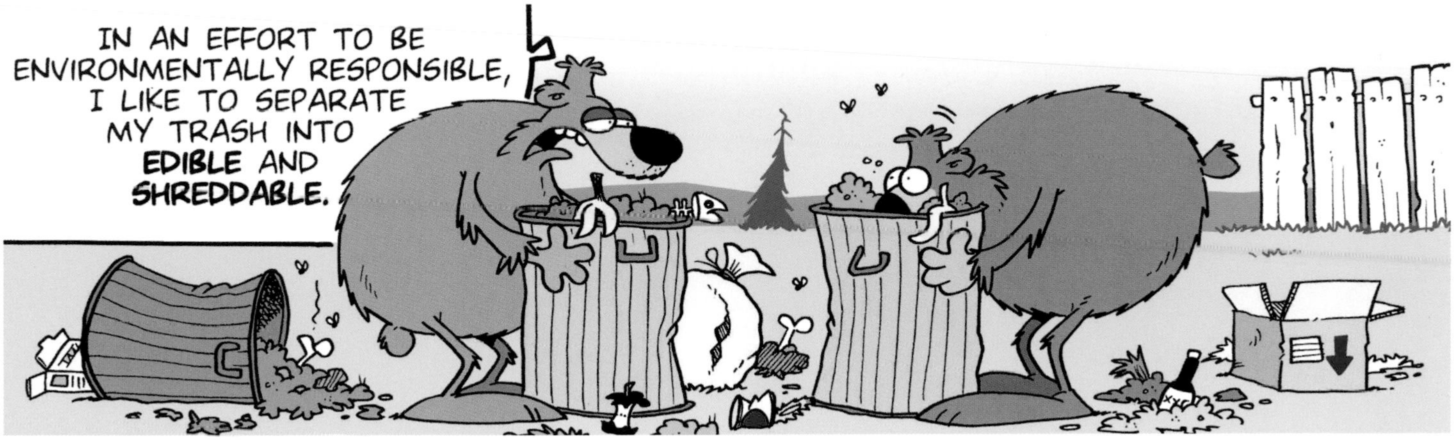
IN AN EFFORT TO BE ENVIRONMENTALLY RESPONSIBLE, I LIKE TO SEPARATE MY TRASH INTO EDIBLE AND SHREDDABLE.

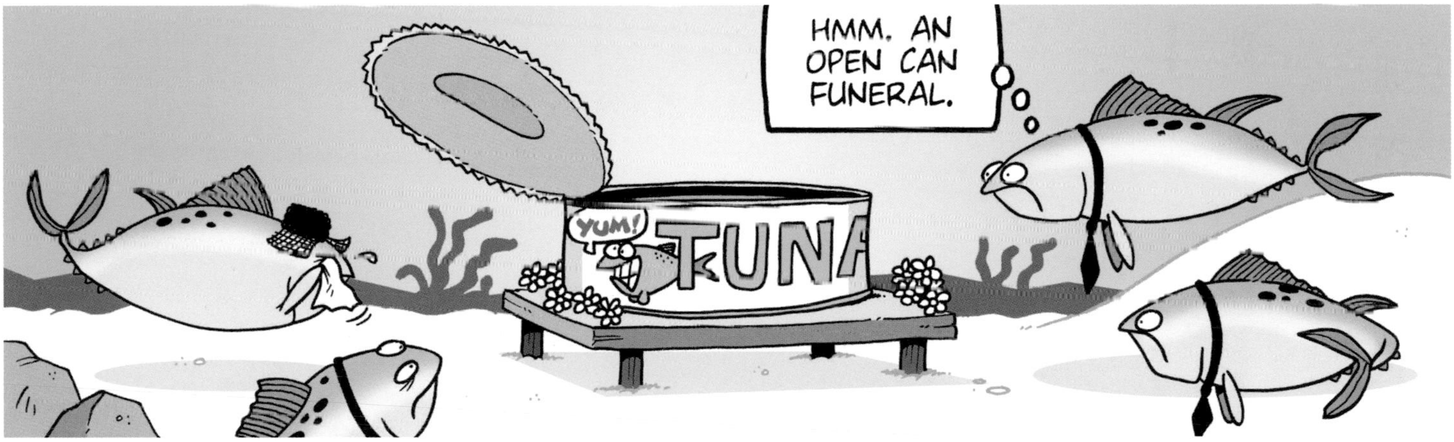
HMM. AN OPEN CAN FUNERAL.
YUM!
TUNA

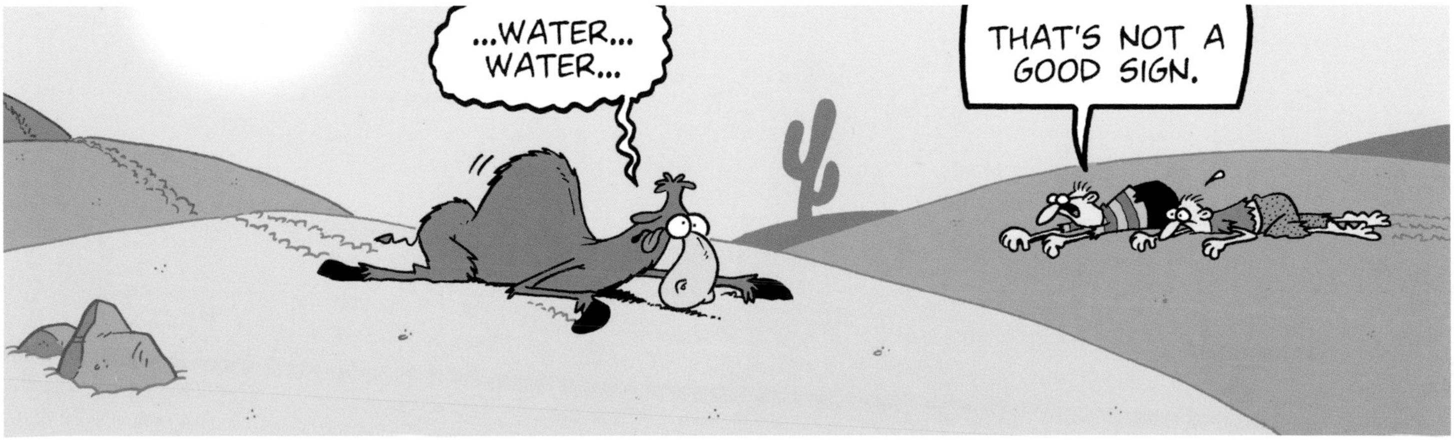
...WATER... WATER...
THAT'S NOT A GOOD SIGN.

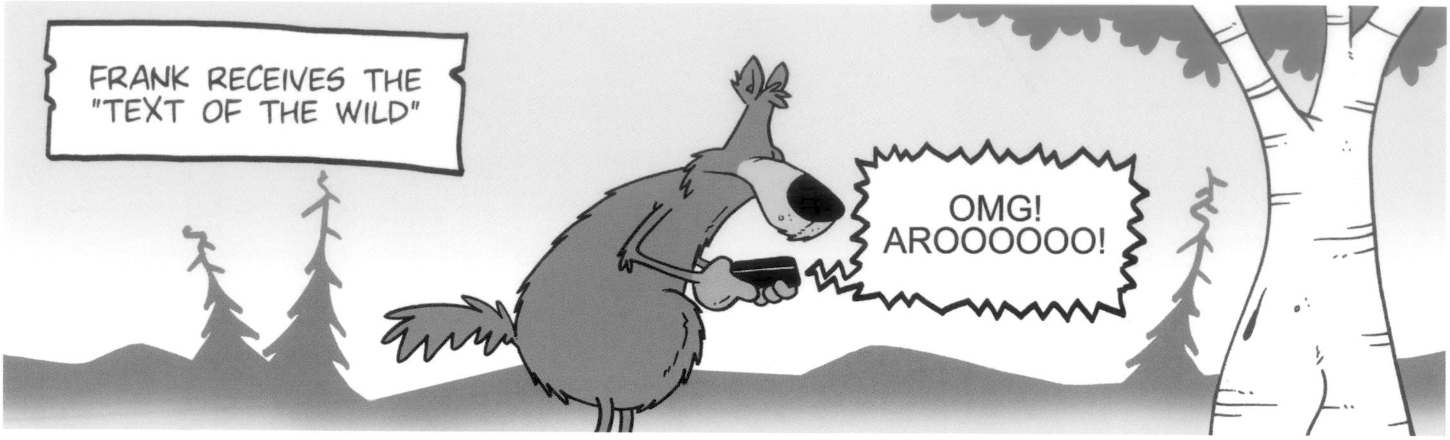
FRANK RECEIVES THE "TEXT OF THE WILD"
OMG! AROOOOOO!

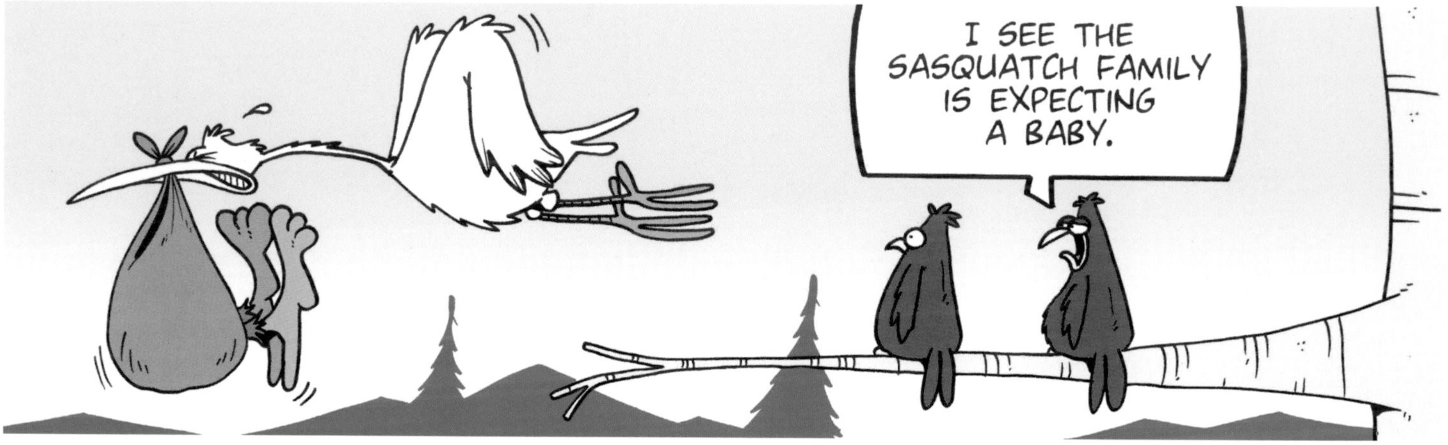
I SEE THE SASQUATCH FAMILY IS EXPECTING A BABY.

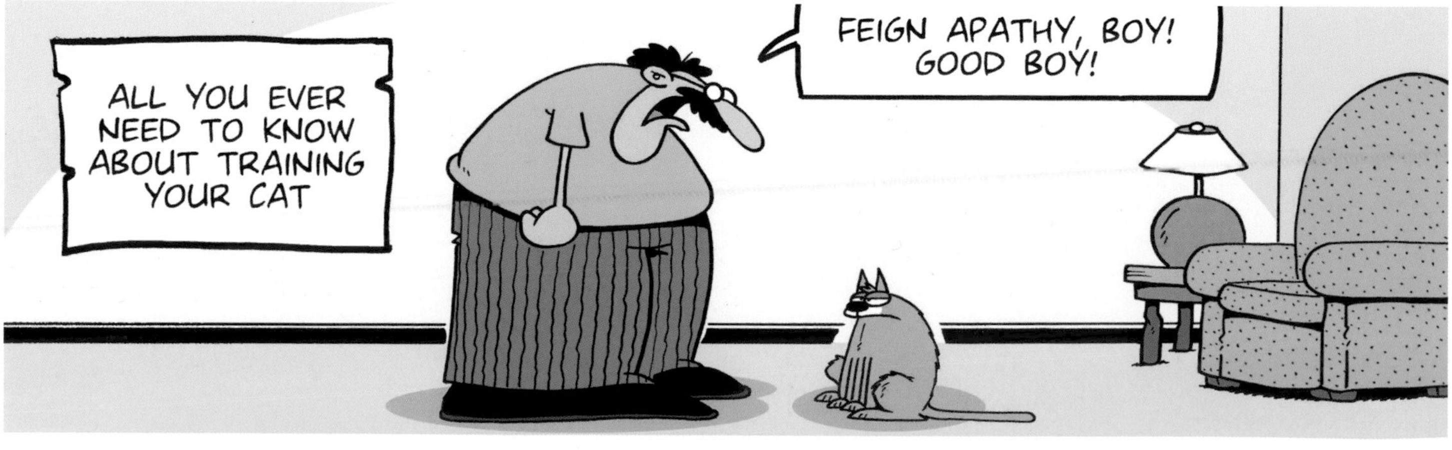
ALL YOU EVER NEED TO KNOW ABOUT TRAINING YOUR CAT
FEIGN APATHY, BOY! GOOD BOY!

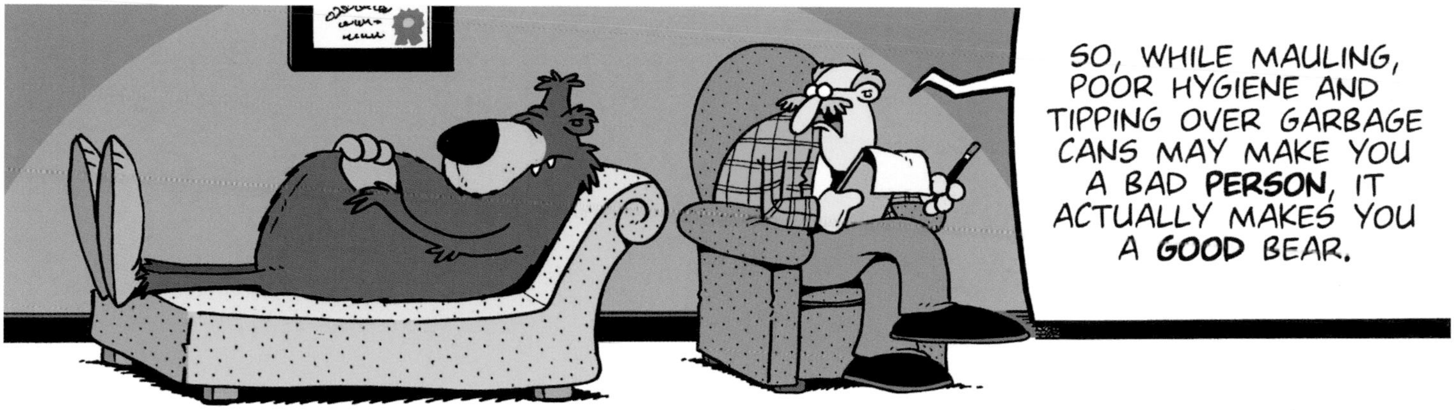
SO, WHILE MAULING, POOR HYGIENE AND TIPPING OVER GARBAGE CANS MAY MAKE YOU A BAD PERSON, IT ACTUALLY MAKES YOU A GOOD BEAR.

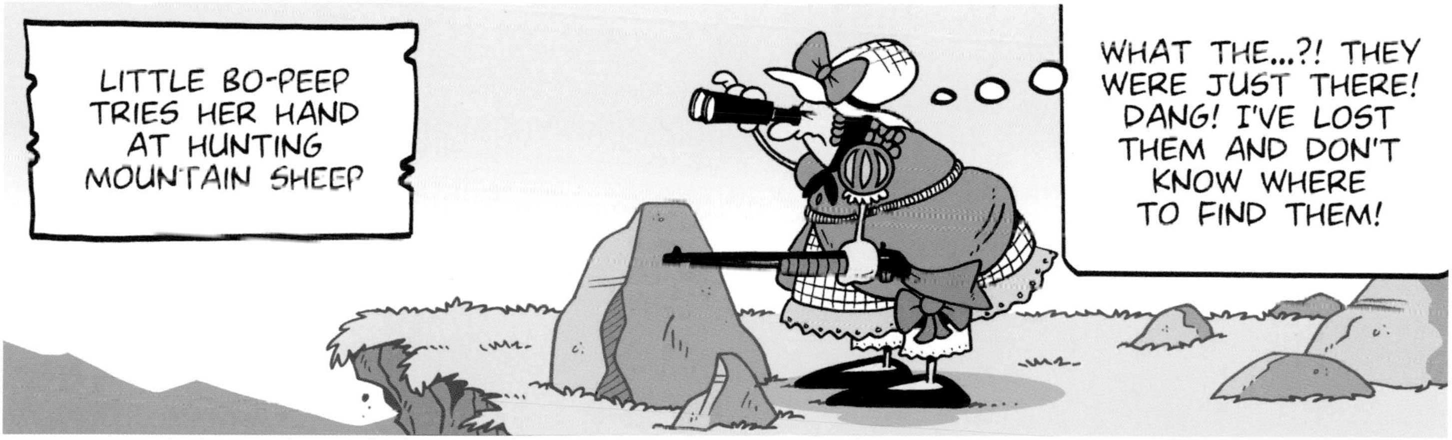
LITTLE BO-PEEP TRIES HER HAND AT HUNTING MOUNTAIN SHEEP
WHAT THE...?! THEY WERE JUST THERE! DANG! I'VE LOST THEM AND DON'T KNOW WHERE TO FIND THEM!

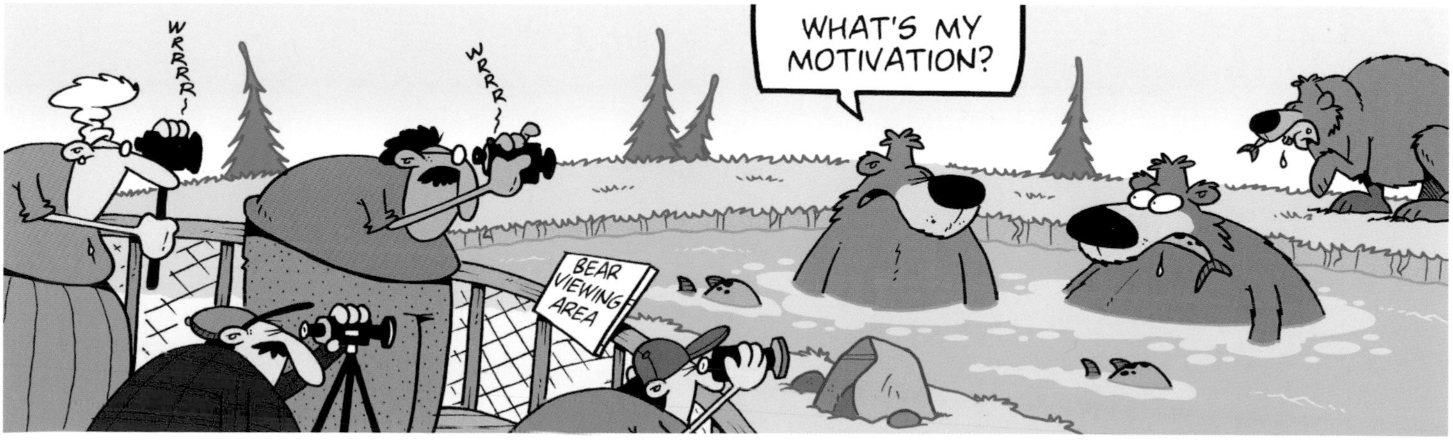
WRRRR~
WRRR~
BEAR VIEWING AREA
WHAT'S MY MOTIVATION?

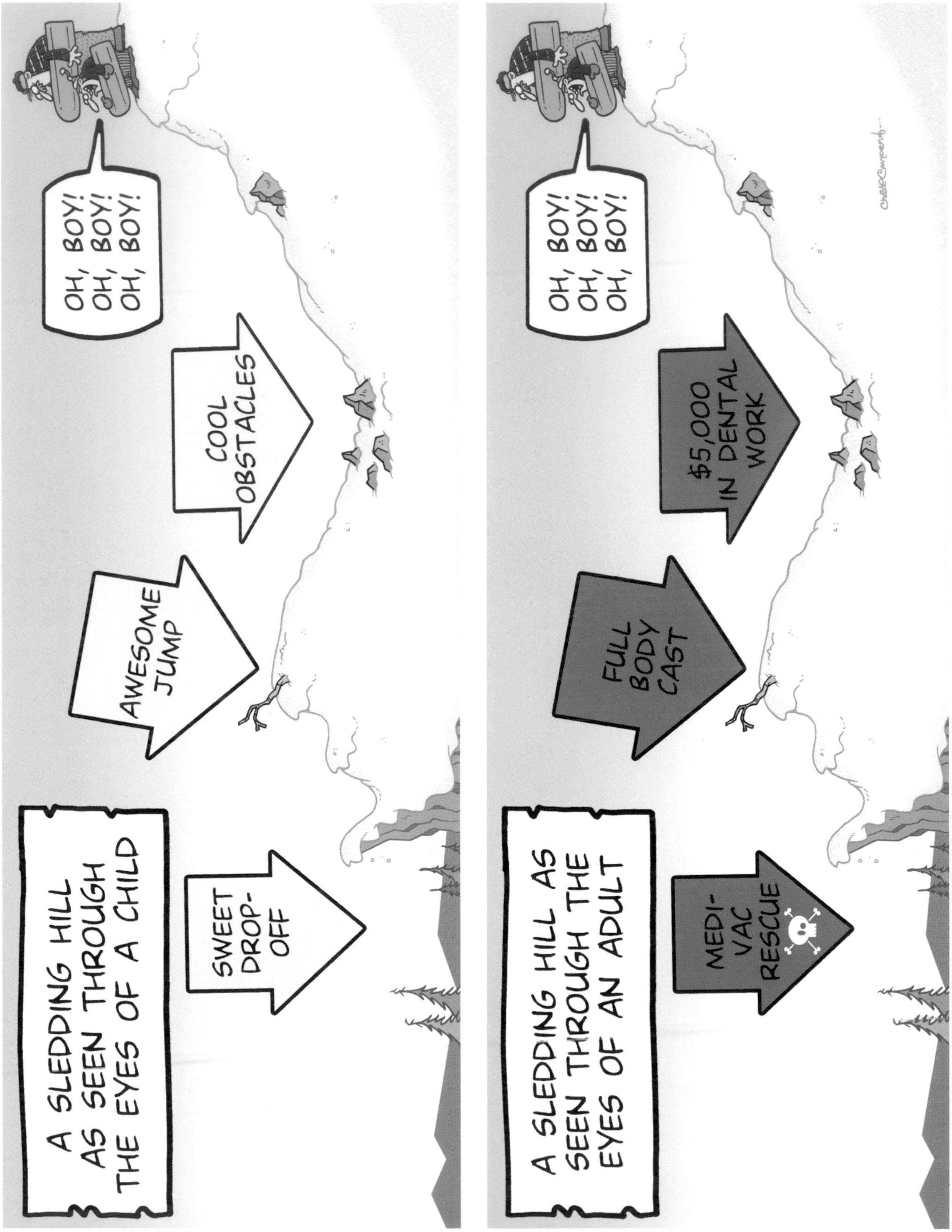
A SLEDDING HILL AS SEEN THROUGH THE EYES OF A CHILD
SWEET DROP-OFF
AWESOME JUMP
COOL OBSTACLES
OH, BOY! OH, BOY! OH, BOY!
A SLEDDING HILL AS SEEN THROUGH THE EYES OF AN ADULT
MEDI-VAC RESCUE
FULL BODY CAST
$5,000 IN DENTAL WORK
OH, BOY! OH, BOY! OH, BOY!

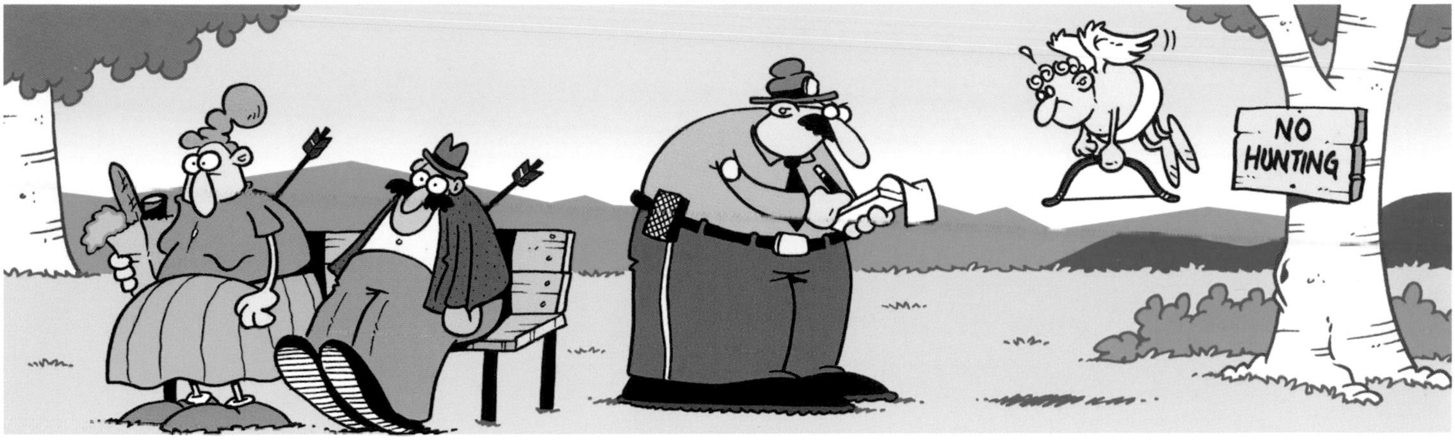
NO HUNTING

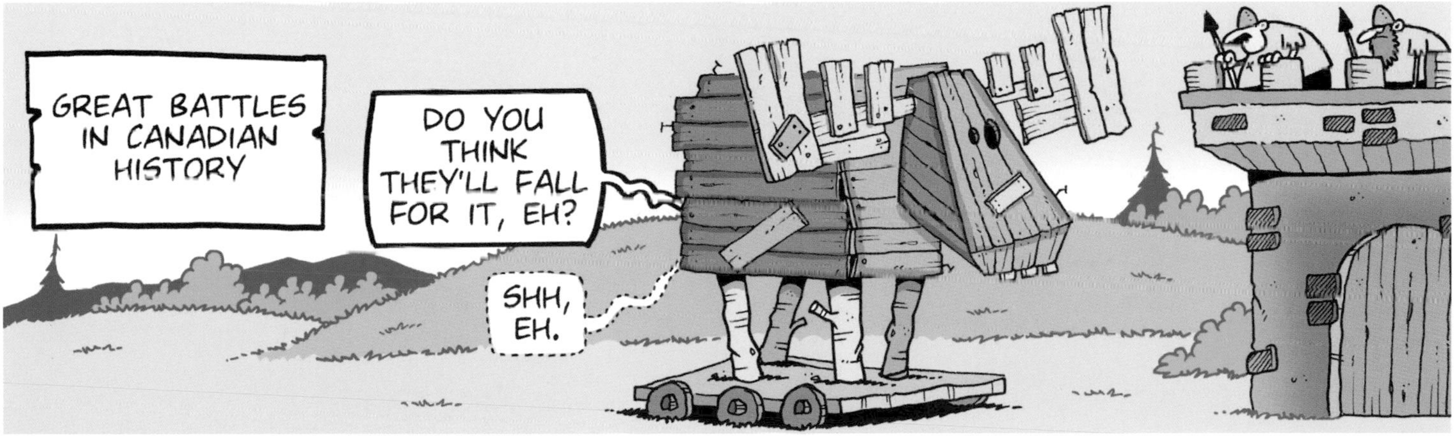
GREAT BATTLES IN CANADIAN HISTORY
DO YOU THINK THEY'LL FALL FOR IT, EH?
SHH, EH.

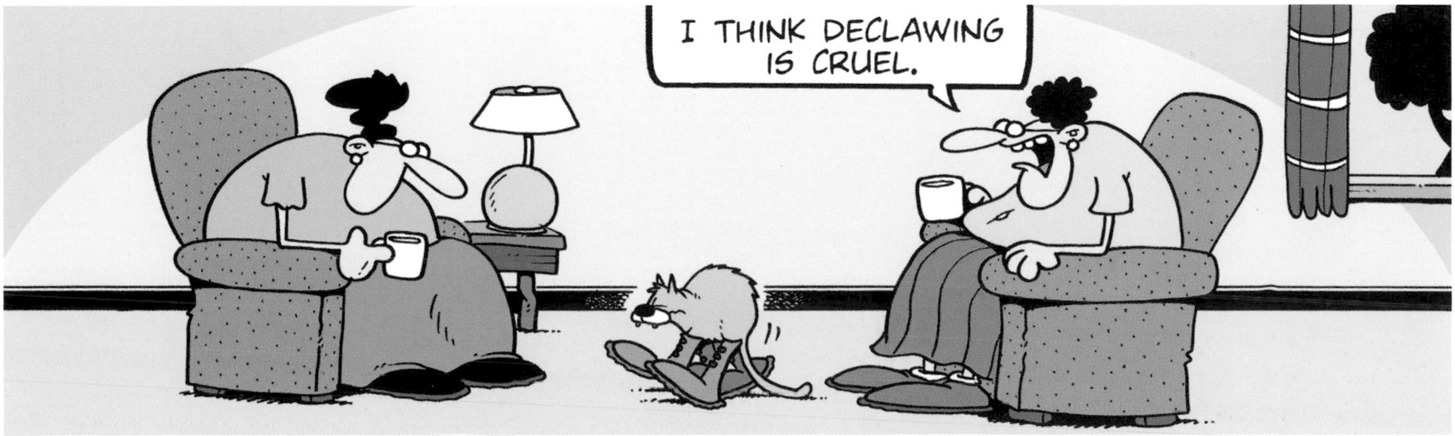
I THINK DECLAWING IS CRUEL.

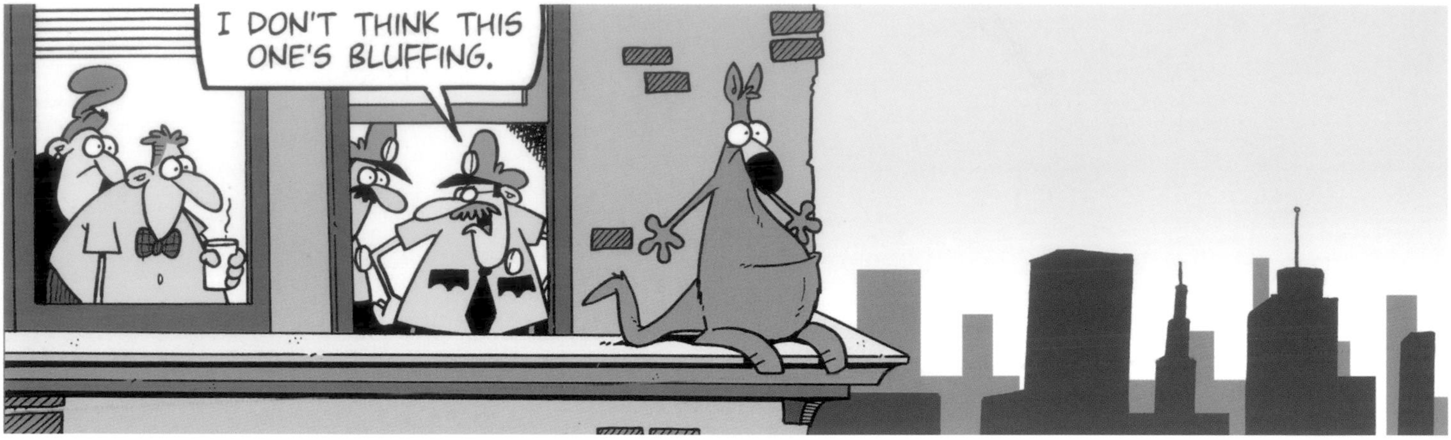
I DON'T THINK THIS ONE'S BLUFFING.

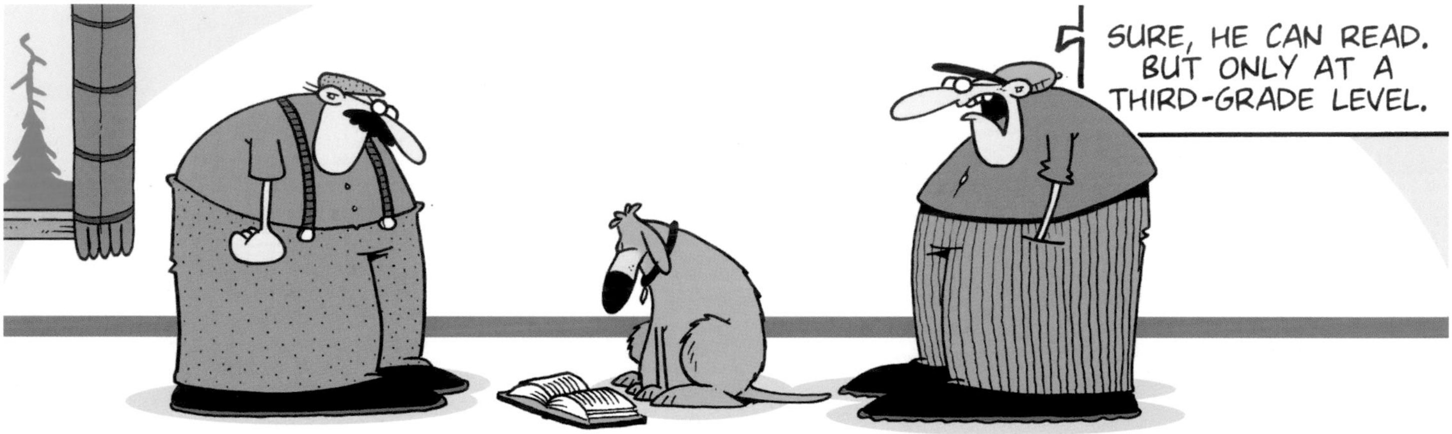
SURE, HE CAN READ. BUT ONLY AT A THIRD-GRADE LEVEL.

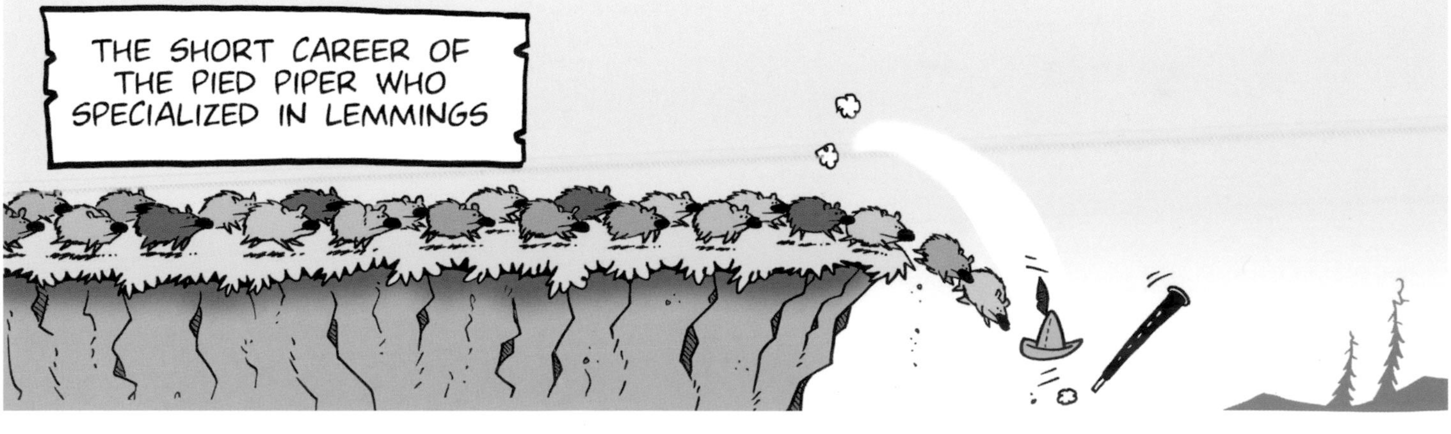
THE SHORT CAREER OF THE PIED PIPER WHO SPECIALIZED IN LEMMINGS

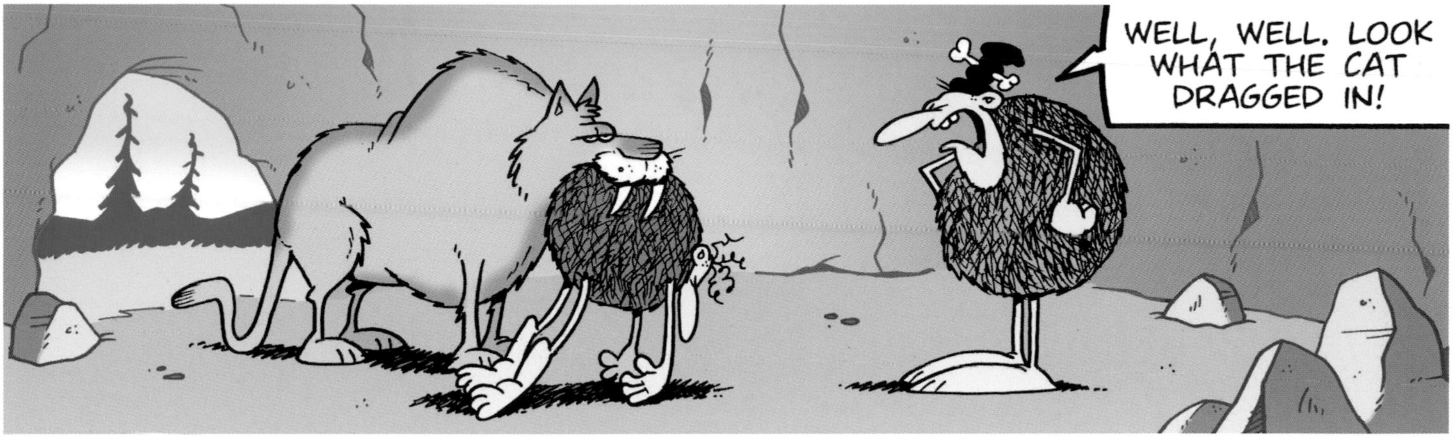
WELL, WELL. LOOK WHAT THE CAT DRAGGED IN!

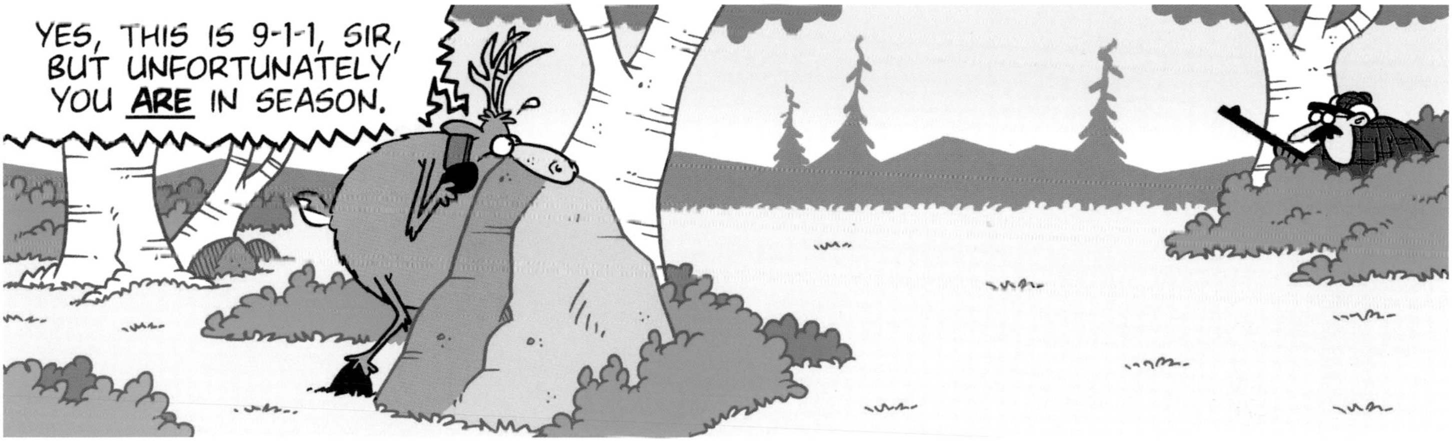
YES, THIS IS 9-1-1, SIR, BUT UNFORTUNATELY YOU ARE IN SEASON.

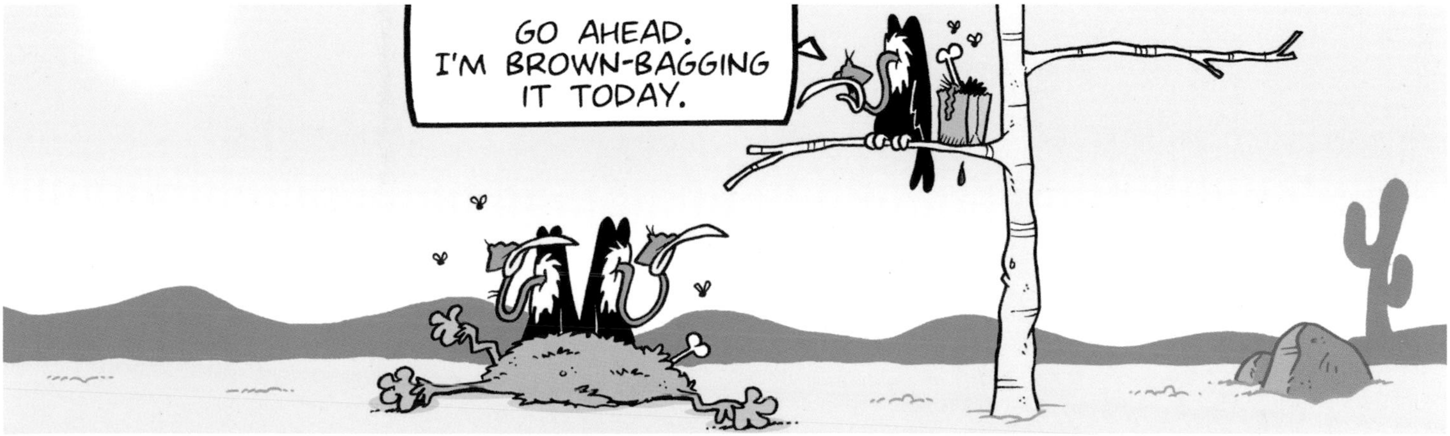
GO AHEAD. I'M BROWN-BAGGING IT TODAY.

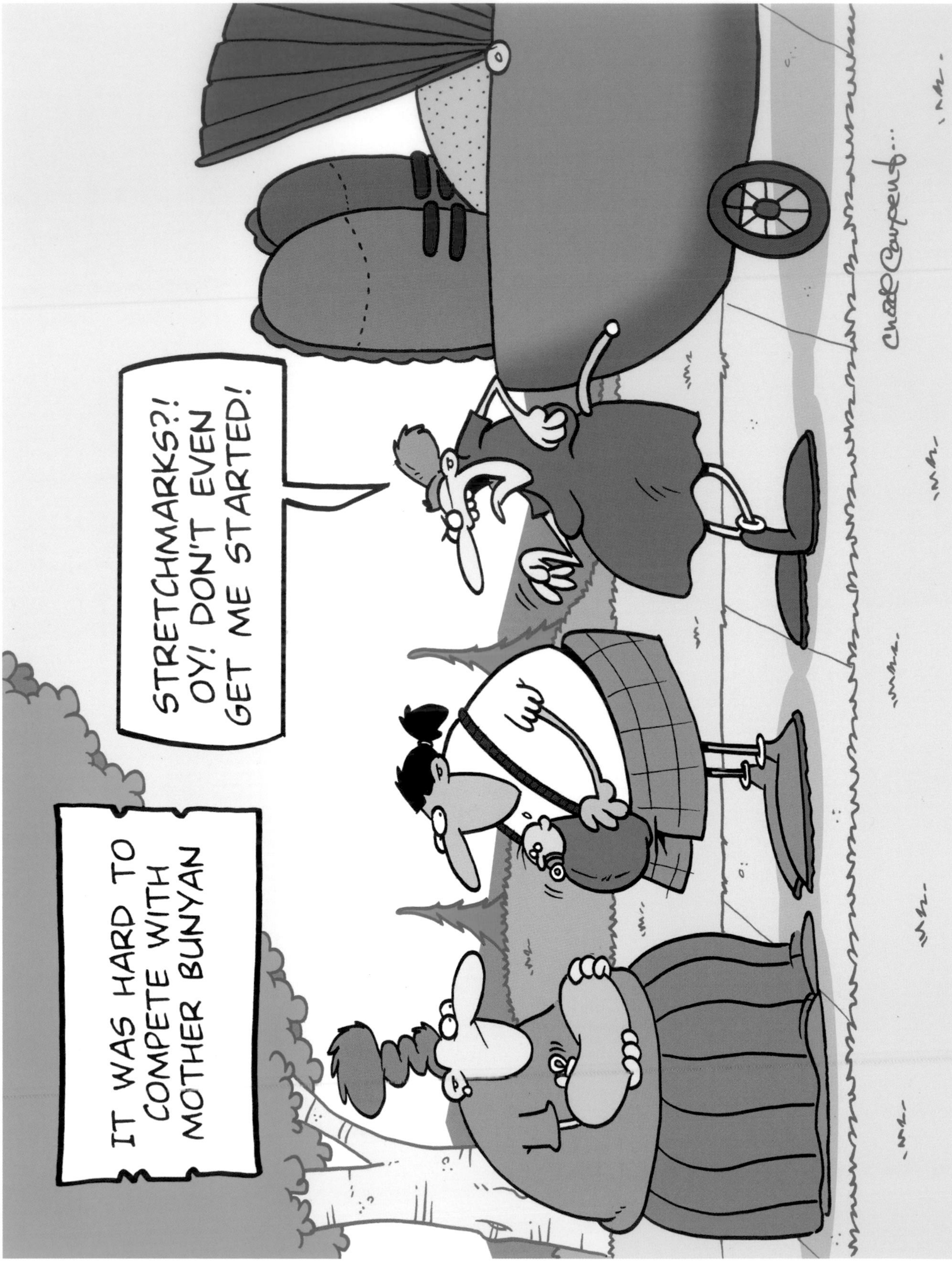
IT WAS HARD TO COMPETE WITH MOTHER BUNYAN
STRETCHMARKS?! OY! DON'T EVEN GET ME STARTED!

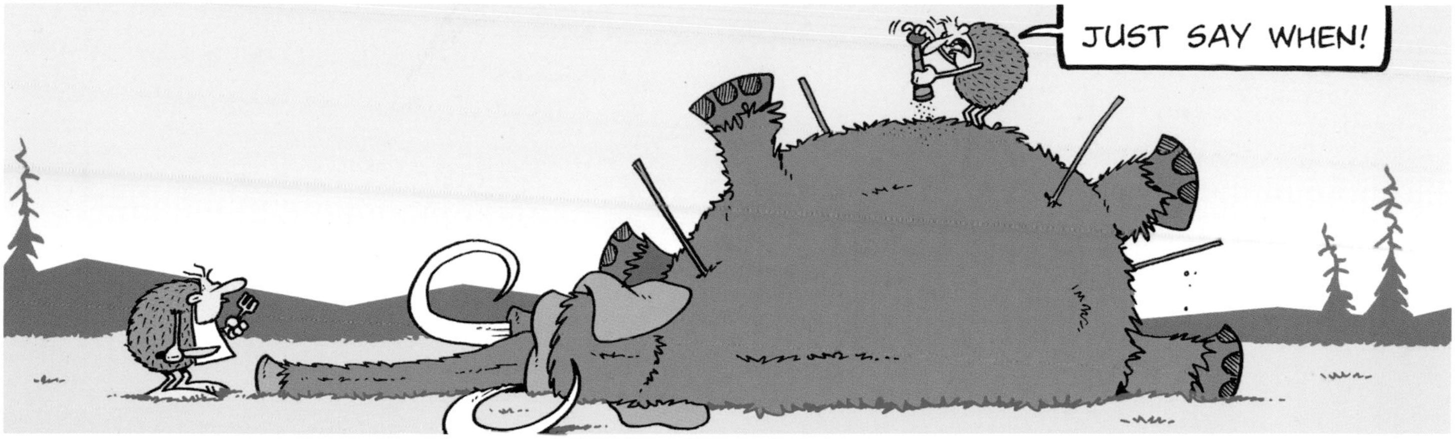
JUST SAY WHEN!

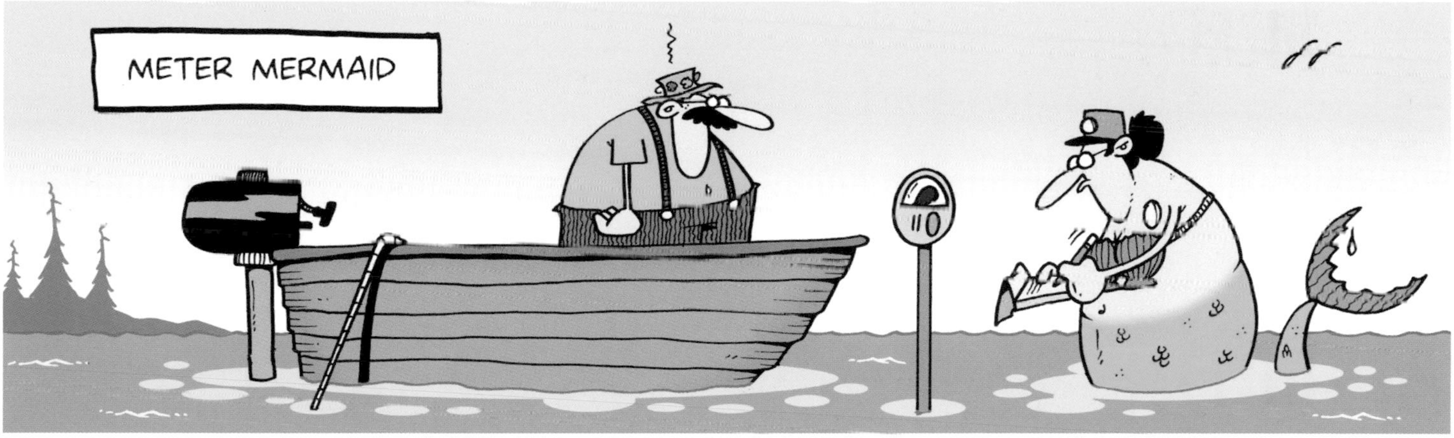
METER MERMAID
110

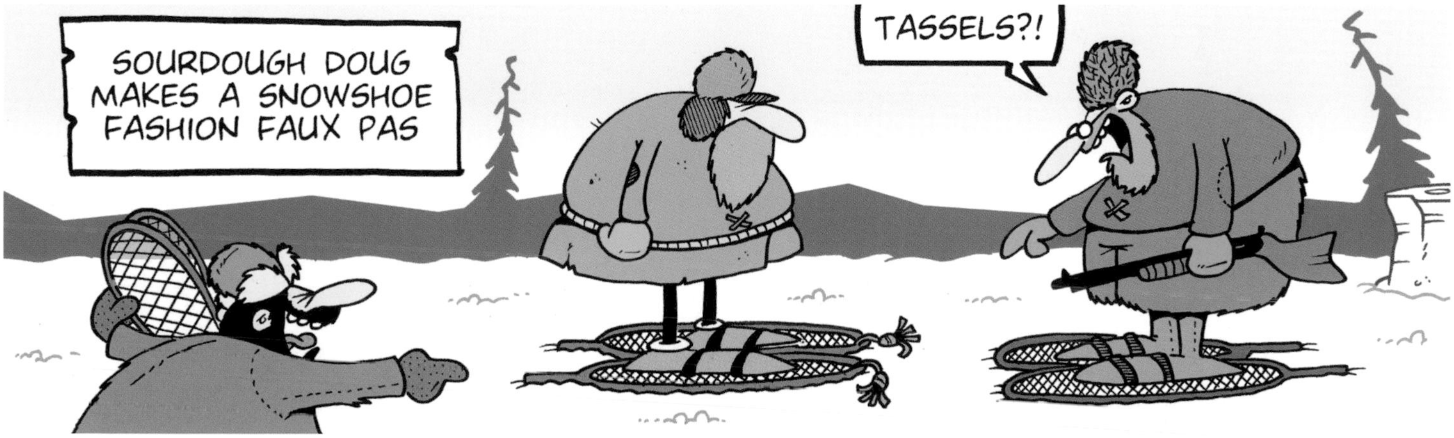
SOURDOUGH DOUG MAKES A SNOWSHOE FASHION FAUX PAS
TASSELS?!

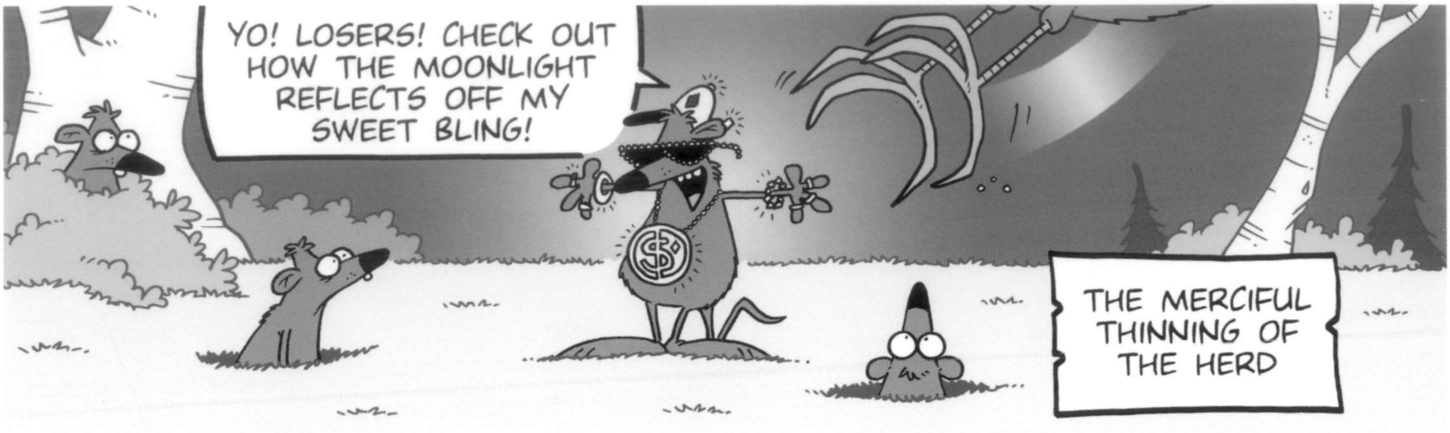
YO! LOSERS! CHECK OUT HOW THE MOONLIGHT REFLECTS OFF MY SWEET BLING!
THE MERCIFUL THINNING OF THE HERD

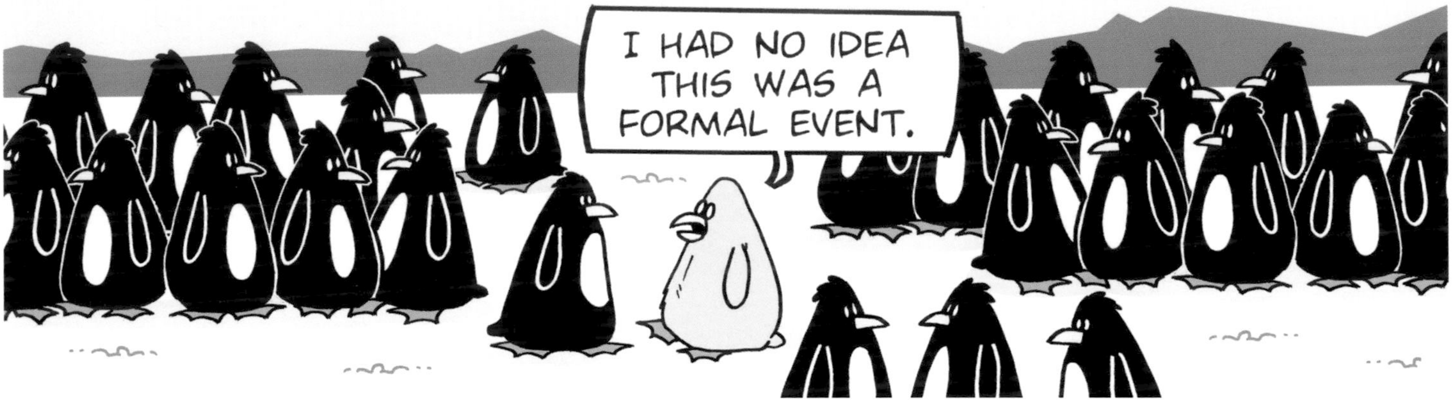
I HAD NO IDEA THIS WAS A FORMAL EVENT.

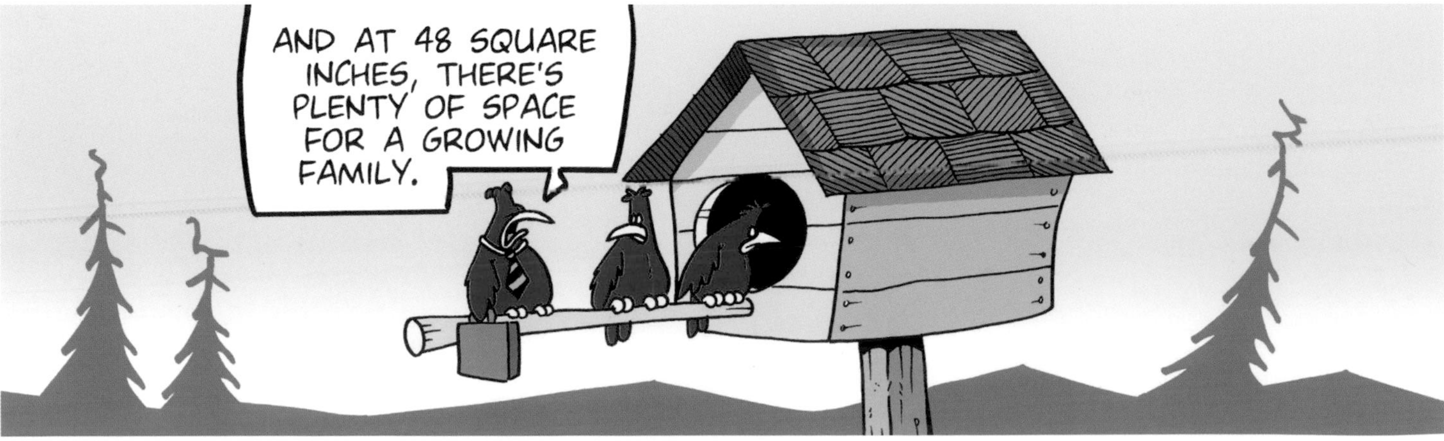
AND AT 48 SQUARE INCHES, THERE'S PLENTY OF SPACE FOR A GROWING FAMILY.

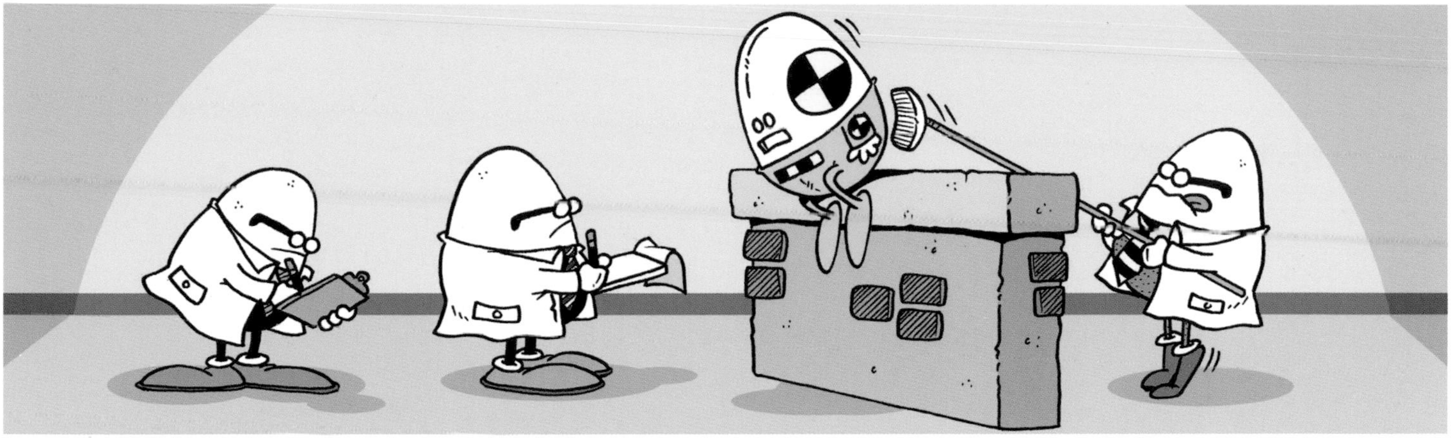

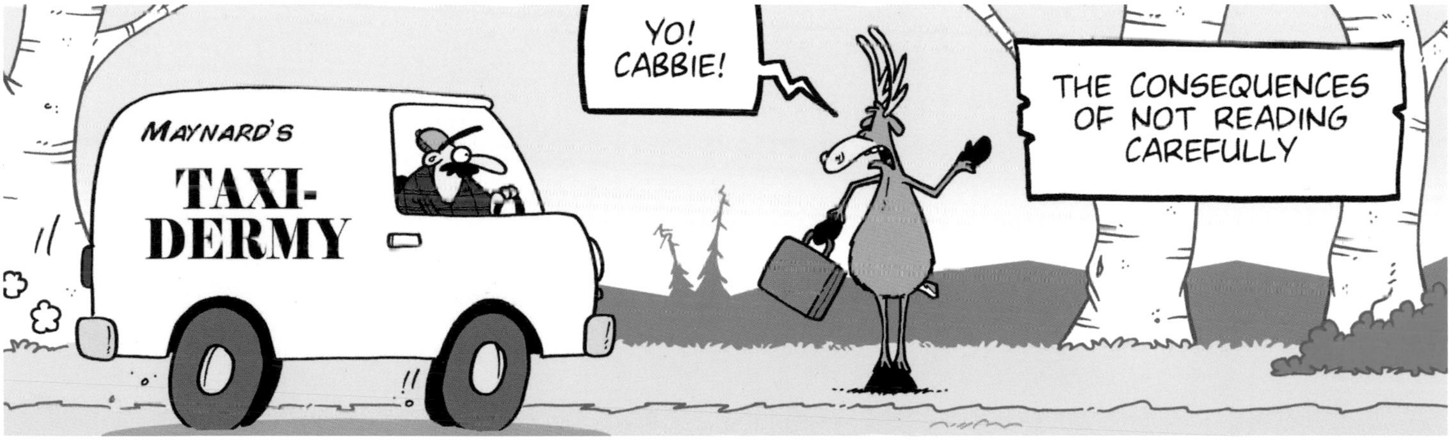
YO! CABBIE!
MAYNARD'S
TAXI-DERMY
THE CONSEQUENCES OF NOT READING CAREFULLY

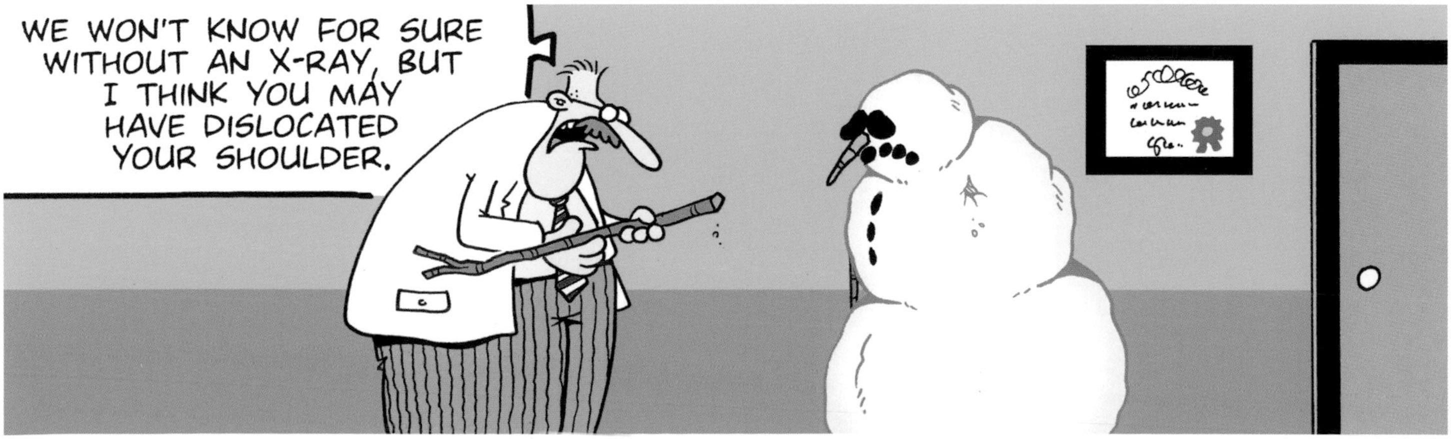
WE WON'T KNOW FOR SURE WITHOUT AN X-RAY, BUT I THINK YOU MAY HAVE DISLOCATED YOUR SHOULDER.

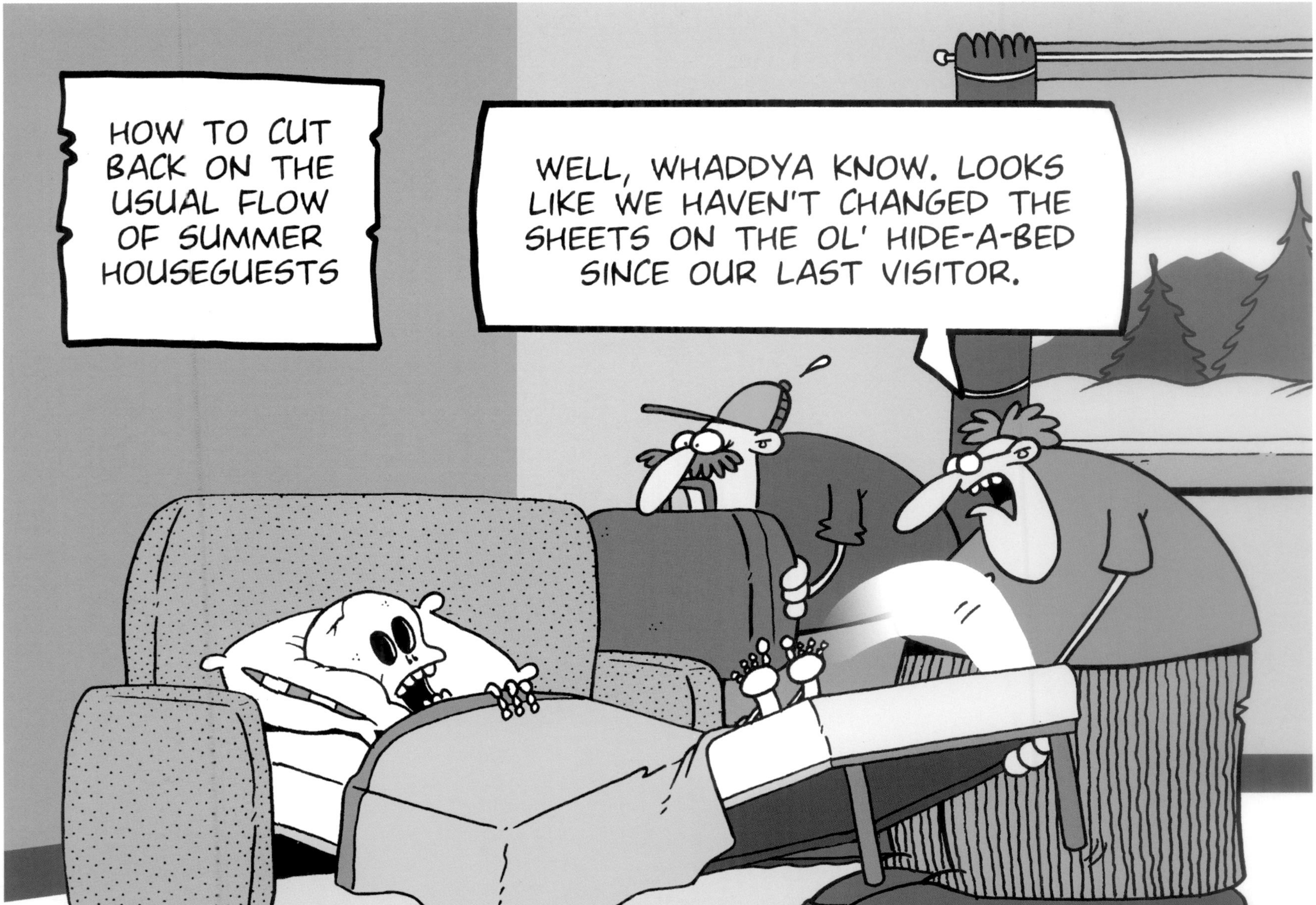
HOW TO CUT BACK ON THE USUAL FLOW OF SUMMER HOUSEGUESTS
WELL, WHADDYA KNOW. LOOKS LIKE WE HAVEN'T CHANGED THE SHEETS ON THE OL' HIDE-A-BED SINCE OUR LAST VISITOR.

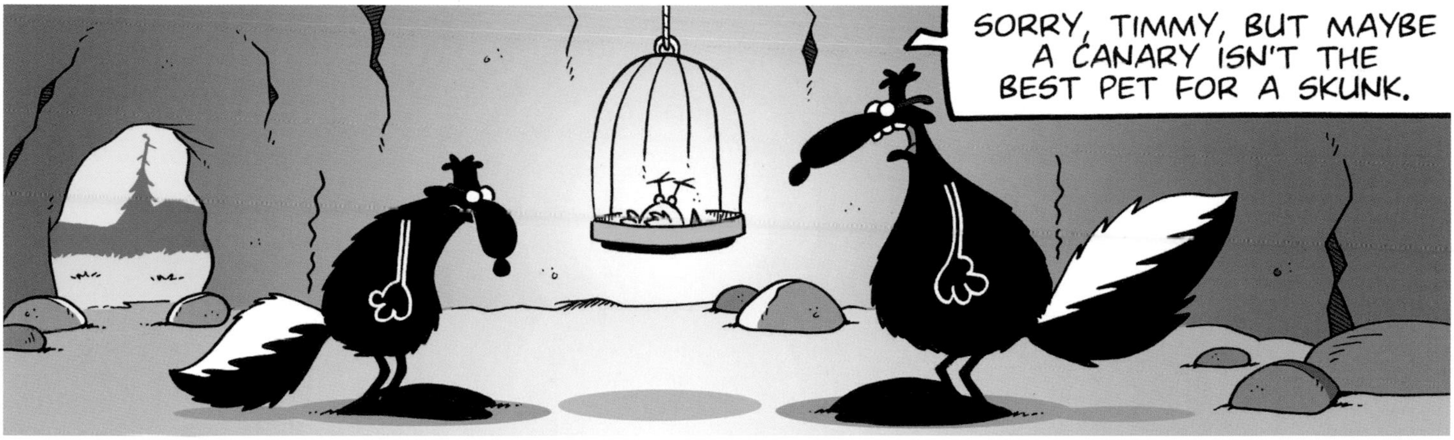
SORRY, TIMMY, BUT MAYBE A CANARY ISN'T THE BEST PET FOR A SKUNK.

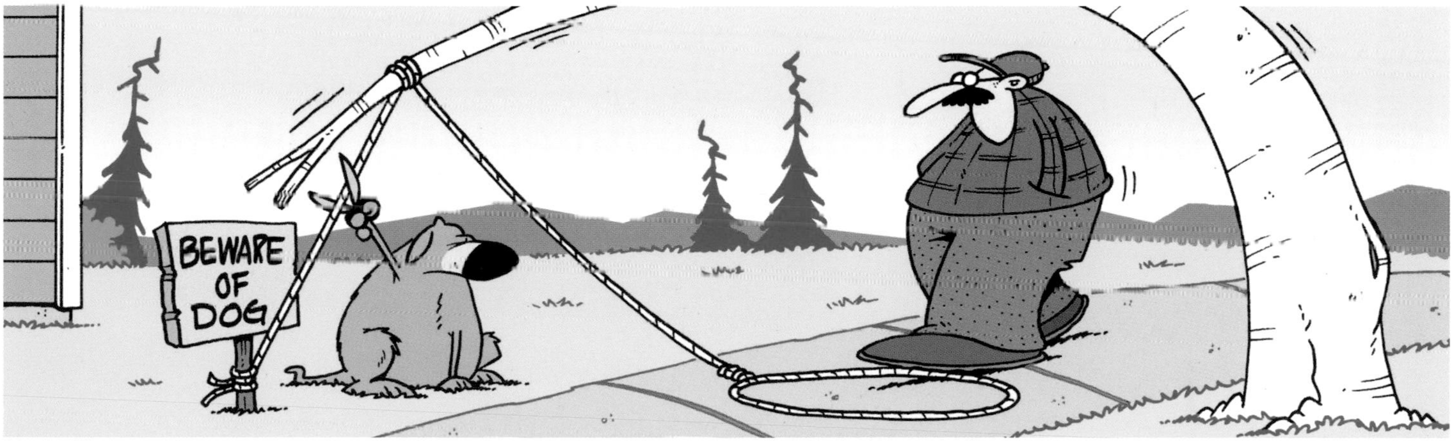
BEWARE OF DOG

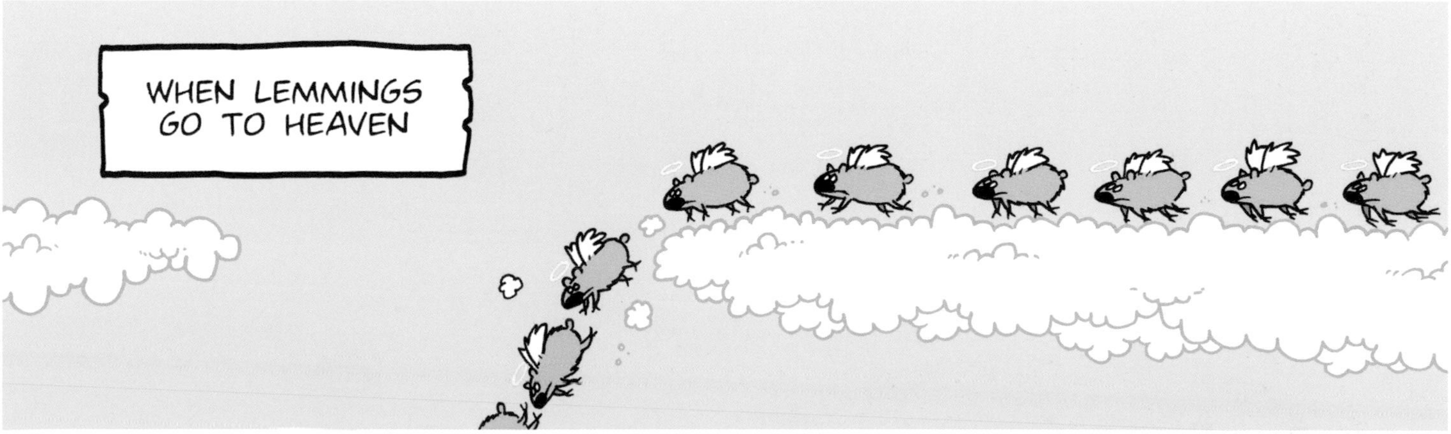
WHEN LEMMINGS GO TO HEAVEN

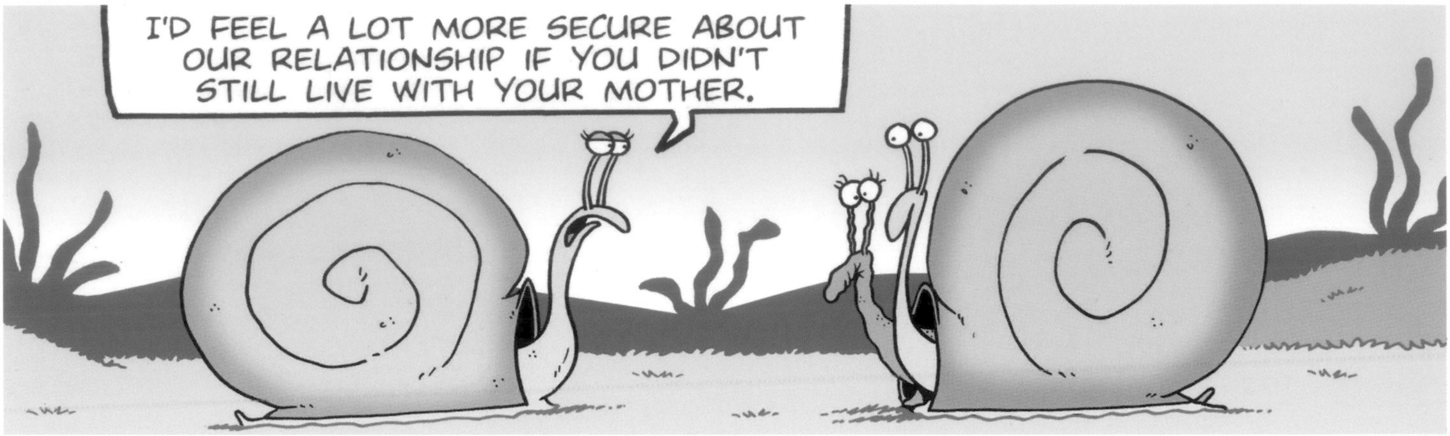
I'D FEEL A LOT MORE SECURE ABOUT OUR RELATIONSHIP IF YOU DIDN'T STILL LIVE WITH YOUR MOTHER.

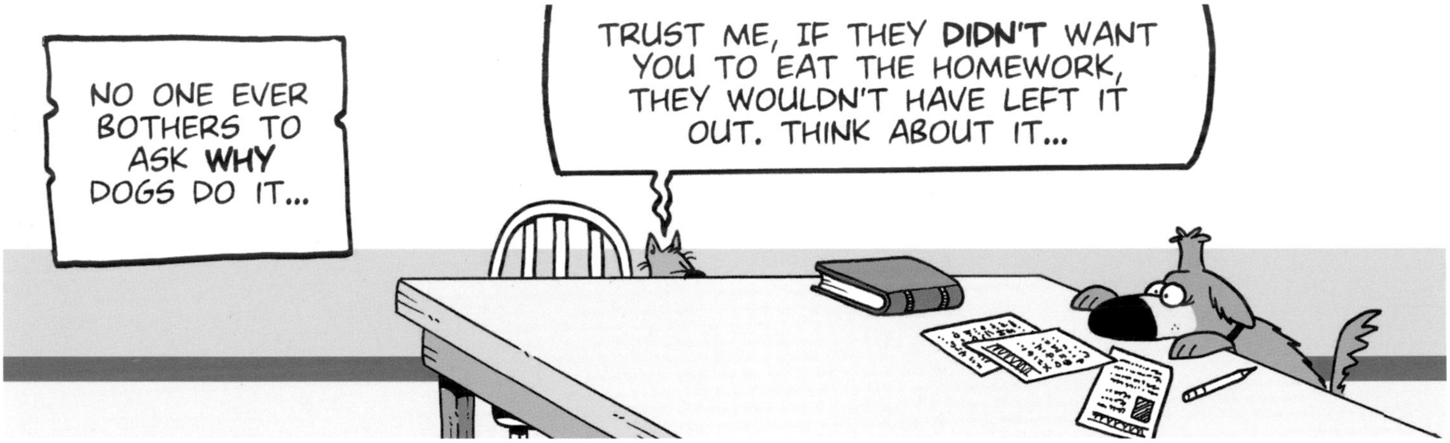
NO ONE EVER BOTHERS TO ASK **WHY** DOGS DO IT...
TRUST ME, IF THEY **DIDN'T** WANT YOU TO EAT THE HOMEWORK, THEY WOULDN'T HAVE LEFT IT OUT. THINK ABOUT IT...

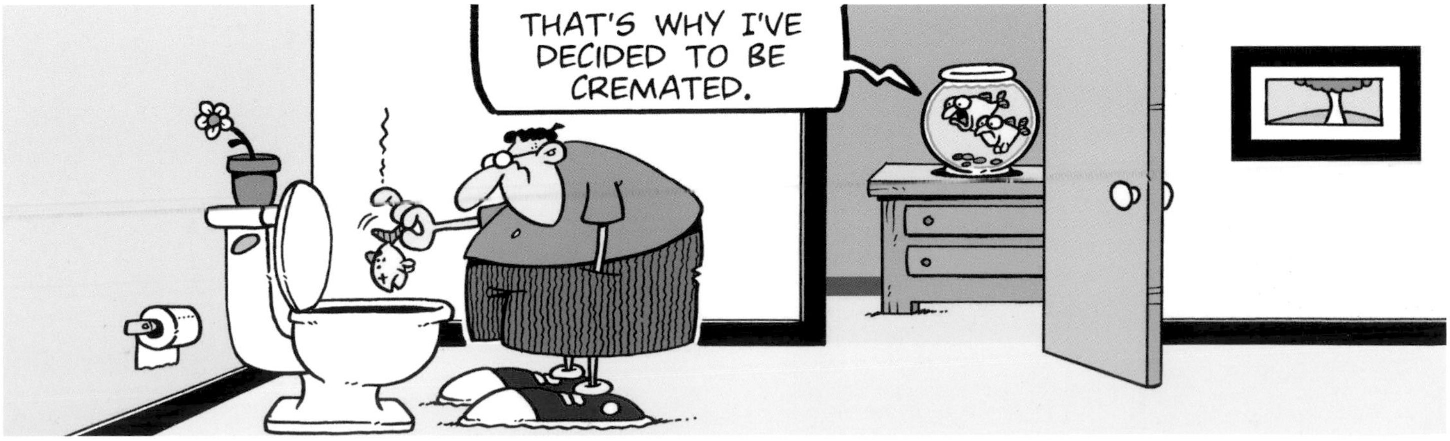
THAT'S WHY I'VE DECIDED TO BE CREMATED.

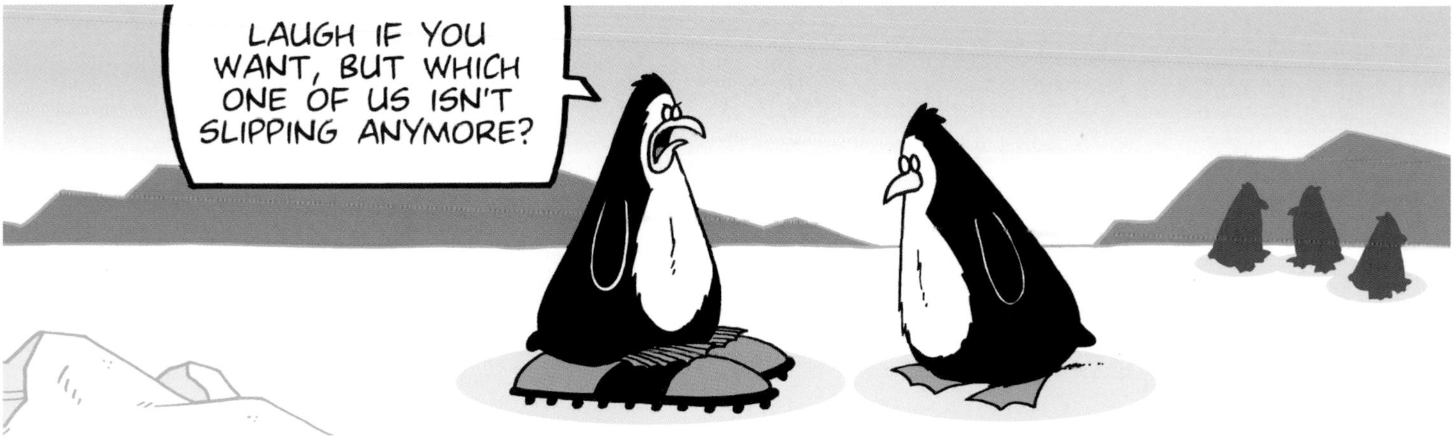
LAUGH IF YOU WANT, BUT WHICH ONE OF US ISN'T SLIPPING ANYMORE?

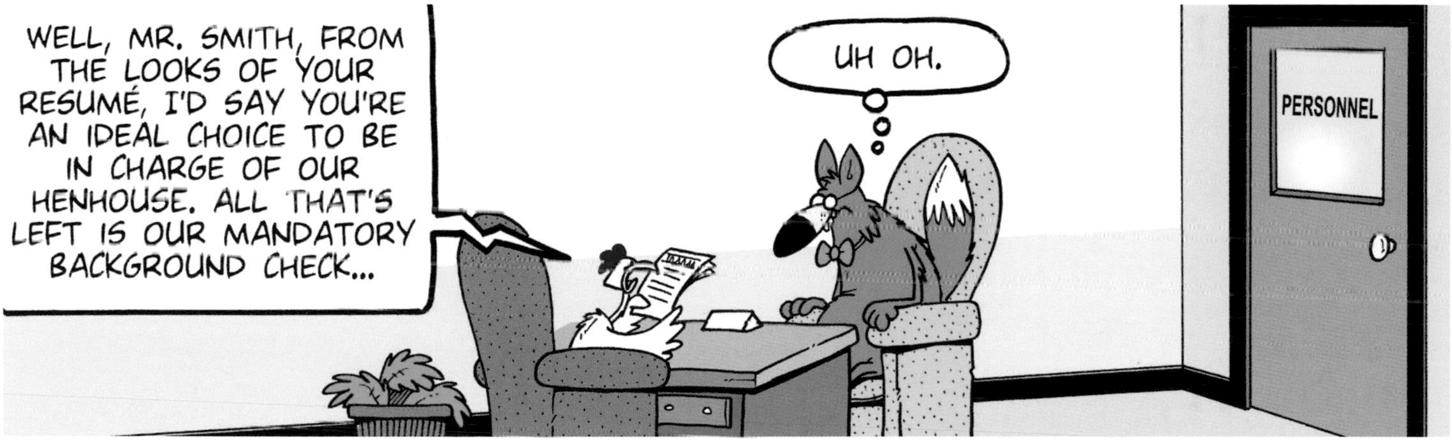
WELL, MR. SMITH, FROM THE LOOKS OF YOUR RESUMÉ, I'D SAY YOU'RE AN IDEAL CHOICE TO BE IN CHARGE OF OUR HENHOUSE. ALL THAT'S LEFT IS OUR MANDATORY BACKGROUND CHECK...
UH OH.
PERSONNEL

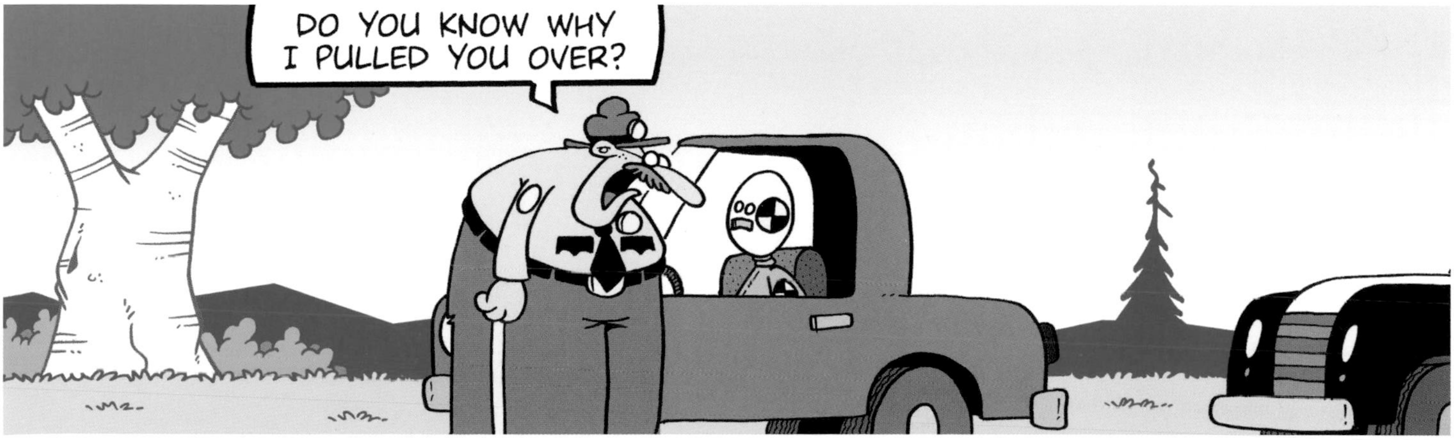
DO YOU KNOW WHY I PULLED YOU OVER?

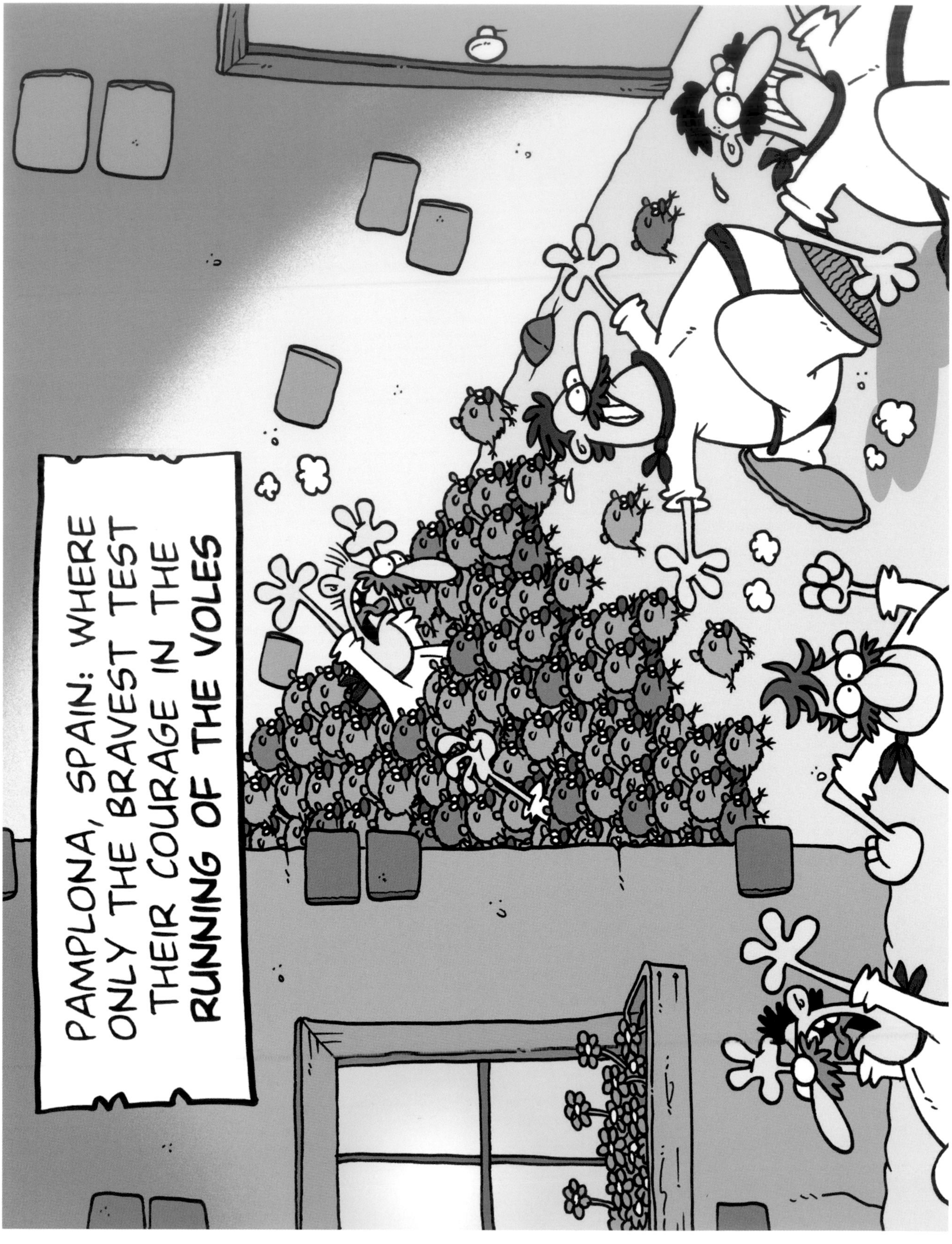
PAMPLONA, SPAIN: WHERE ONLY THE BRAVEST TEST THEIR COURAGE IN THE **RUNNING OF THE VOLES**

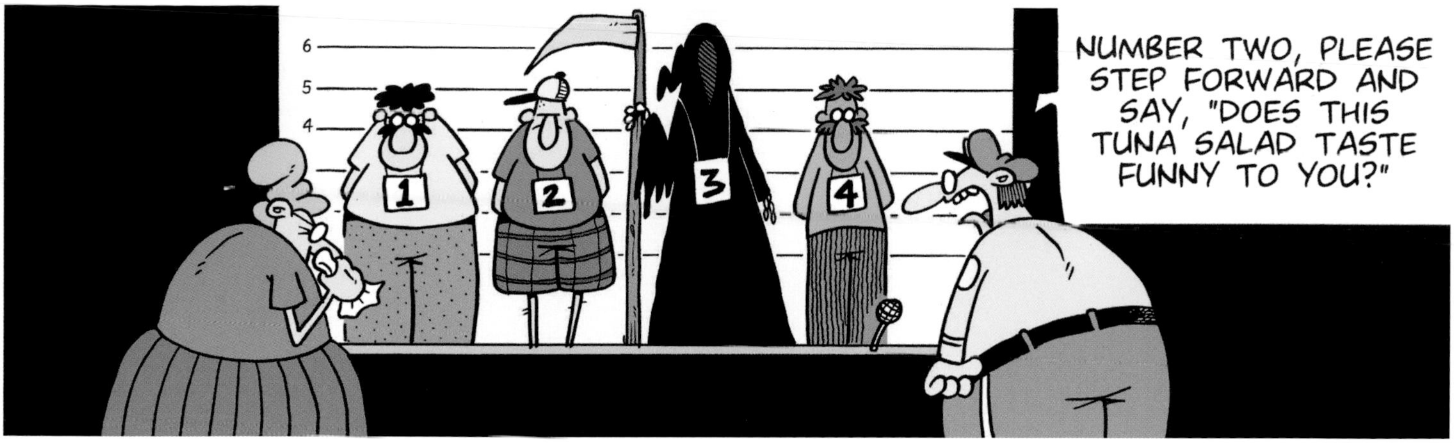
6
5
4
1
2
3
4
NUMBER TWO, PLEASE STEP FORWARD AND SAY, "DOES THIS TUNA SALAD TASTE FUNNY TO YOU?"

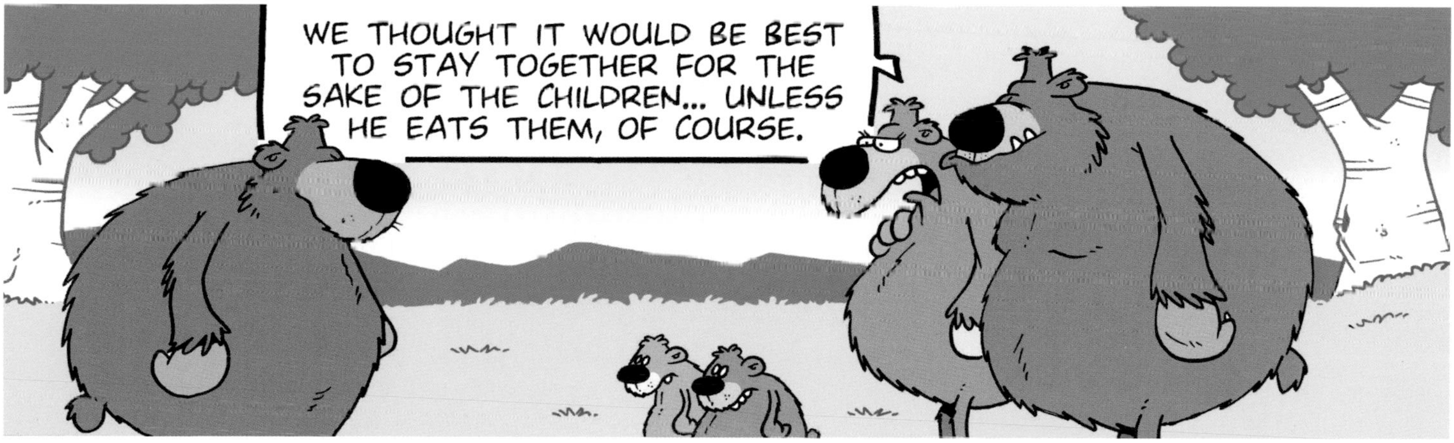
WE THOUGHT IT WOULD BE BEST TO STAY TOGETHER FOR THE SAKE OF THE CHILDREN... UNLESS HE EATS THEM, OF COURSE.

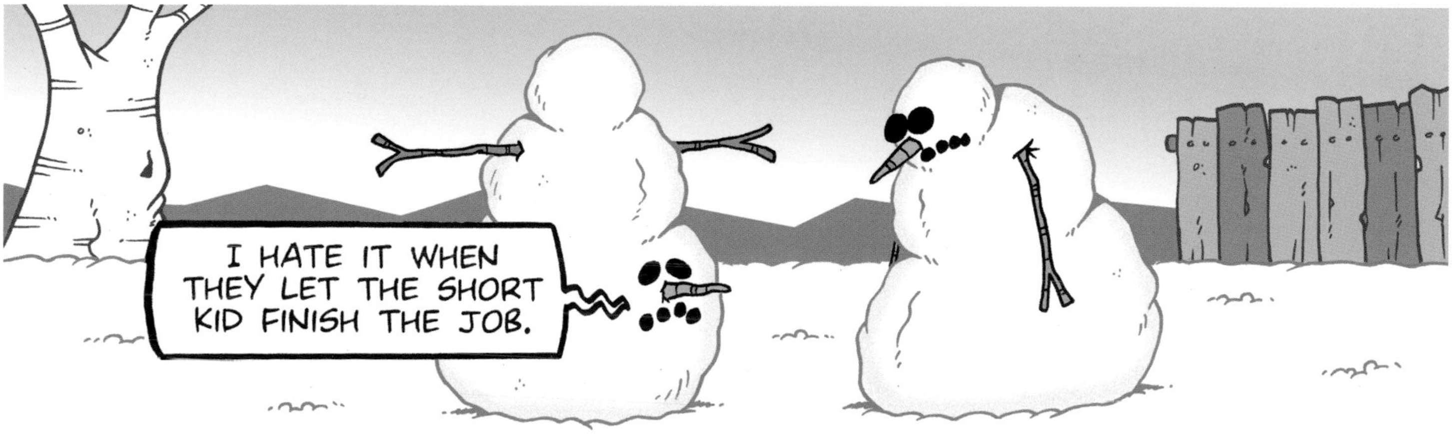
I HATE IT WHEN THEY LET THE SHORT KID FINISH THE JOB.

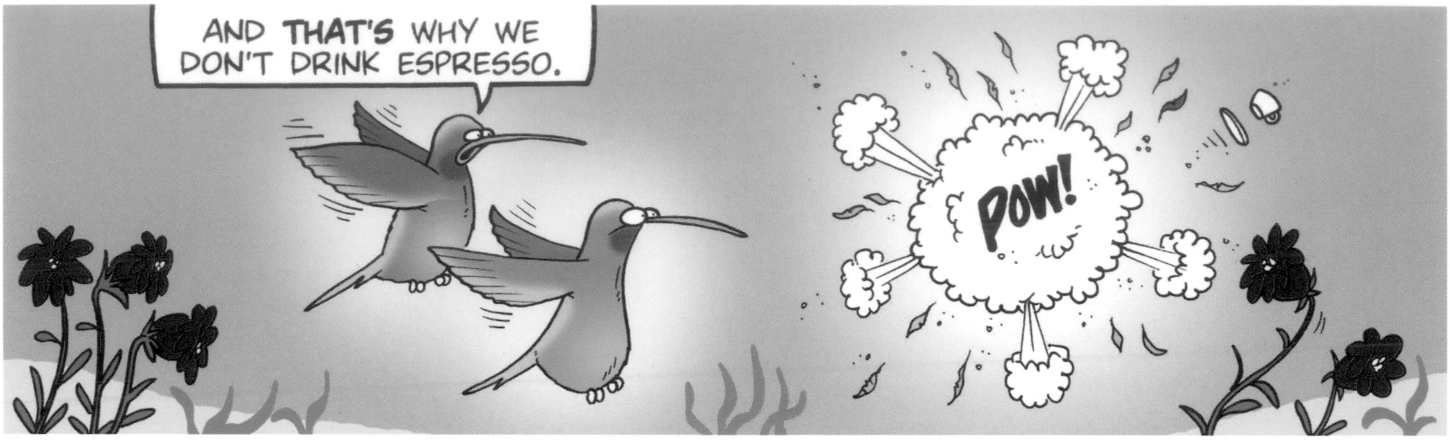
AND THAT'S WHY WE DON'T DRINK ESPRESSO.
POW!

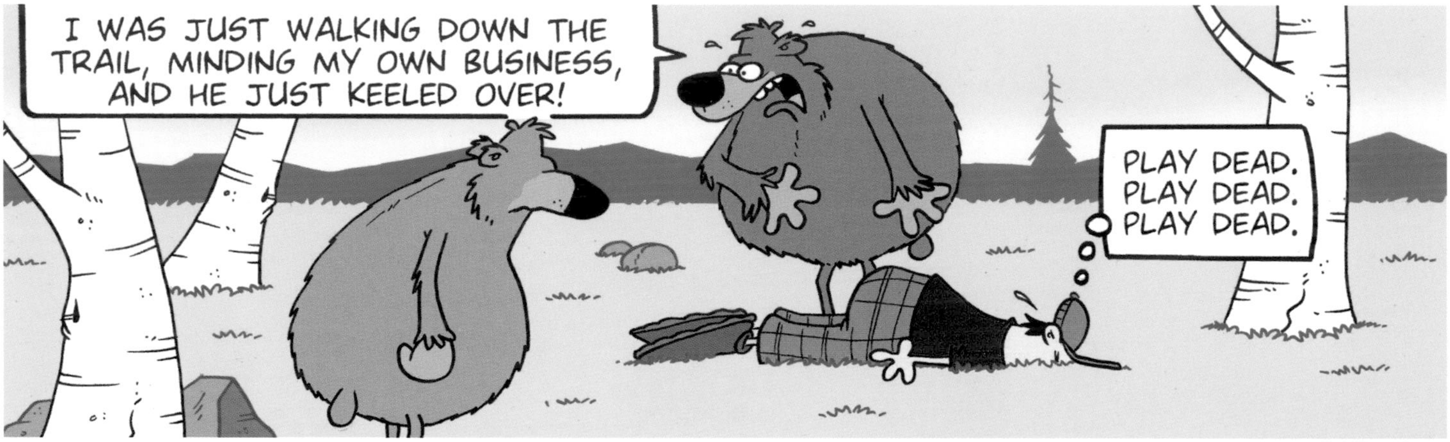
I WAS JUST WALKING DOWN THE TRAIL, MINDING MY OWN BUSINESS, AND HE JUST KEELED OVER!
PLAY DEAD. PLAY DEAD. PLAY DEAD.

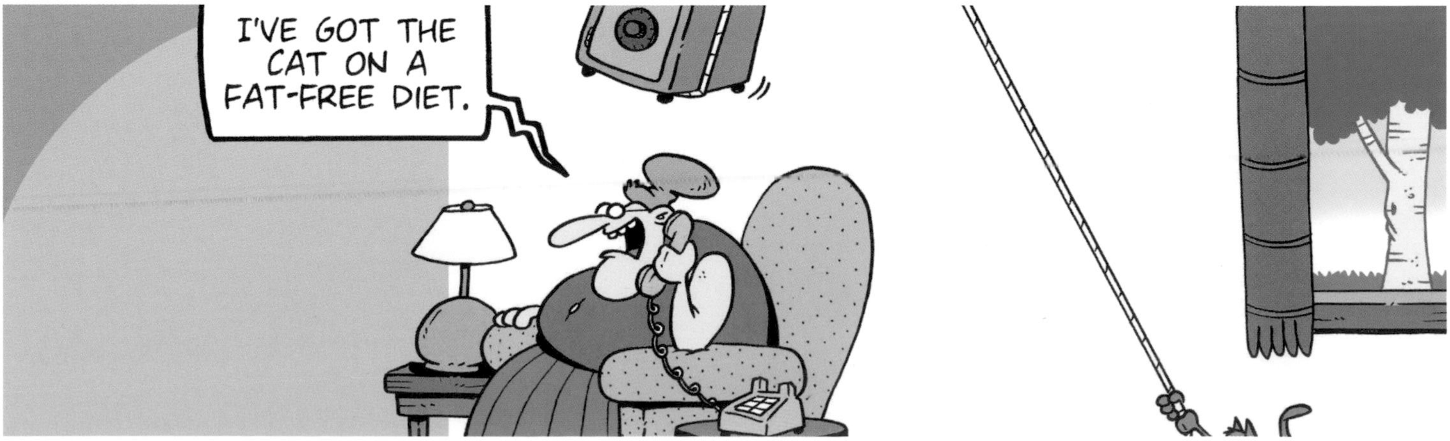
I'VE GOT THE CAT ON A FAT-FREE DIET.

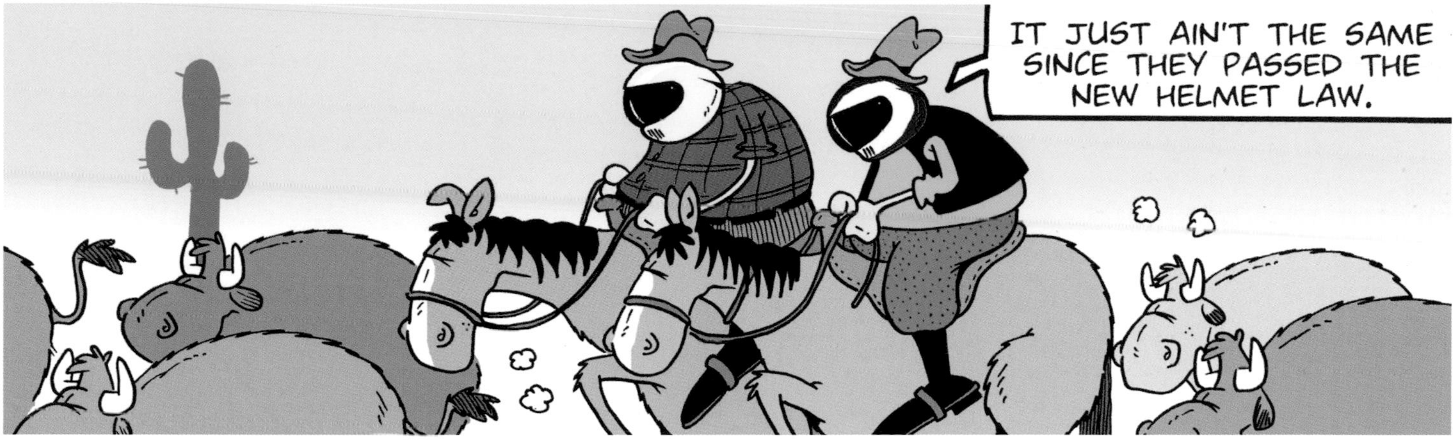
IT JUST AIN'T THE SAME SINCE THEY PASSED THE NEW HELMET LAW.

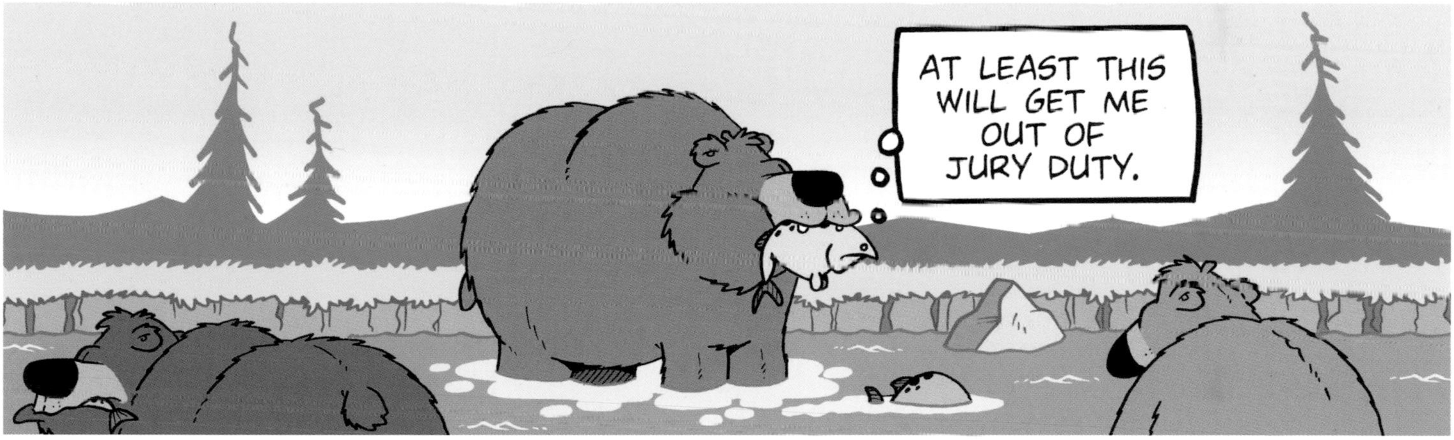
AT LEAST THIS WILL GET ME OUT OF JURY DUTY.

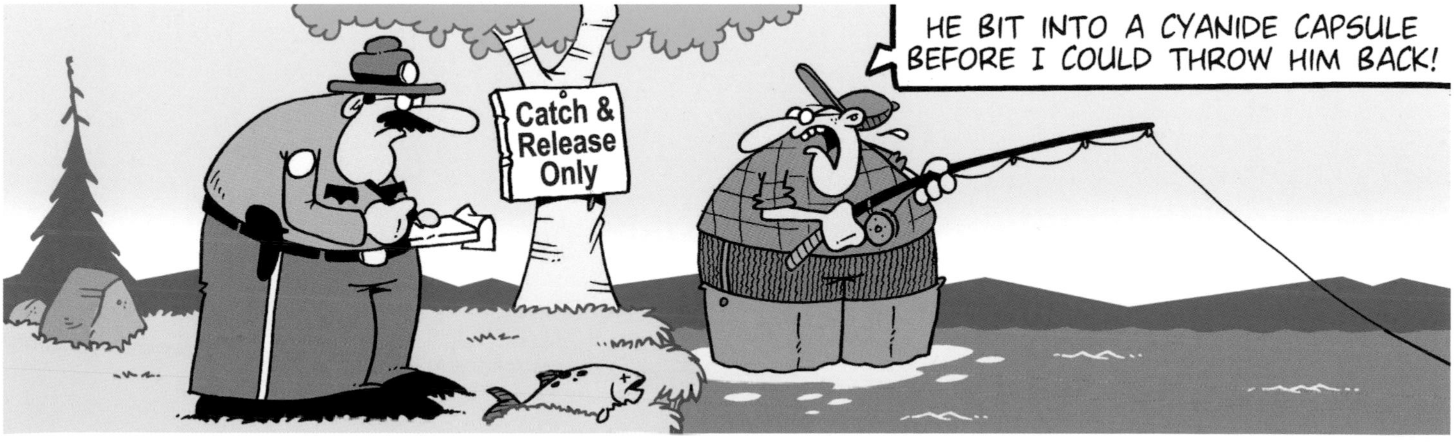
Catch & Release Only
HE BIT INTO A CYANIDE CAPSULE BEFORE I COULD THROW HIM BACK!

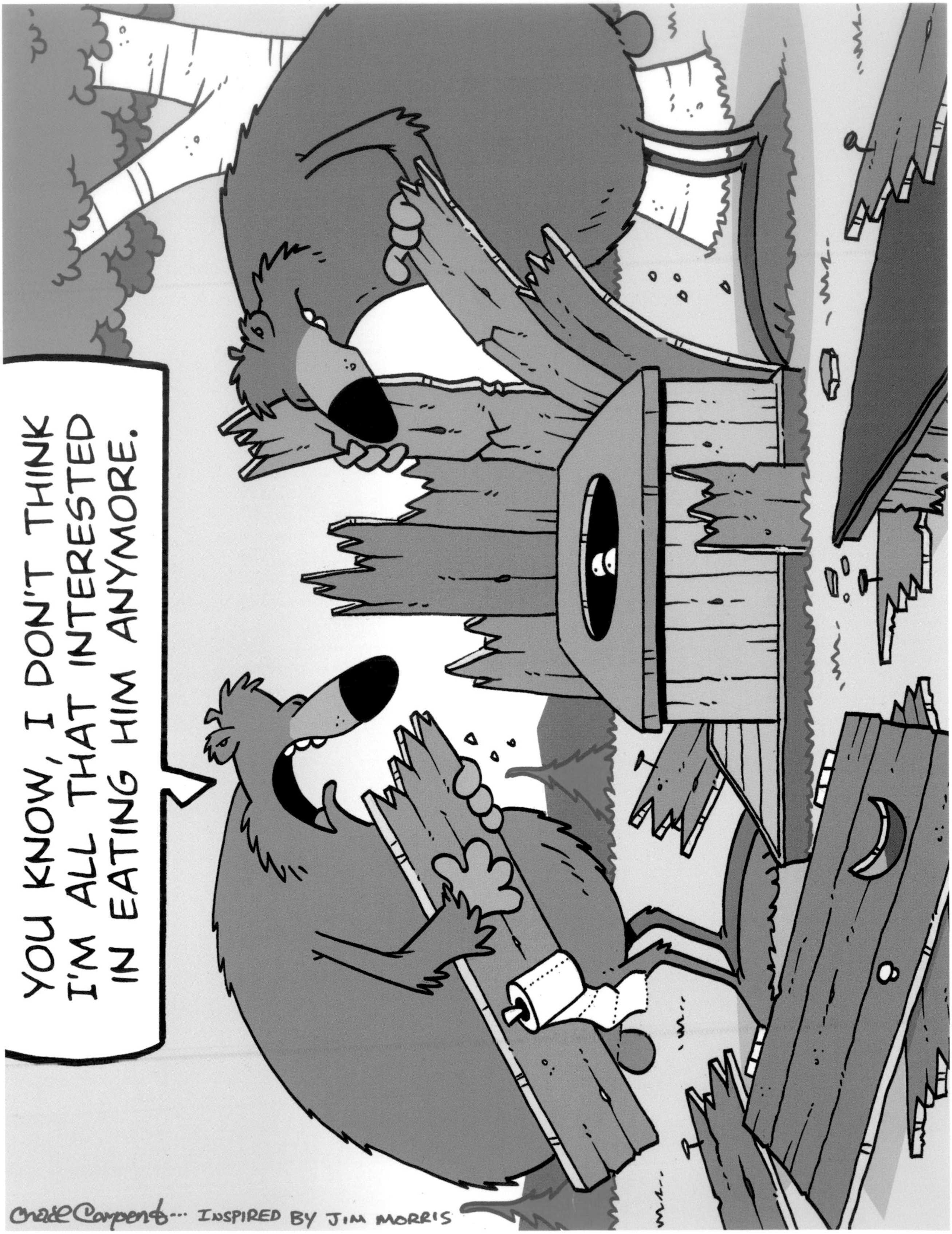
YOU KNOW, I DON'T THINK I'M ALL THAT INTERESTED IN EATING HIM ANYMORE.
Chad Carpenter... INSPIRED BY JIM MORRIS

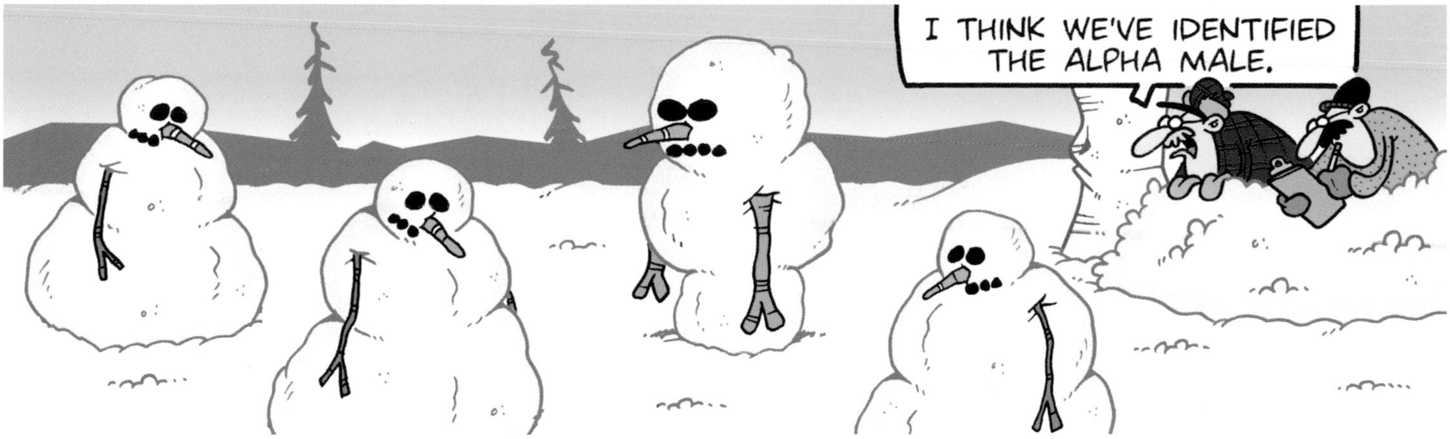
I THINK WE'VE IDENTIFIED THE ALPHA MALE.

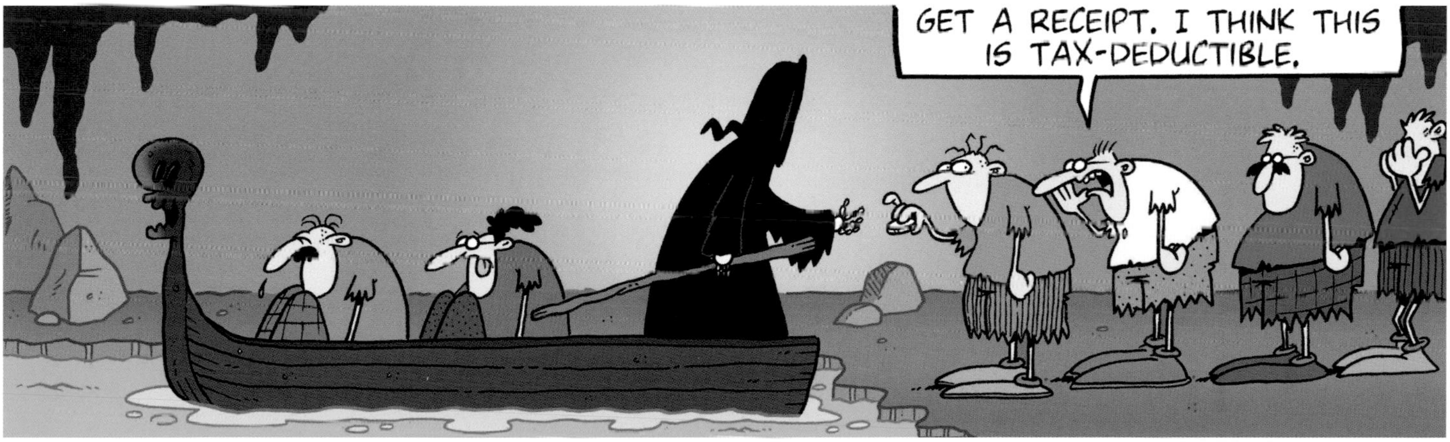
GET A RECEIPT. I THINK THIS IS TAX-DEDUCTIBLE.

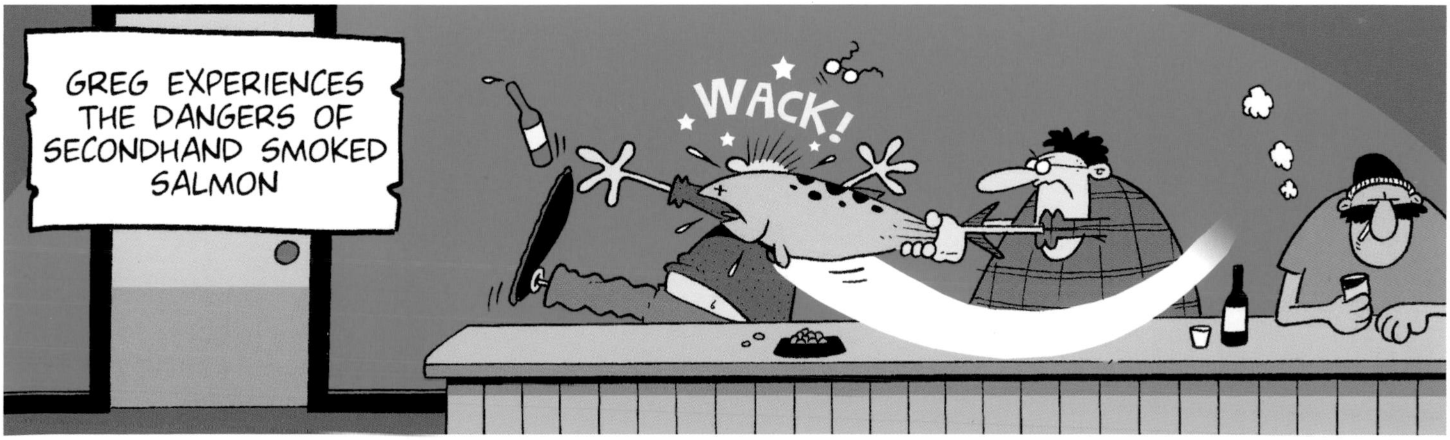
GREG EXPERIENCES THE DANGERS OF SECONDHAND SMOKED SALMON
WACK!

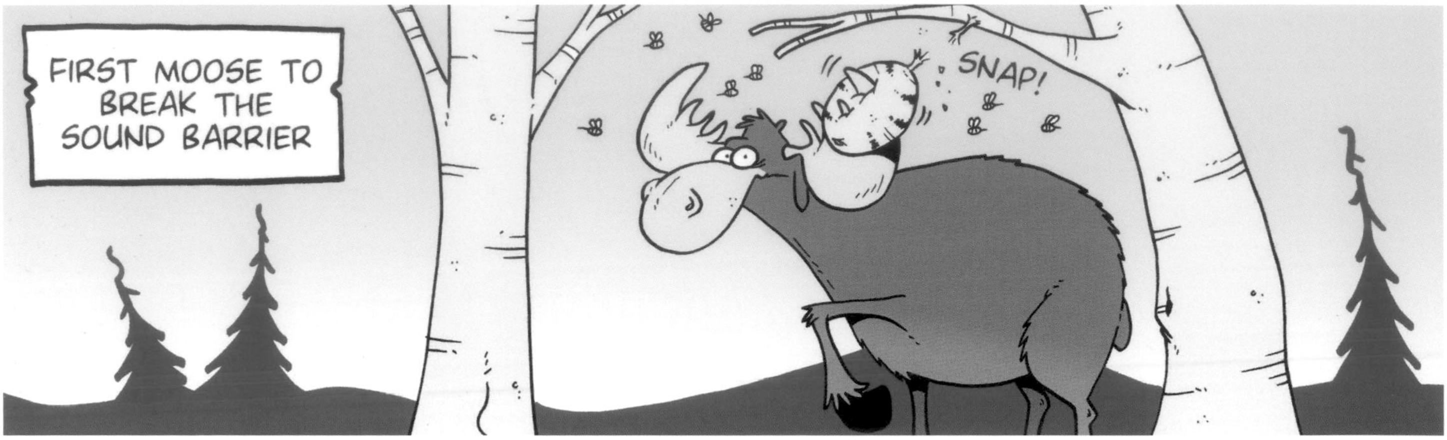
FIRST MOOSE TO BREAK THE SOUND BARRIER
SNAP!

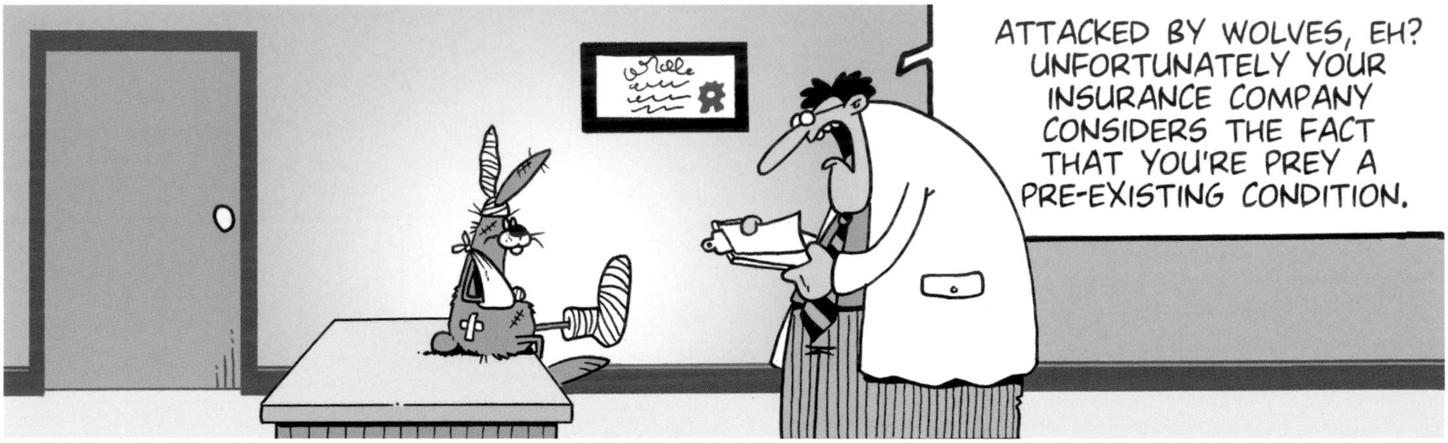
ATTACKED BY WOLVES, EH? UNFORTUNATELY YOUR INSURANCE COMPANY CONSIDERS THE FACT THAT YOU'RE PREY A PRE-EXISTING CONDITION.

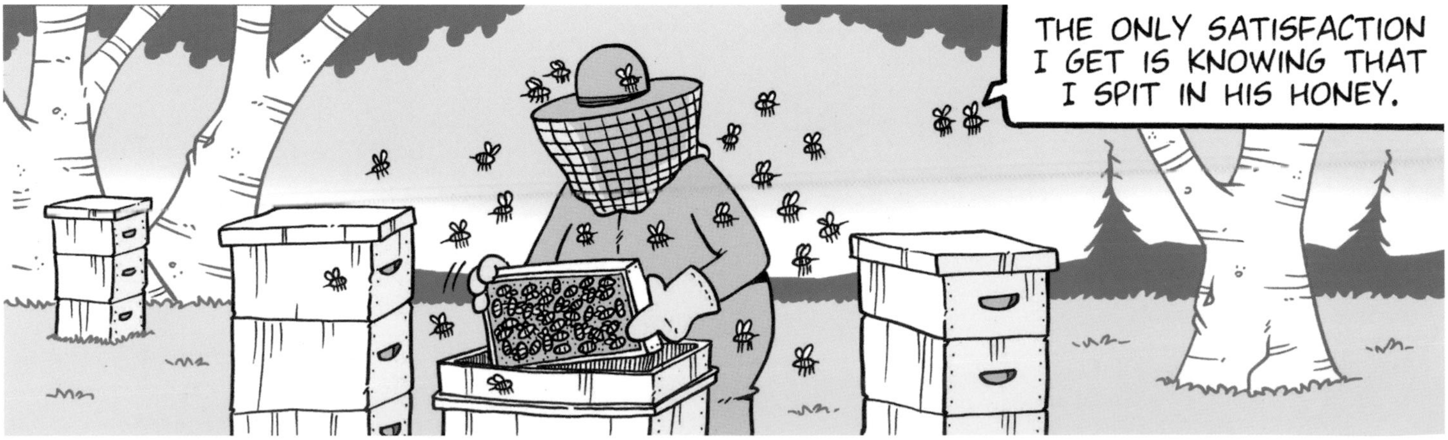
THE ONLY SATISFACTION I GET IS KNOWING THAT I SPIT IN HIS HONEY.

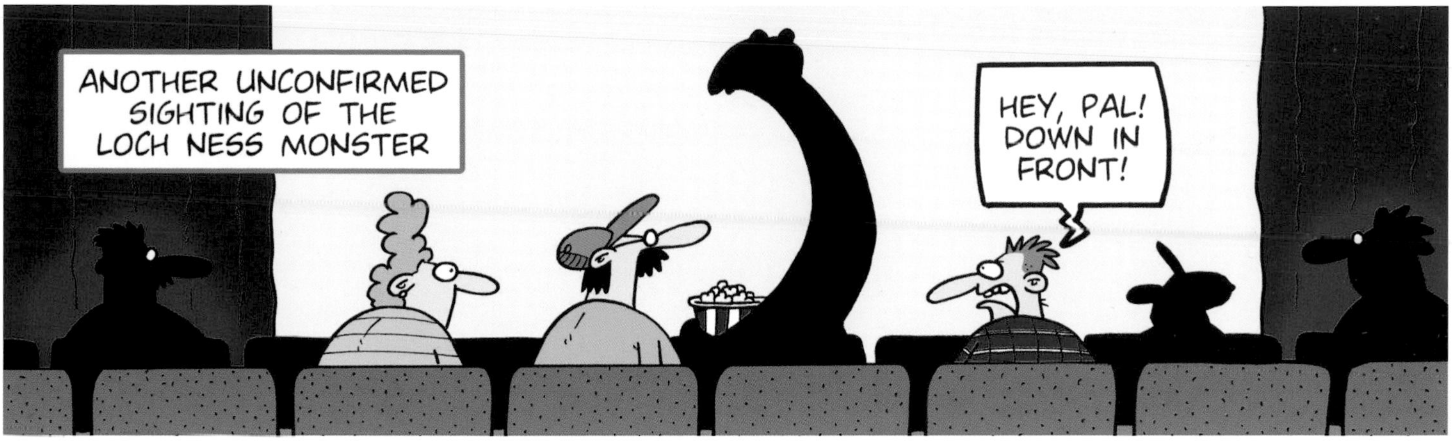
ANOTHER UNCONFIRMED SIGHTING OF THE LOCH NESS MONSTER
HEY, PAL! DOWN IN FRONT!

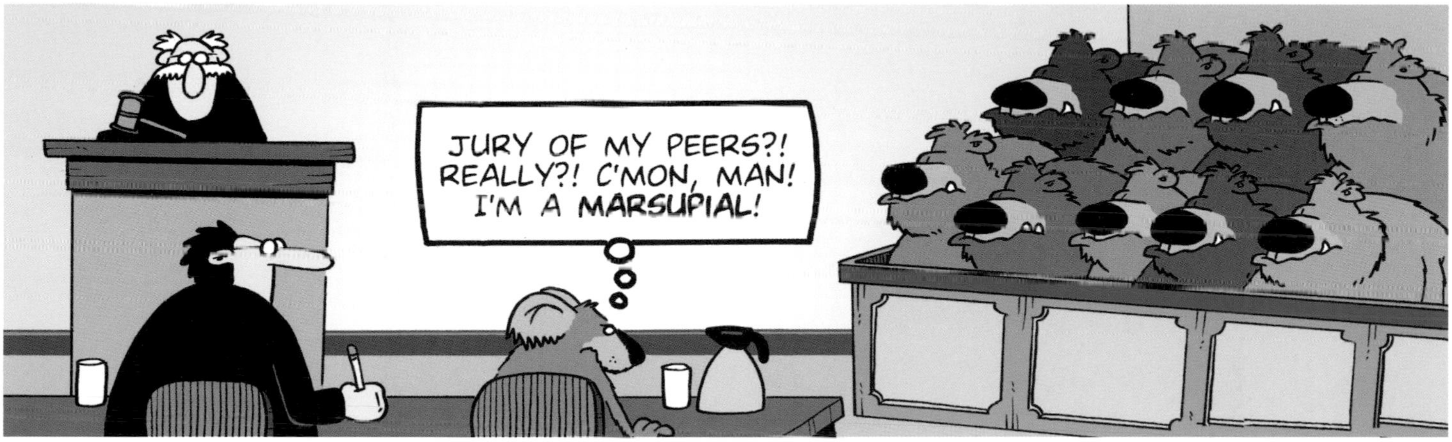
JURY OF MY PEERS?! REALLY?! C'MON, MAN! I'M A MARSUPIAL!

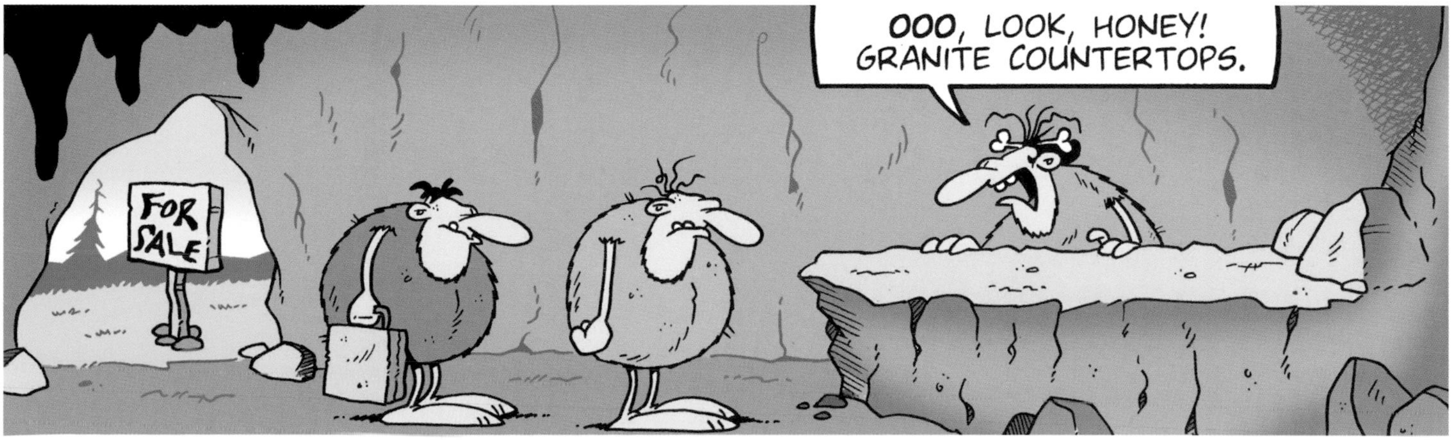
OOO, LOOK, HONEY! GRANITE COUNTERTOPS.
FOR SALE

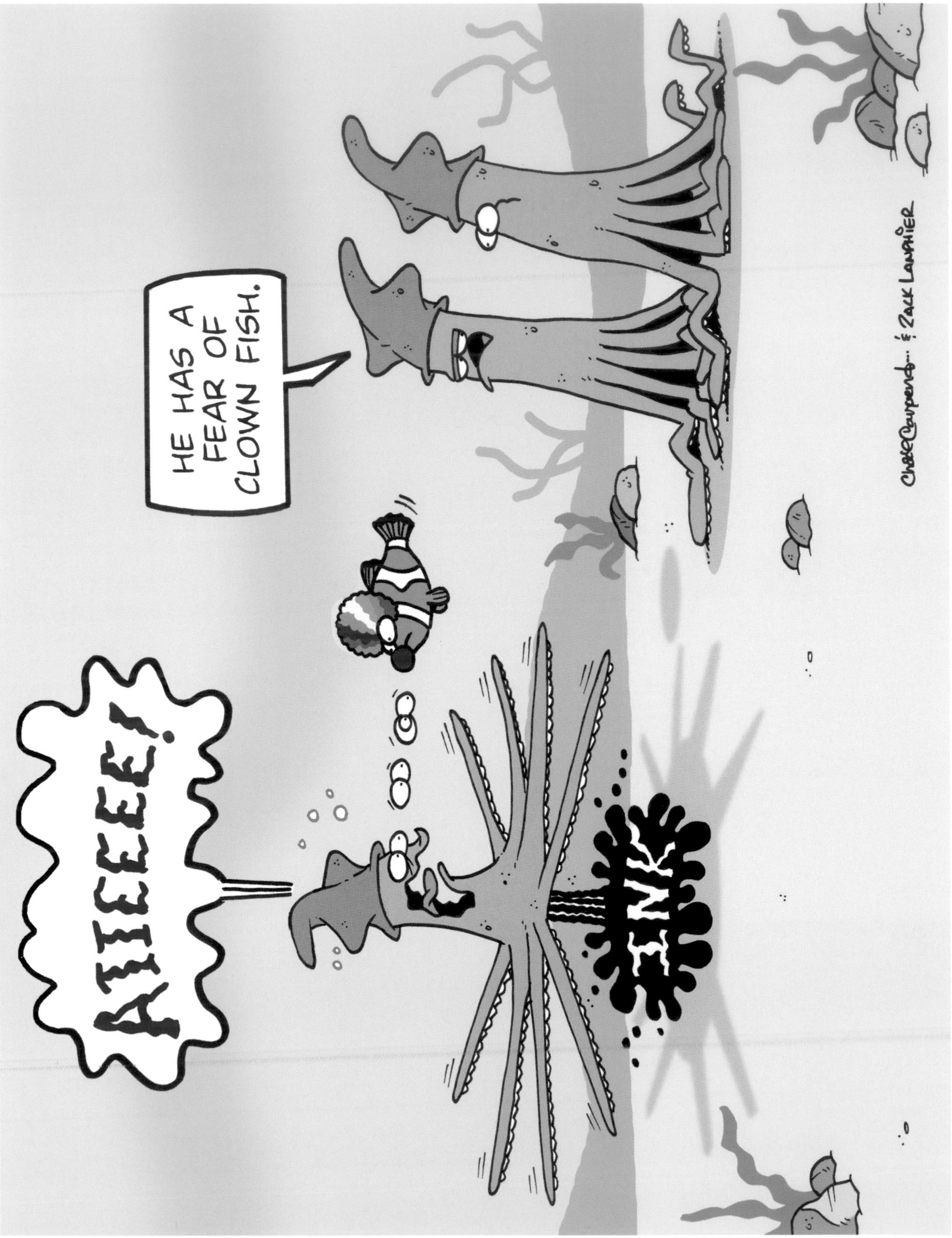
AIIEEEE!
INK
HE HAS A FEAR OF CLOWN FISH.

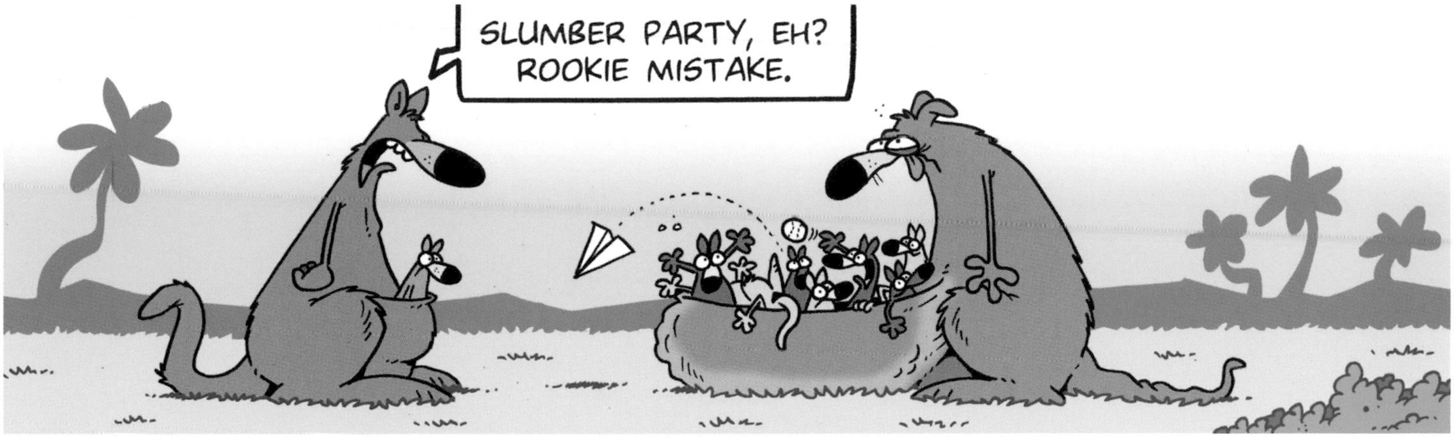
SLUMBER PARTY, EH?
ROOKIE MISTAKE.

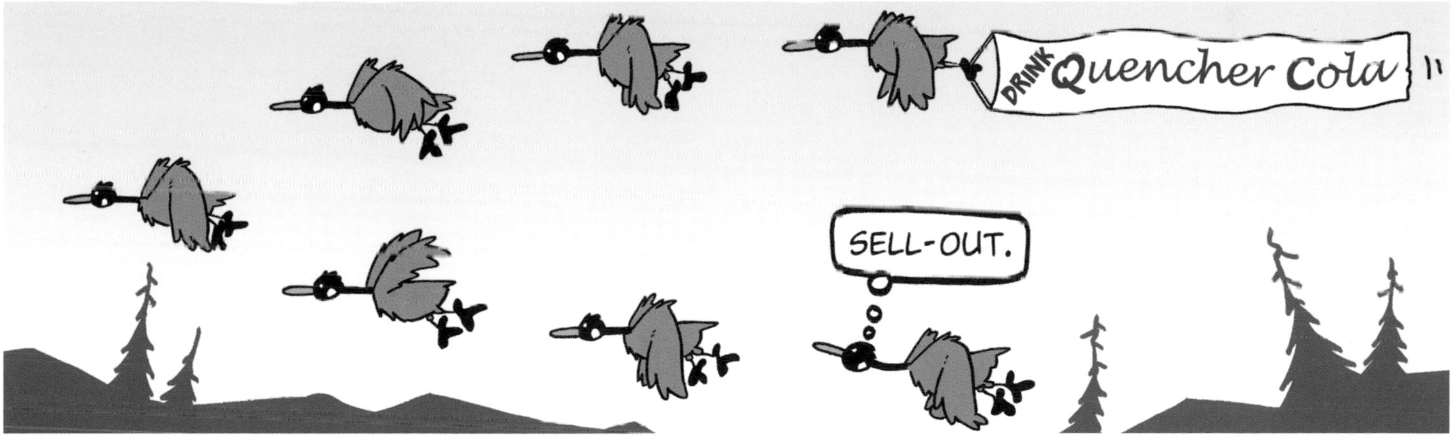
DRINK Quencher Cola
SELL-OUT.

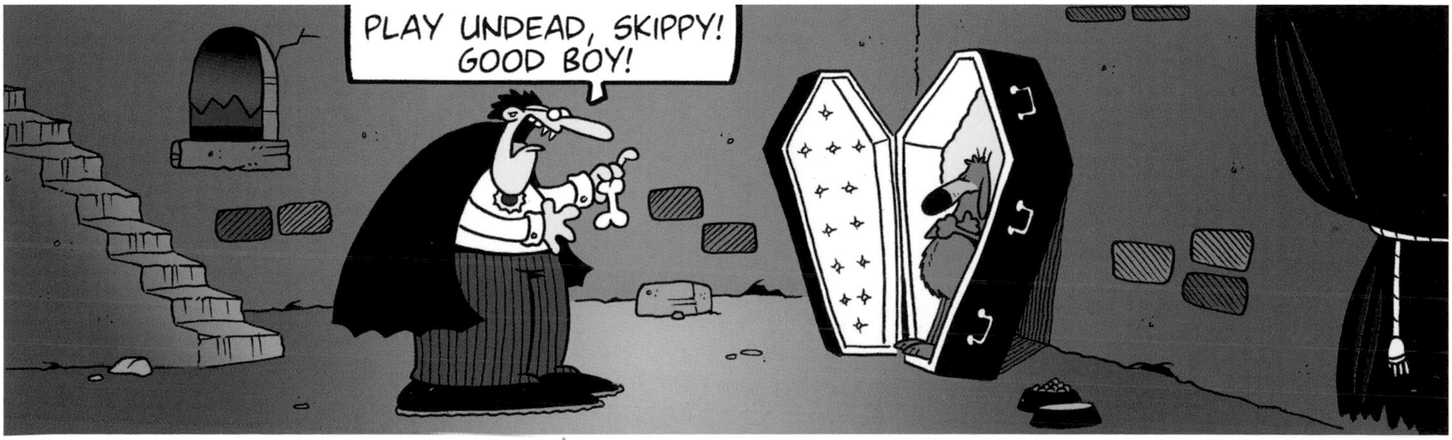
PLAY UNDEAD, SKIPPY!
GOOD BOY!

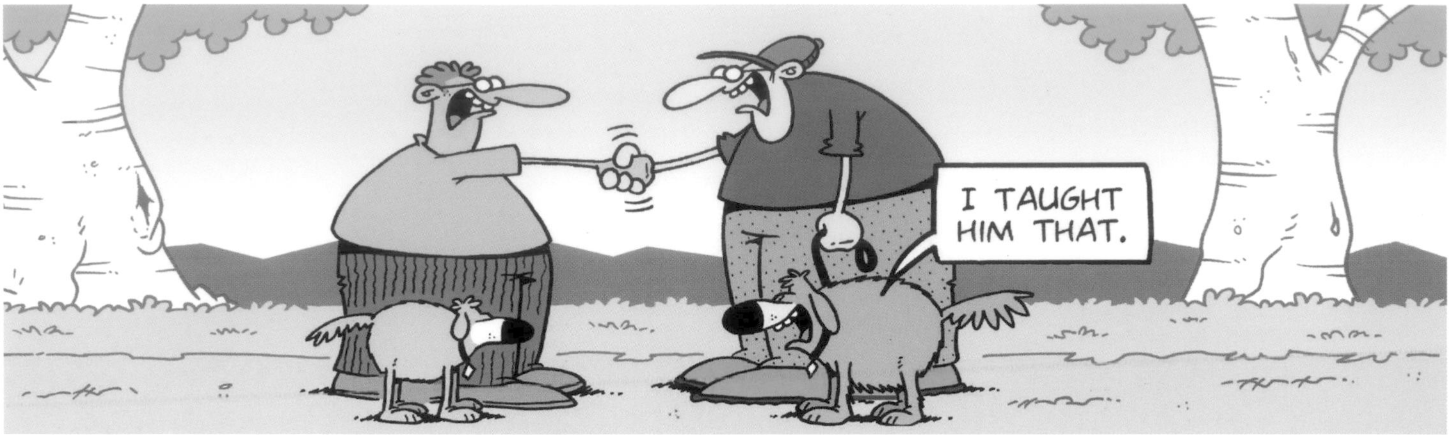
I TAUGHT HIM THAT.

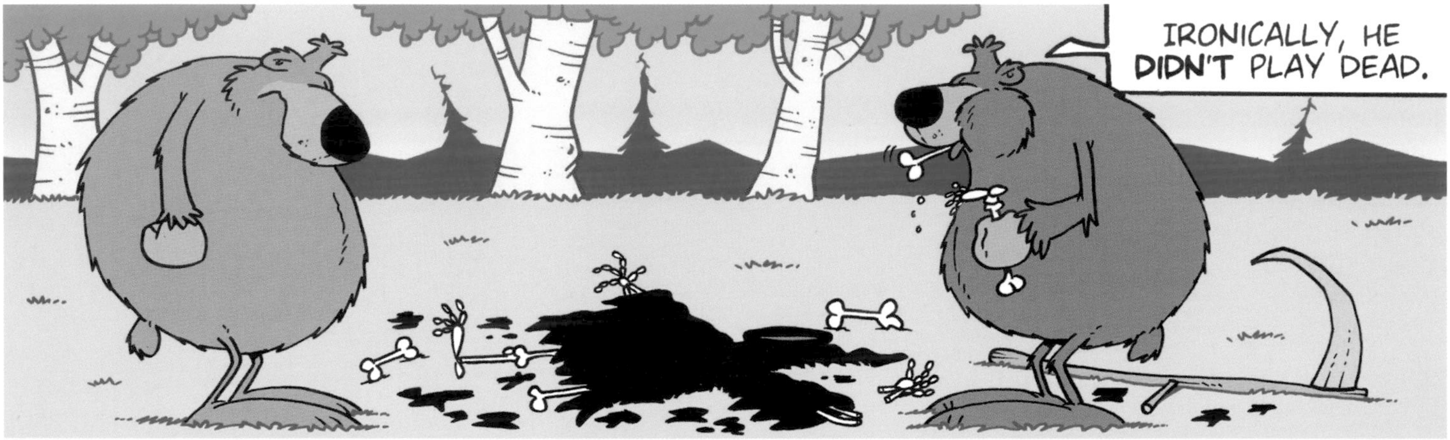
IRONICALLY, HE DIDN'T PLAY DEAD.

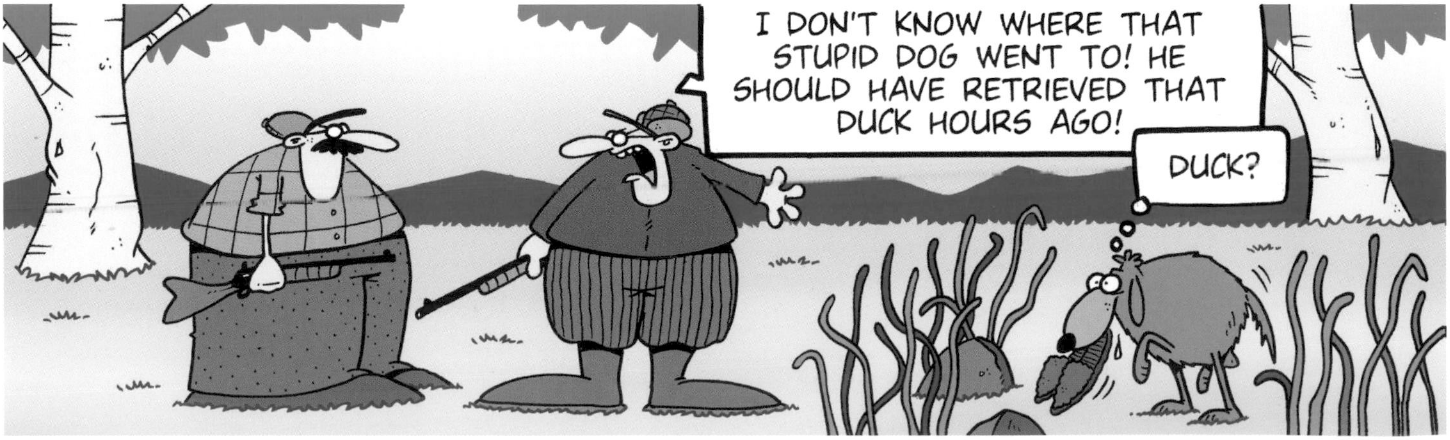
I DON'T KNOW WHERE THAT STUPID DOG WENT TO! HE SHOULD HAVE RETRIEVED THAT DUCK HOURS AGO!
DUCK?

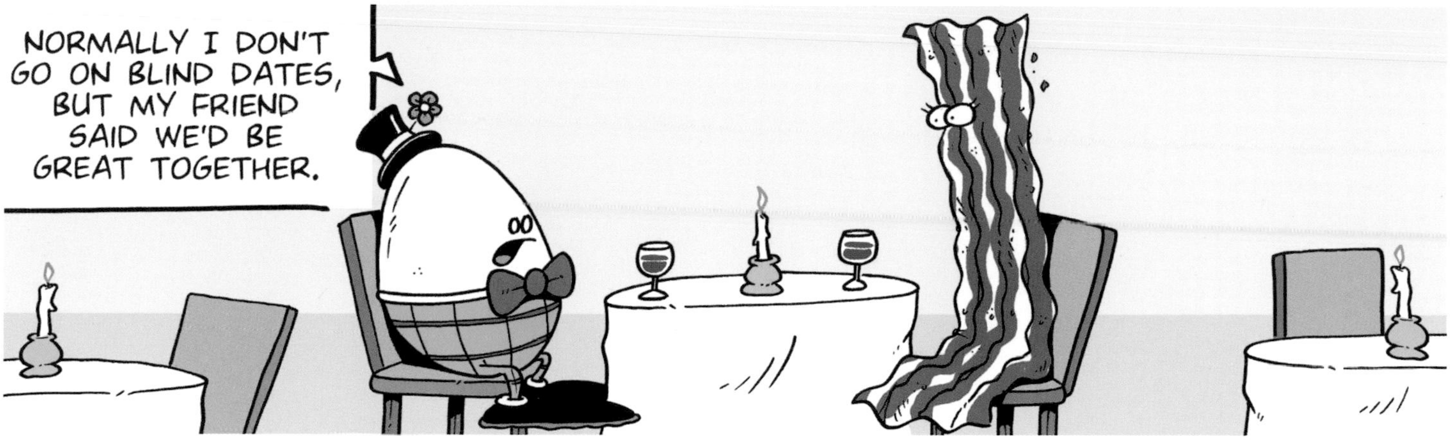
NORMALLY I DON'T GO ON BLIND DATES, BUT MY FRIEND SAID WE'D BE GREAT TOGETHER.

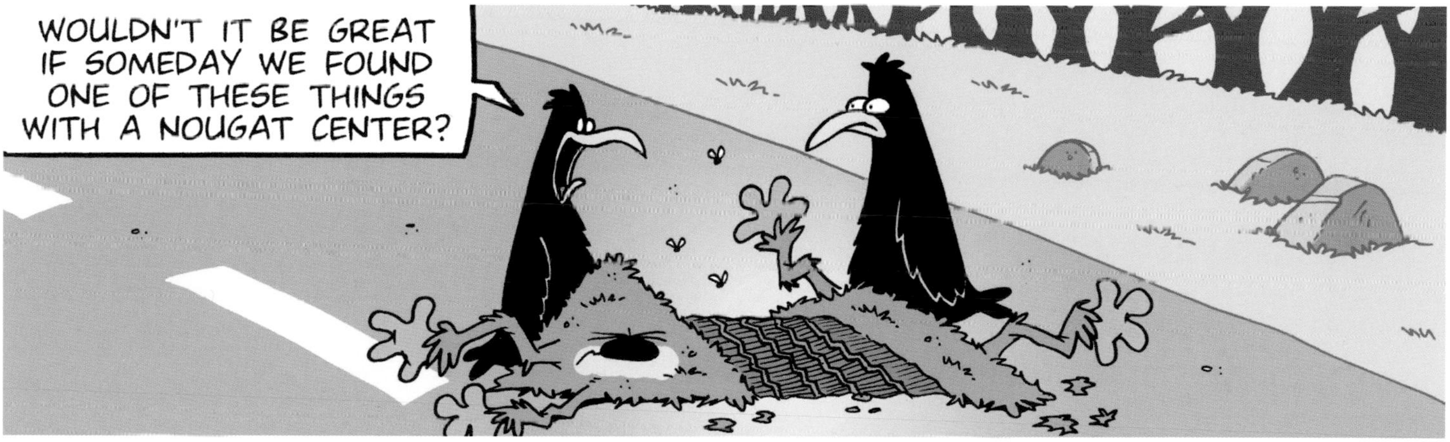
WOULDN'T IT BE GREAT IF SOMEDAY WE FOUND ONE OF THESE THINGS WITH A NOUGAT CENTER?

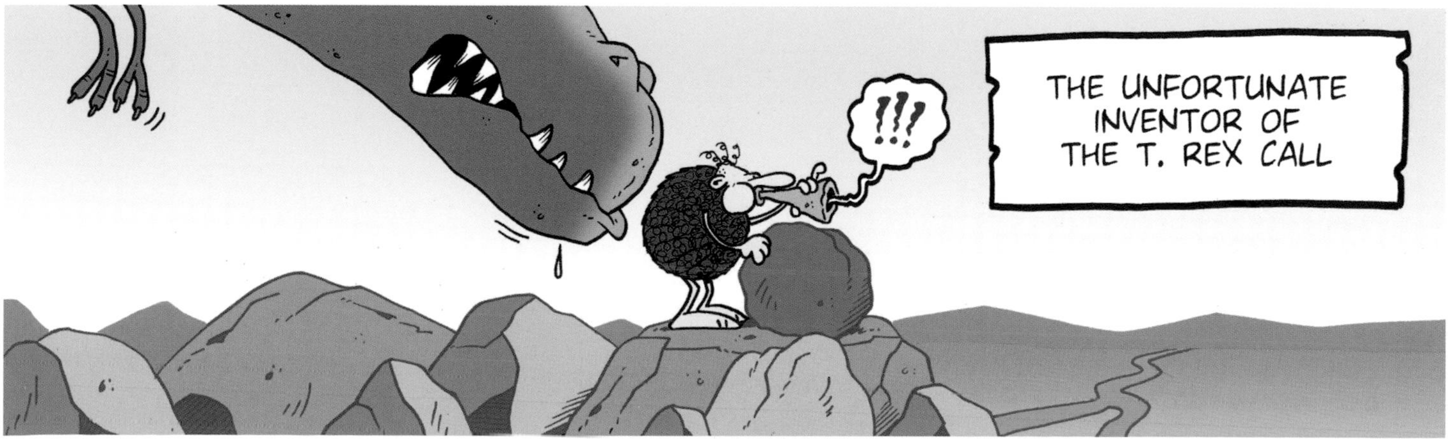
!!!
THE UNFORTUNATE INVENTOR OF THE T. REX CALL

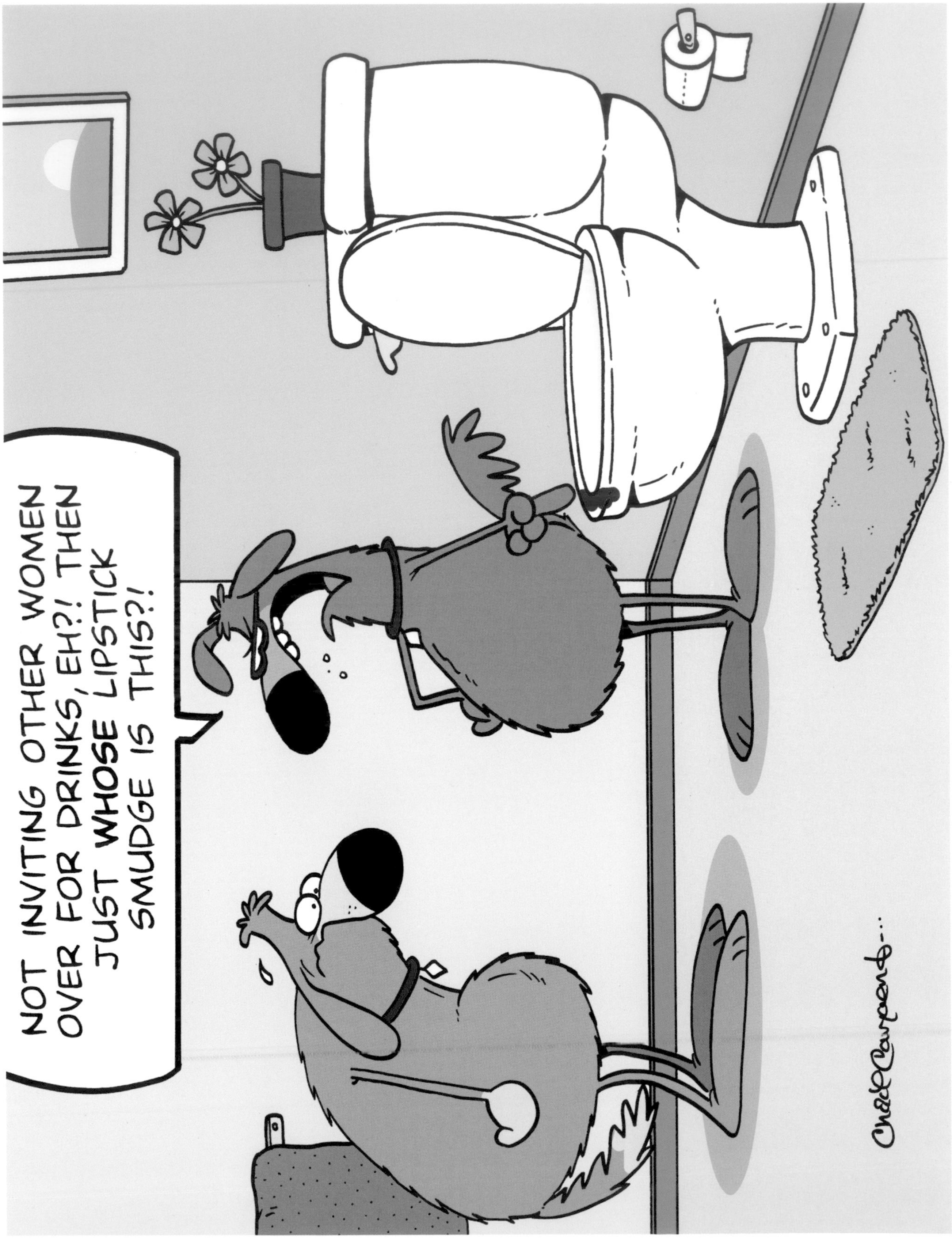
NOT INVITING OTHER WOMEN OVER FOR DRINKS, EH?! THEN JUST WHOSE LIPSTICK SMUDGE IS THIS?!

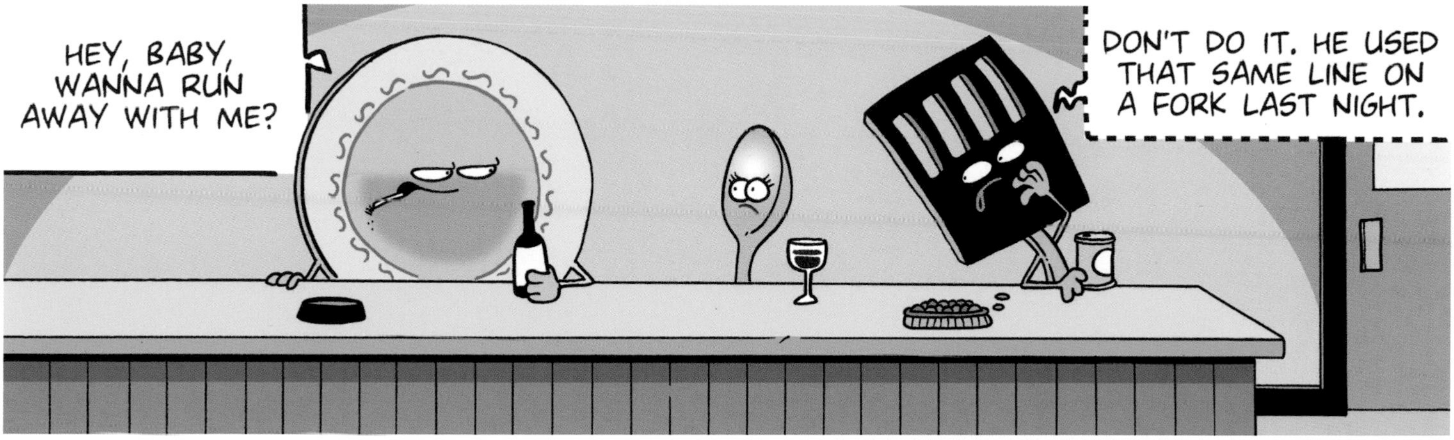
HEY, BABY, WANNA RUN AWAY WITH ME?
DON'T DO IT. HE USED THAT SAME LINE ON A FORK LAST NIGHT.

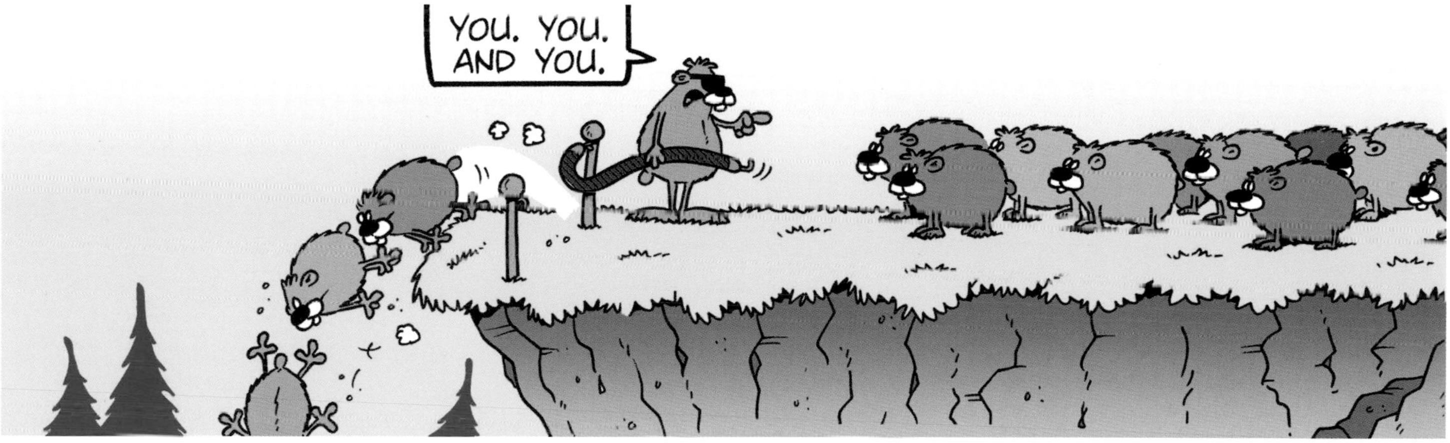
YOU. YOU. AND YOU.

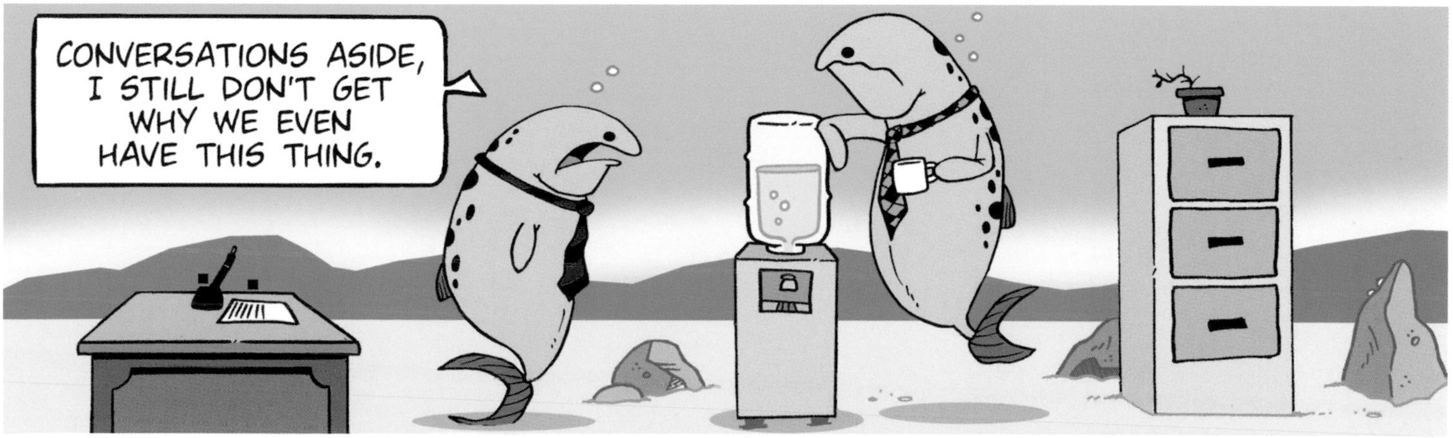
CONVERSATIONS ASIDE, I STILL DON'T GET WHY WE EVEN HAVE THIS THING.

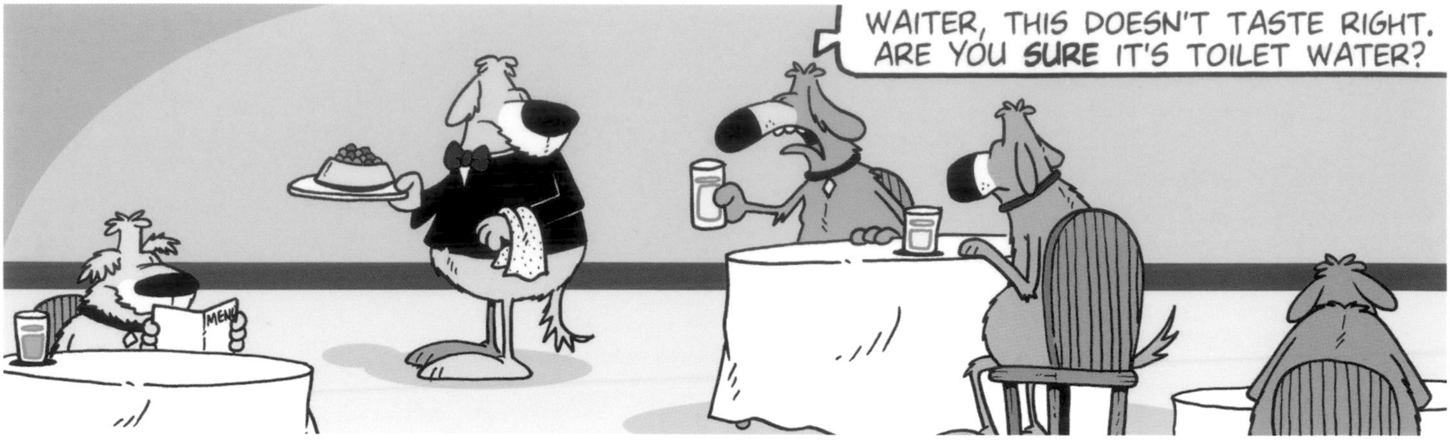
WAITER, THIS DOESN'T TASTE RIGHT. ARE YOU **SURE** IT'S TOILET WATER?
MENU

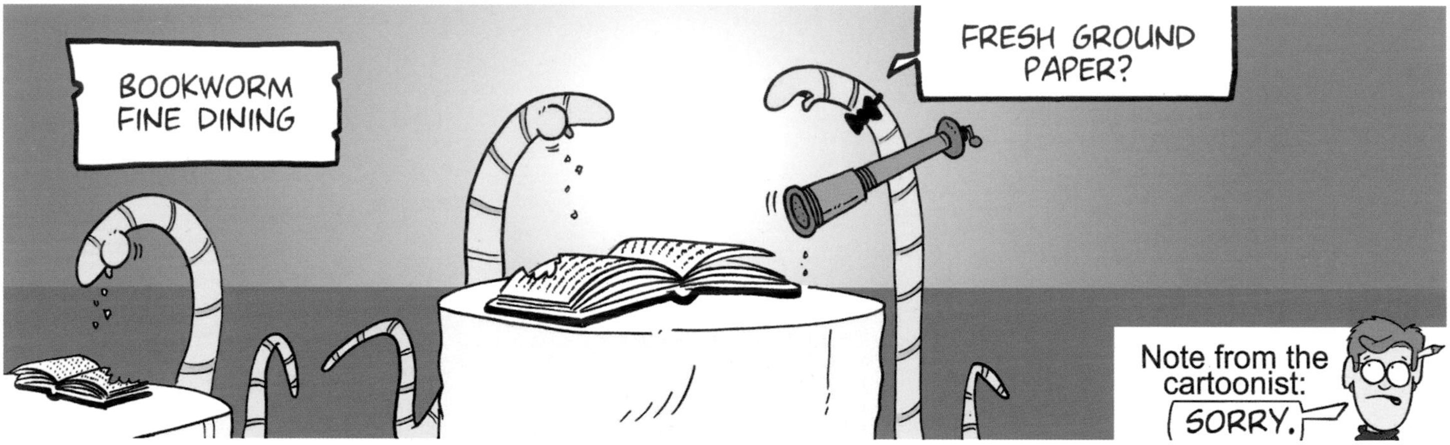
BOOKWORM FINE DINING
FRESH GROUND PAPER?
Note from the cartoonist:
SORRY.

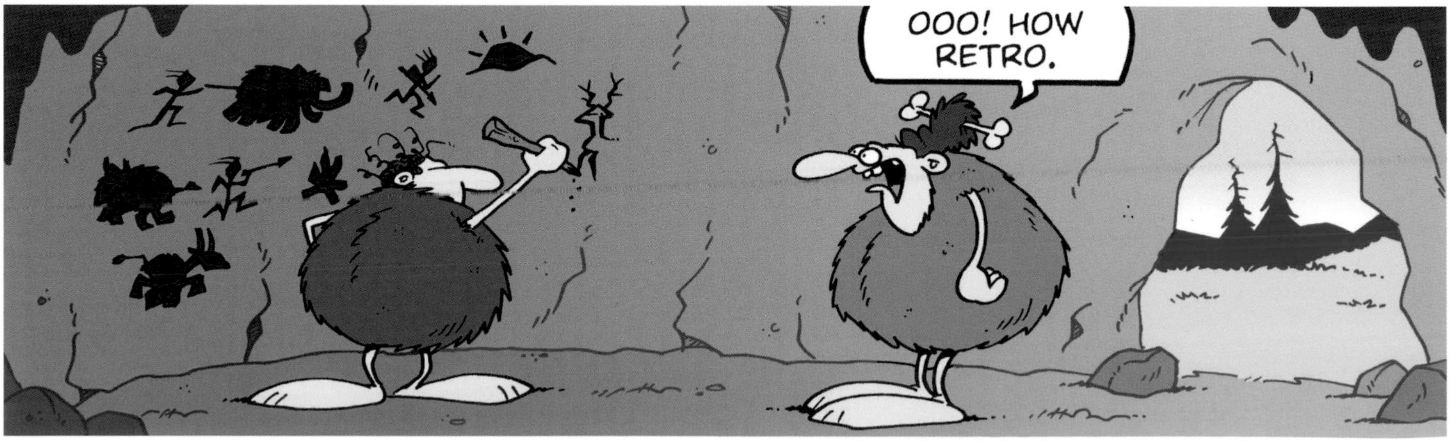
OOO! HOW RETRO.

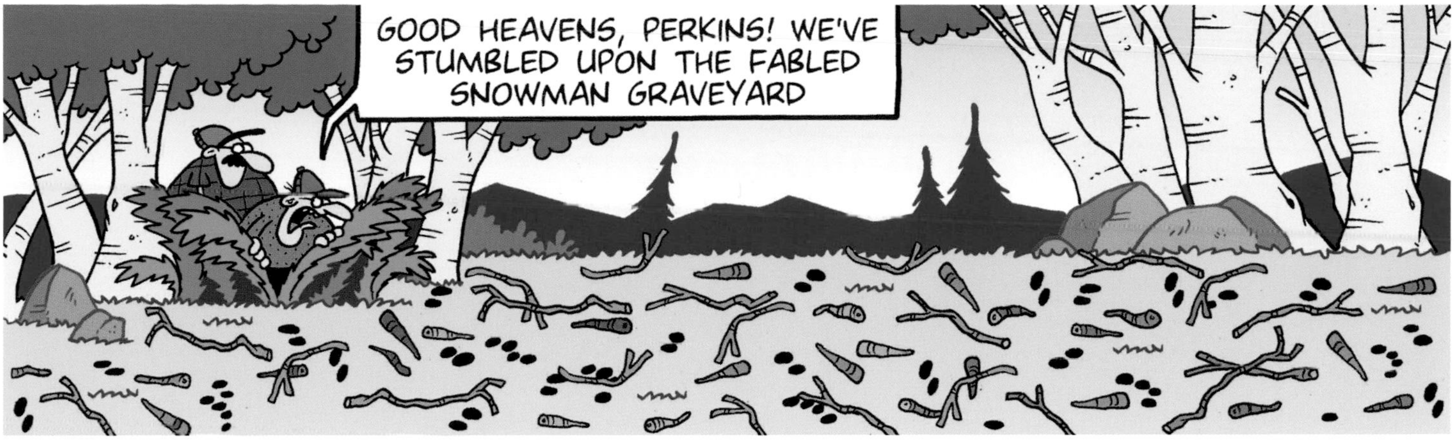
GOOD HEAVENS, PERKINS! WE'VE STUMBLED UPON THE FABLED SNOWMAN GRAVEYARD

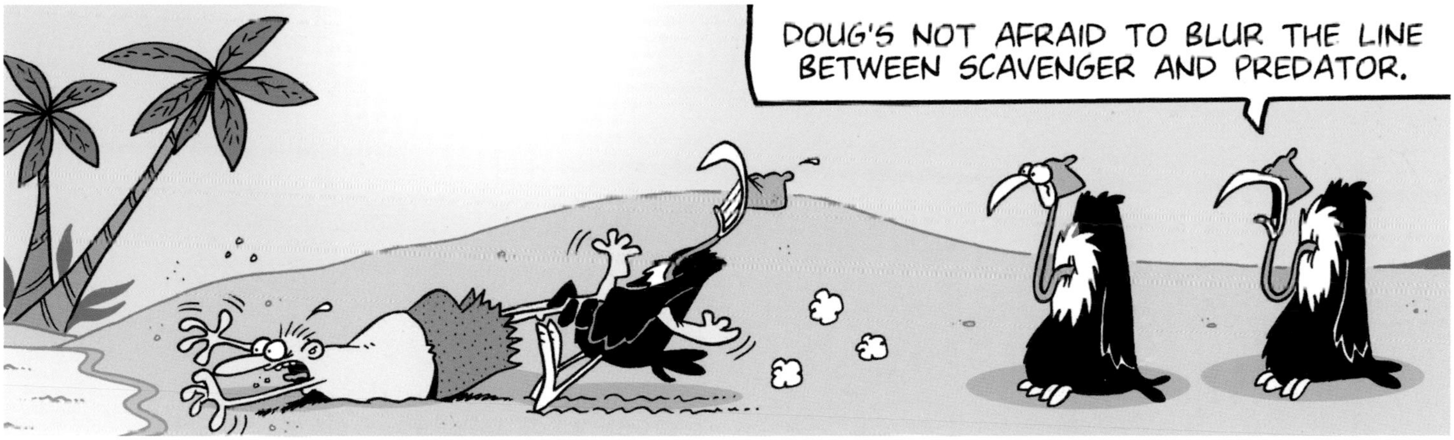
DOUG'S NOT AFRAID TO BLUR THE LINE BETWEEN SCAVENGER AND PREDATOR.

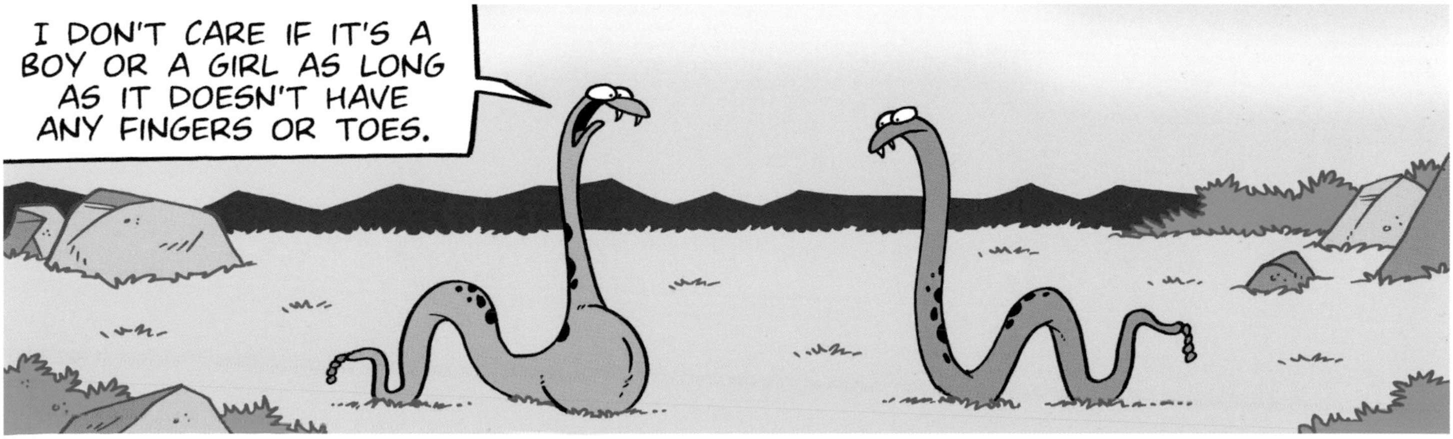
I DON'T CARE IF IT'S A BOY OR A GIRL AS LONG AS IT DOESN'T HAVE ANY FINGERS OR TOES.

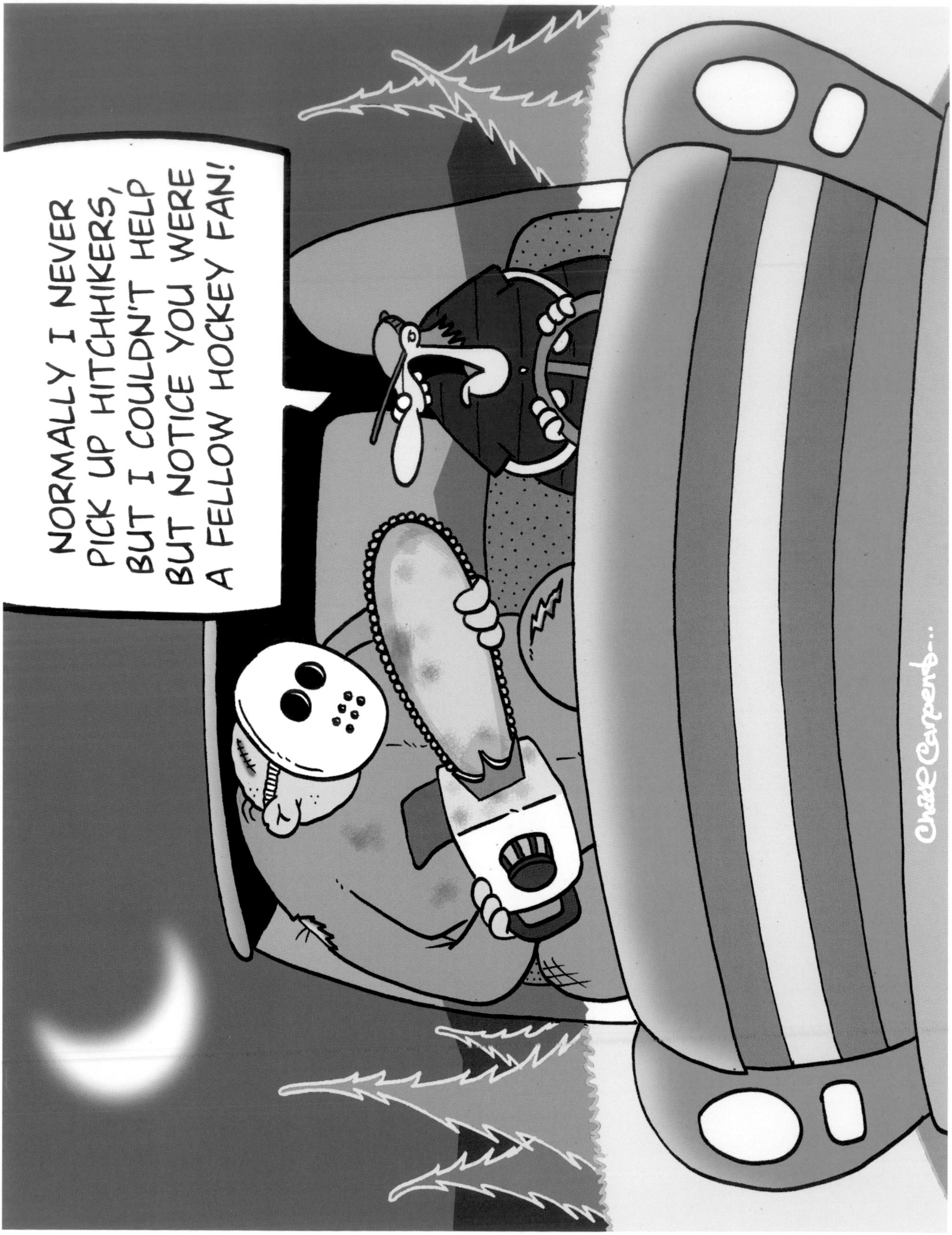
NORMALLY I NEVER PICK UP HITCHHIKERS, BUT I COULDN'T HELP BUT NOTICE YOU WERE A FELLOW HOCKEY FAN!
Chad Carpenter...

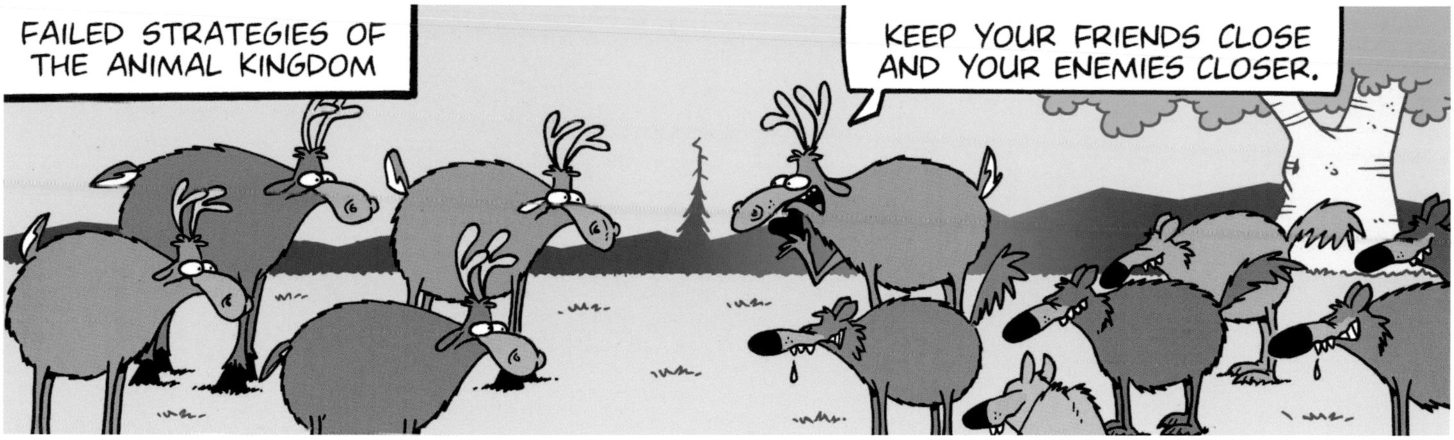
FAILED STRATEGIES OF THE ANIMAL KINGDOM
KEEP YOUR FRIENDS CLOSE AND YOUR ENEMIES CLOSER.

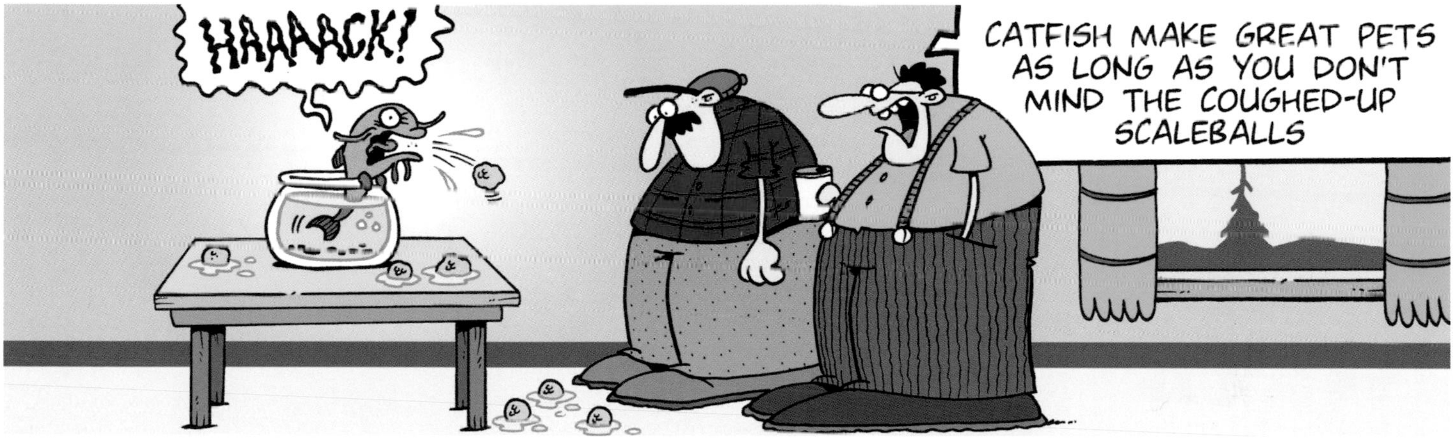
HAAAACK!
CATFISH MAKE GREAT PETS AS LONG AS YOU DON'T MIND THE COUGHED-UP SCALEBALLS

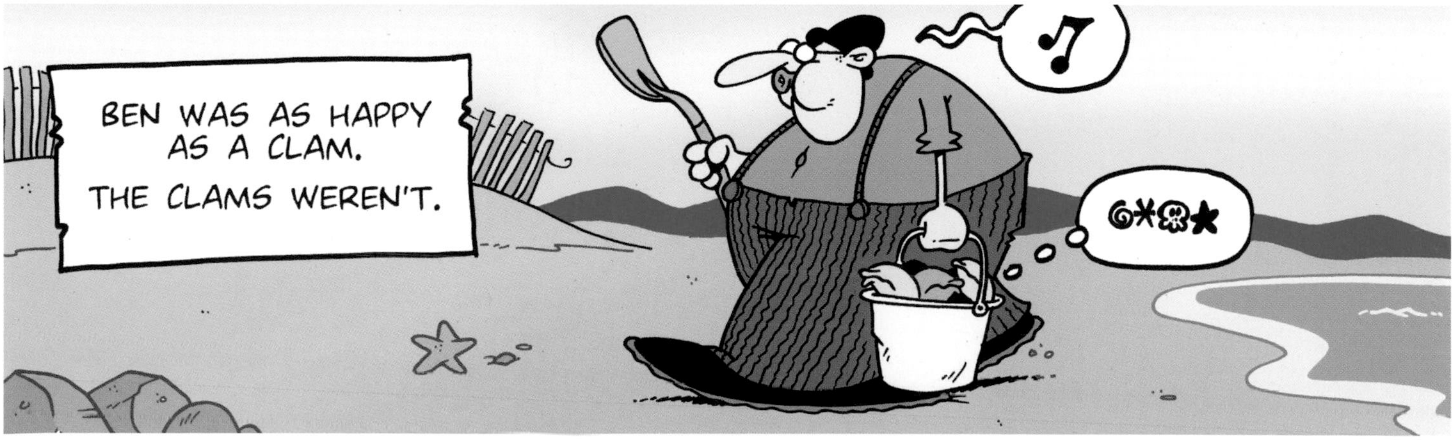
BEN WAS AS HAPPY AS A CLAM.
THE CLAMS WEREN'T.

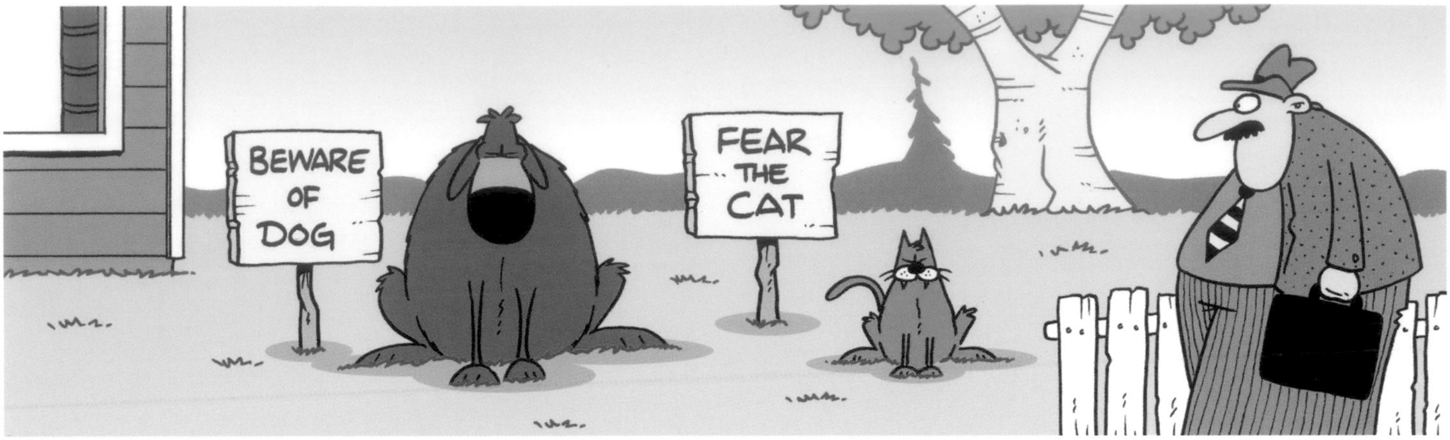
BEWARE OF DOG
FEAR THE CAT

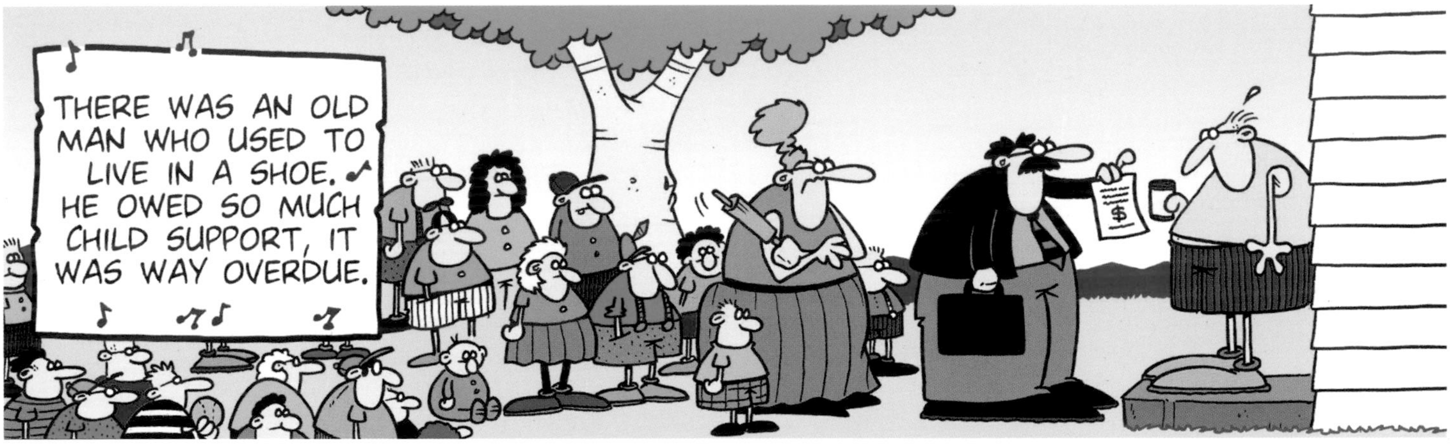
THERE WAS AN OLD MAN WHO USED TO LIVE IN A SHOE. HE OWED SO MUCH CHILD SUPPORT, IT WAS WAY OVERDUE.

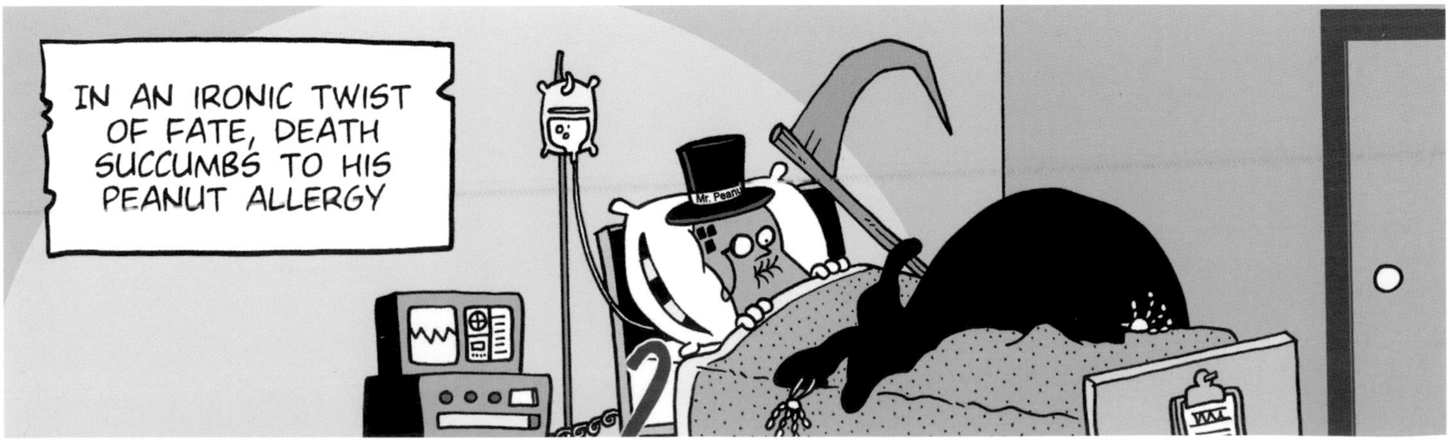
IN AN IRONIC TWIST OF FATE, DEATH SUCCUMBS TO HIS PEANUT ALLERGY

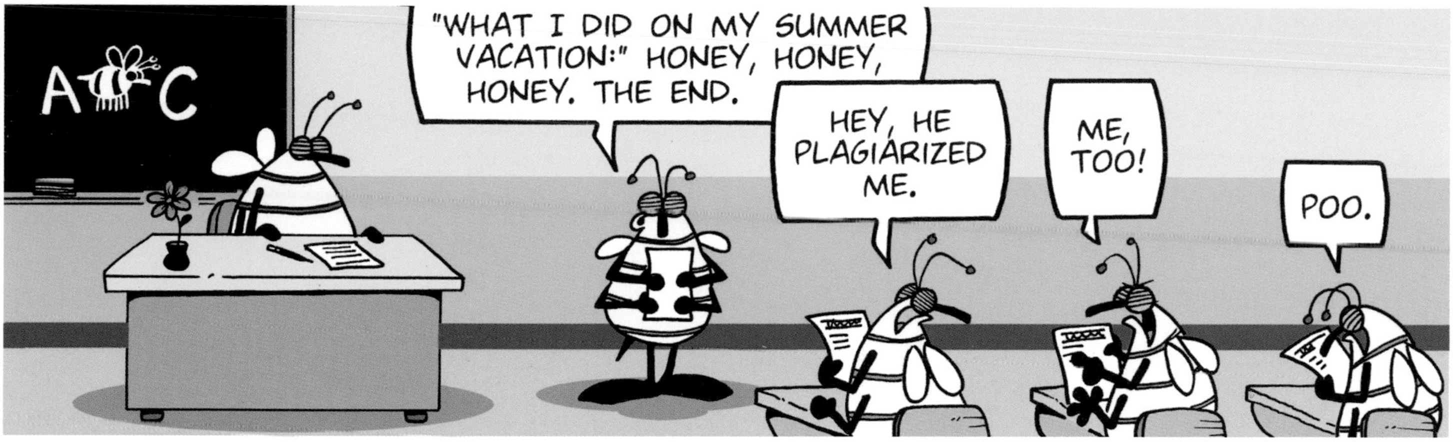
A C
"WHAT I DID ON MY SUMMER VACATION:" HONEY, HONEY, HONEY. THE END.
HEY, HE PLAGIARIZED ME.
ME, TOO!
POO.

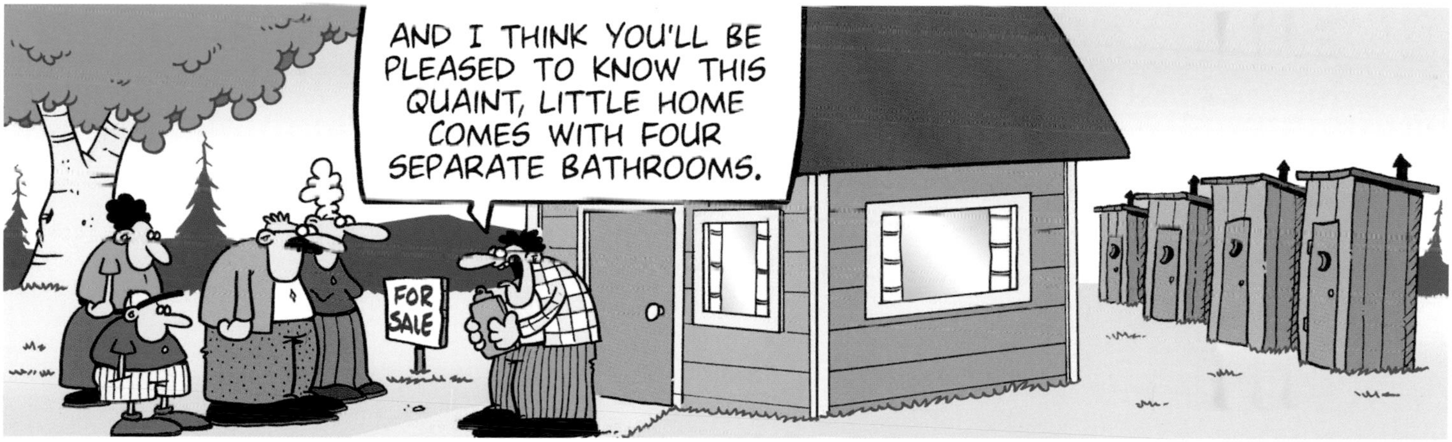
AND I THINK YOU'LL BE PLEASED TO KNOW THIS QUAINT, LITTLE HOME COMES WITH FOUR SEPARATE BATHROOMS.
FOR SALE

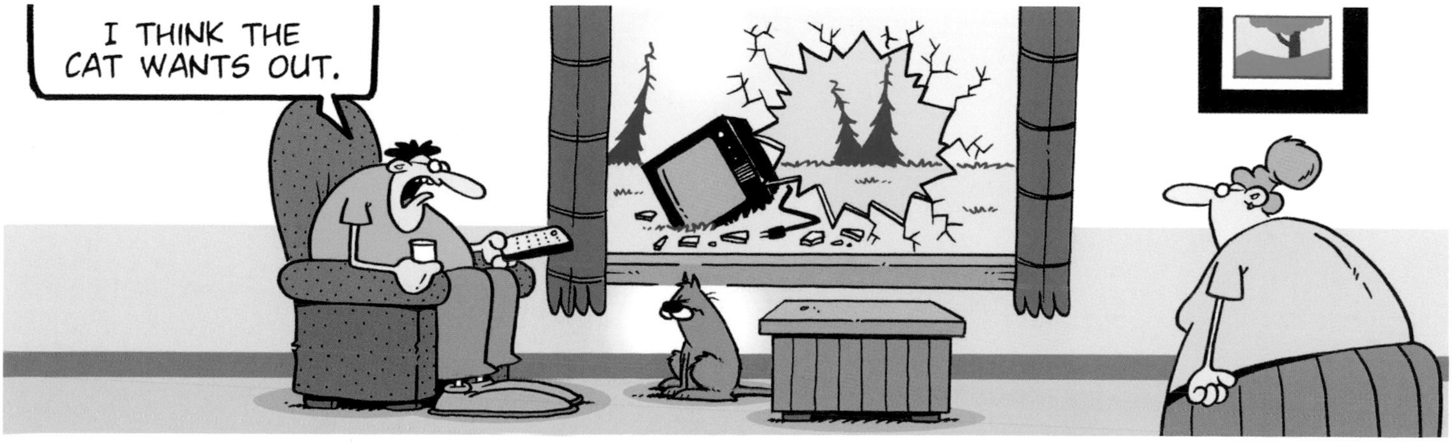
I THINK THE CAT WANTS OUT.

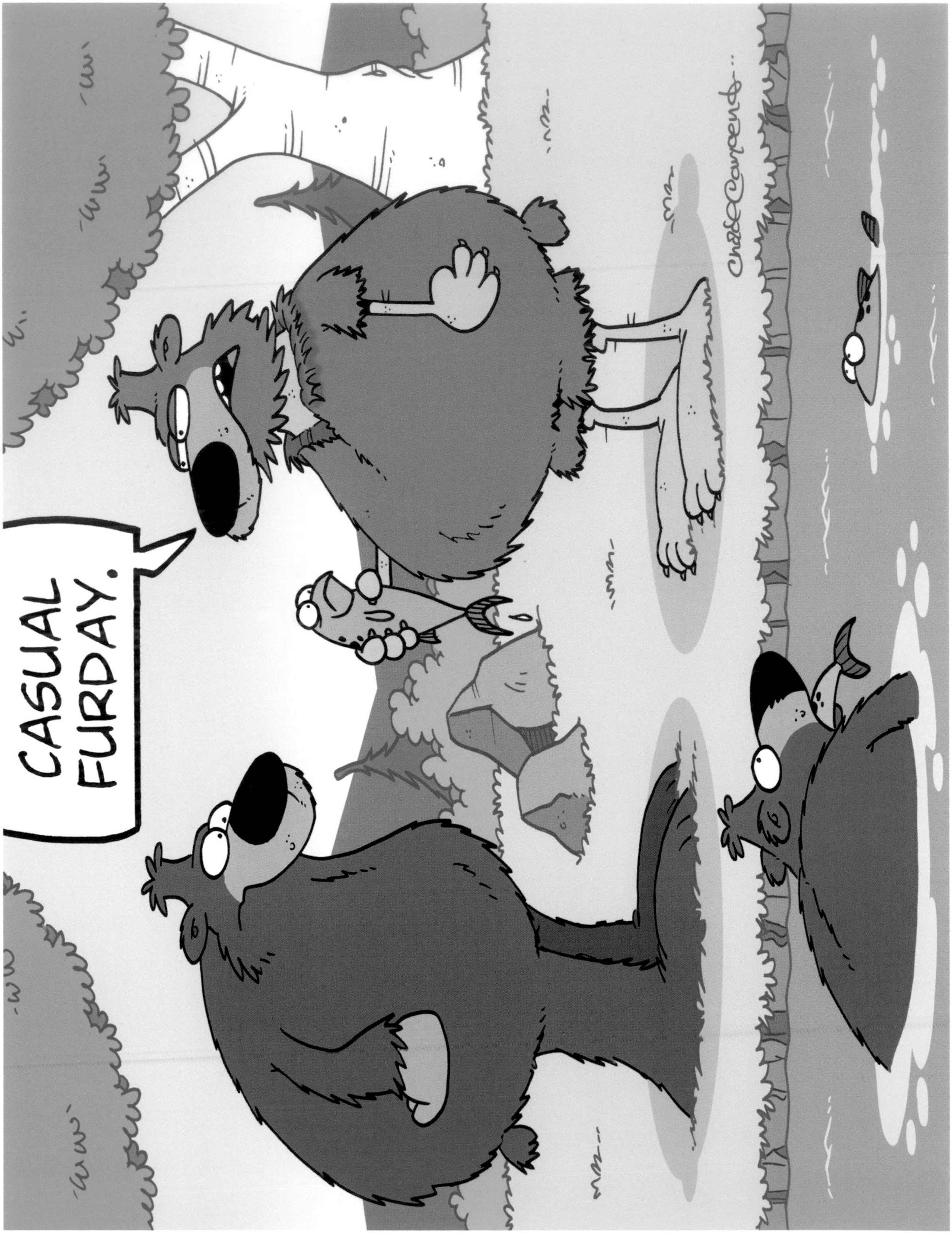
CASUAL FURDAY.

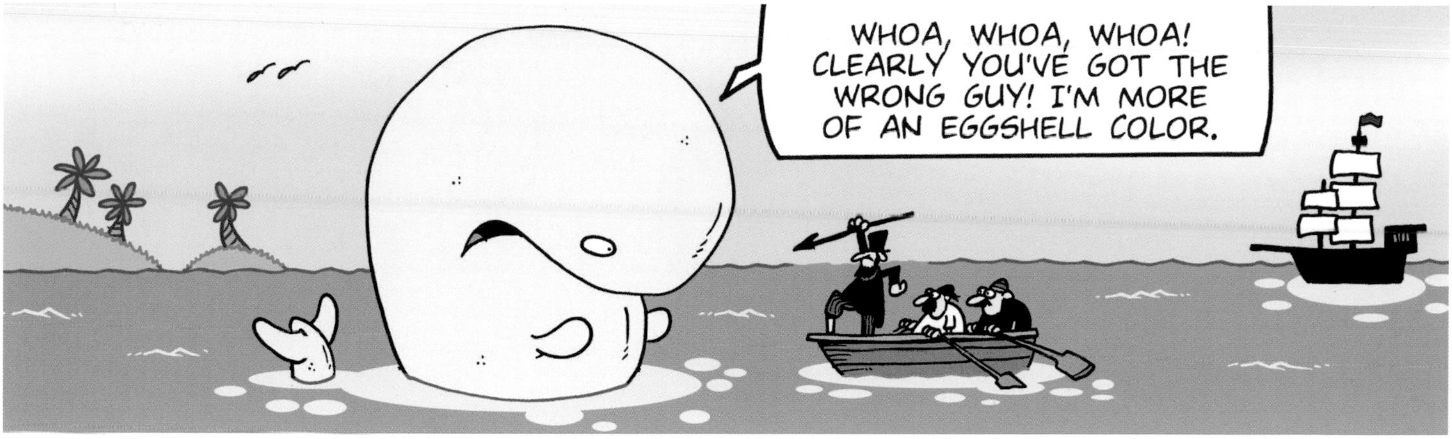
WHOA, WHOA, WHOA! CLEARLY YOU'VE GOT THE WRONG GUY! I'M MORE OF AN EGGSHELL COLOR.

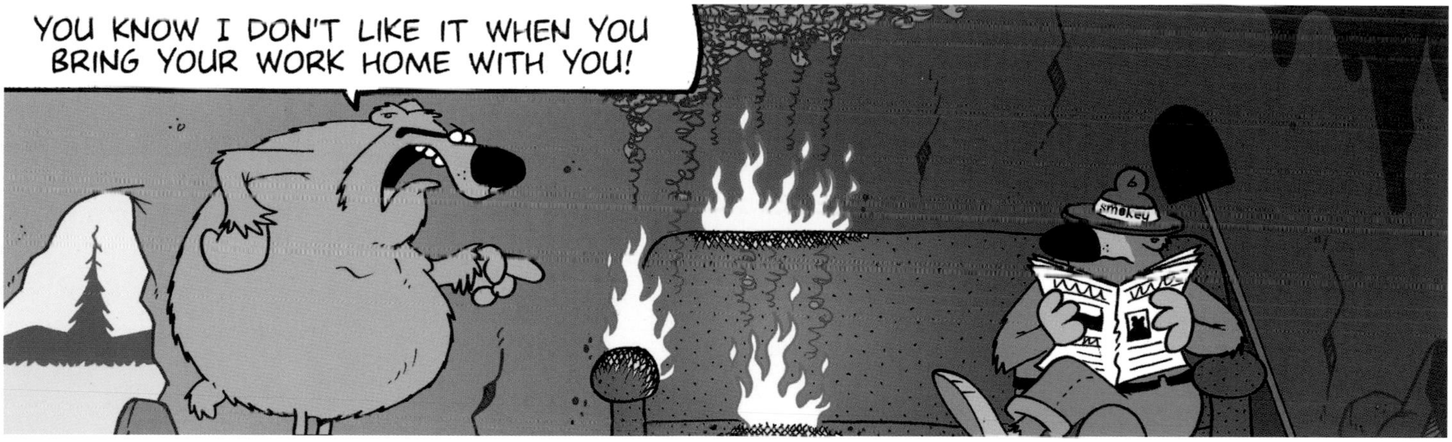
YOU KNOW I DON'T LIKE IT WHEN YOU BRING YOUR WORK HOME WITH YOU!
SMOKEY

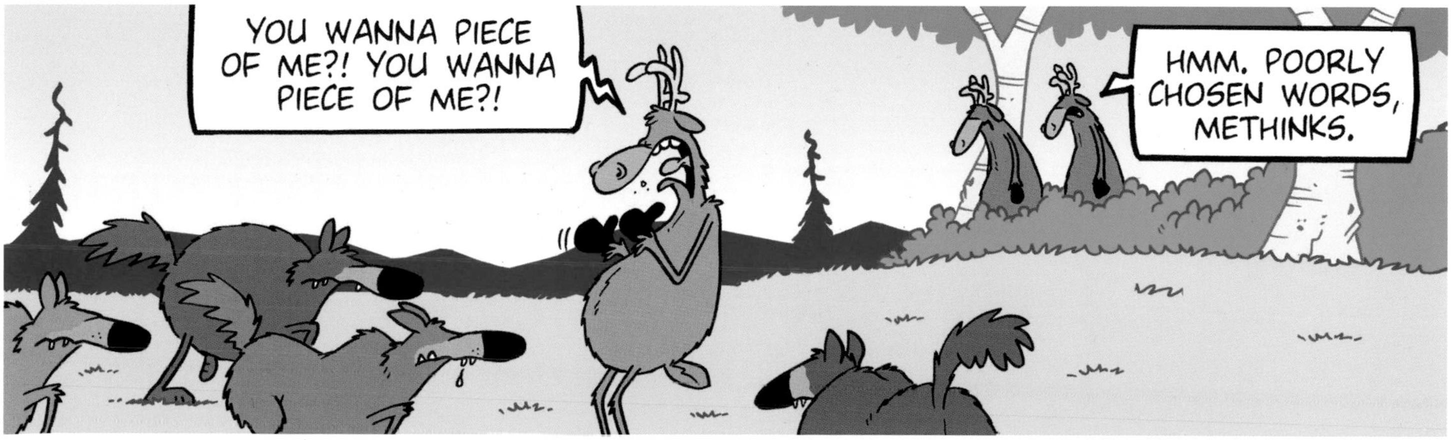
YOU WANNA PIECE OF ME?! YOU WANNA PIECE OF ME?!
HMM. POORLY CHOSEN WORDS, METHINKS.

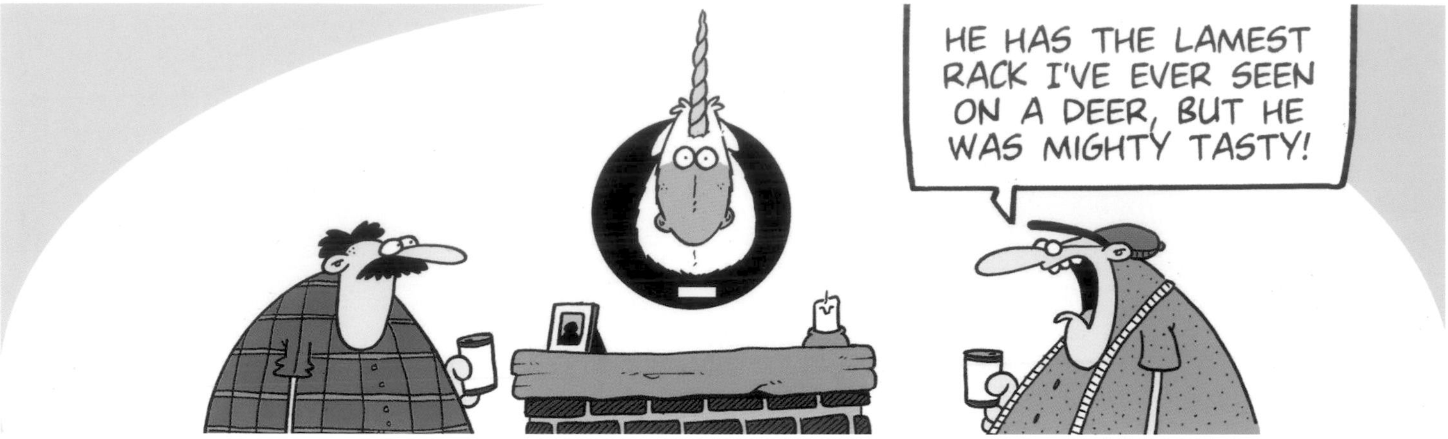
HE HAS THE LAMEST RACK I'VE EVER SEEN ON A DEER, BUT HE WAS MIGHTY TASTY!

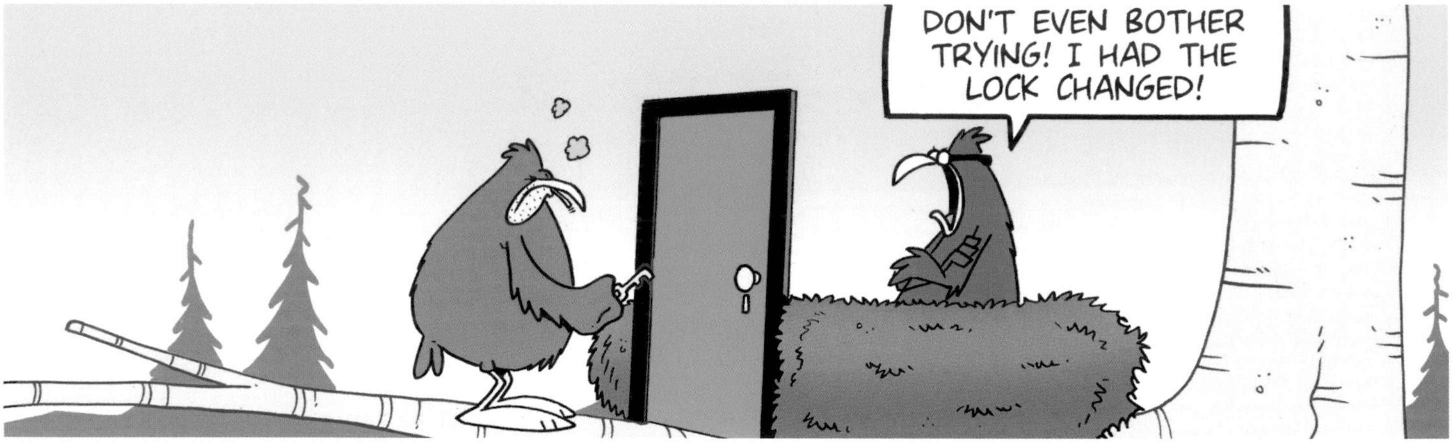
DON'T EVEN BOTHER TRYING! I HAD THE LOCK CHANGED!

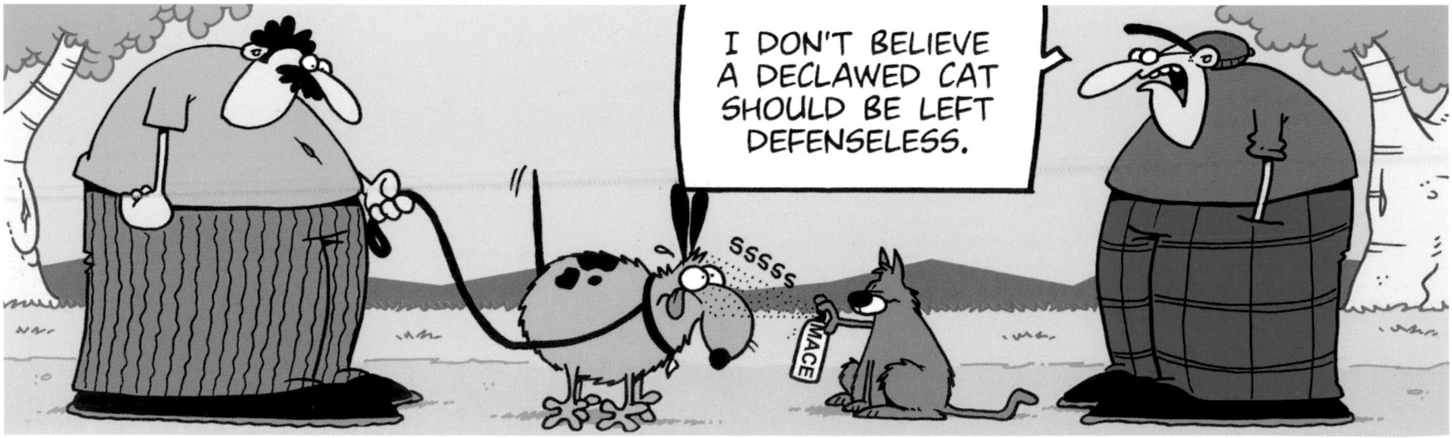
I DON'T BELIEVE A DECLAWED CAT SHOULD BE LEFT DEFENSELESS.
SSSSS
MACE

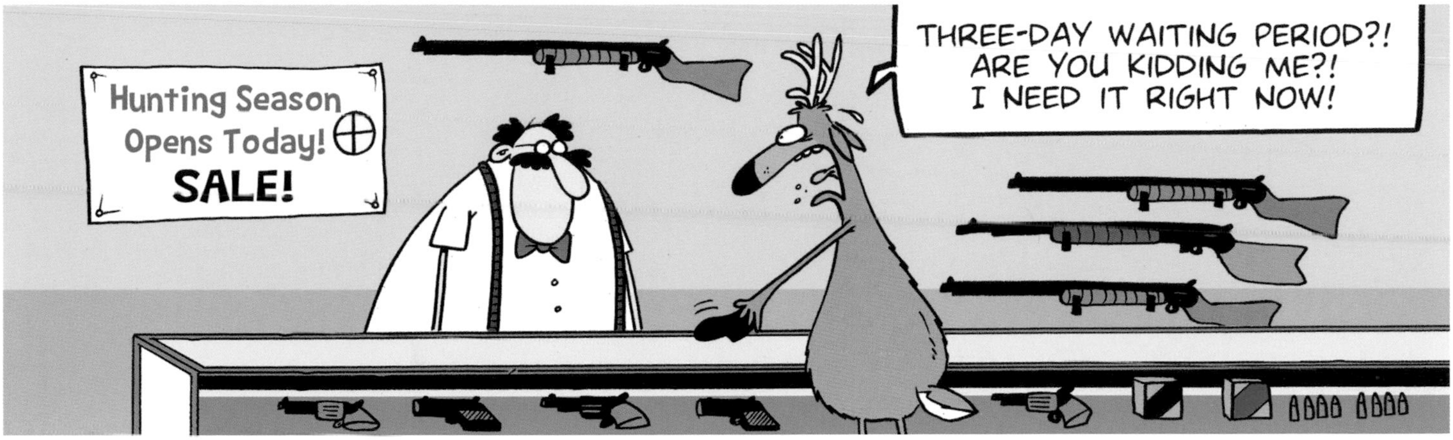
Hunting Season
Opens Today!
SALE!
THREE-DAY WAITING PERIOD?! ARE YOU KIDDING ME?! I NEED IT RIGHT NOW!

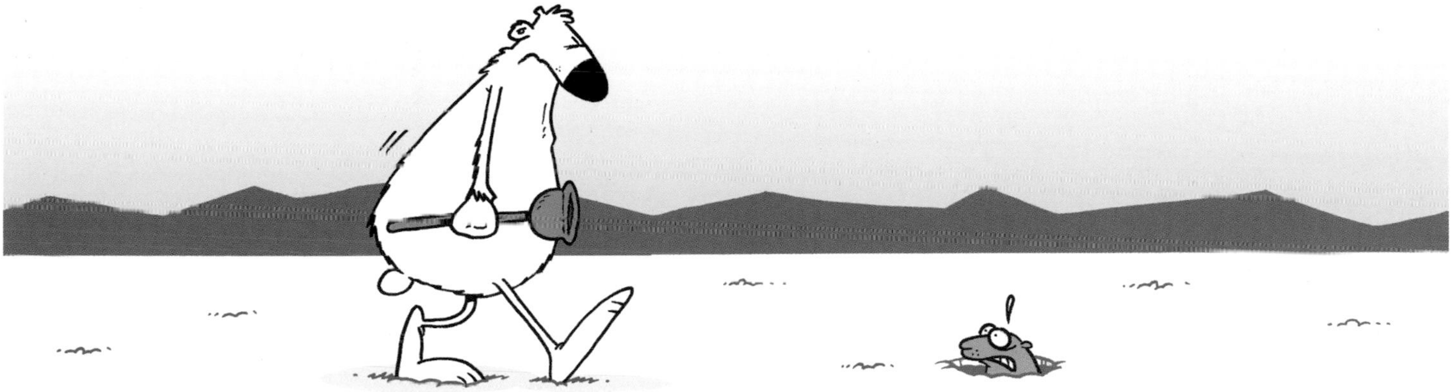

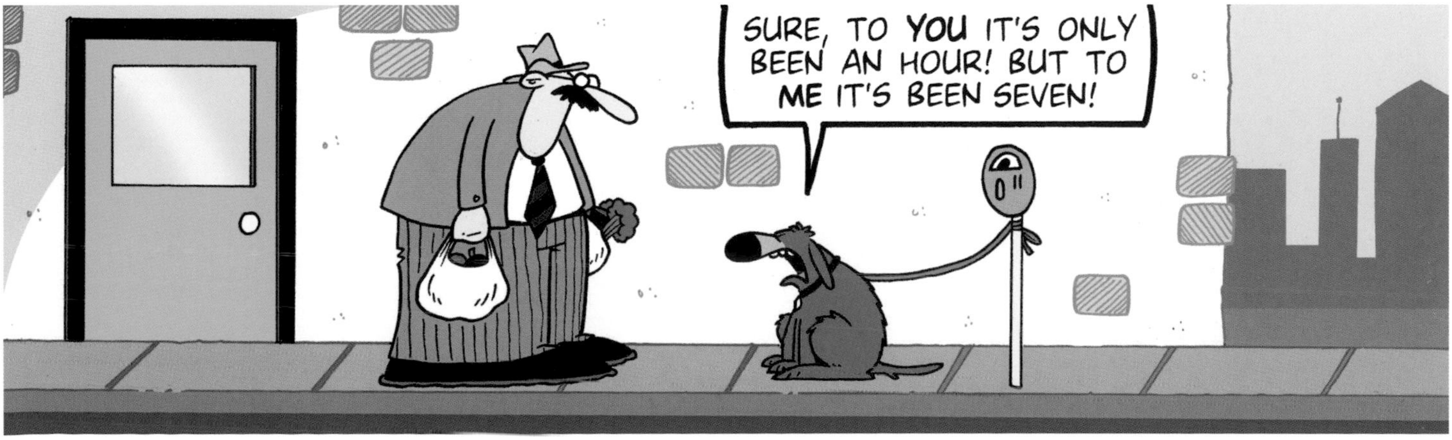
SURE, TO **YOU** IT'S ONLY BEEN AN HOUR! BUT TO **ME** IT'S BEEN SEVEN!

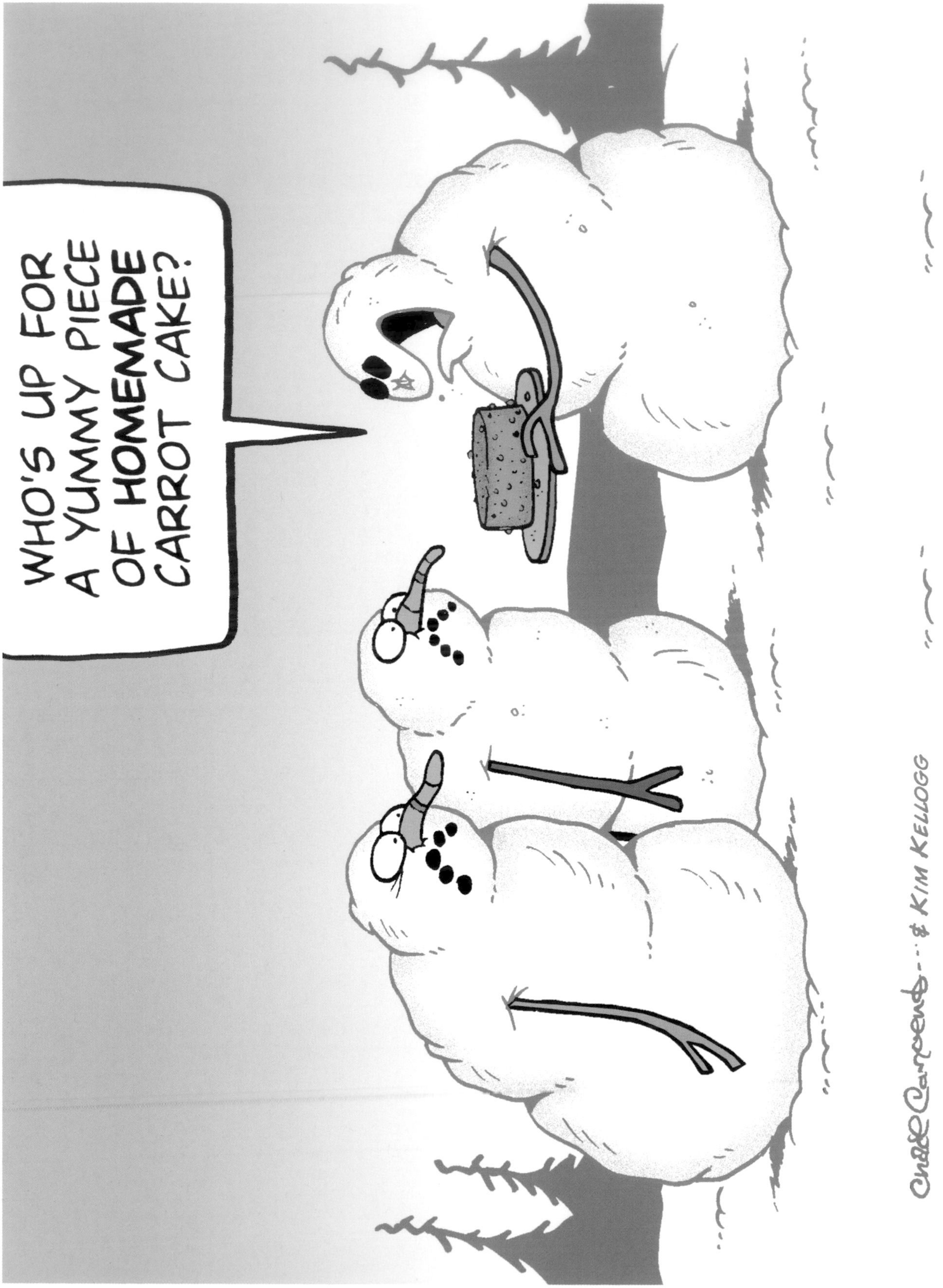
WHO'S UP FOR A YUMMY PIECE OF HOMEMADE CARROT CAKE?
Chad Carpenter ... & KIM KELLOGG

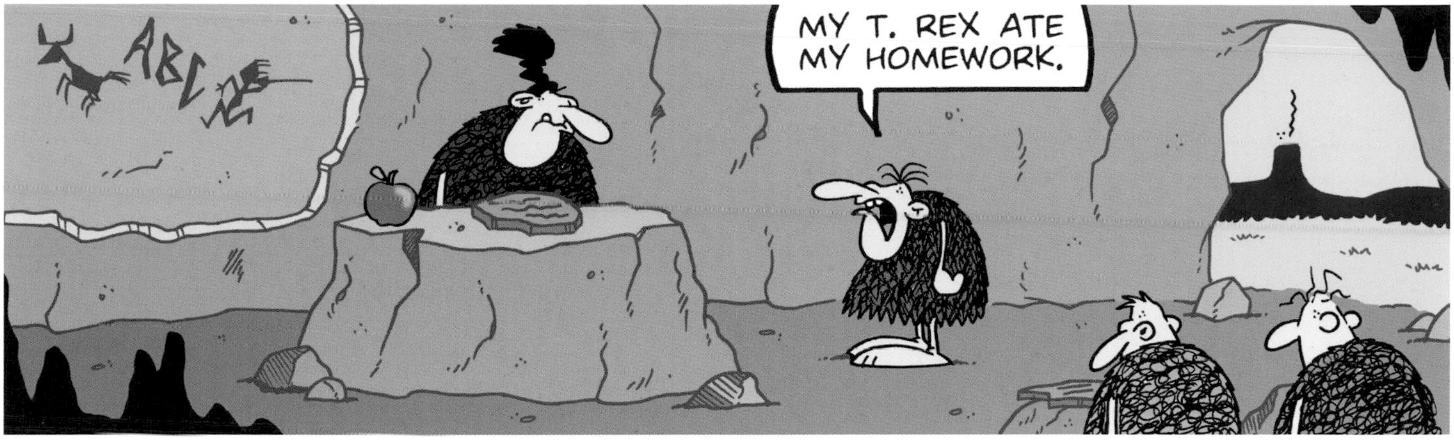
MY T. REX ATE MY HOMEWORK.

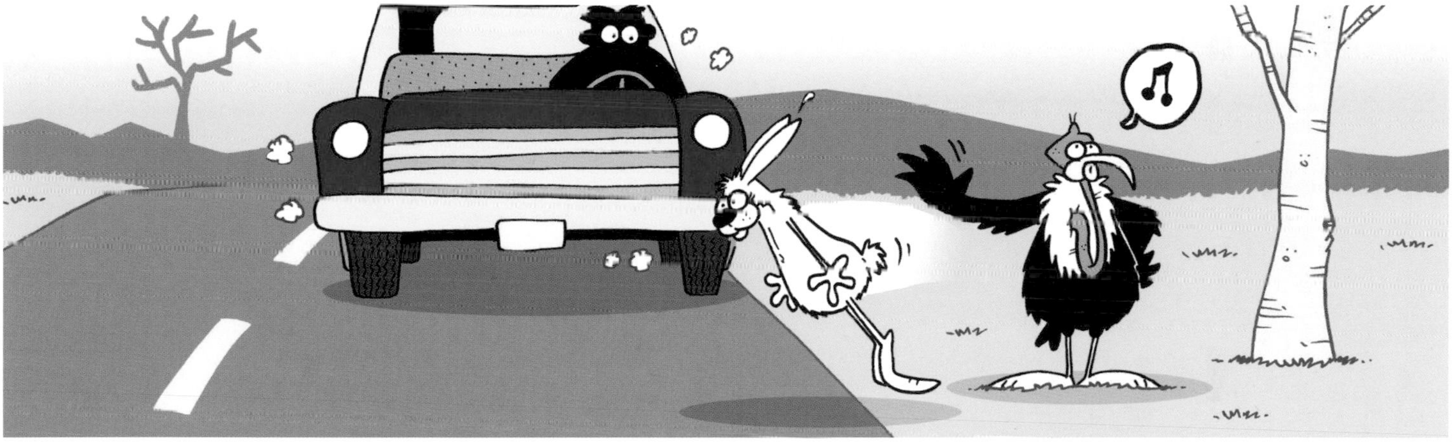

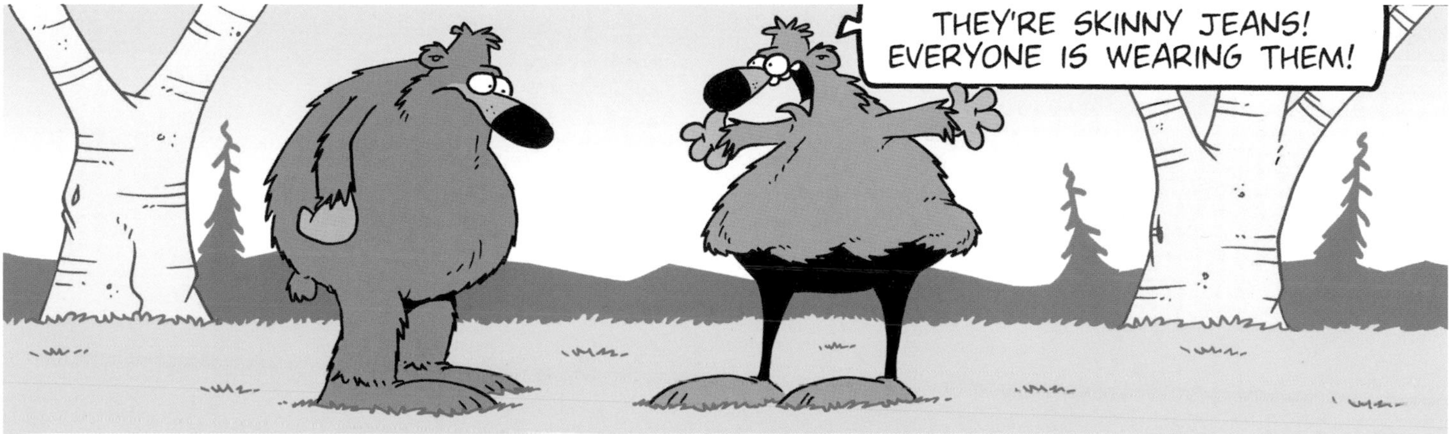
THEY'RE SKINNY JEANS! EVERYONE IS WEARING THEM!

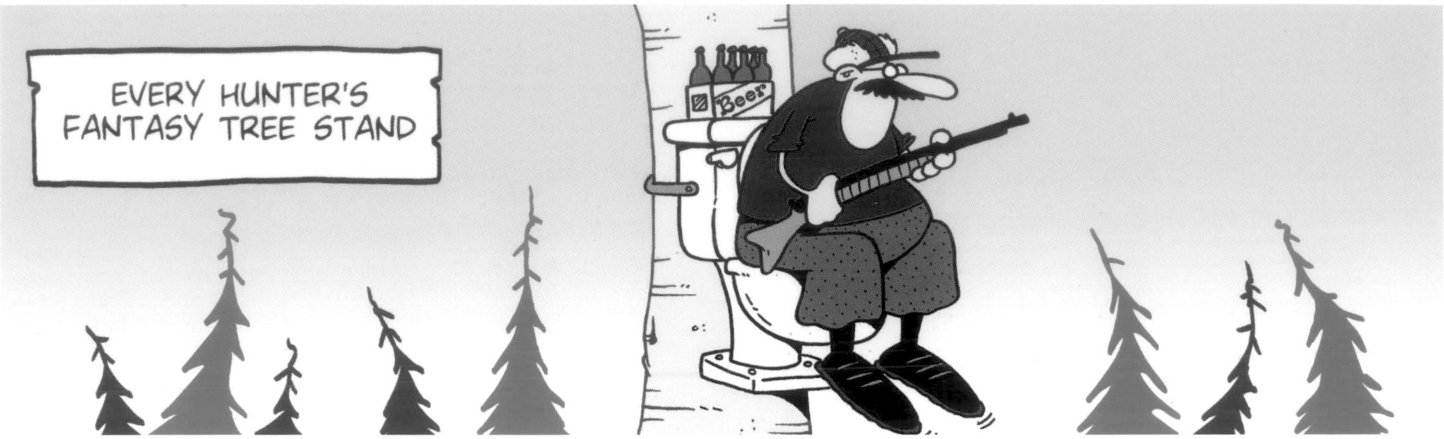
EVERY HUNTER'S FANTASY TREE STAND
Beer

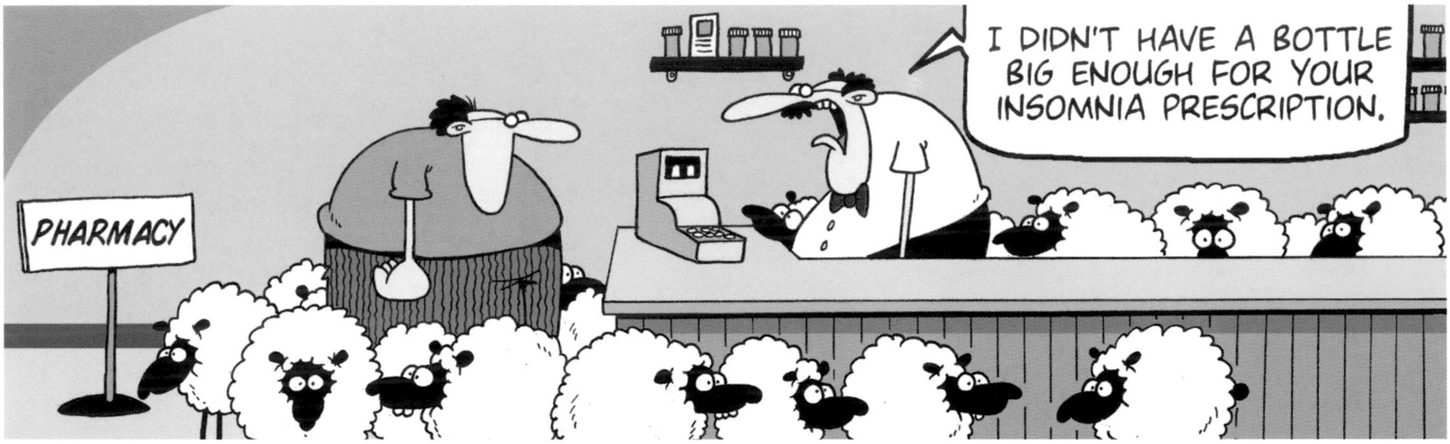
I DIDN'T HAVE A BOTTLE BIG ENOUGH FOR YOUR INSOMNIA PRESCRIPTION.
PHARMACY

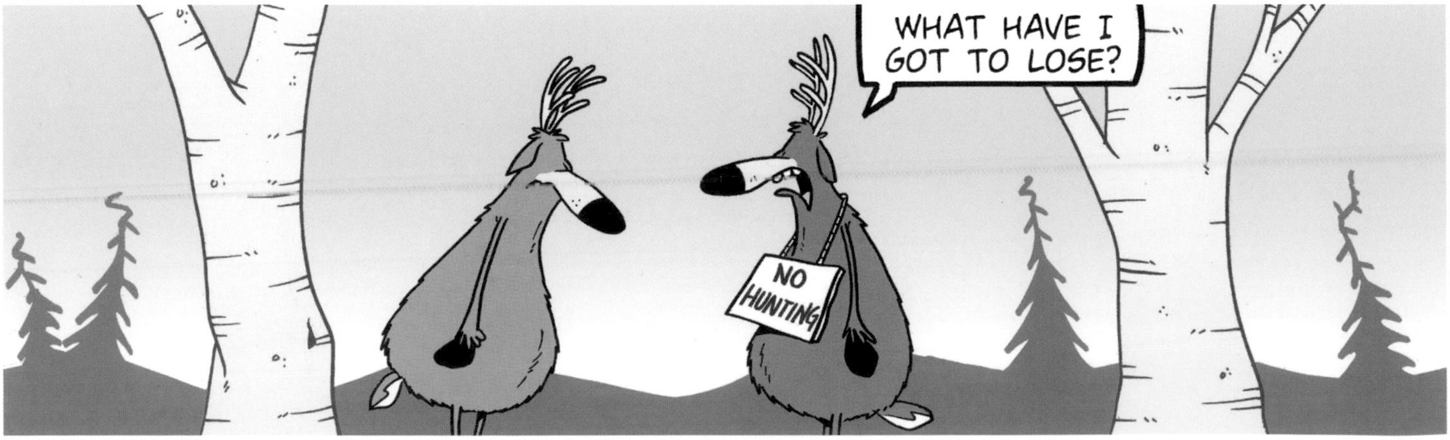
WHAT HAVE I GOT TO LOSE?
NO HUNTING

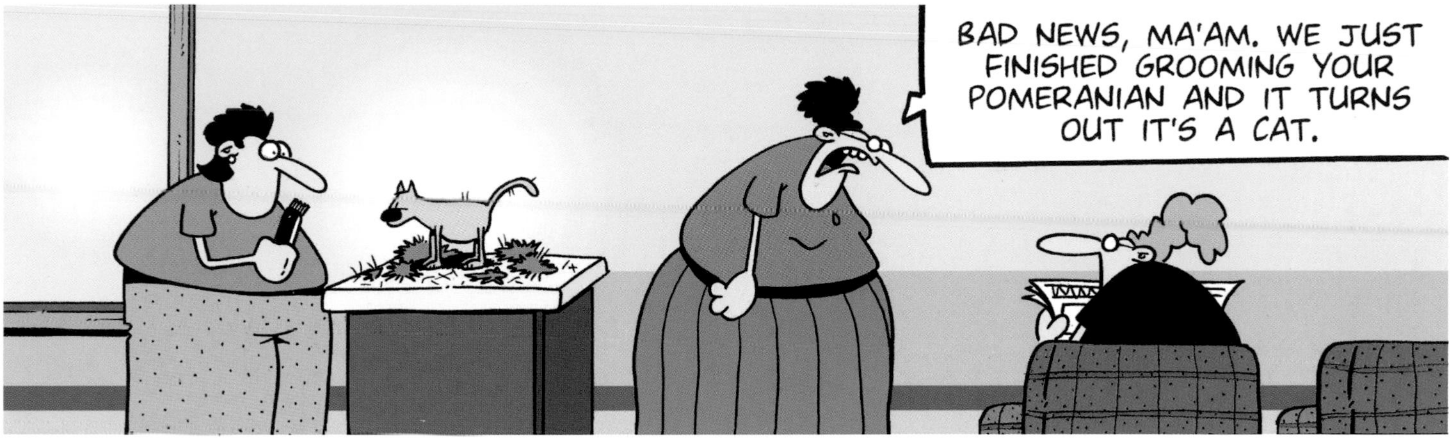
BAD NEWS, MA'AM. WE JUST FINISHED GROOMING YOUR POMERANIAN AND IT TURNS OUT IT'S A CAT.

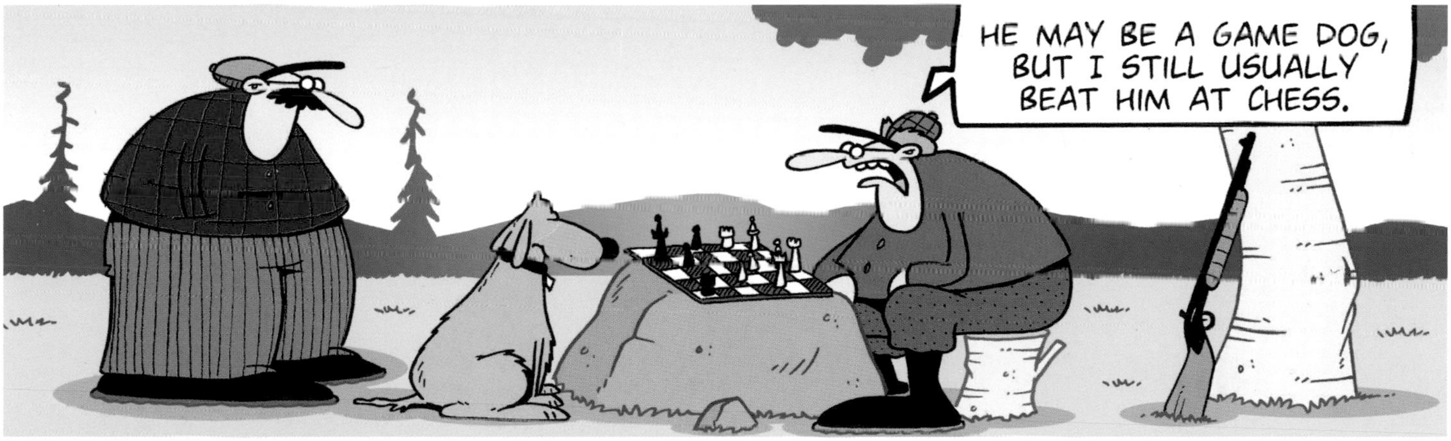
HE MAY BE A GAME DOG, BUT I STILL USUALLY BEAT HIM AT CHESS.

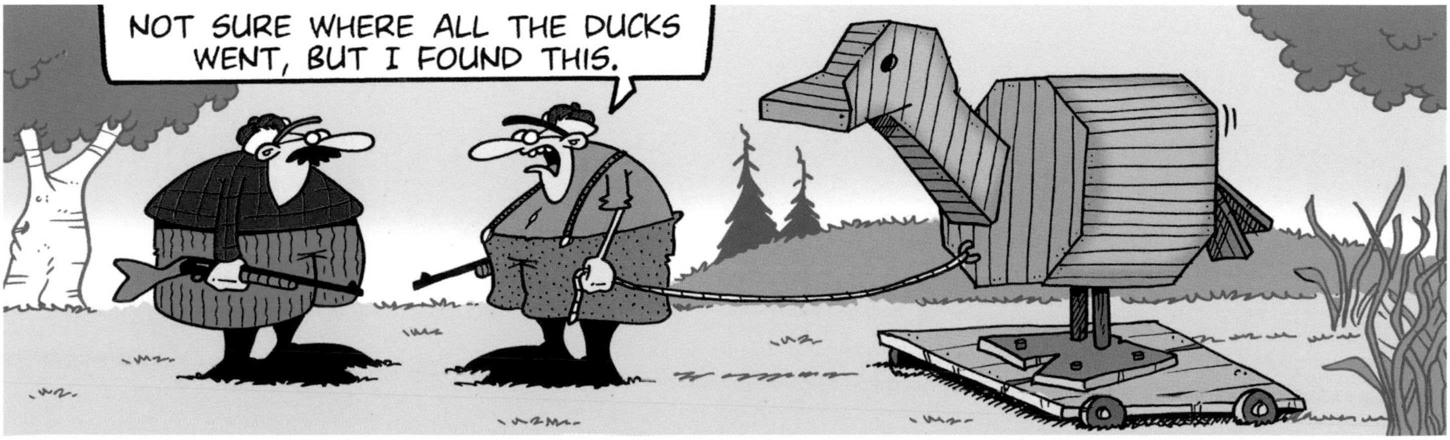
NOT SURE WHERE ALL THE DUCKS WENT, BUT I FOUND THIS.

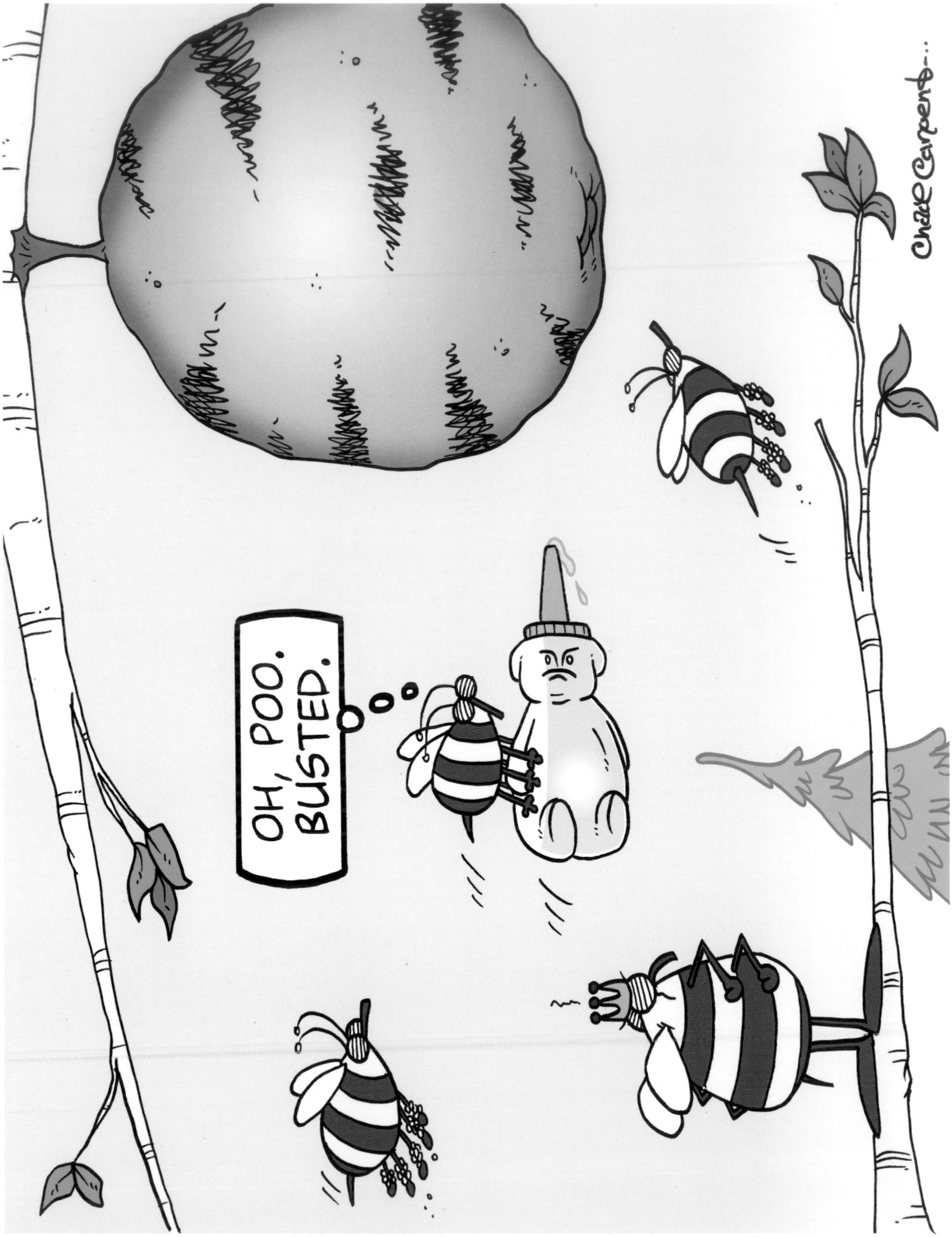
OH, POO. BUSTED.
Chad Carpenter

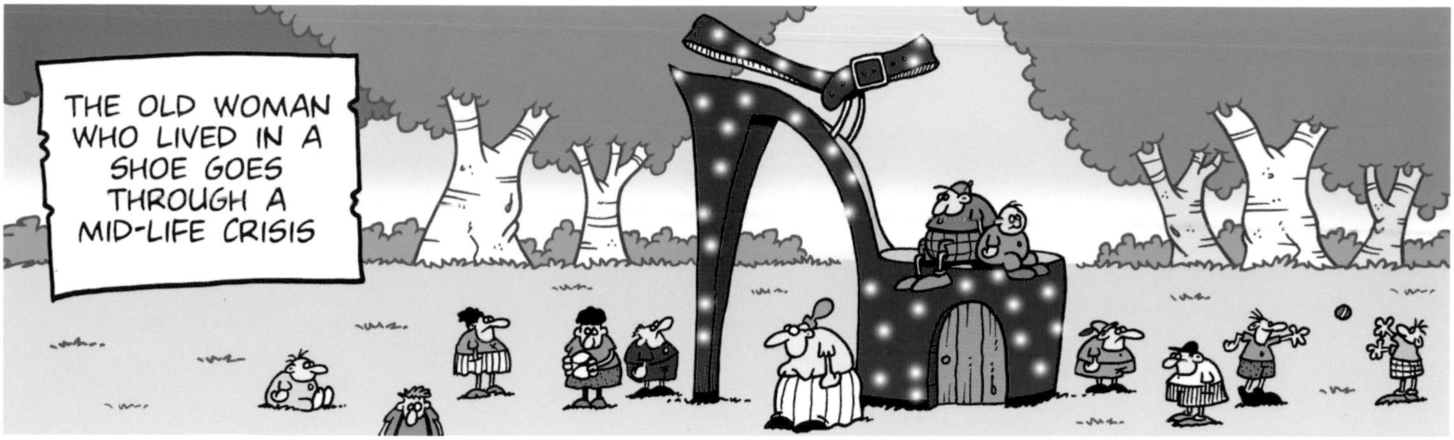
THE OLD WOMAN WHO LIVED IN A SHOE GOES THROUGH A MID-LIFE CRISIS

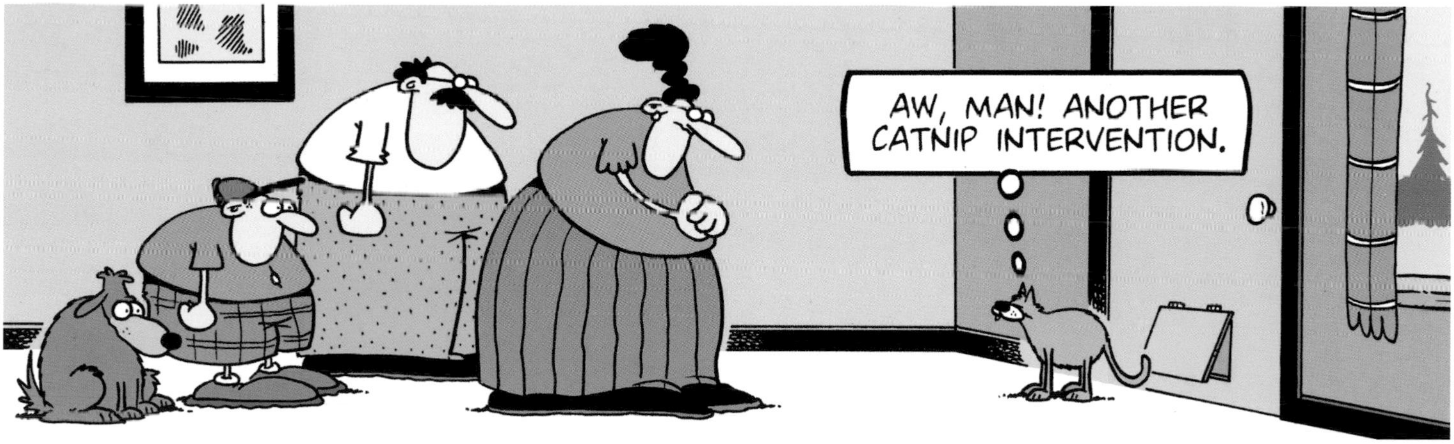
AW, MAN! ANOTHER CATNIP INTERVENTION.

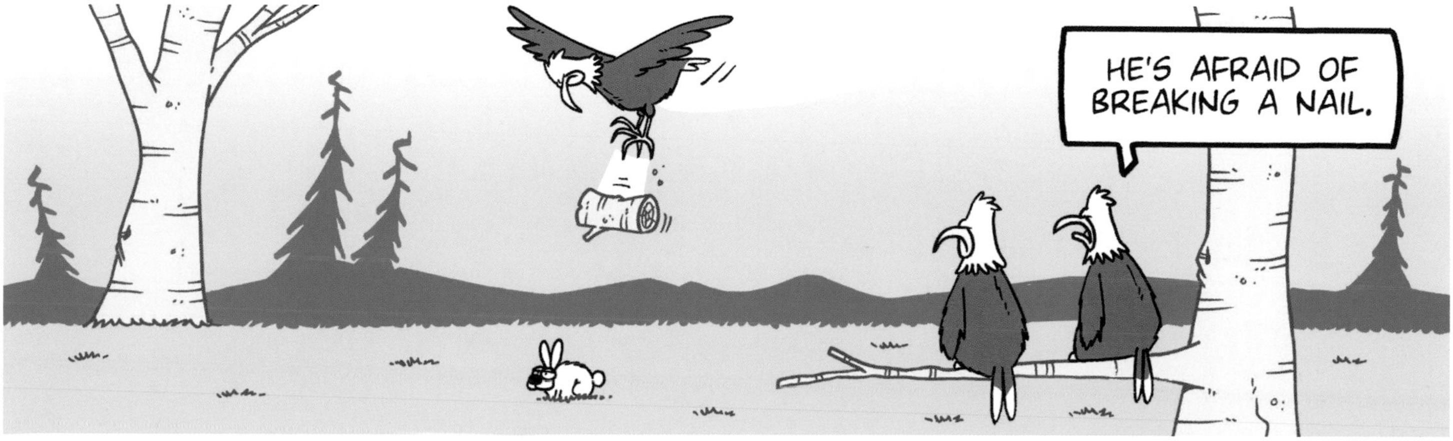
HE'S AFRAID OF BREAKING A NAIL.

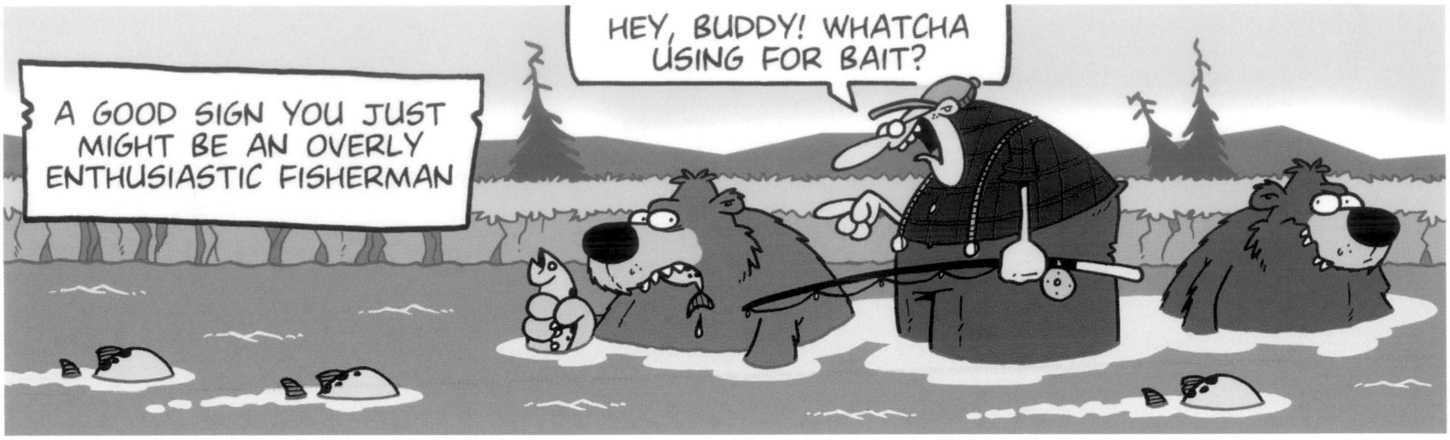
A GOOD SIGN YOU JUST MIGHT BE AN OVERLY ENTHUSIASTIC FISHERMAN
HEY, BUDDY! WHATCHA USING FOR BAIT?

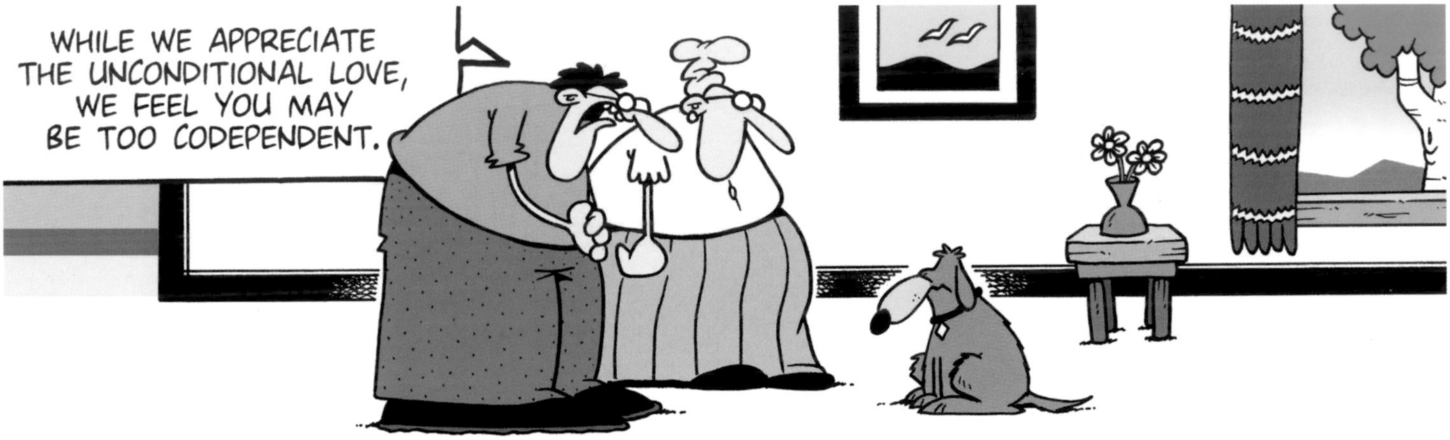
WHILE WE APPRECIATE THE UNCONDITIONAL LOVE, WE FEEL YOU MAY BE TOO CODEPENDENT.

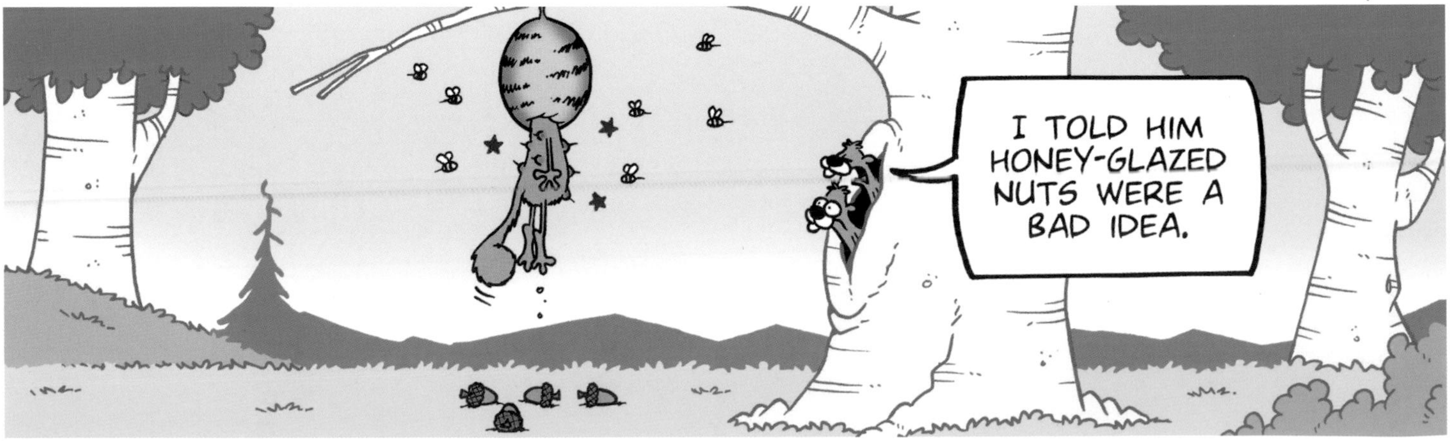
I TOLD HIM HONEY-GLAZED NUTS WERE A BAD IDEA.

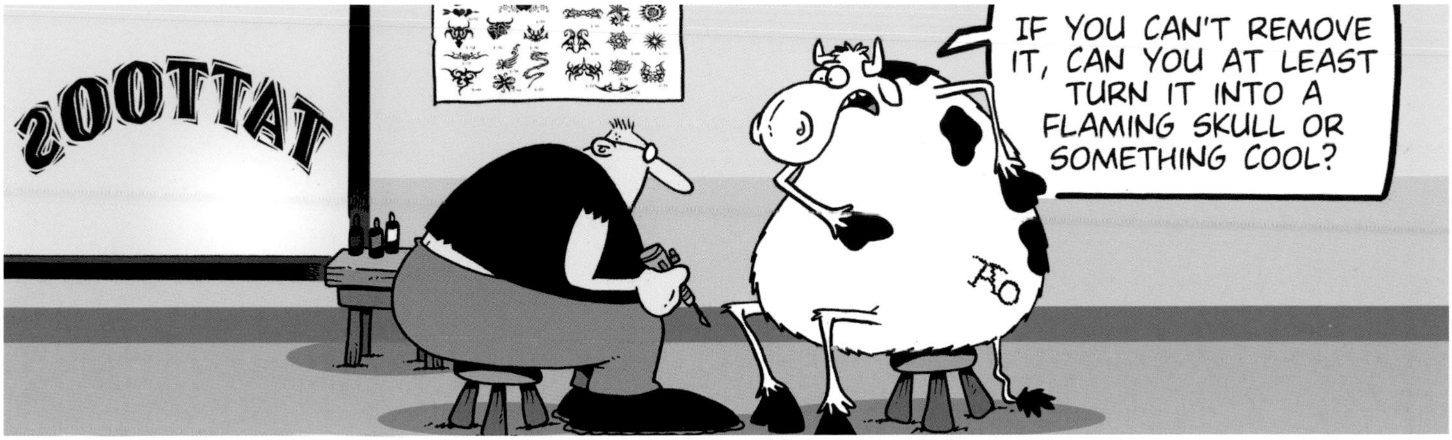
IF YOU CAN'T REMOVE IT, CAN YOU AT LEAST TURN IT INTO A FLAMING SKULL OR SOMETHING COOL?

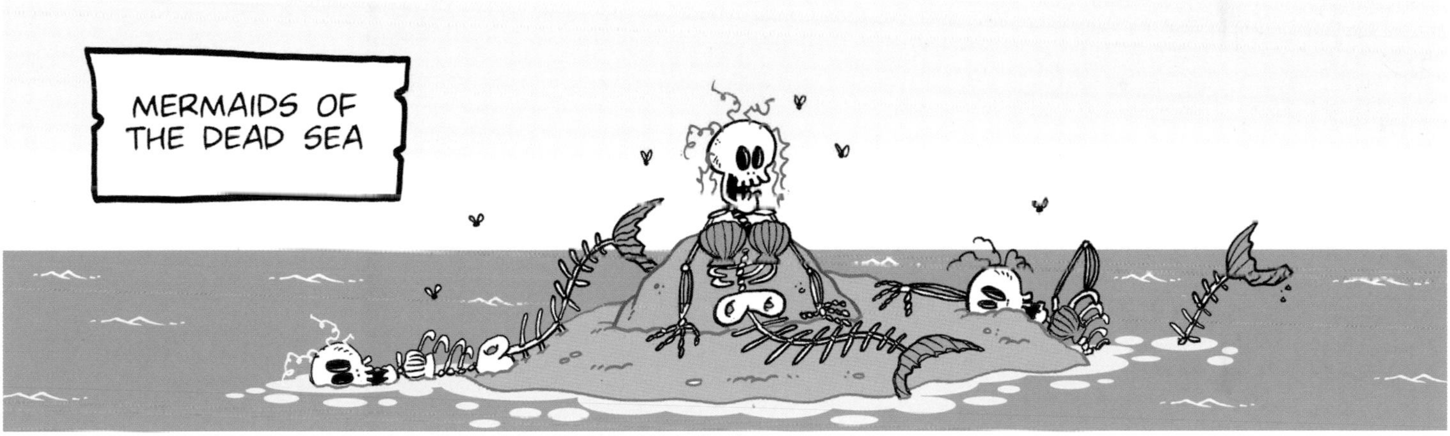
MERMAIDS OF THE DEAD SEA

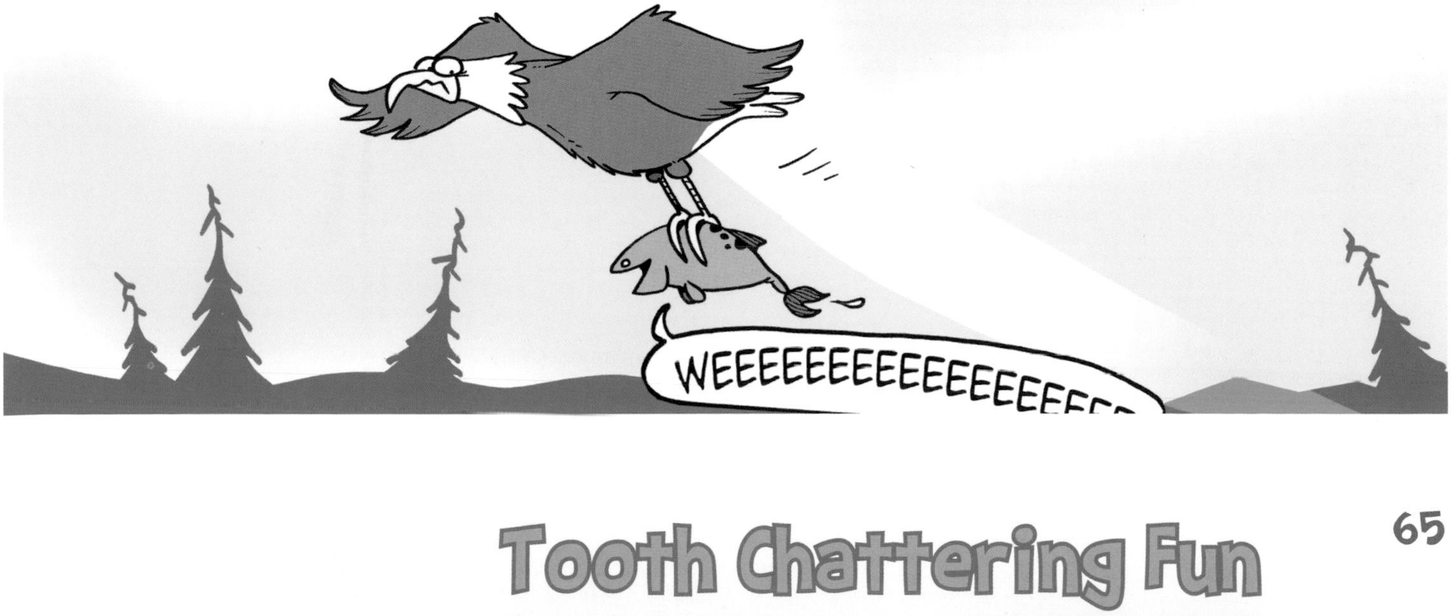
WEEEEEEEEEEEEEEEEE

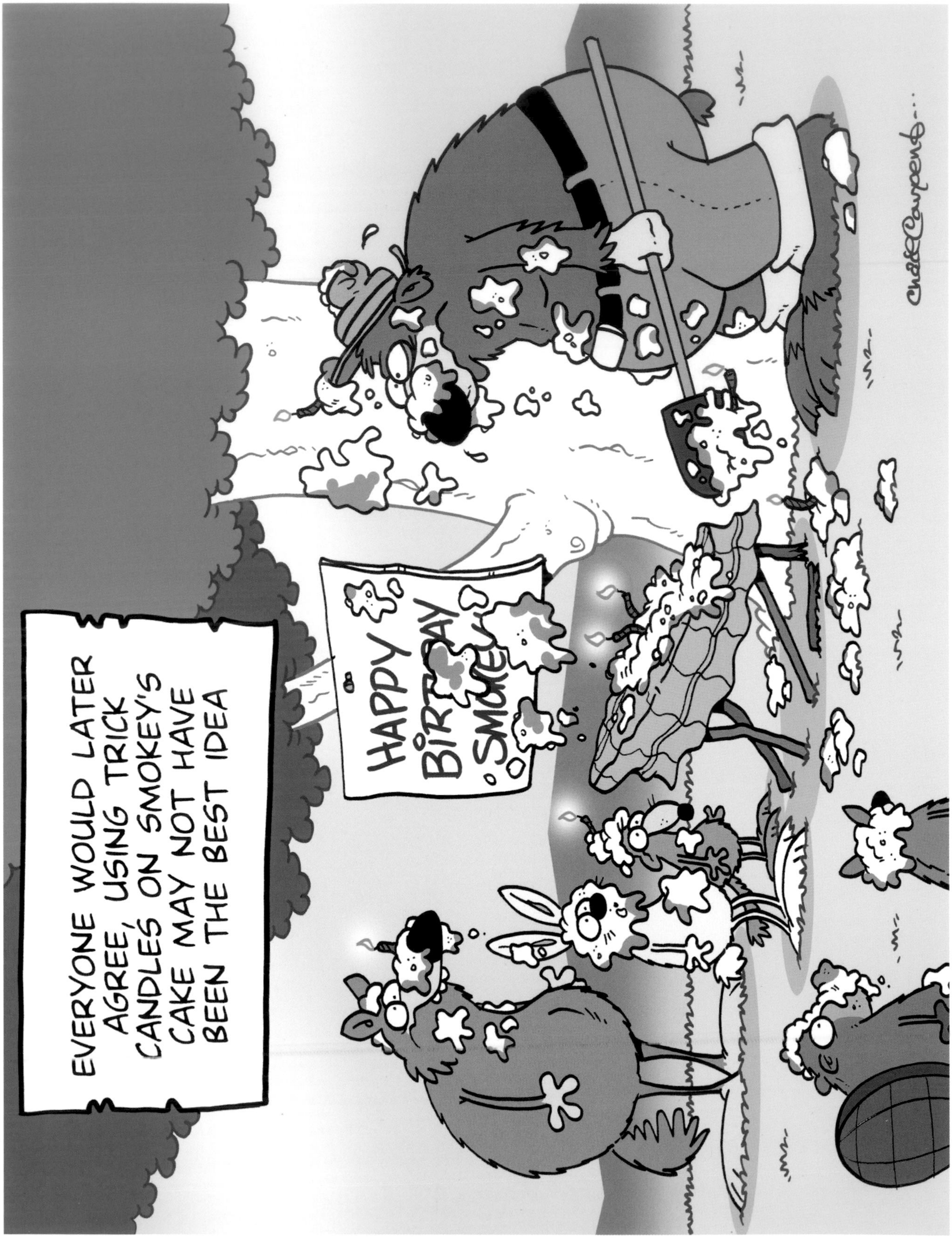
EVERYONE WOULD LATER AGREE, USING TRICK CANDLES ON SMOKEY'S CAKE MAY NOT HAVE BEEN THE BEST IDEA
HAPPY BIRTHDAY SMOKEY

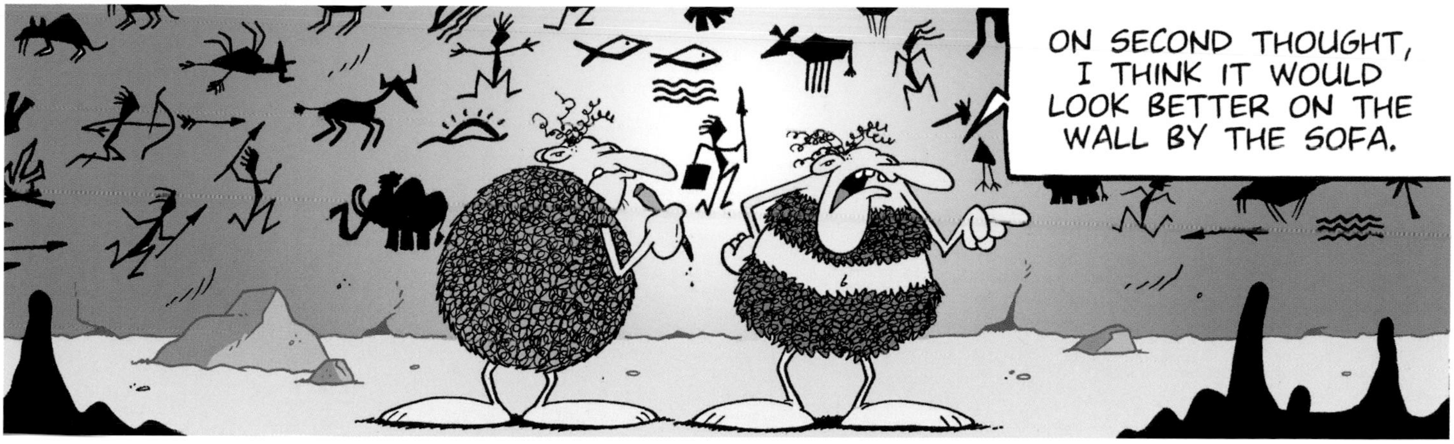
ON SECOND THOUGHT, I THINK IT WOULD LOOK BETTER ON THE WALL BY THE SOFA.

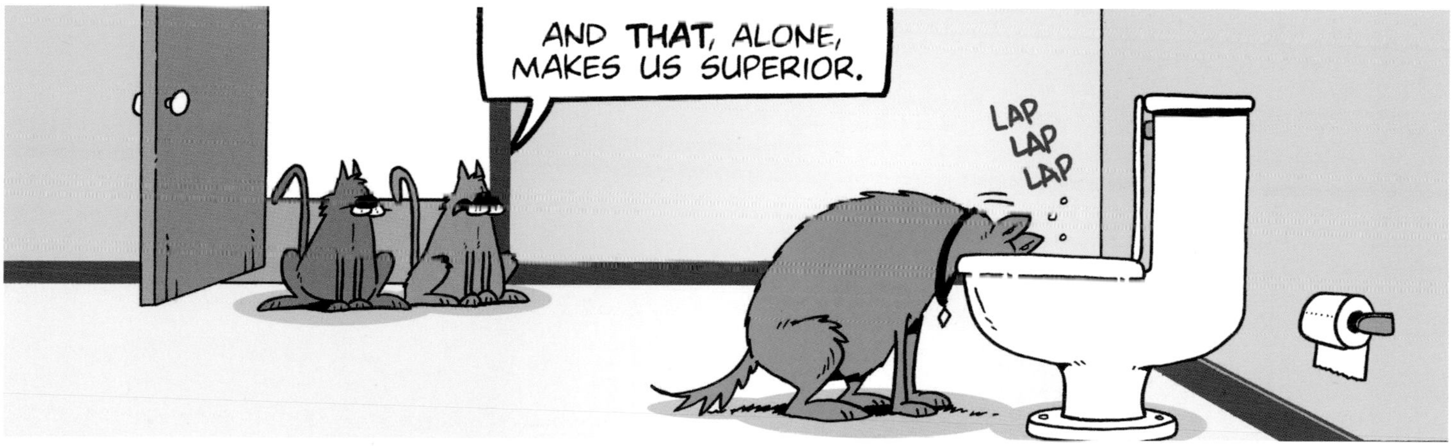
AND THAT, ALONE, MAKES US SUPERIOR.
LAP
LAP
LAP

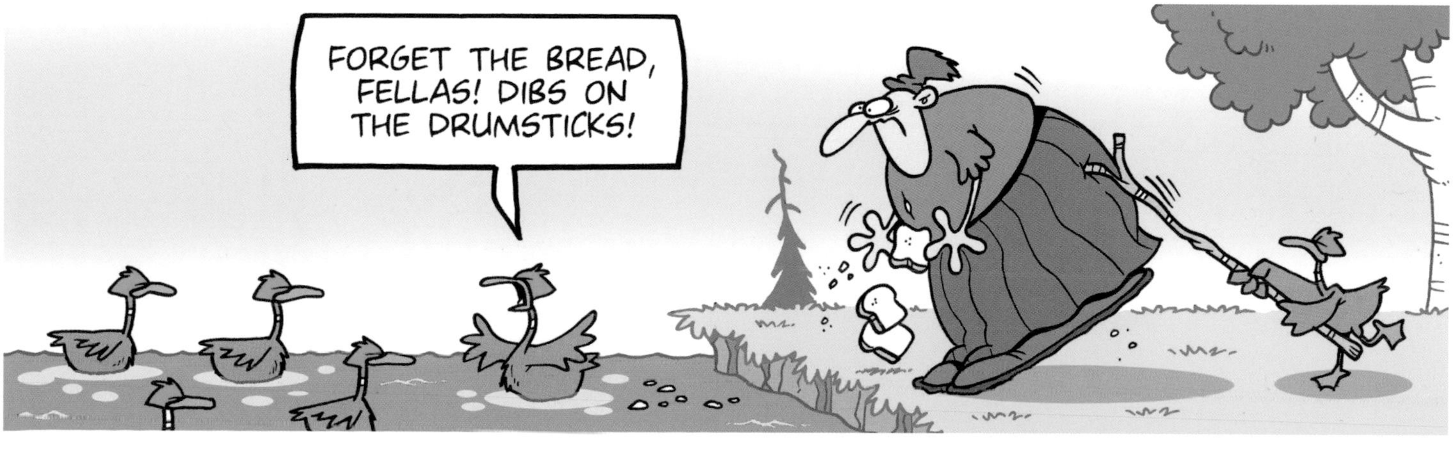
FORGET THE BREAD, FELLAS! DIBS ON THE DRUMSTICKS!

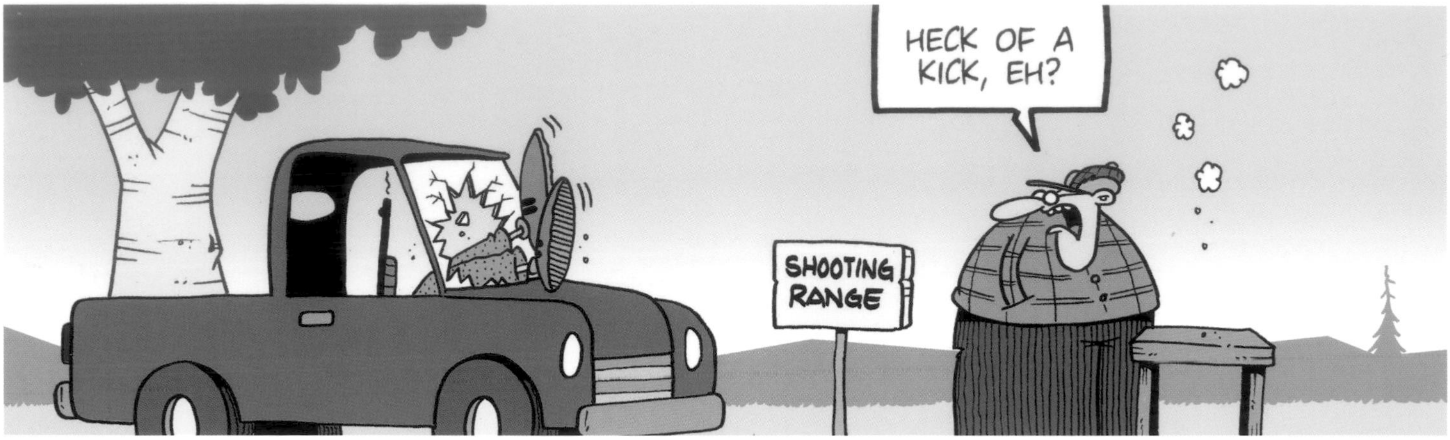
HECK OF A KICK, EH?
SHOOTING RANGE

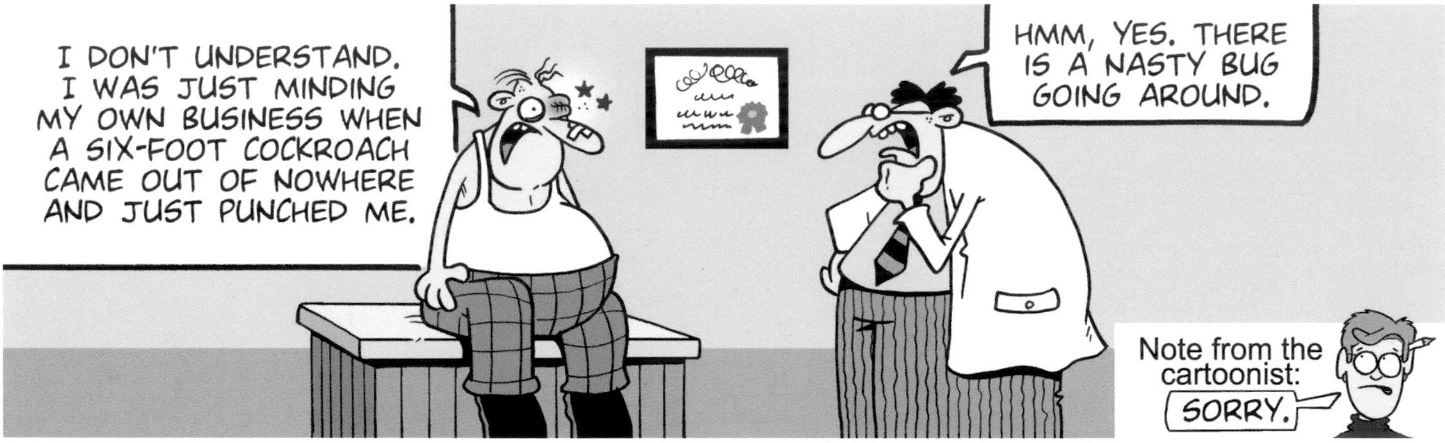
I DON'T UNDERSTAND. I WAS JUST MINDING MY OWN BUSINESS WHEN A SIX-FOOT COCKROACH CAME OUT OF NOWHERE AND JUST PUNCHED ME.
HMM, YES. THERE IS A NASTY BUG GOING AROUND.
Note from the cartoonist:
SORRY.

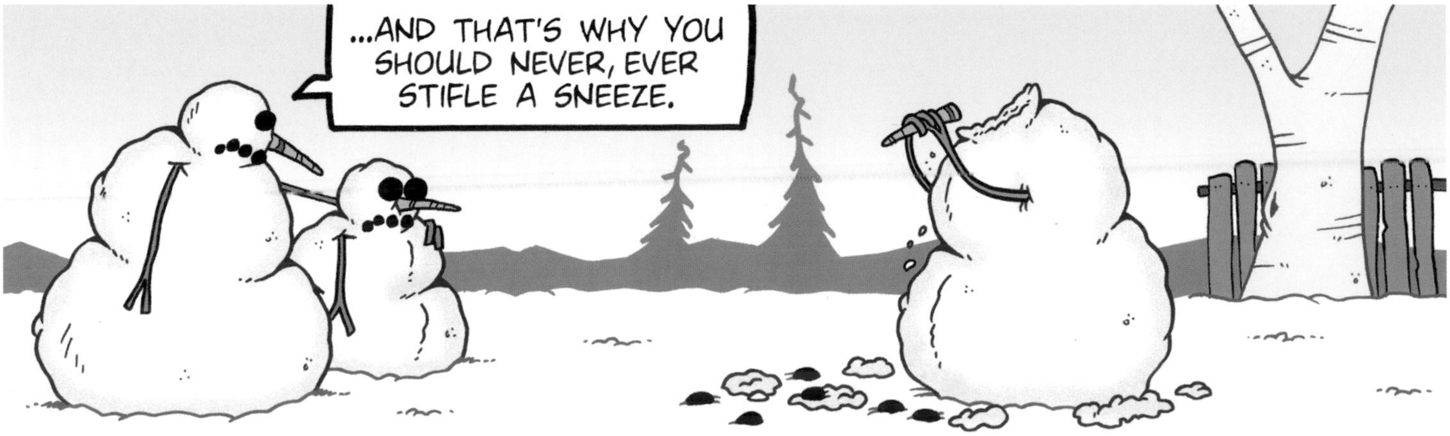
...AND THAT'S WHY YOU SHOULD NEVER, EVER STIFLE A SNEEZE.

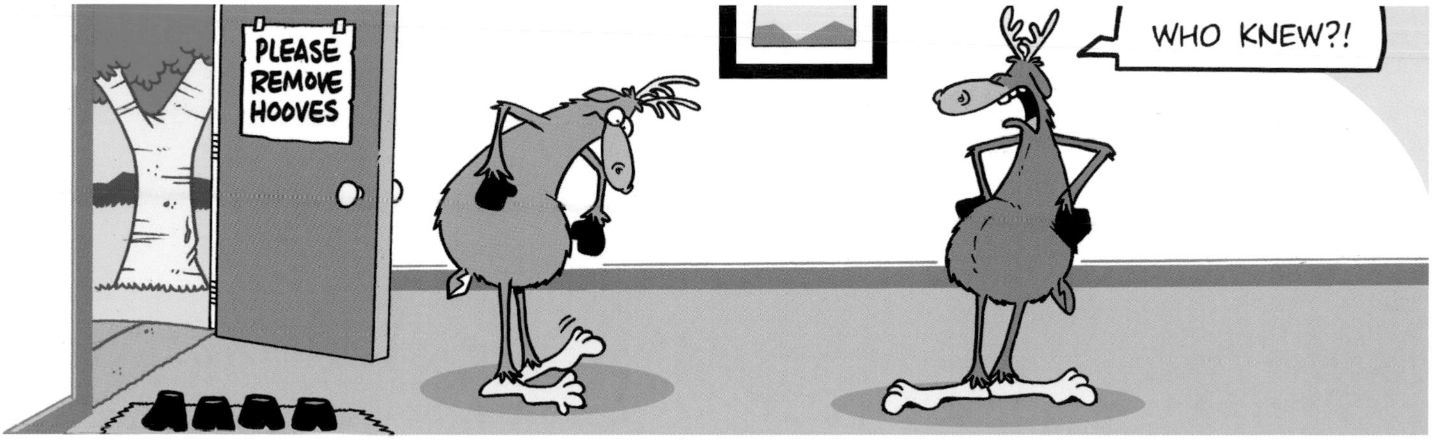
PLEASE REMOVE HOOVES
WHO KNEW?!

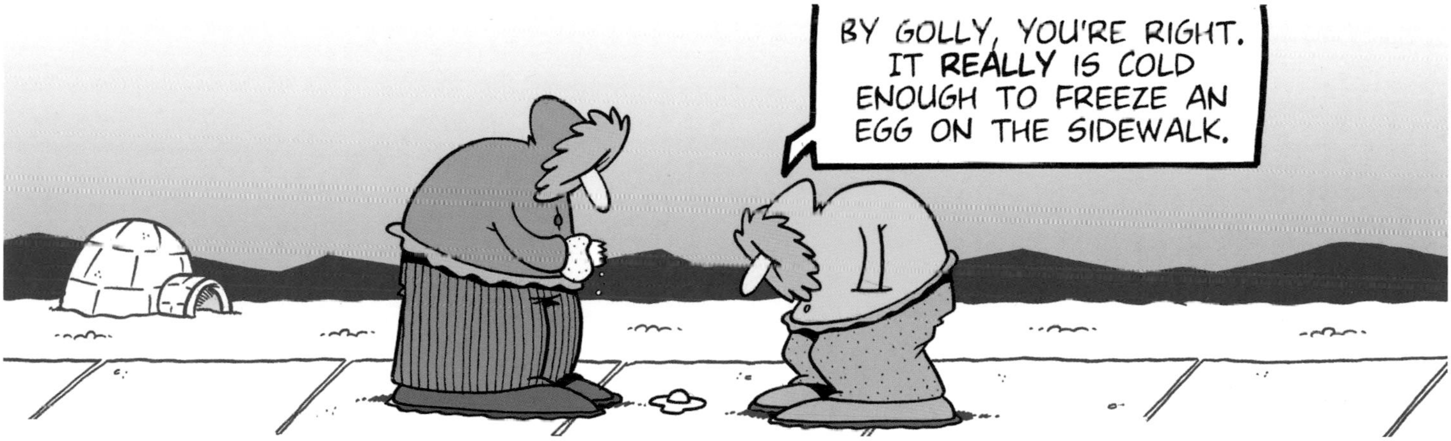
BY GOLLY, YOU'RE RIGHT. IT **REALLY** IS COLD ENOUGH TO FREEZE AN EGG ON THE SIDEWALK.

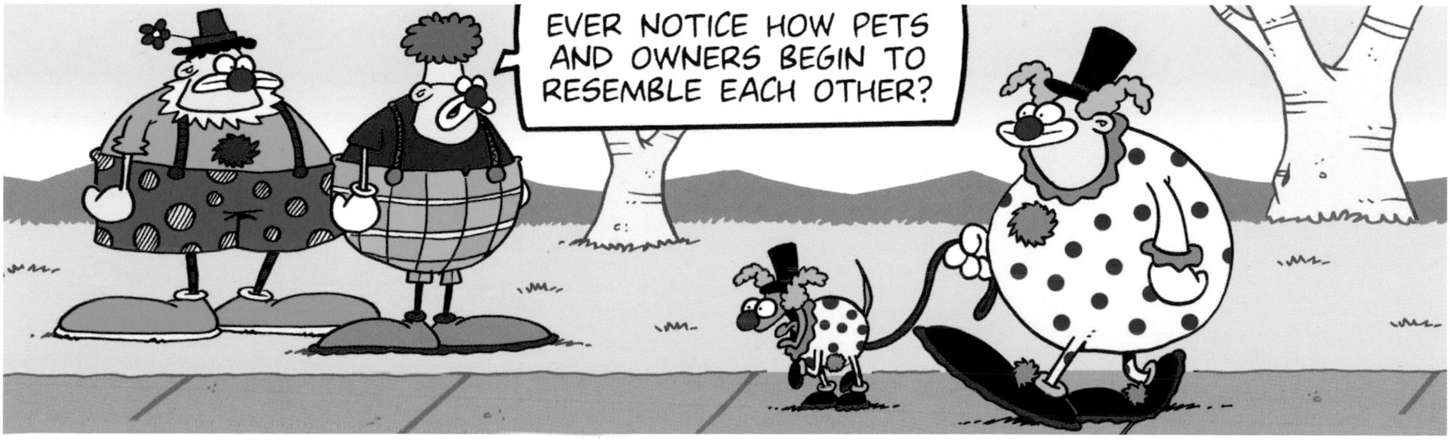
EVER NOTICE HOW PETS AND OWNERS BEGIN TO RESEMBLE EACH OTHER?

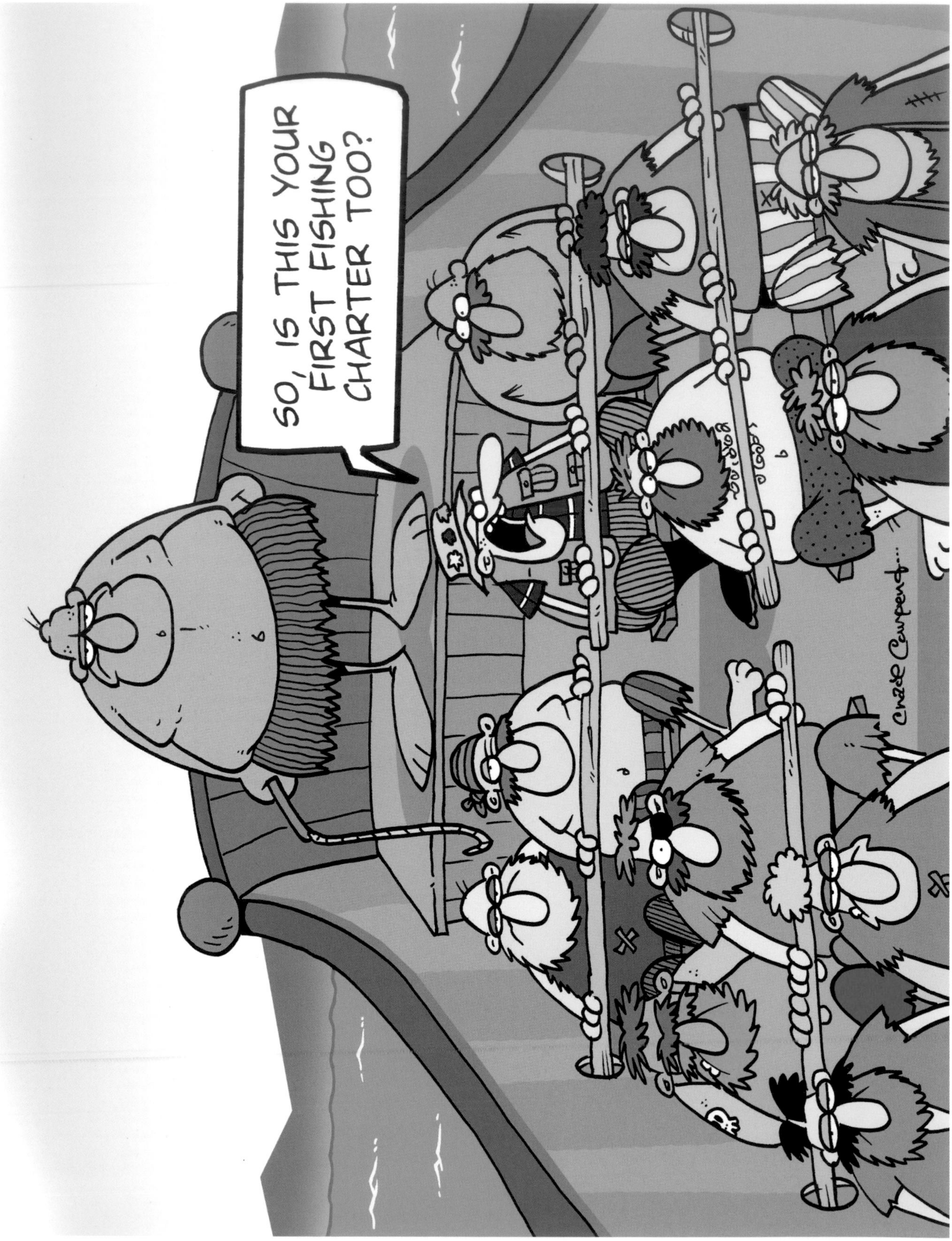
SO, IS THIS YOUR FIRST FISHING CHARTER TOO?

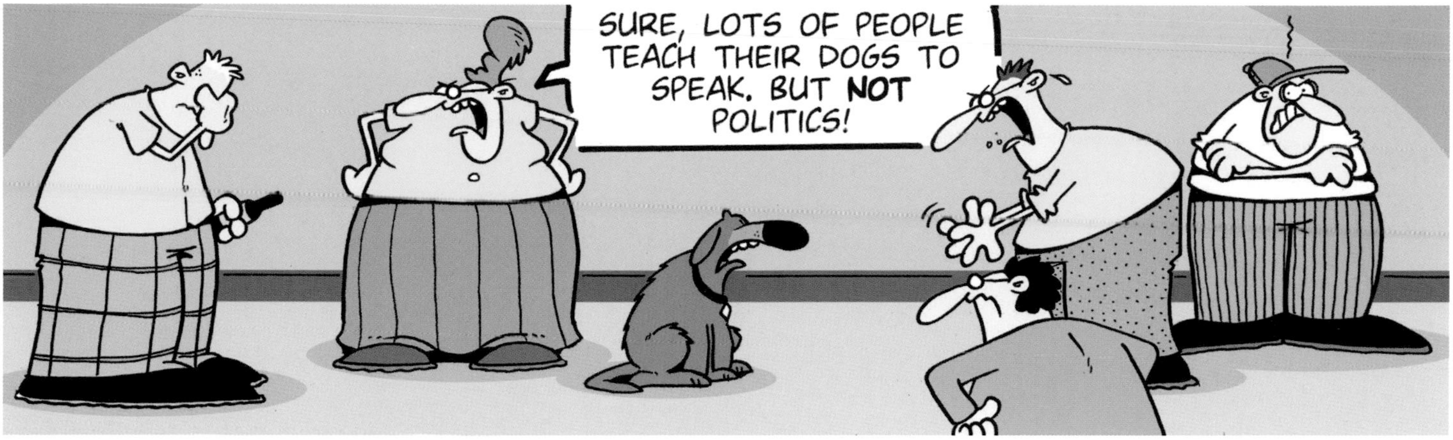
SURE, LOTS OF PEOPLE TEACH THEIR DOGS TO SPEAK. BUT **NOT** POLITICS!

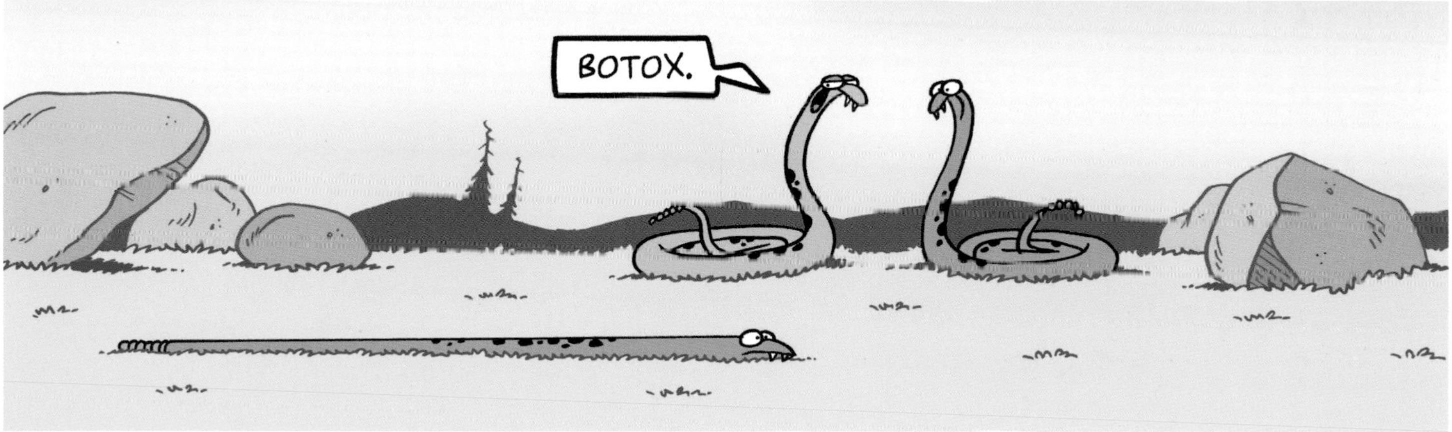
BOTOX.

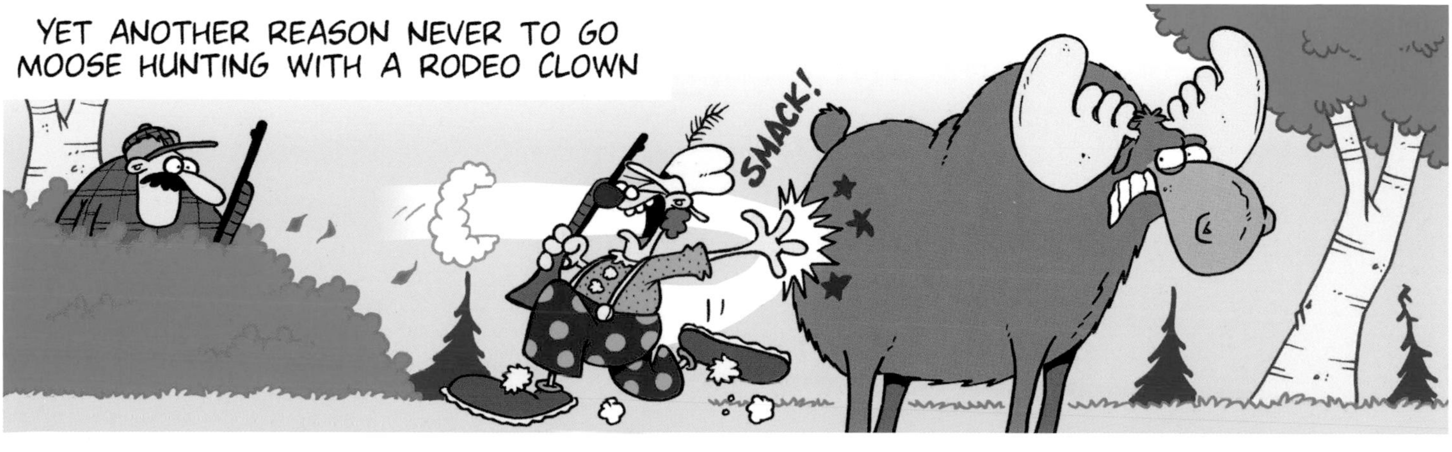
YET ANOTHER REASON NEVER TO GO MOOSE HUNTING WITH A RODEO CLOWN
SMACK!

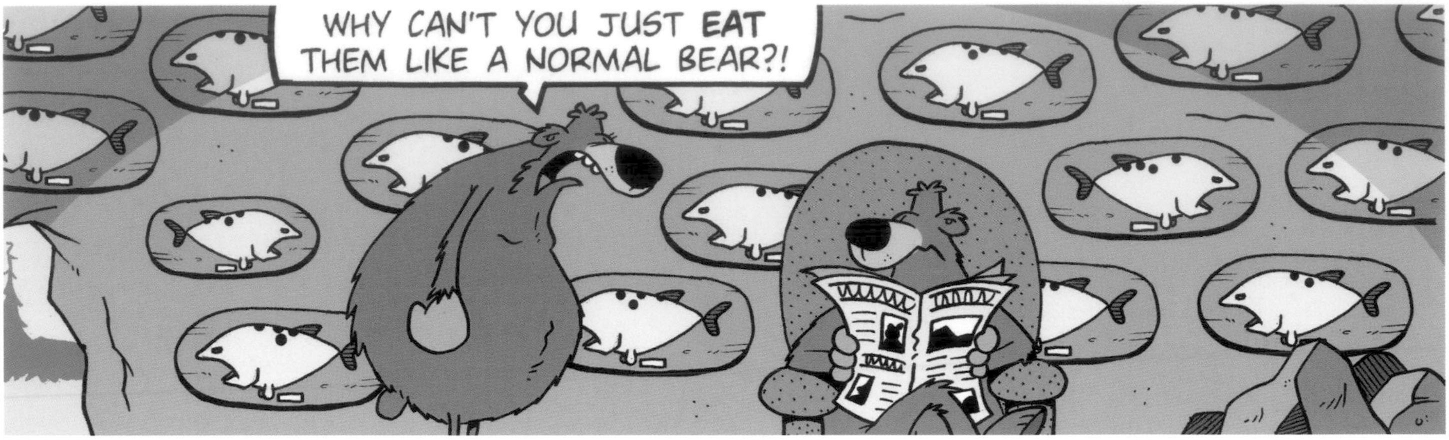
WHY CAN'T YOU JUST **EAT** THEM LIKE A NORMAL BEAR?!

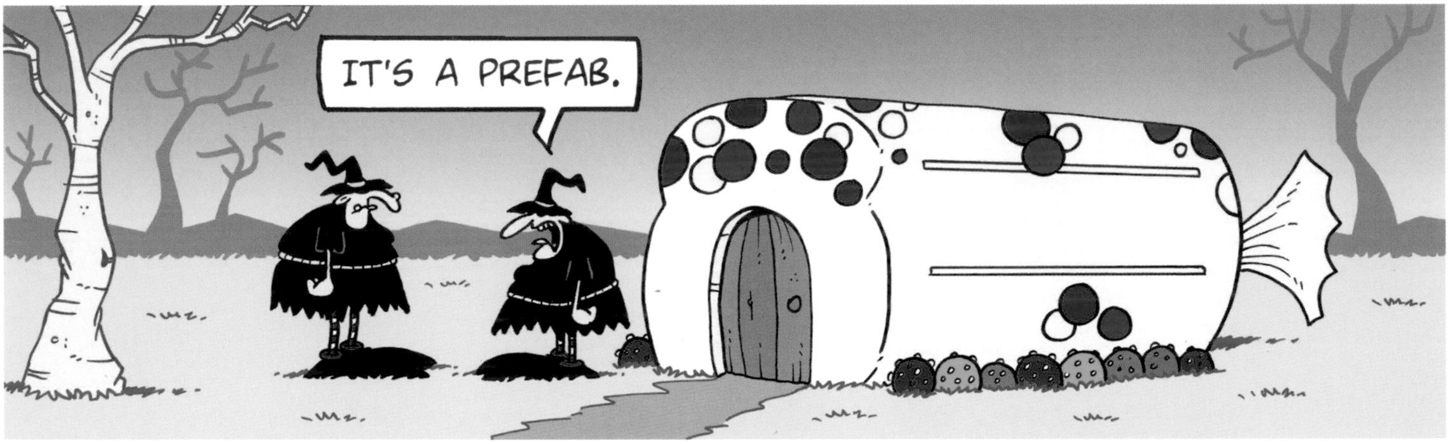
IT'S A PREFAB.

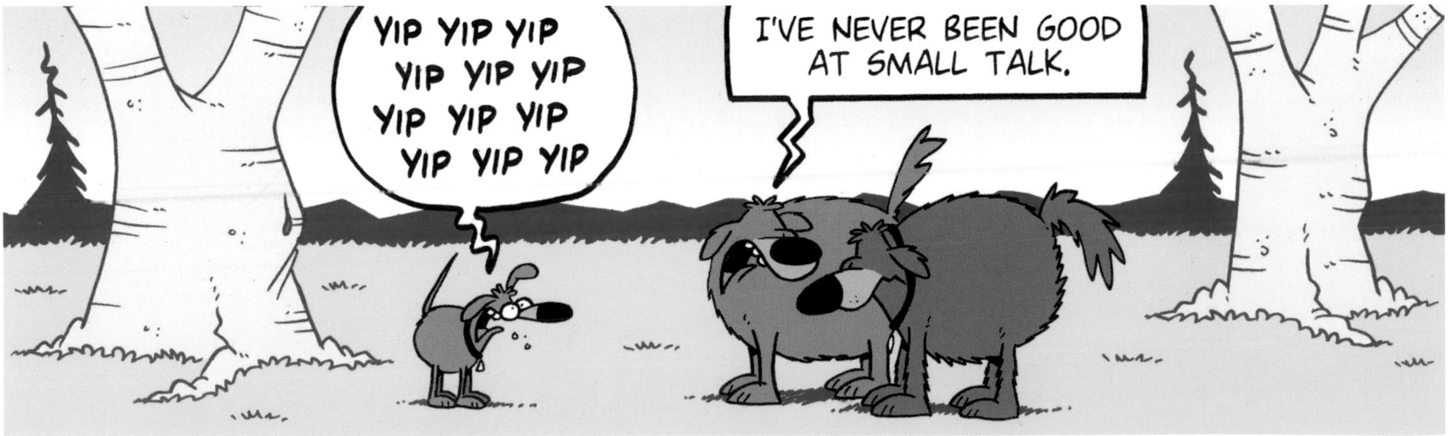
YIP YIP YIP YIP YIP YIP YIP YIP YIP YIP YIP YIP
I'VE NEVER BEEN GOOD AT SMALL TALK.

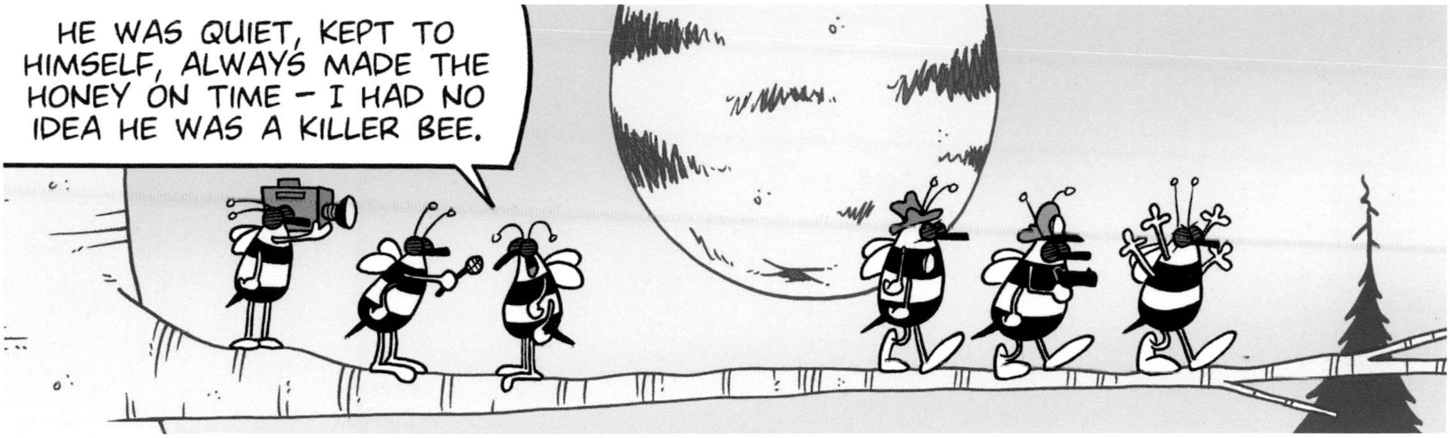
HE WAS QUIET, KEPT TO HIMSELF, ALWAYS MADE THE HONEY ON TIME – I HAD NO IDEA HE WAS A KILLER BEE.

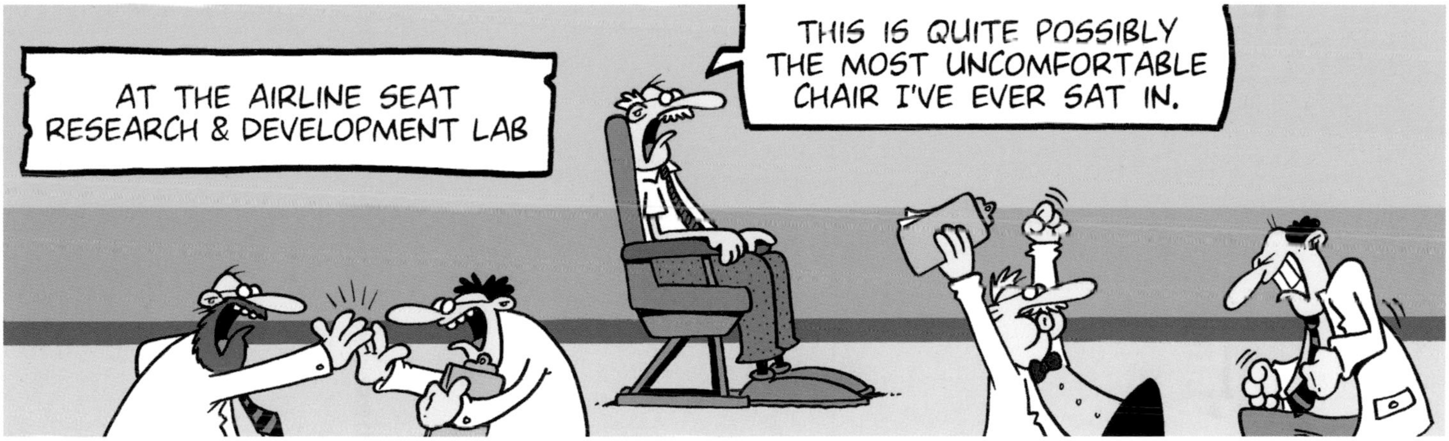
AT THE AIRLINE SEAT RESEARCH & DEVELOPMENT LAB
THIS IS QUITE POSSIBLY THE MOST UNCOMFORTABLE CHAIR I'VE EVER SAT IN.

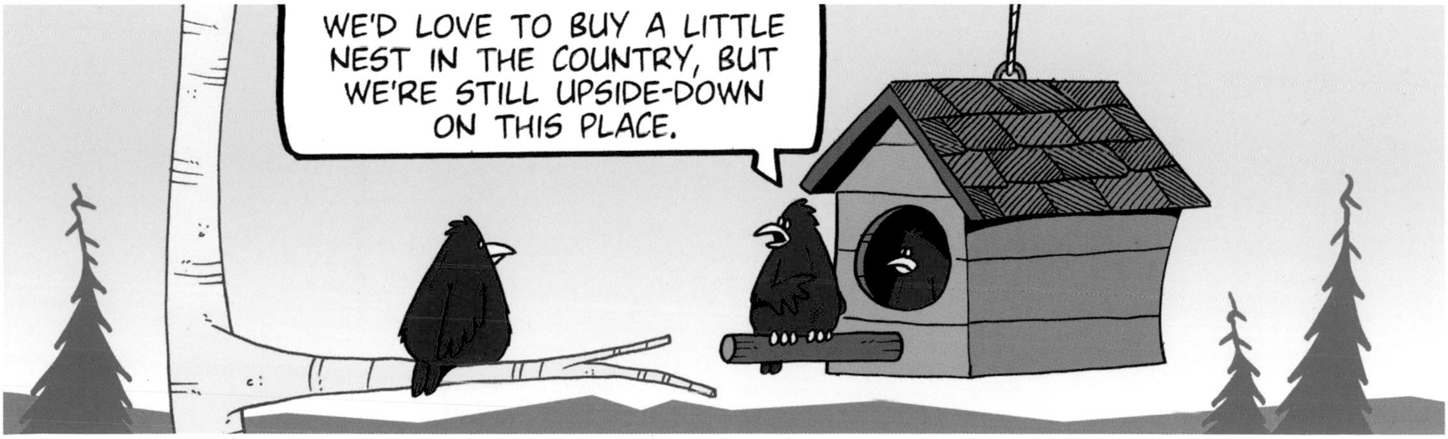
WE'D LOVE TO BUY A LITTLE NEST IN THE COUNTRY, BUT WE'RE STILL UPSIDE-DOWN ON THIS PLACE.

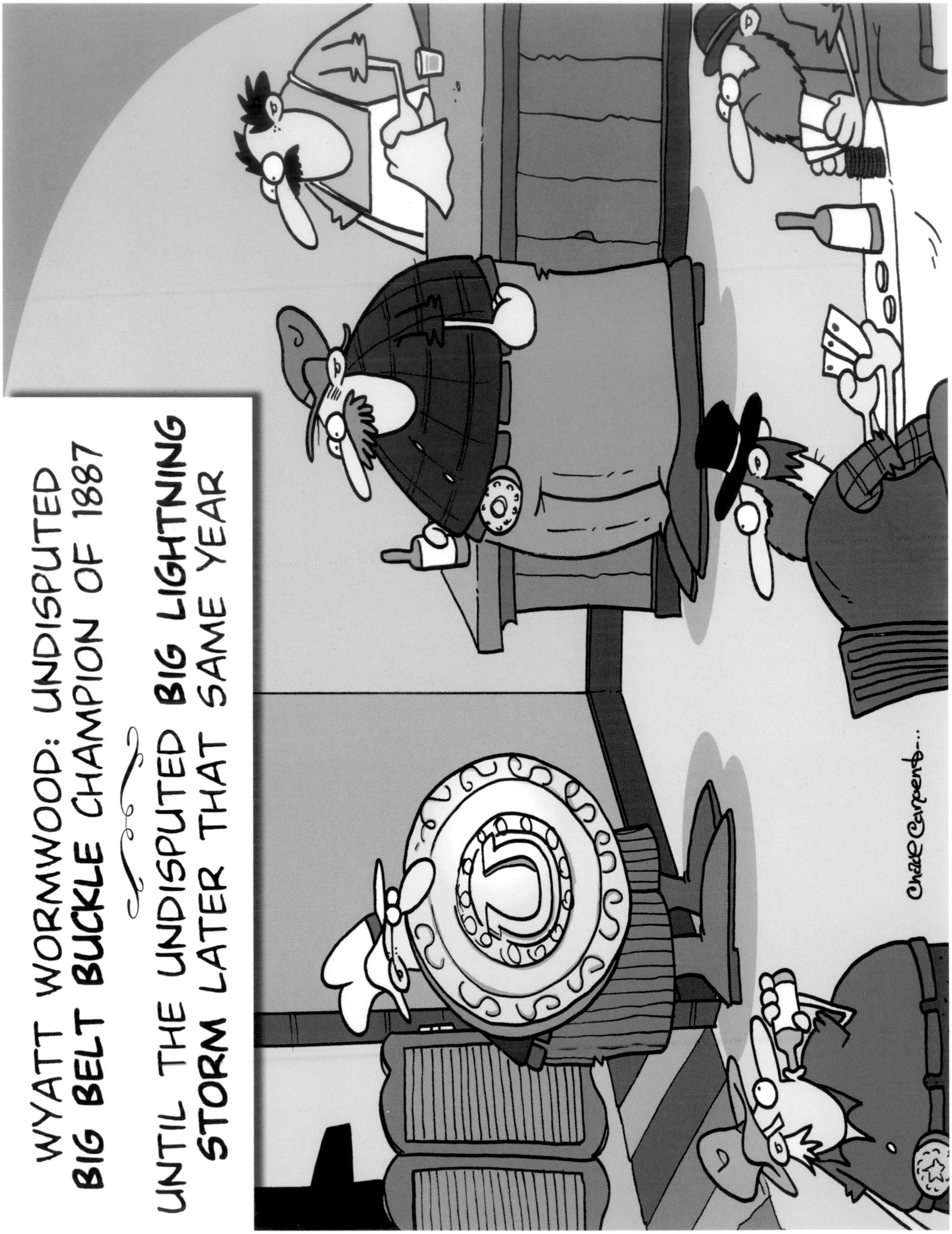
WYATT WORMWOOD: UNDISPUTED BIG BELT BUCKLE CHAMPION OF 1887
UNTIL THE UNDISPUTED BIG LIGHTNING STORM LATER THAT SAME YEAR
Chad Carpenter...

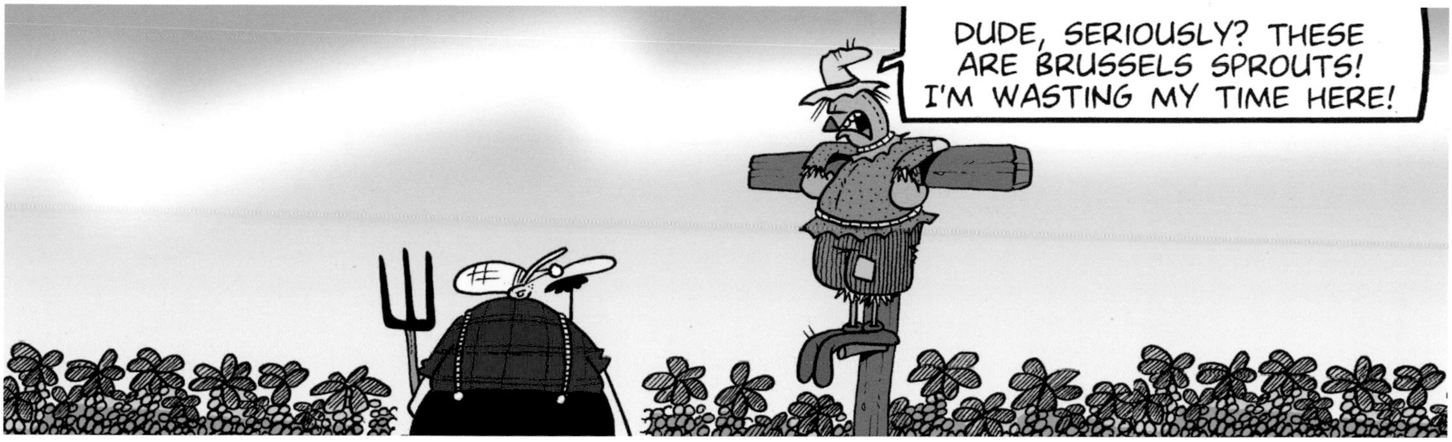
DUDE, SERIOUSLY? THESE ARE BRUSSELS SPROUTS! I'M WASTING MY TIME HERE!

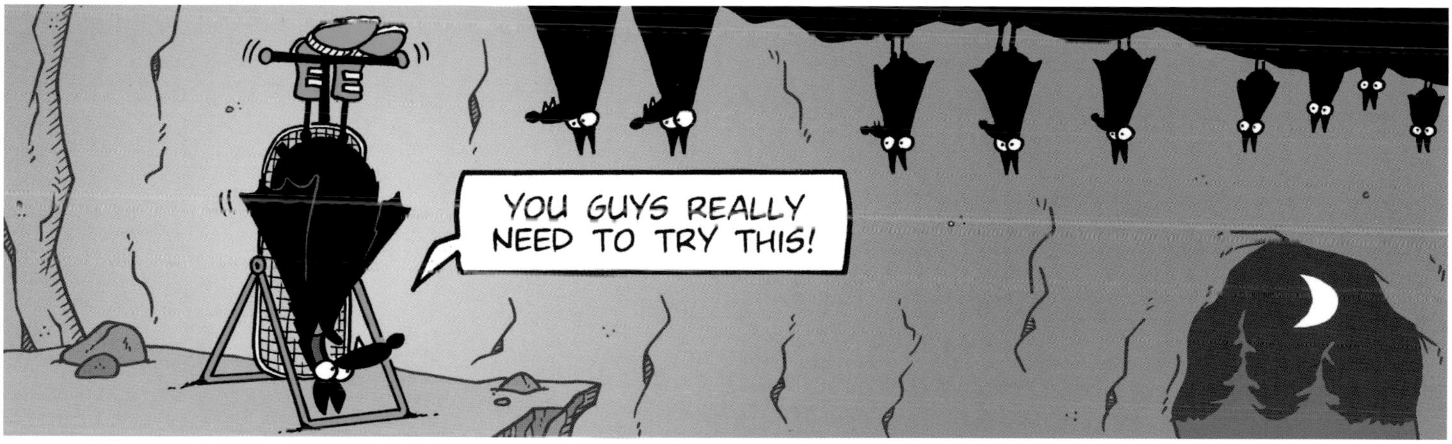
YOU GUYS REALLY NEED TO TRY THIS!

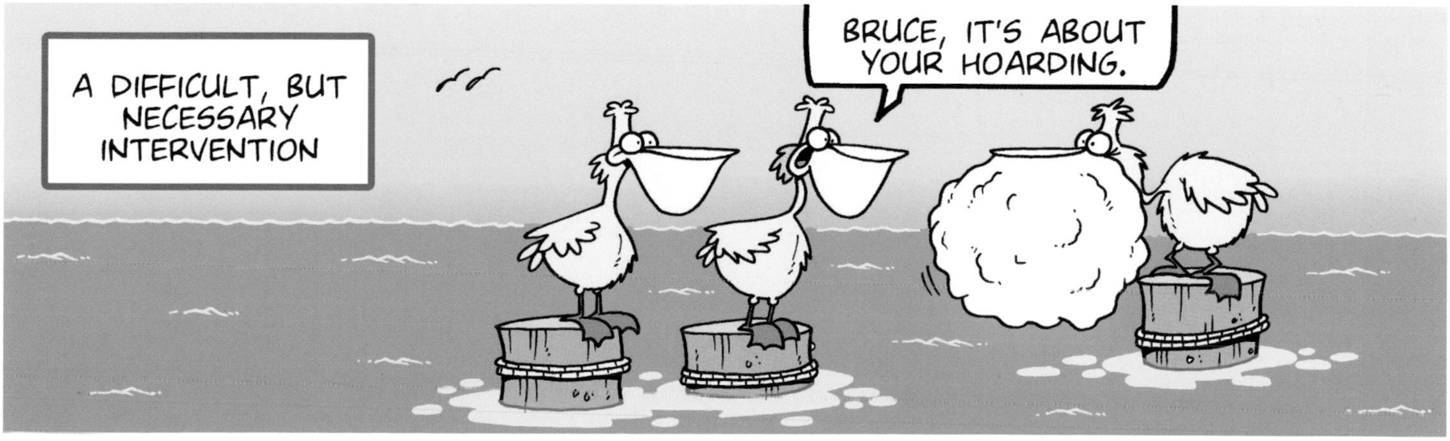
A DIFFICULT, BUT NECESSARY INTERVENTION
BRUCE, IT'S ABOUT YOUR HOARDING.

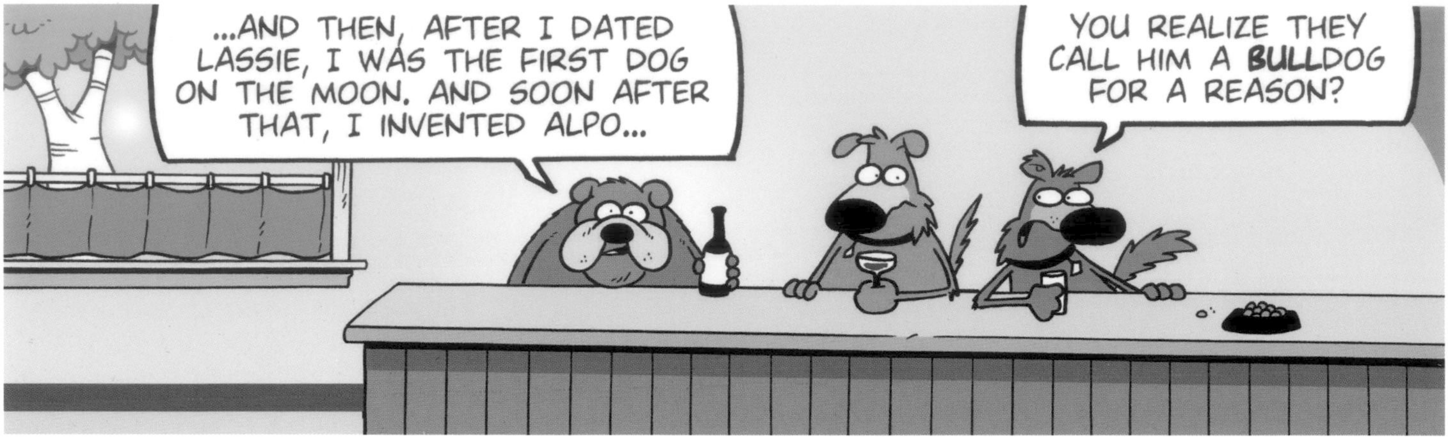
...AND THEN, AFTER I DATED LASSIE, I WAS THE FIRST DOG ON THE MOON. AND SOON AFTER THAT, I INVENTED ALPO...
YOU REALIZE THEY CALL HIM A **BULL**DOG FOR A REASON?

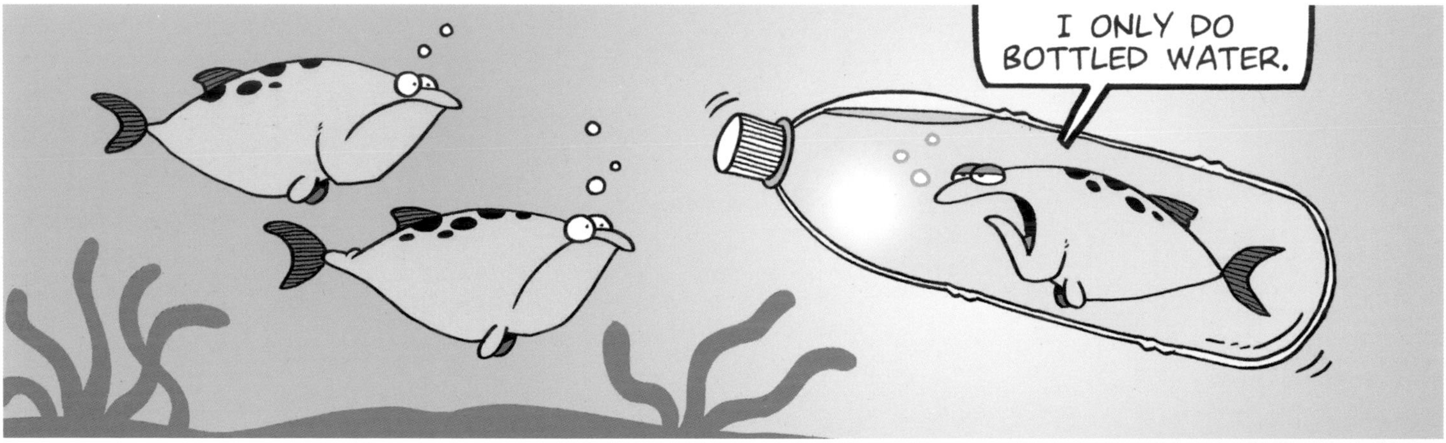
I ONLY DO BOTTLED WATER.

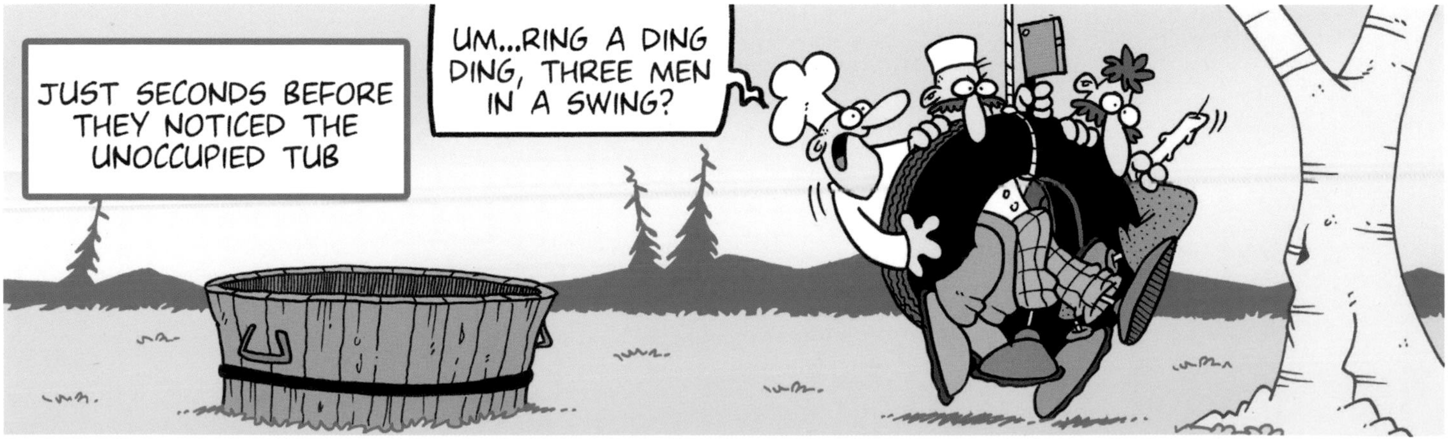
JUST SECONDS BEFORE THEY NOTICED THE UNOCCUPIED TUB
UM...RING A DING DING, THREE MEN IN A SWING?

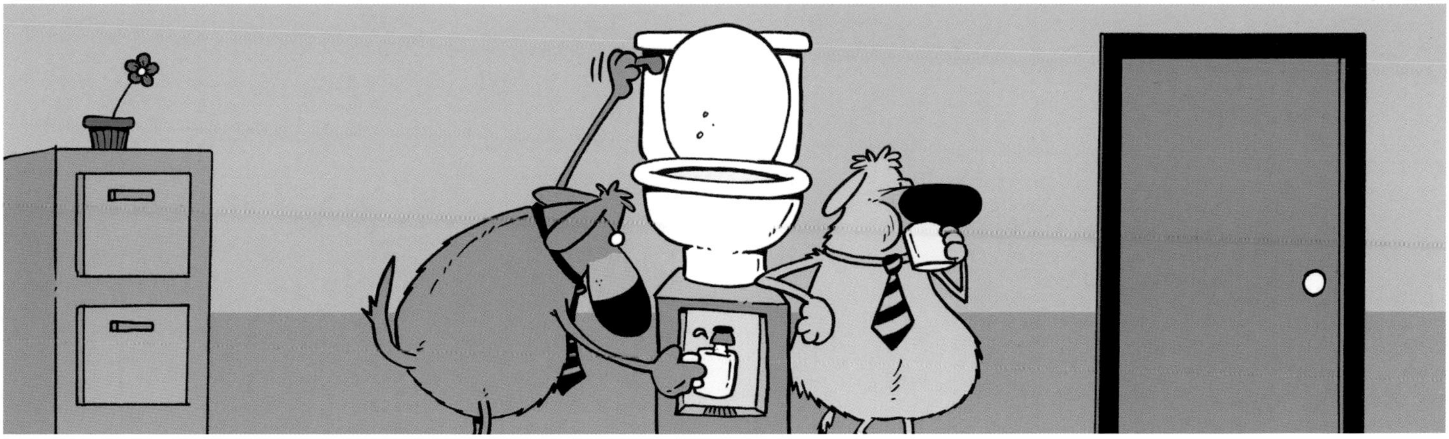

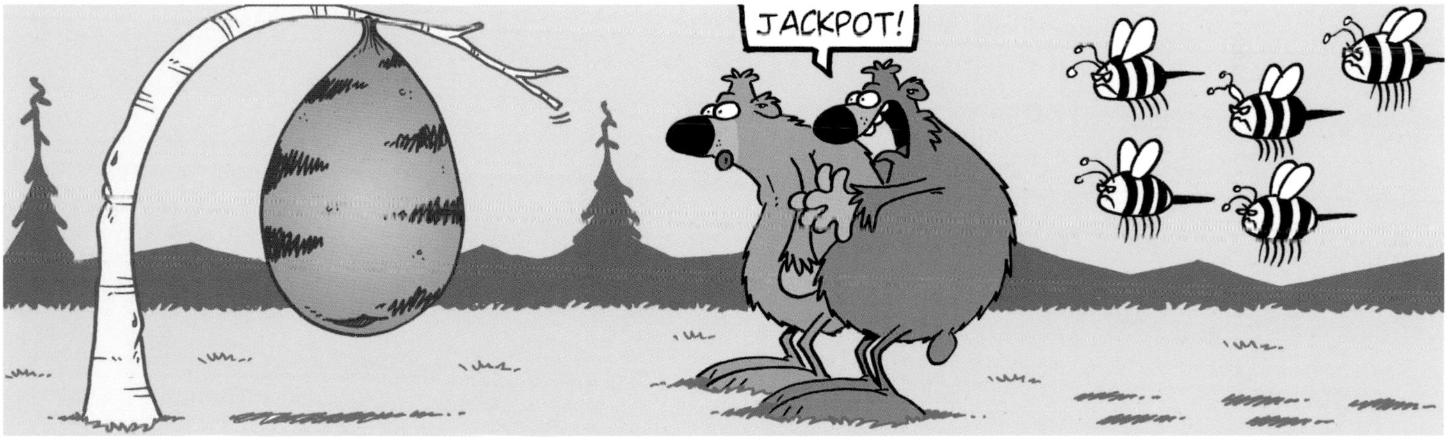
JACKPOT!

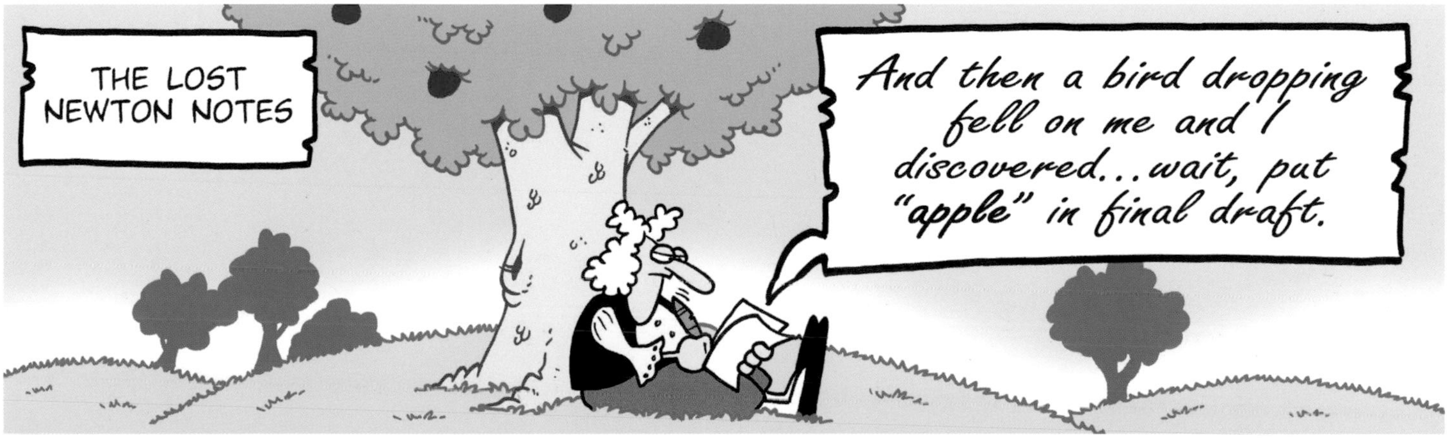
THE LOST NEWTON NOTES
And then a bird dropping fell on me and I discovered...wait, put "apple" in final draft.

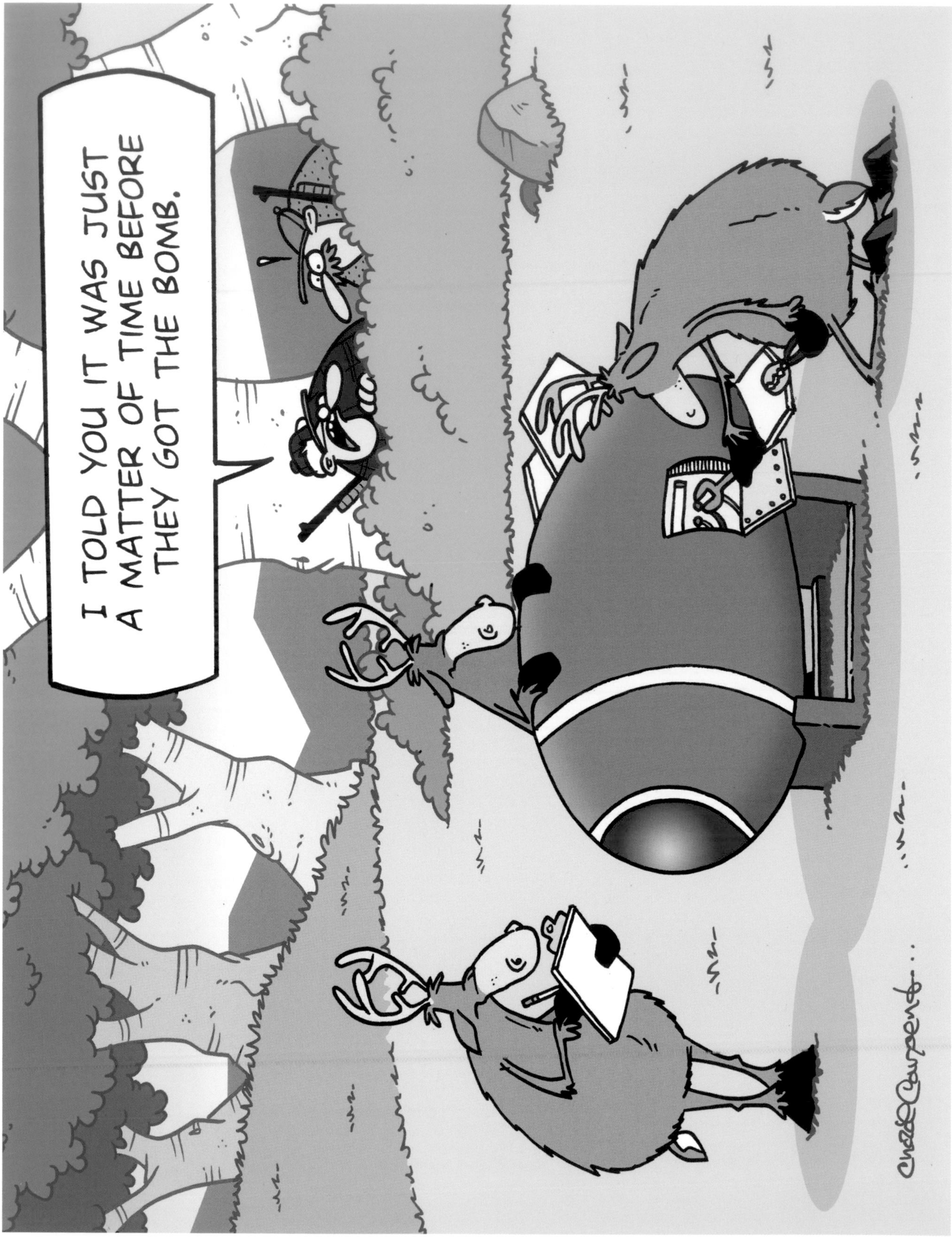
I TOLD YOU IT WAS JUST A MATTER OF TIME BEFORE THEY GOT THE BOMB.

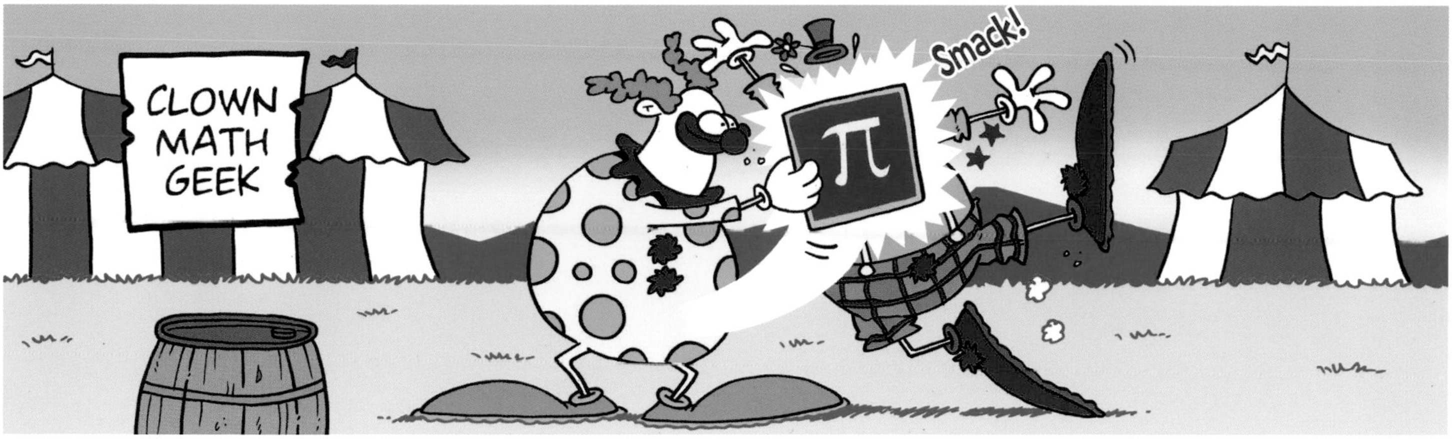
CLOWN MATH GEEK
Smack!
π

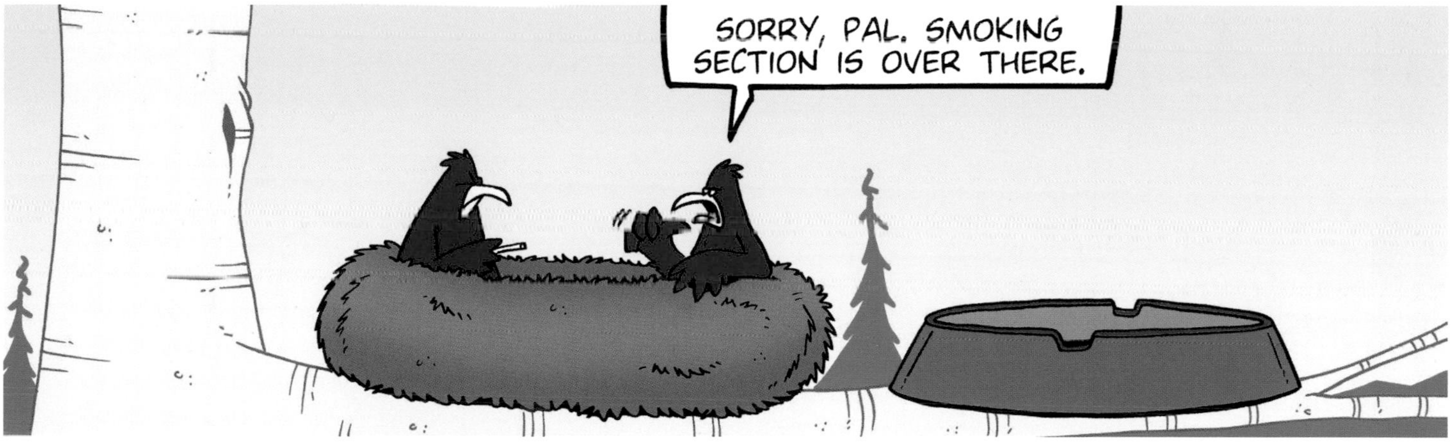
SORRY, PAL. SMOKING SECTION IS OVER THERE.

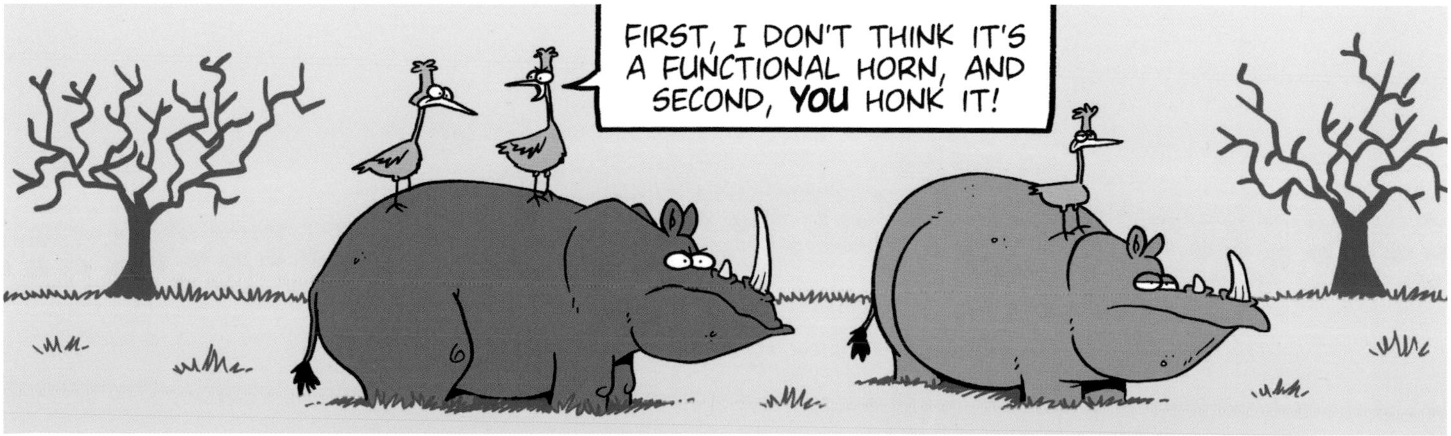
FIRST, I DON'T THINK IT'S A FUNCTIONAL HORN, AND SECOND, **YOU** HONK IT!

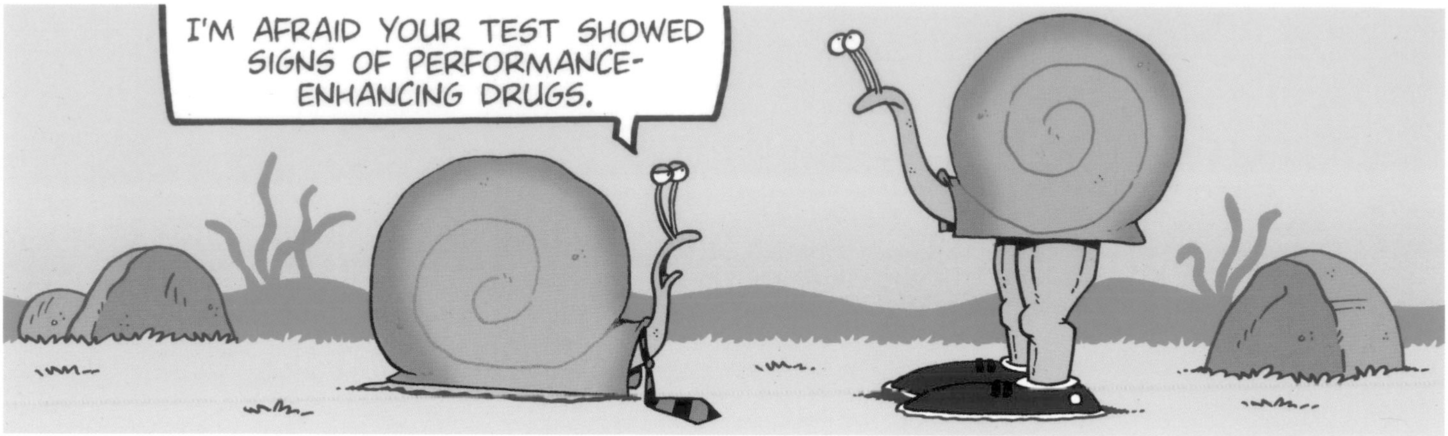
I'M AFRAID YOUR TEST SHOWED SIGNS OF PERFORMANCE-ENHANCING DRUGS.

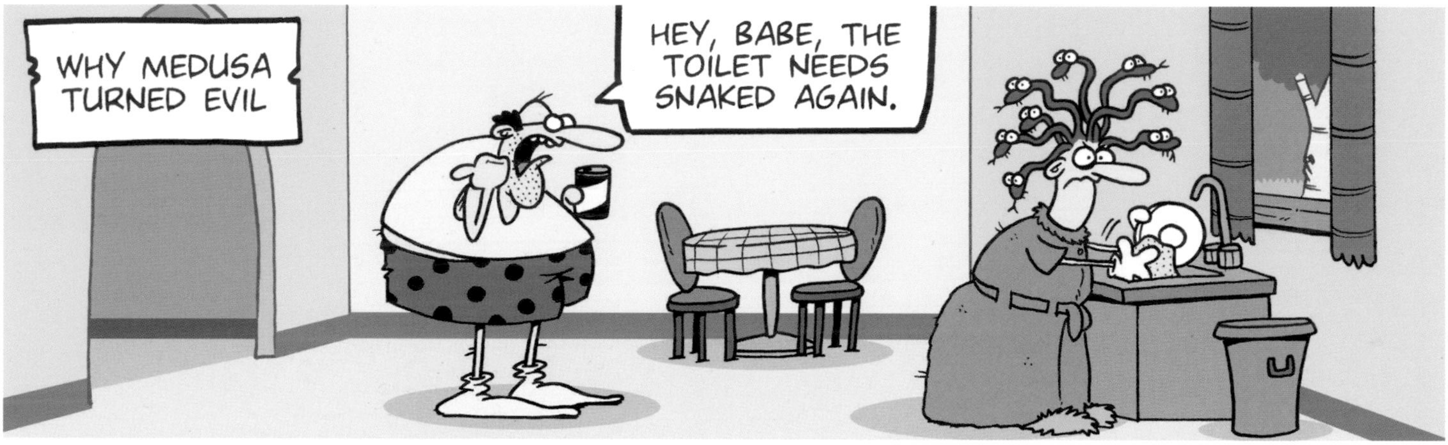
WHY MEDUSA TURNED EVIL
HEY, BABE, THE TOILET NEEDS SNAKED AGAIN.

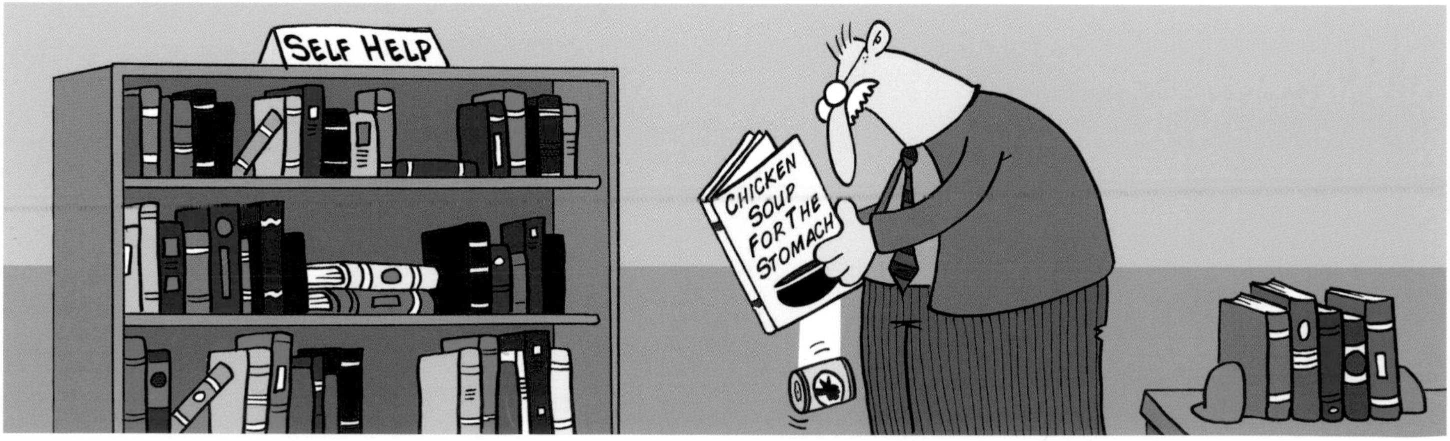
SELF HELP
CHICKEN SOUP FOR THE STOMACH

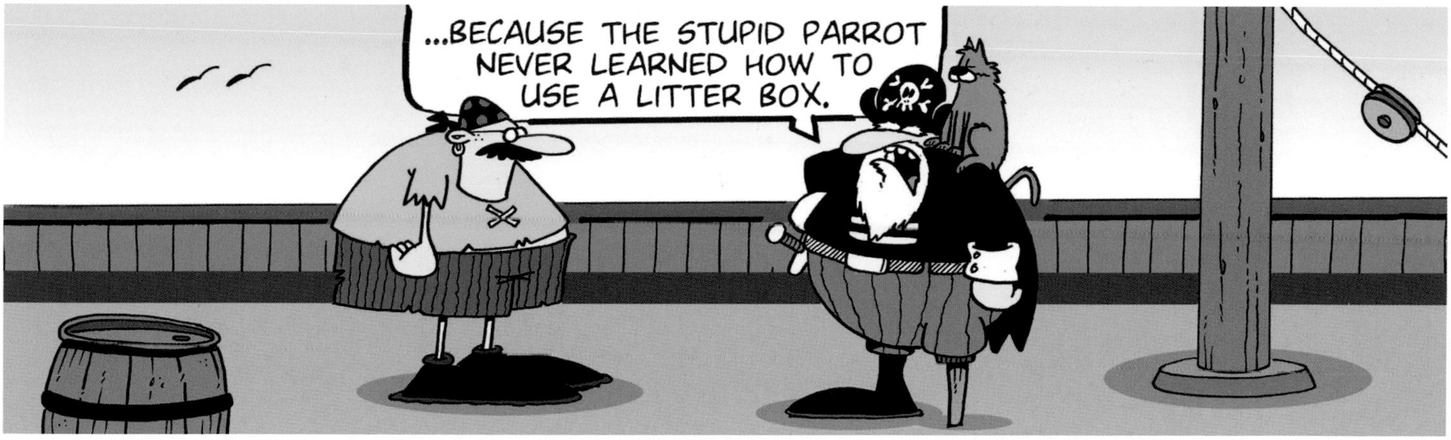
...BECAUSE THE STUPID PARROT NEVER LEARNED HOW TO USE A LITTER BOX.

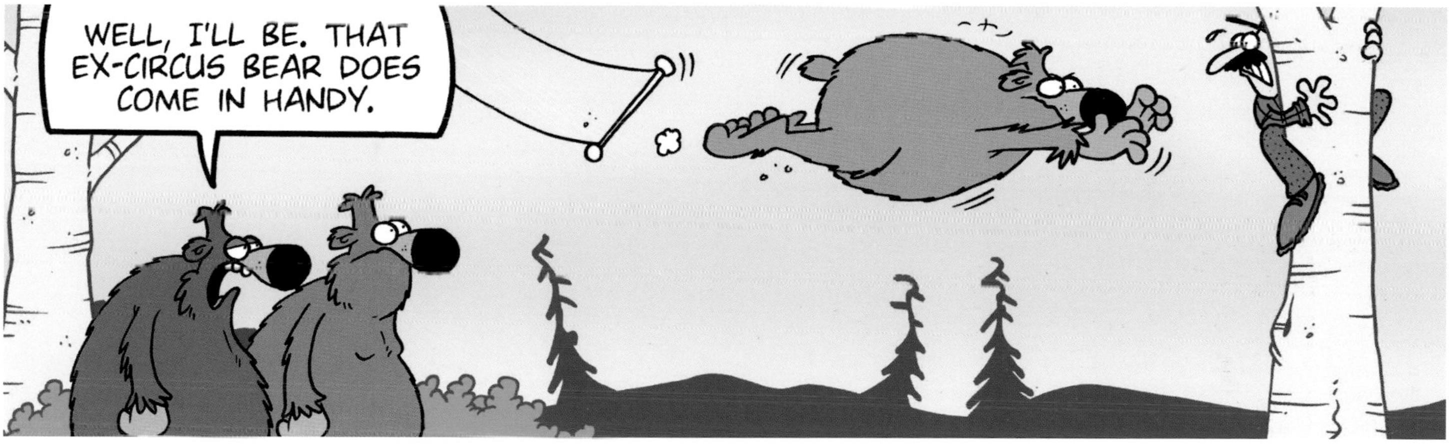
WELL, I'LL BE. THAT EX-CIRCUS BEAR DOES COME IN HANDY.

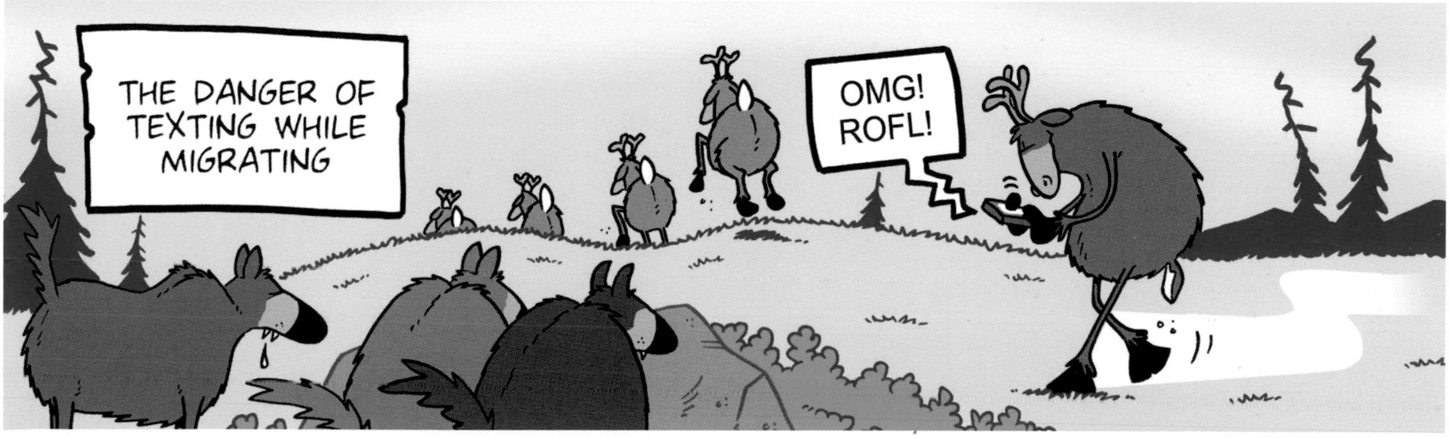
THE DANGER OF TEXTING WHILE MIGRATING
OMG! ROFL!

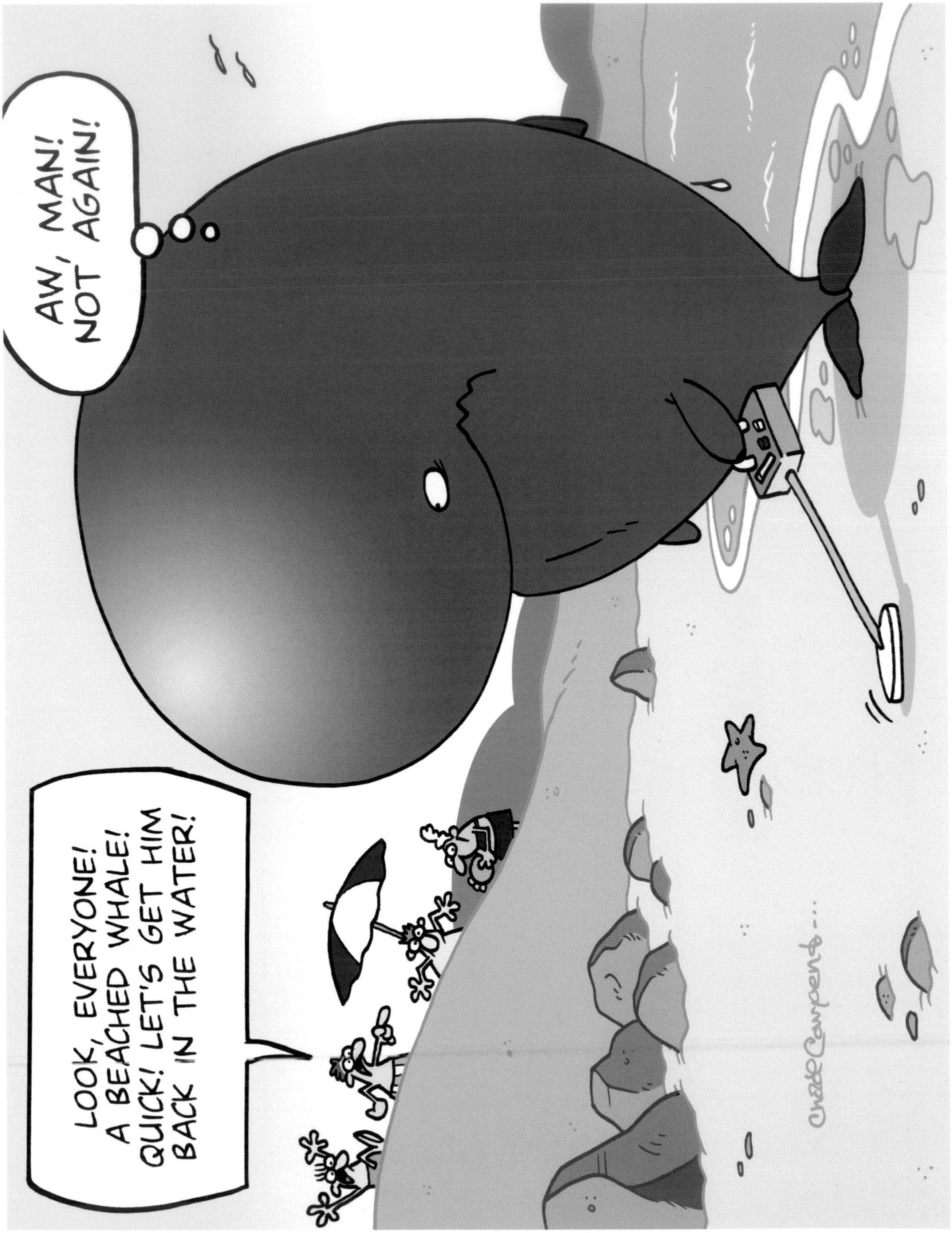
LOOK, EVERYONE! A BEACHED WHALE! QUICK! LET'S GET HIM BACK IN THE WATER!
AW, MAN! NOT AGAIN!

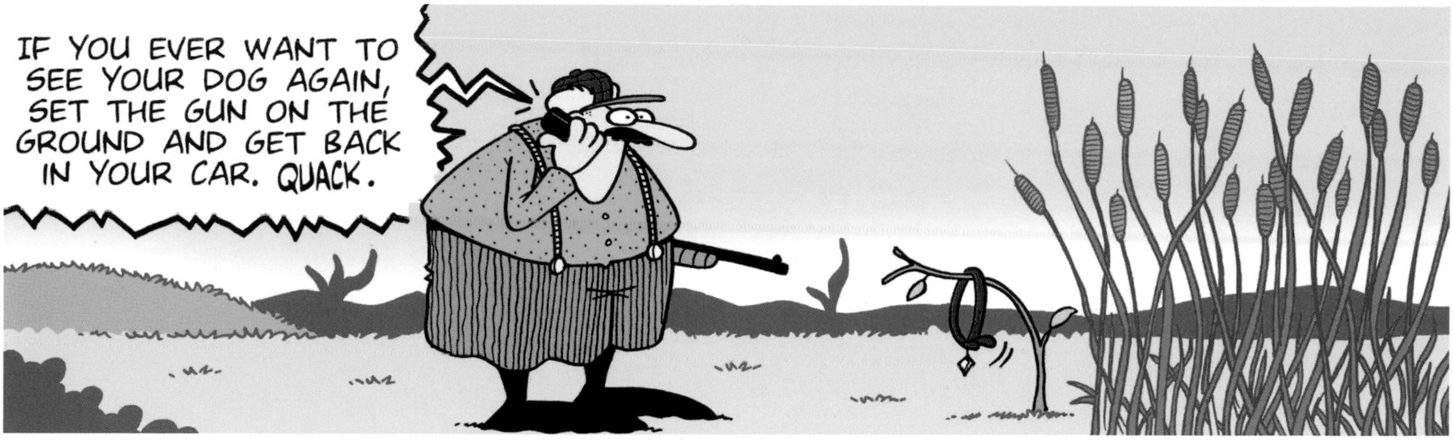
IF YOU EVER WANT TO SEE YOUR DOG AGAIN, SET THE GUN ON THE GROUND AND GET BACK IN YOUR CAR. QUACK.

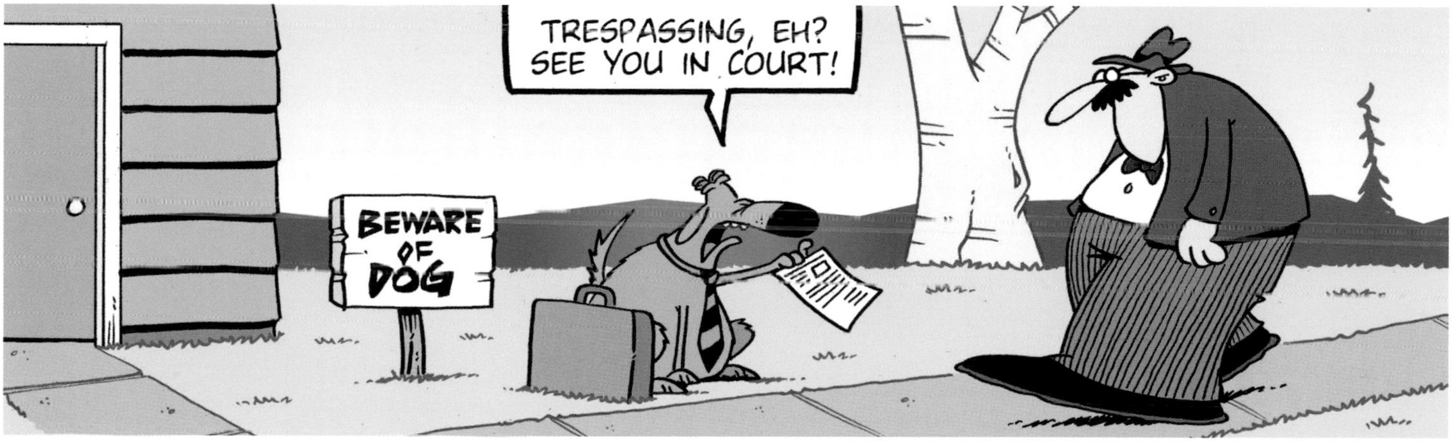
TRESPASSING, EH? SEE YOU IN COURT!
BEWARE OF DOG

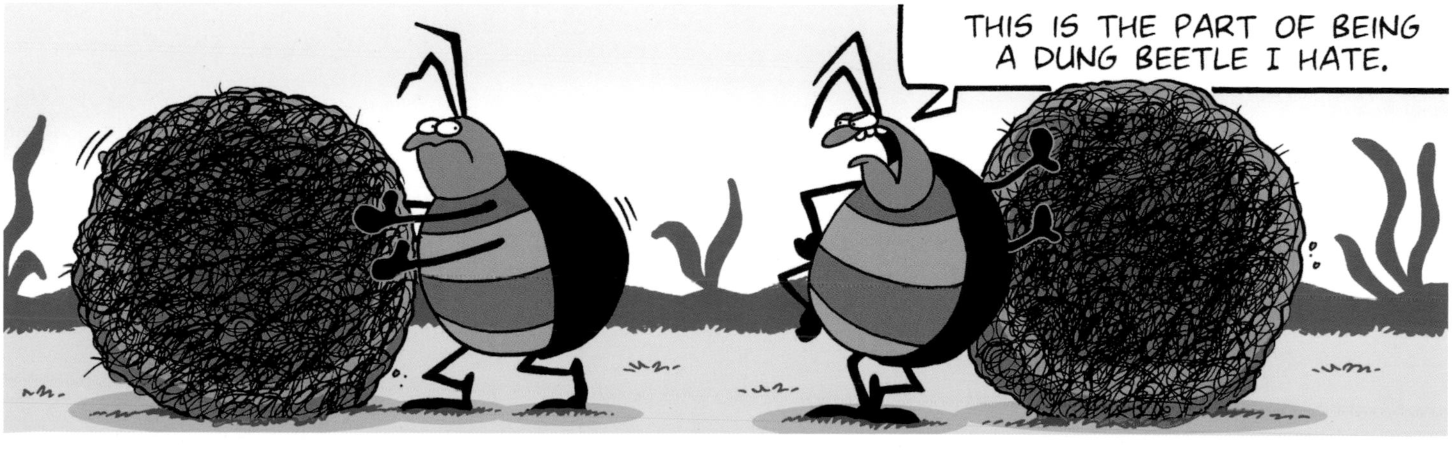
THIS IS THE PART OF BEING A DUNG BEETLE I HATE.

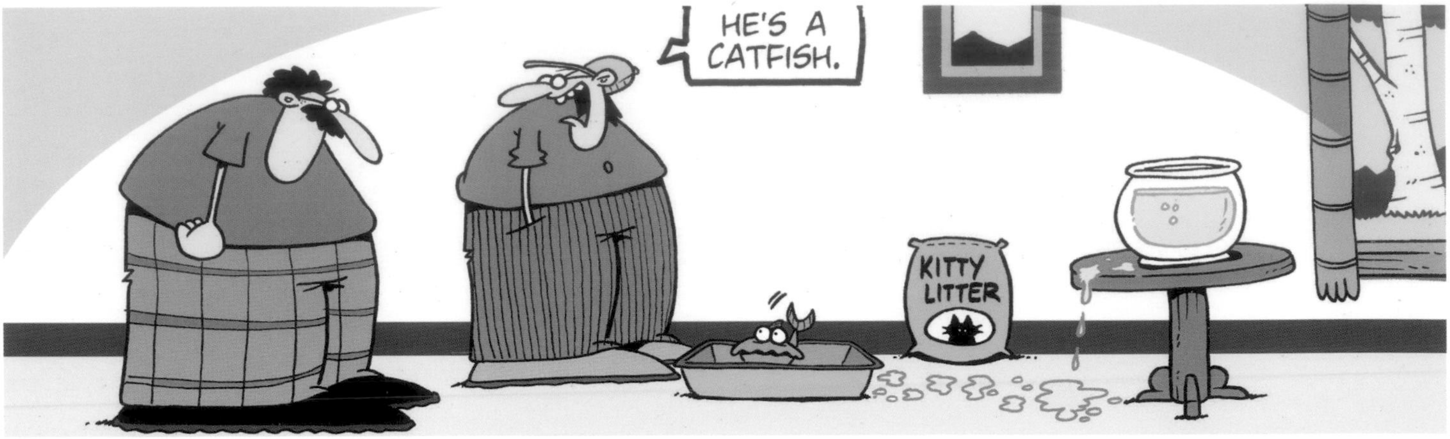
HE'S A CATFISH.
KITTY LITTER

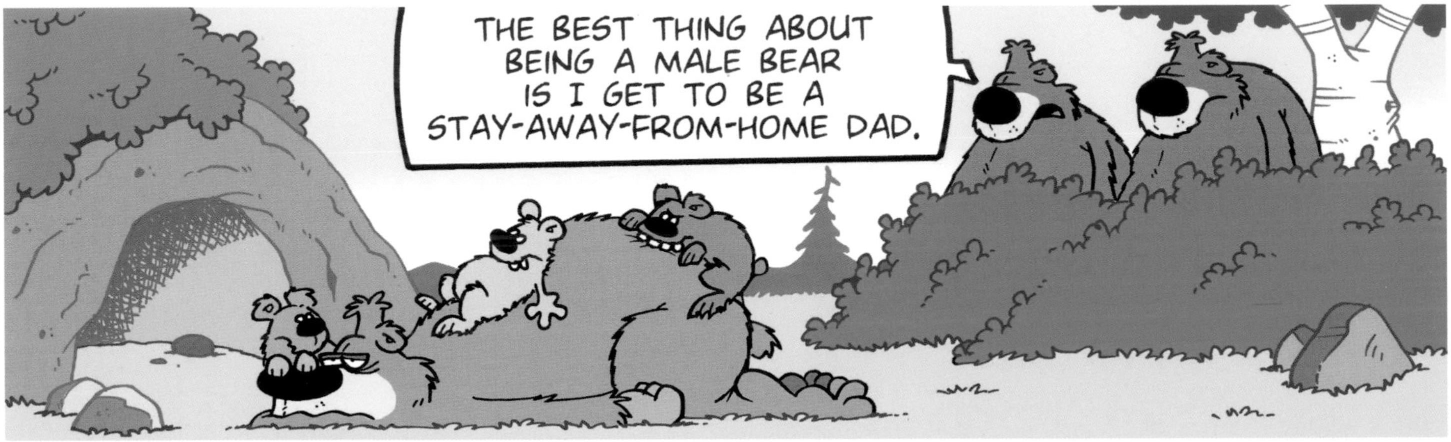
THE BEST THING ABOUT BEING A MALE BEAR IS I GET TO BE A STAY-AWAY-FROM-HOME DAD.

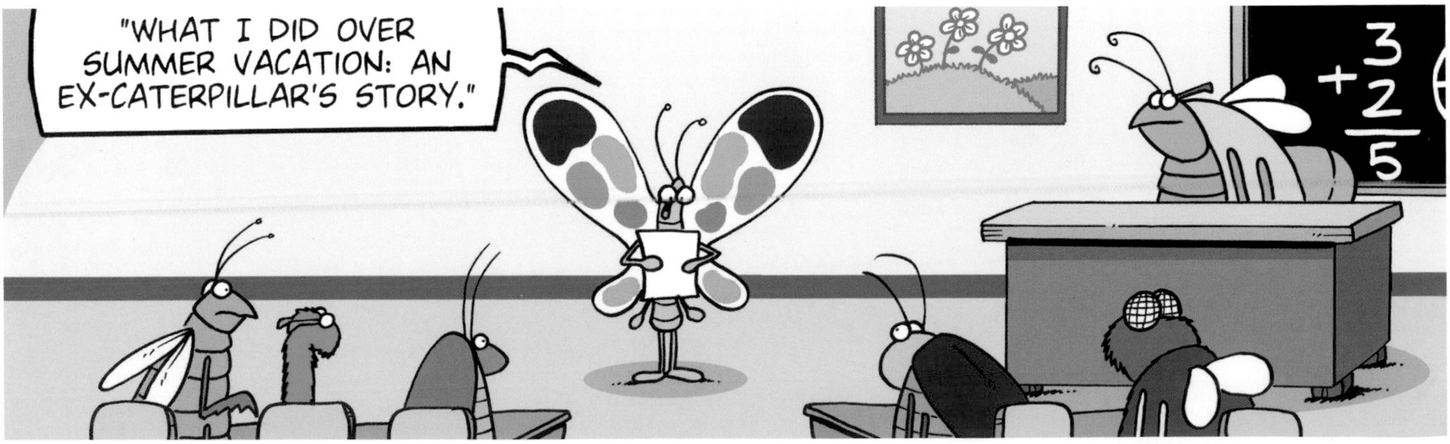
"WHAT I DID OVER SUMMER VACATION: AN EX-CATERPILLAR'S STORY."
3
+2
5

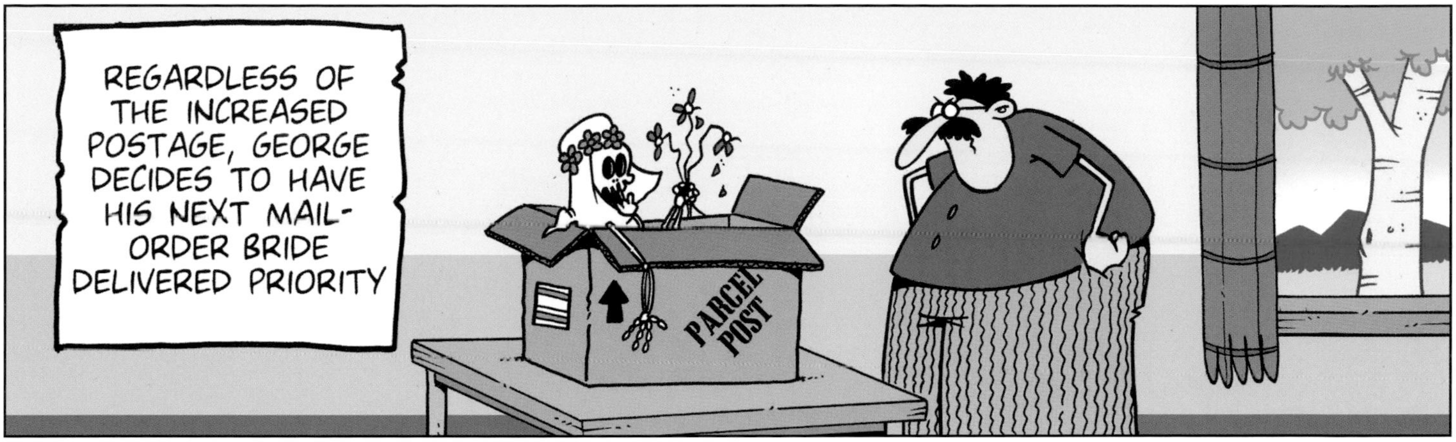
REGARDLESS OF THE INCREASED POSTAGE, GEORGE DECIDES TO HAVE HIS NEXT MAIL-ORDER BRIDE DELIVERED PRIORITY
PARCEL POST

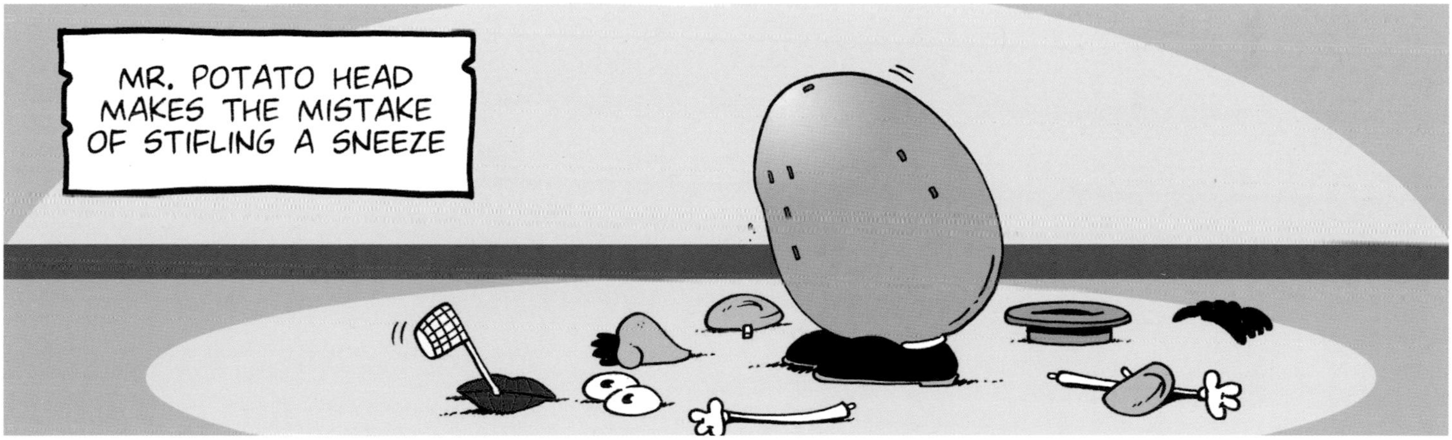
MR. POTATO HEAD MAKES THE MISTAKE OF STIFLING A SNEEZE

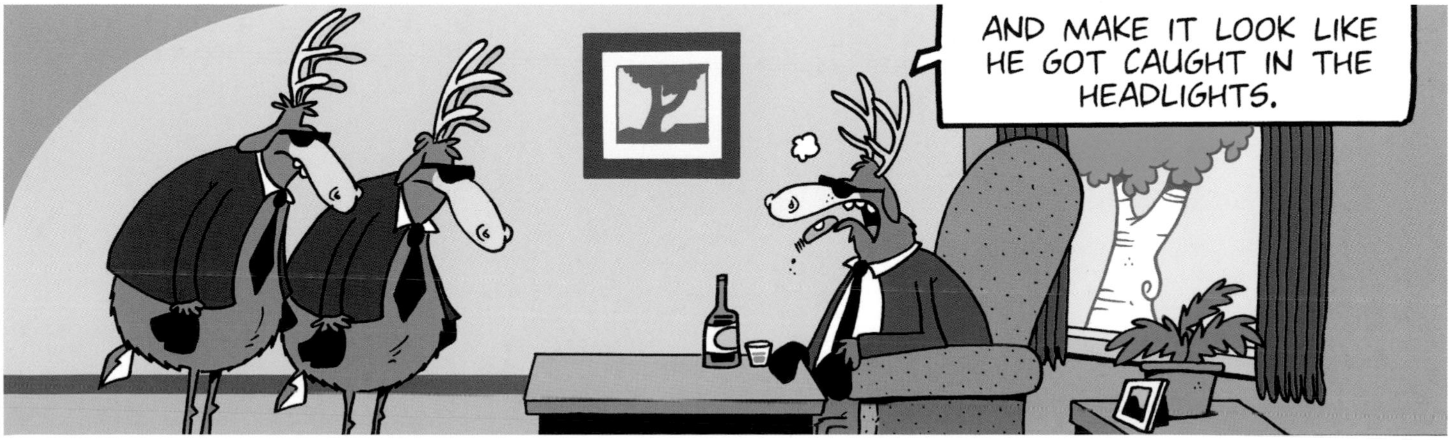
AND MAKE IT LOOK LIKE HE GOT CAUGHT IN THE HEADLIGHTS.

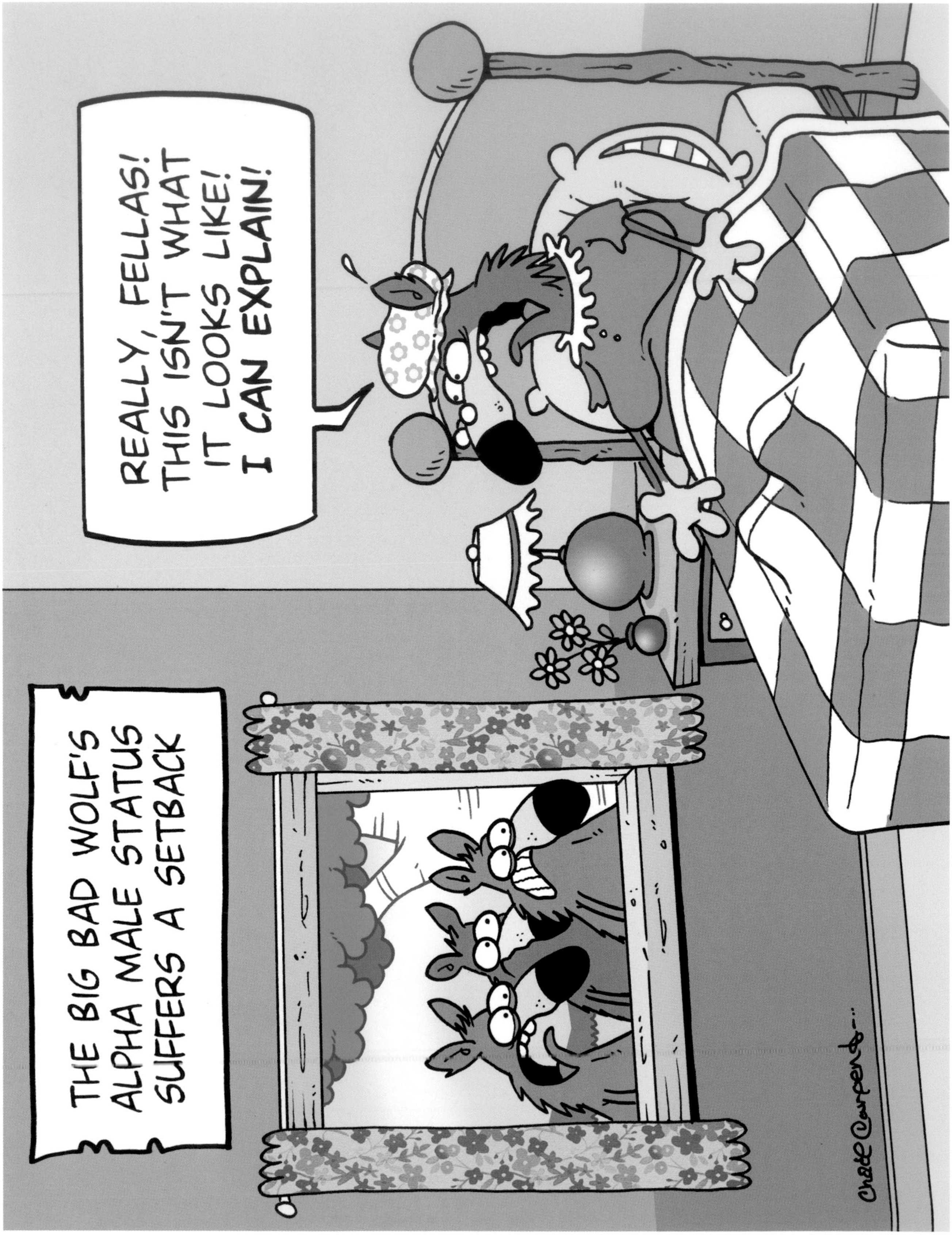
THE BIG BAD WOLF'S ALPHA MALE STATUS SUFFERS A SETBACK
REALLY, FELLAS! THIS ISN'T WHAT IT LOOKS LIKE! I CAN EXPLAIN!
Chad Carpenter

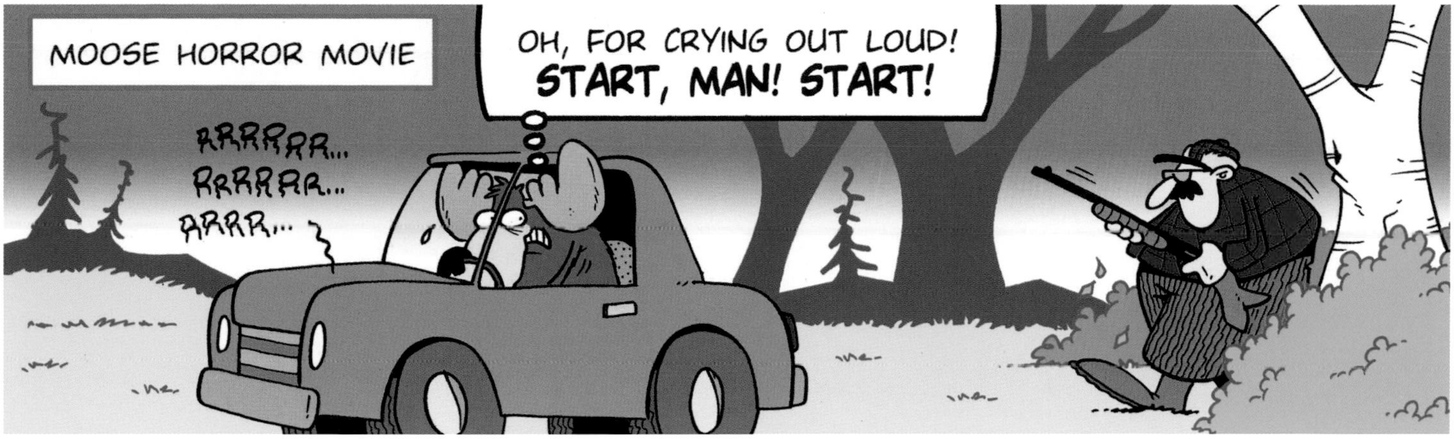
MOOSE HORROR MOVIE
RRRRRRR...
RRRRRR...
RRRR...
OH, FOR CRYING OUT LOUD! START, MAN! START!

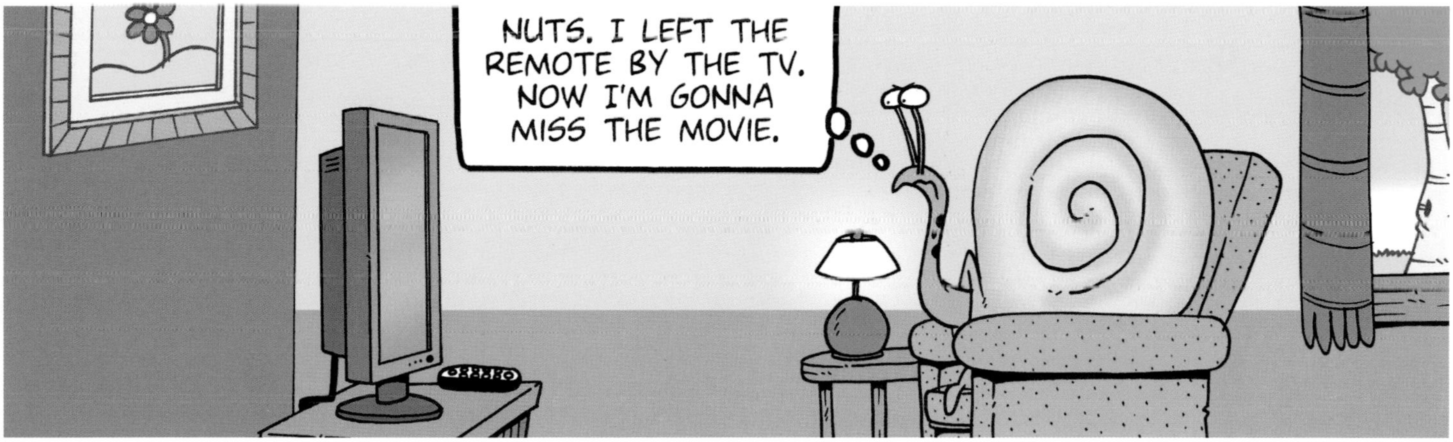
NUTS. I LEFT THE REMOTE BY THE TV. NOW I'M GONNA MISS THE MOVIE.

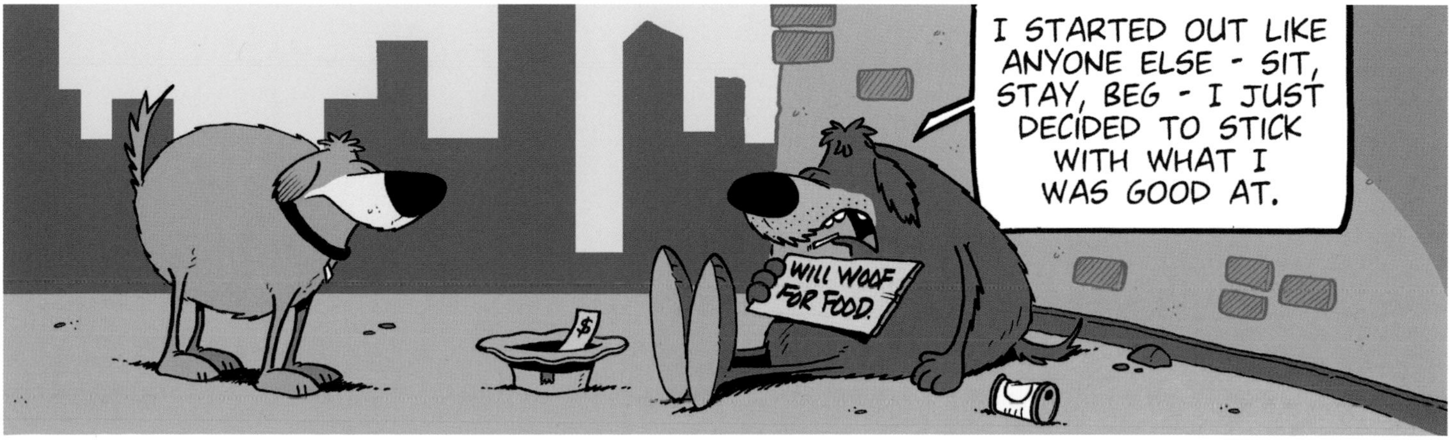
I STARTED OUT LIKE ANYONE ELSE - SIT, STAY, BEG - I JUST DECIDED TO STICK WITH WHAT I WAS GOOD AT.
WILL WOOF FOR FOOD.
$

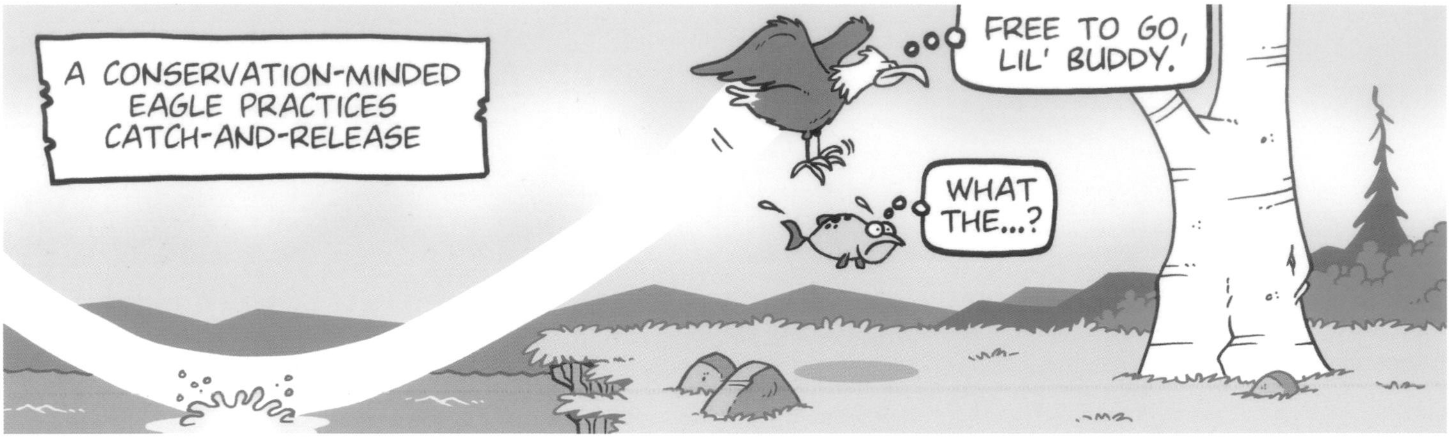
A CONSERVATION-MINDED EAGLE PRACTICES CATCH-AND-RELEASE
FREE TO GO, LIL' BUDDY.
WHAT THE...?

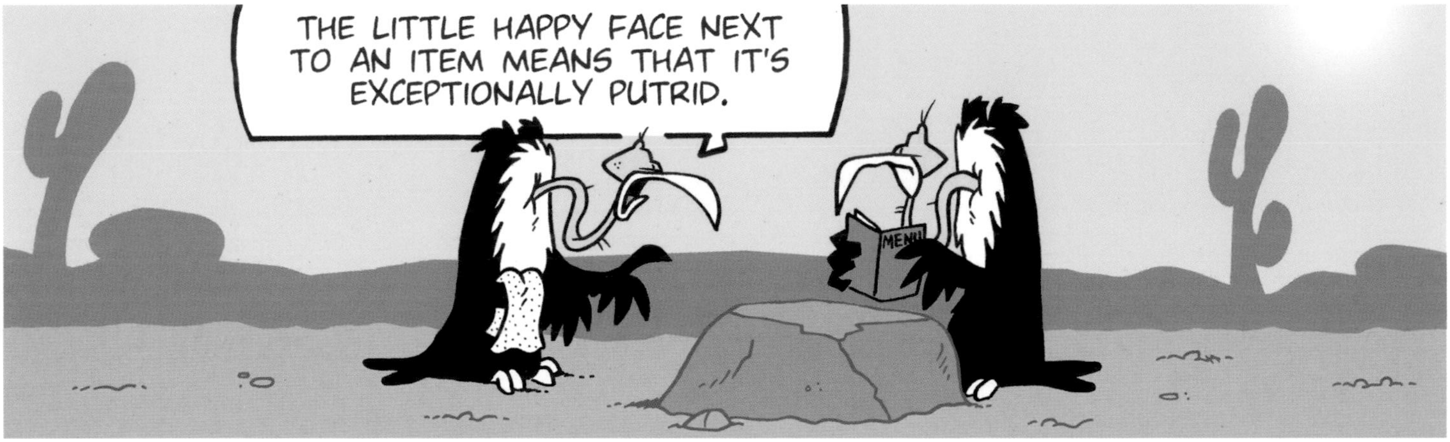
THE LITTLE HAPPY FACE NEXT TO AN ITEM MEANS THAT IT'S EXCEPTIONALLY PUTRID.
MENU

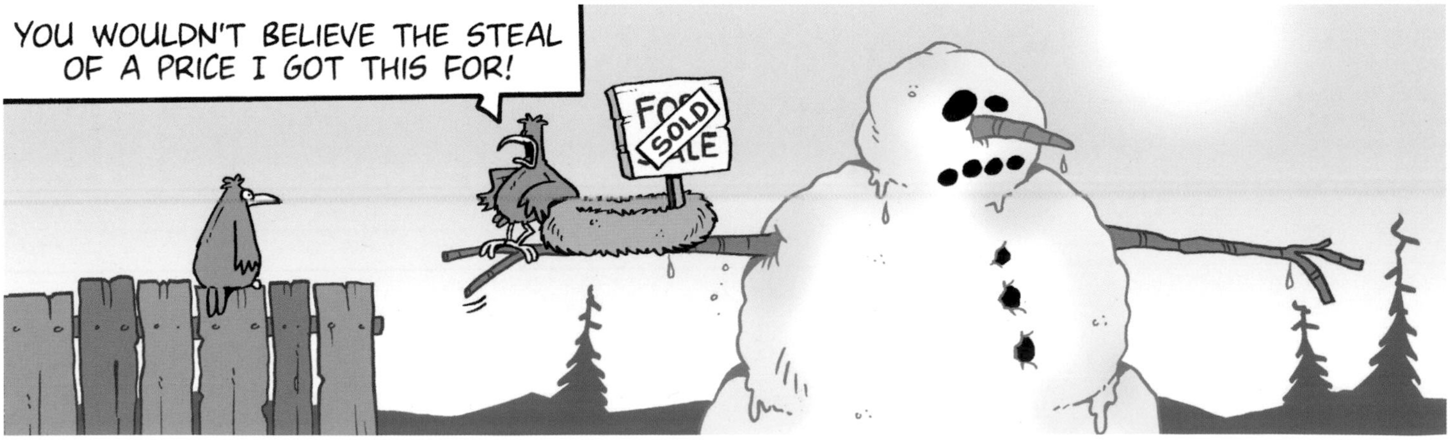
YOU WOULDN'T BELIEVE THE STEAL OF A PRICE I GOT THIS FOR!
SOLD

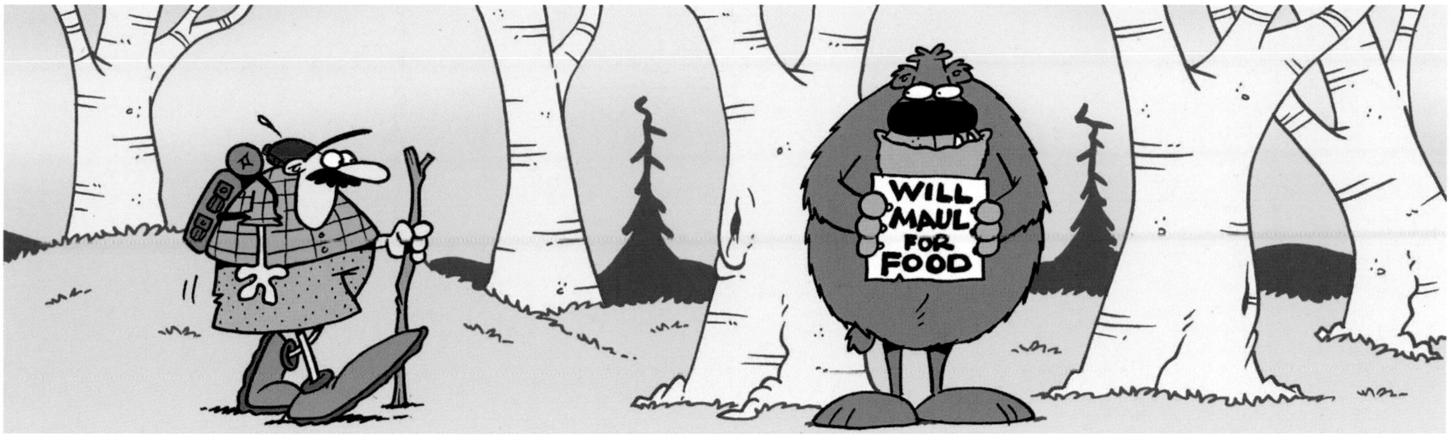
WILL MAUL FOR FOOD

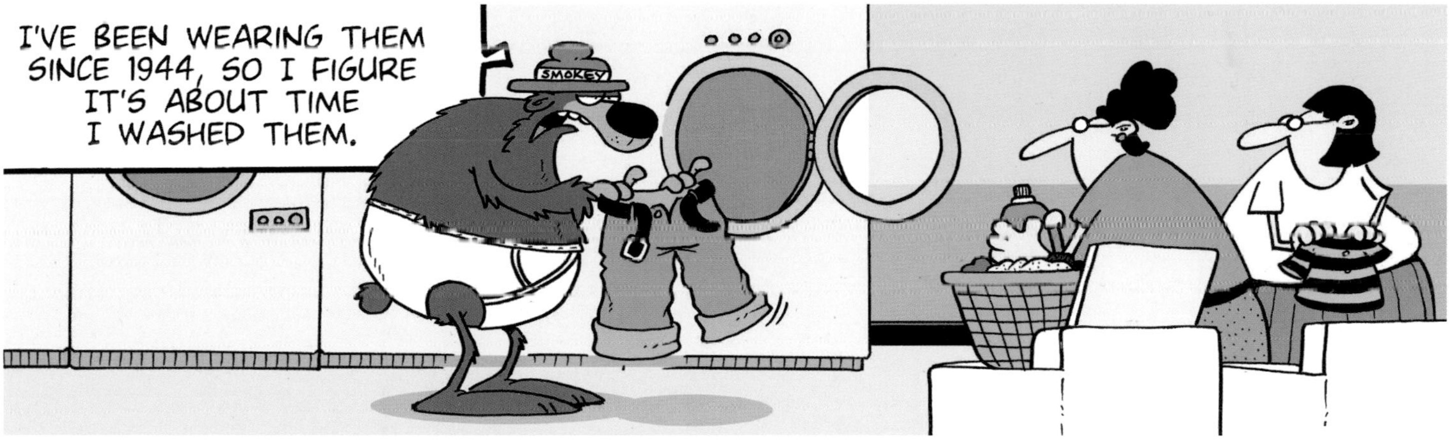
I'VE BEEN WEARING THEM SINCE 1944, SO I FIGURE IT'S ABOUT TIME I WASHED THEM.
SMOKEY

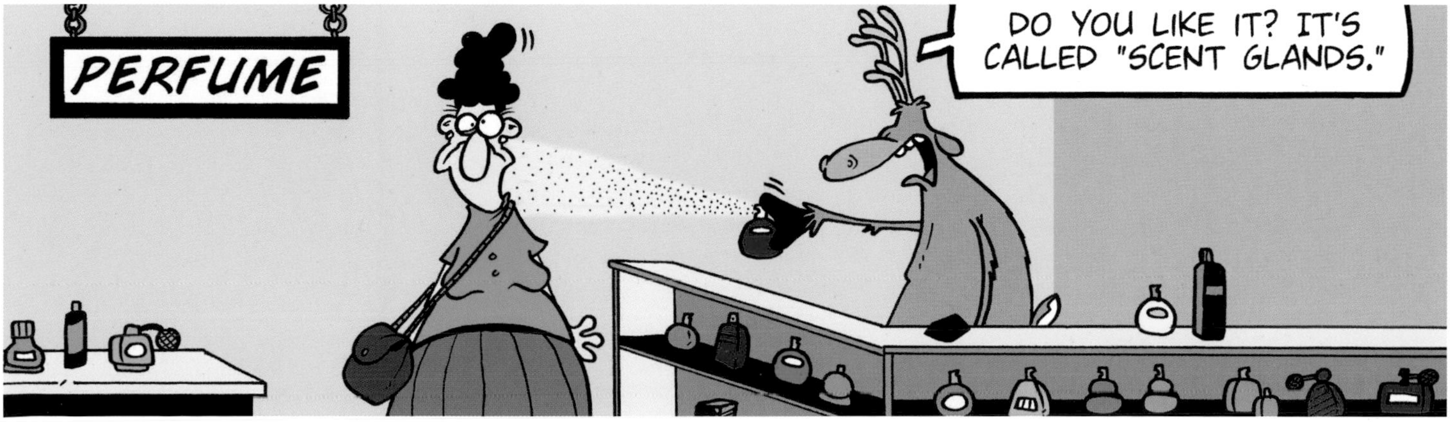
PERFUME
DO YOU LIKE IT? IT'S CALLED "SCENT GLANDS."

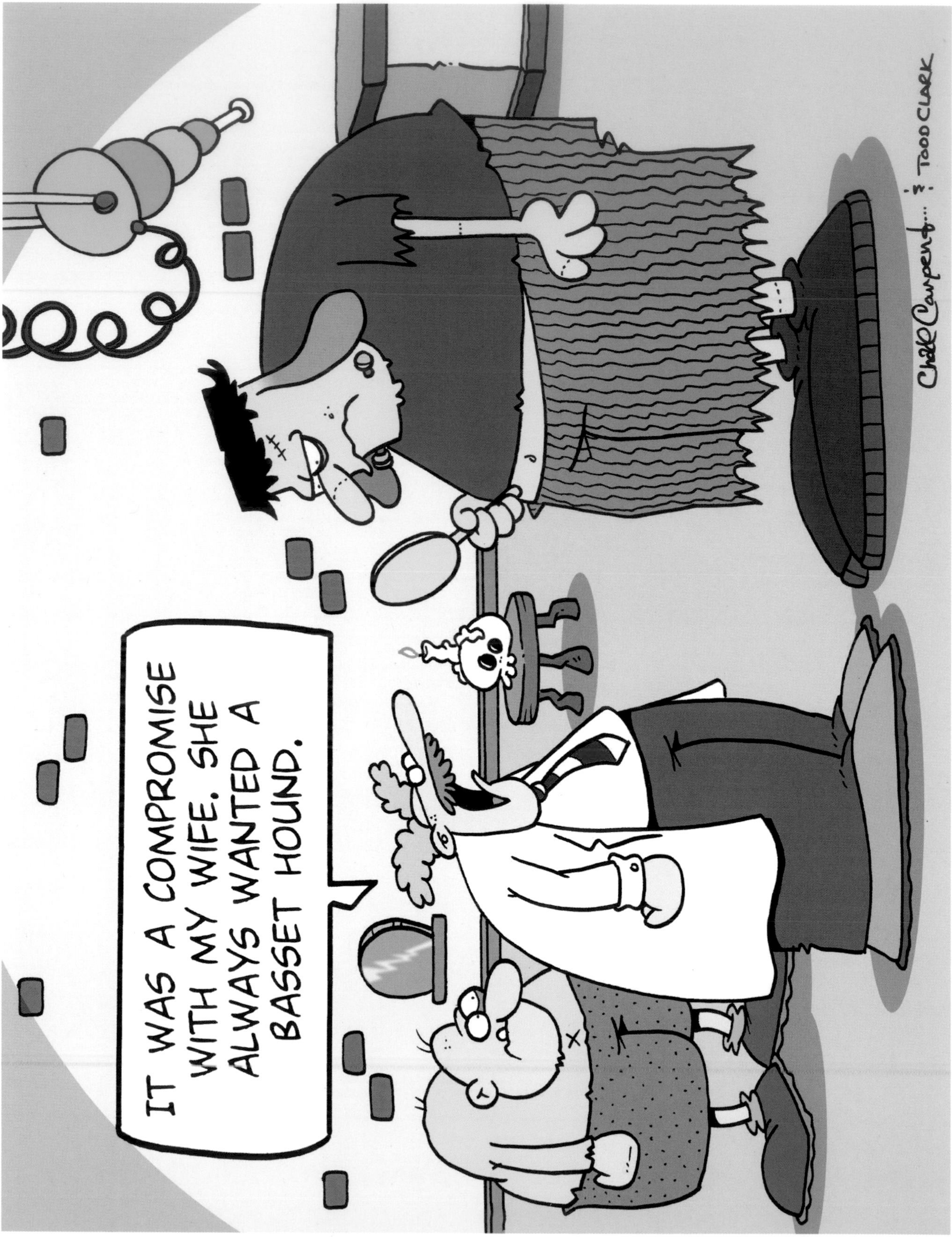
IT WAS A COMPROMISE WITH MY WIFE. SHE ALWAYS WANTED A BASSET HOUND.
Chad Carpenter... & TODD CLARK

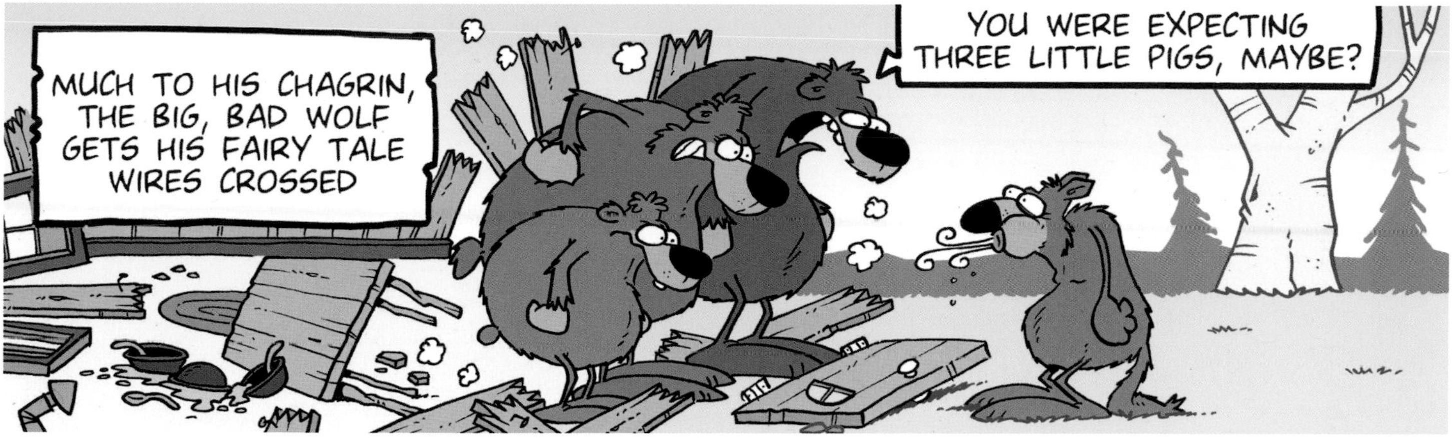
MUCH TO HIS CHAGRIN, THE BIG, BAD WOLF GETS HIS FAIRY TALE WIRES CROSSED
YOU WERE EXPECTING THREE LITTLE PIGS, MAYBE?

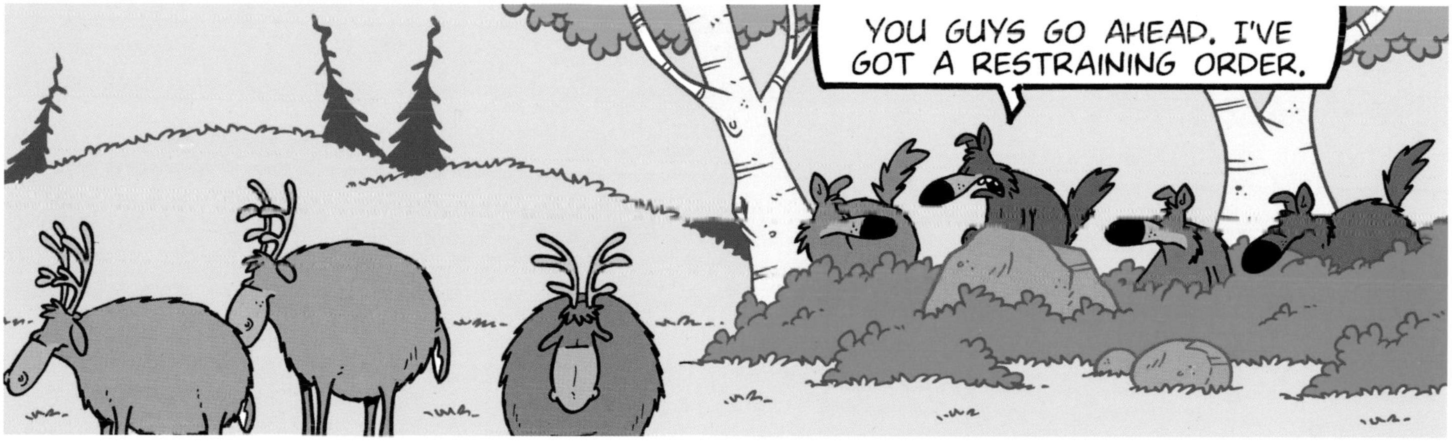
YOU GUYS GO AHEAD. I'VE GOT A RESTRAINING ORDER.

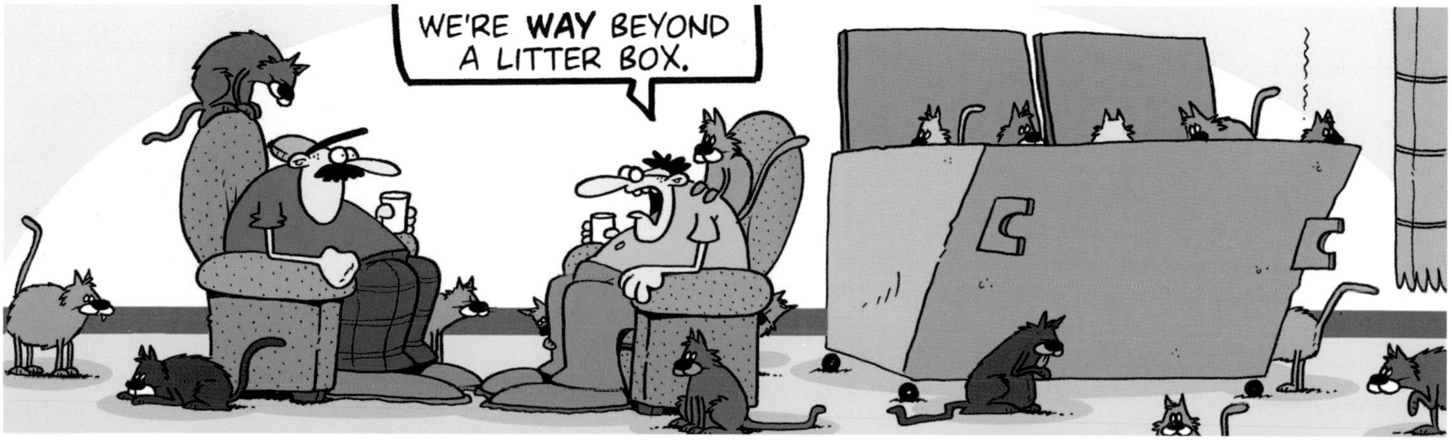
WE'RE **WAY** BEYOND A LITTER BOX.

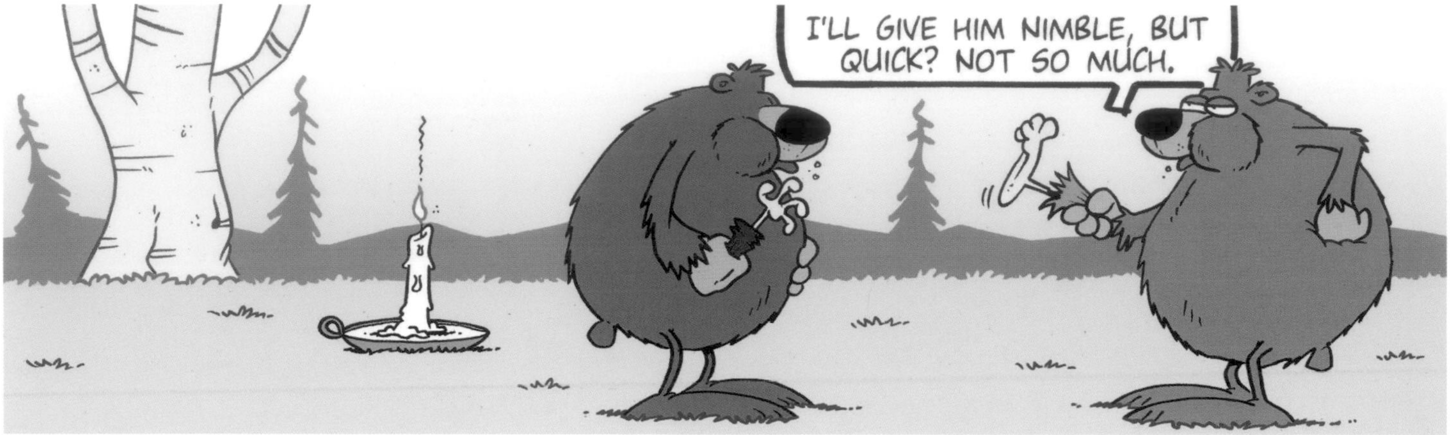
I'LL GIVE HIM NIMBLE, BUT QUICK? NOT SO MUCH.

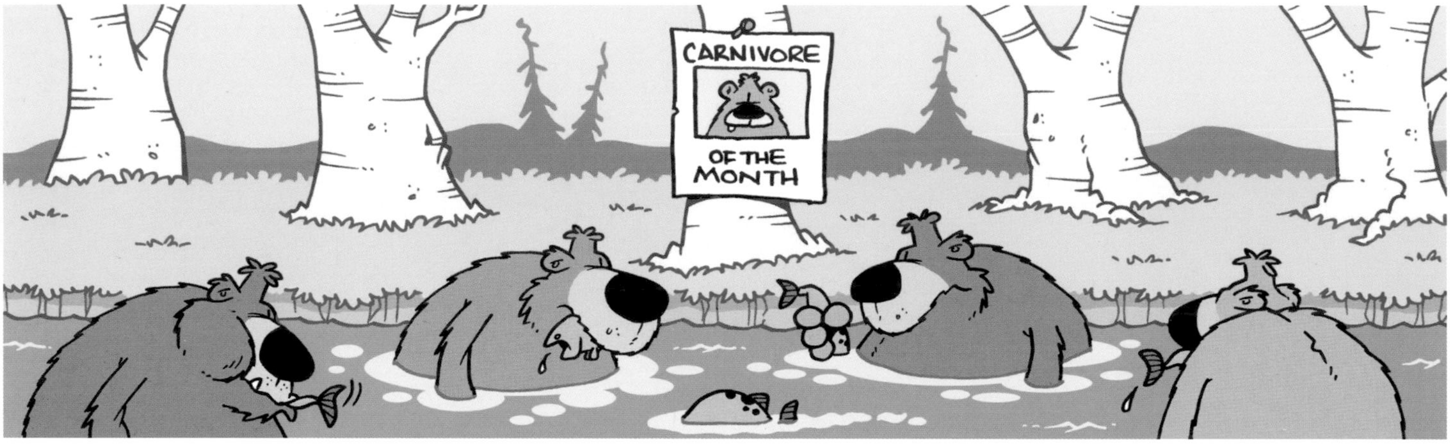
CARNIVORE
OF THE MONTH

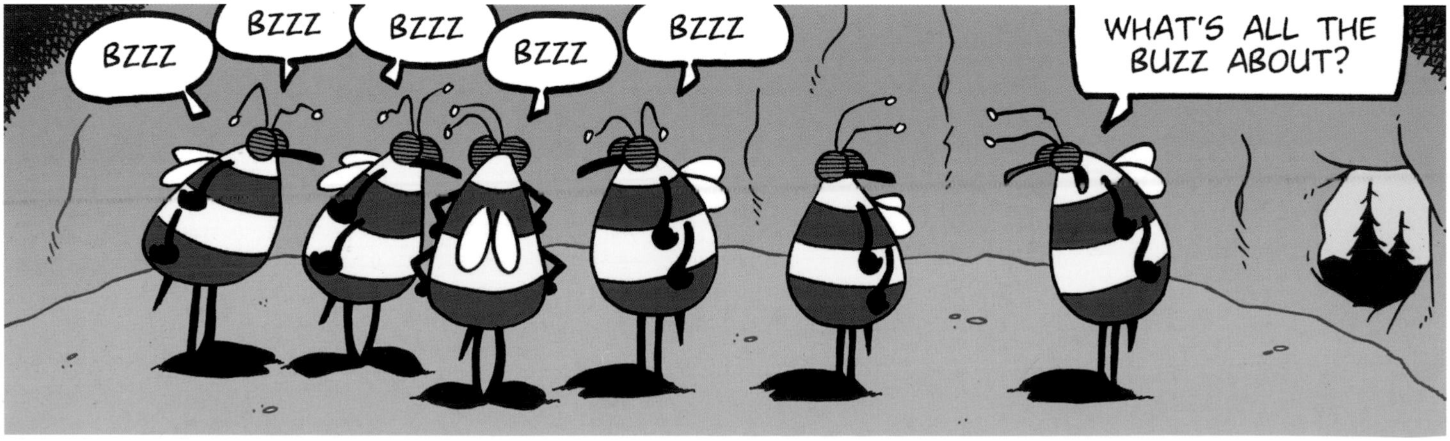
BZZZ
BZZZ
BZZZ
BZZZ
BZZZ
WHAT'S ALL THE BUZZ ABOUT?

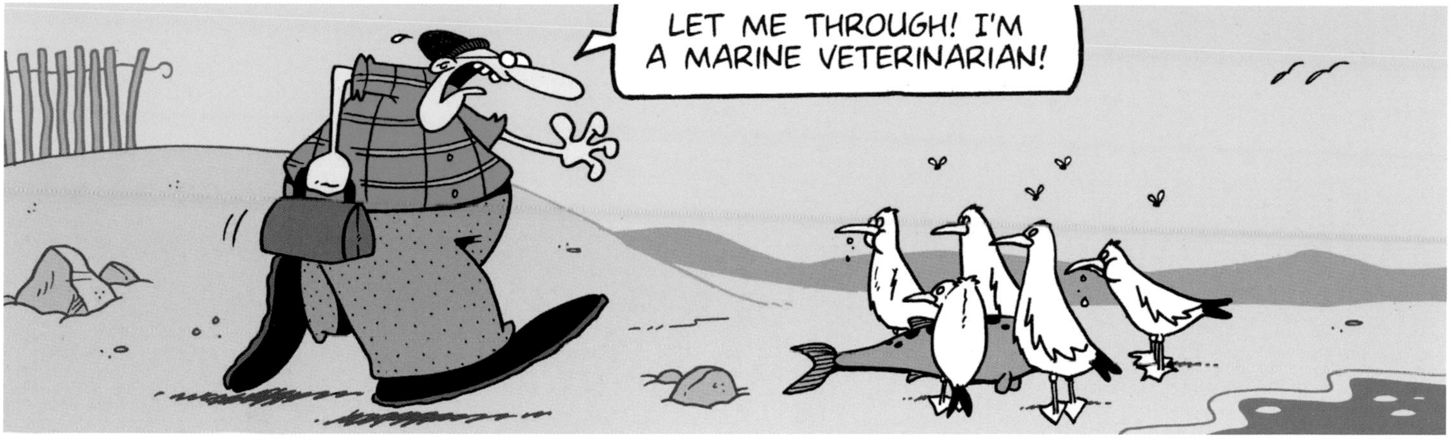
LET ME THROUGH! I'M A MARINE VETERINARIAN!

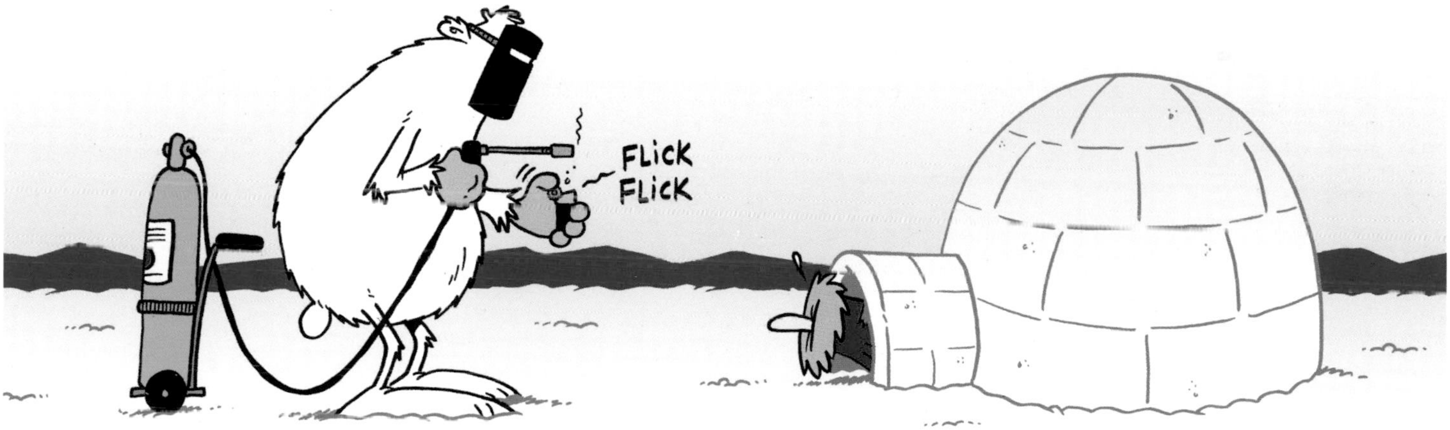
FLICK FLICK

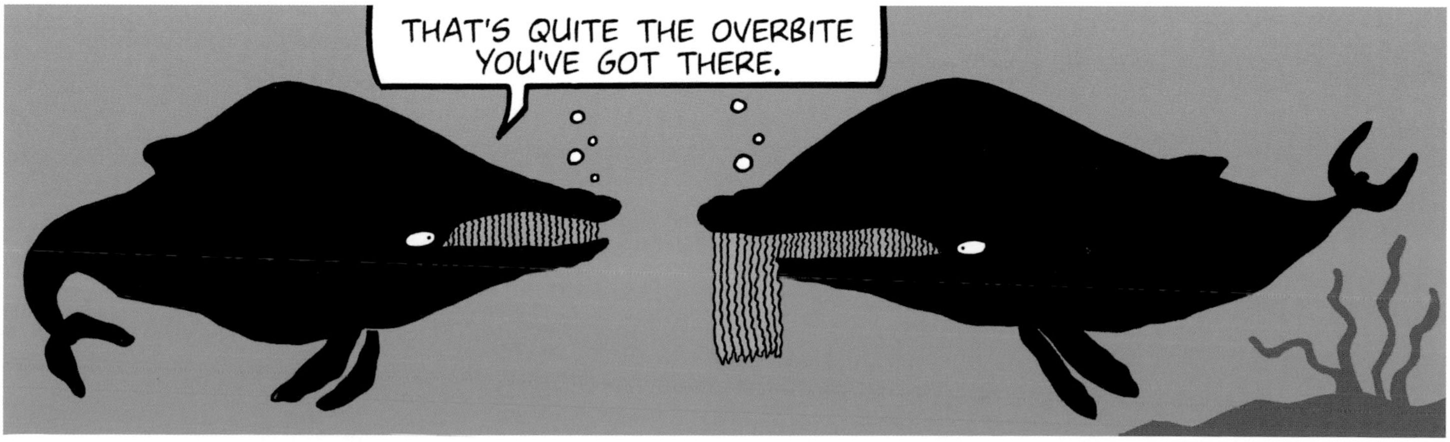
THAT'S QUITE THE OVERBITE YOU'VE GOT THERE.

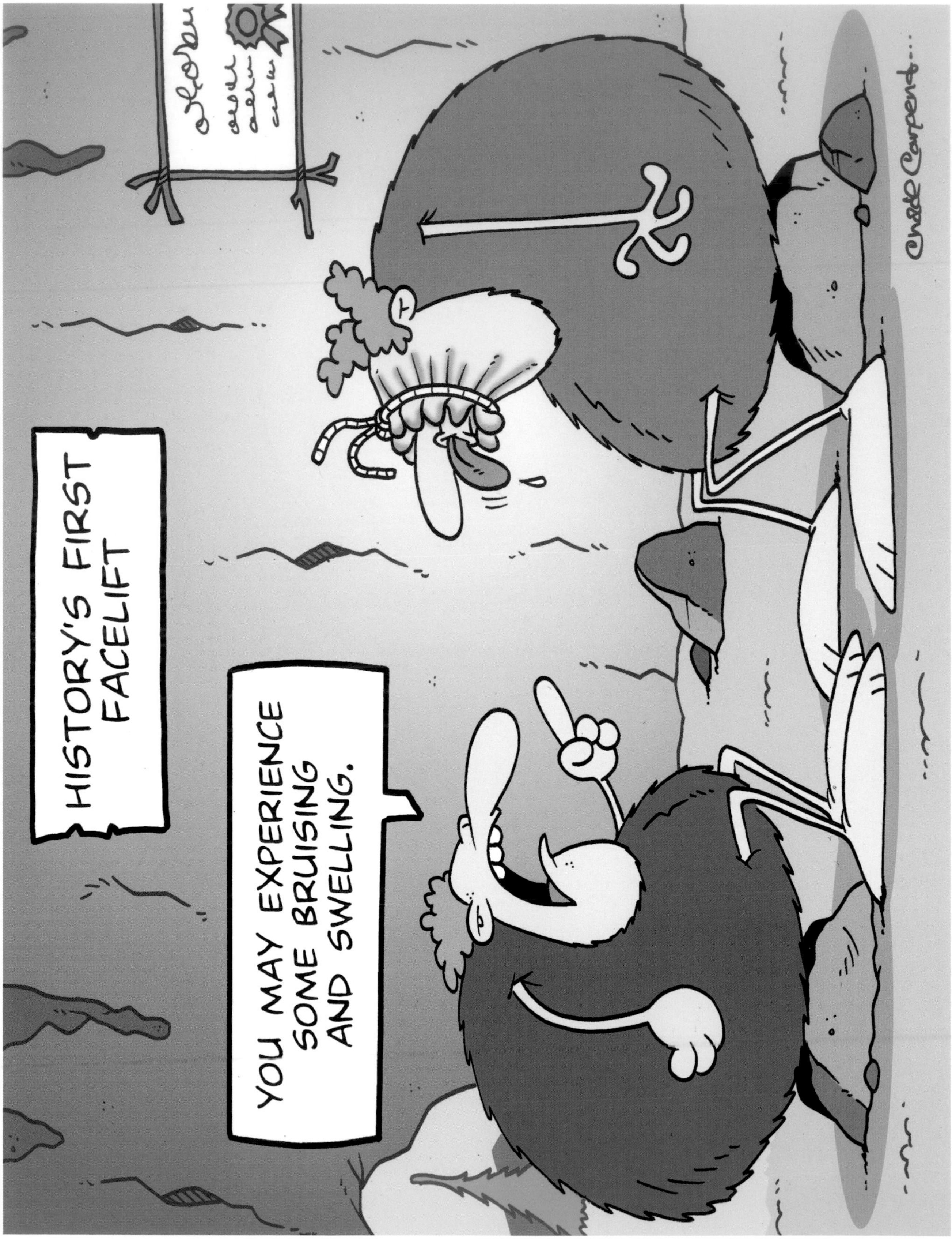
HISTORY'S FIRST FACELIFT
YOU MAY EXPERIENCE SOME BRUISING AND SWELLING.

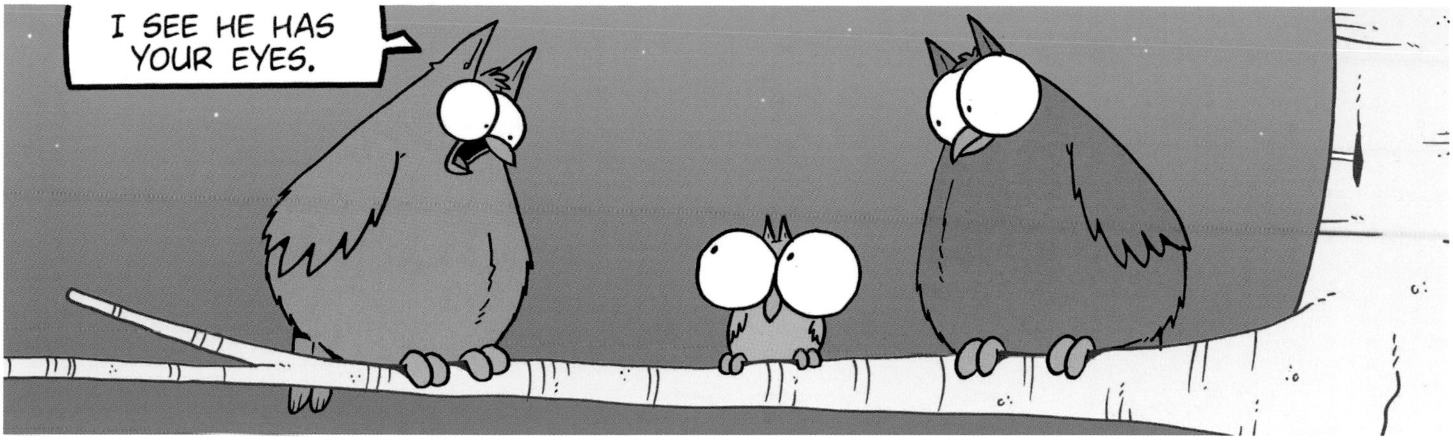
I SEE HE HAS YOUR EYES.

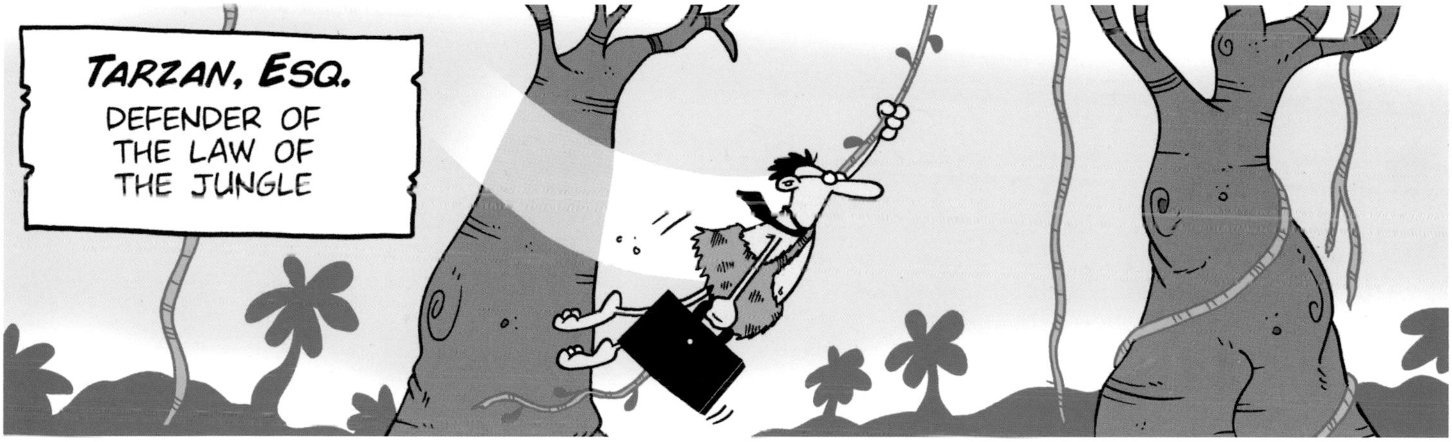
TARZAN, ESQ.
DEFENDER OF THE LAW OF THE JUNGLE

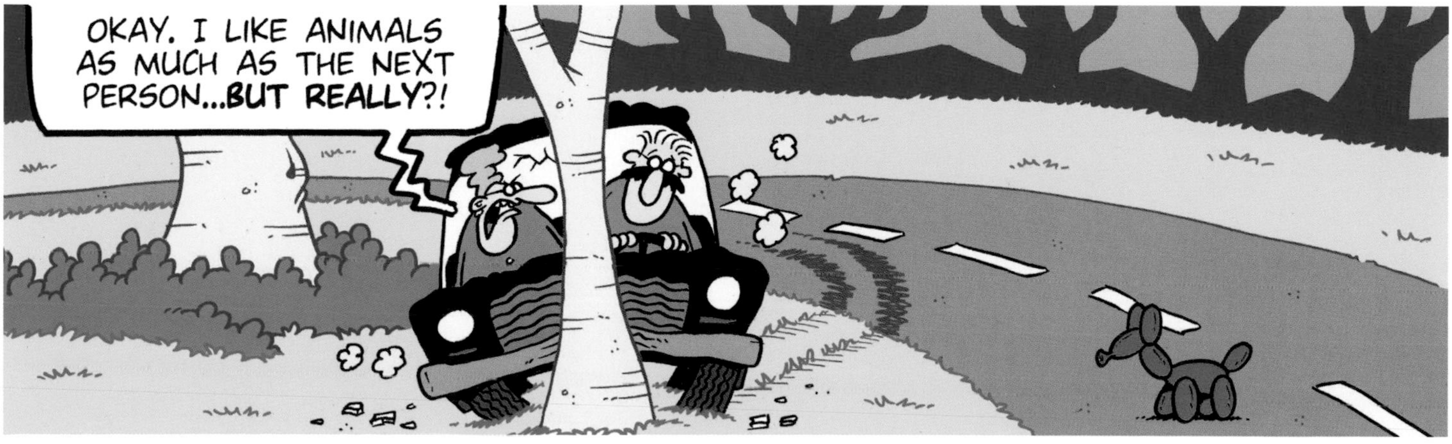
OKAY. I LIKE ANIMALS AS MUCH AS THE NEXT PERSON...BUT REALLY?!

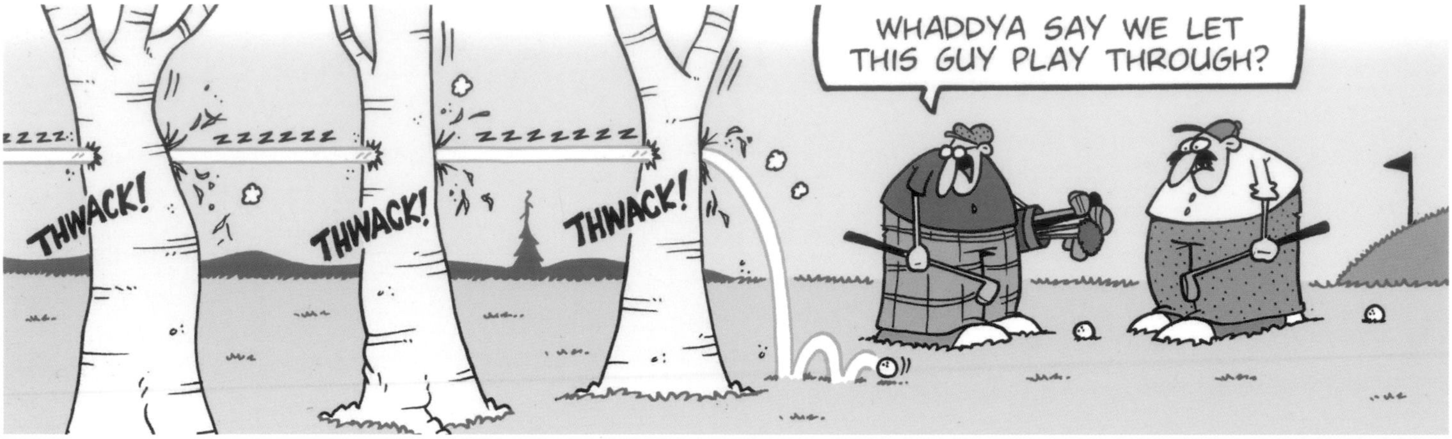
ZZZZ
ZZZZZZ
ZZZZZZZ
THWACK!
THWACK!
THWACK!
WHADDYA SAY WE LET THIS GUY PLAY THROUGH?

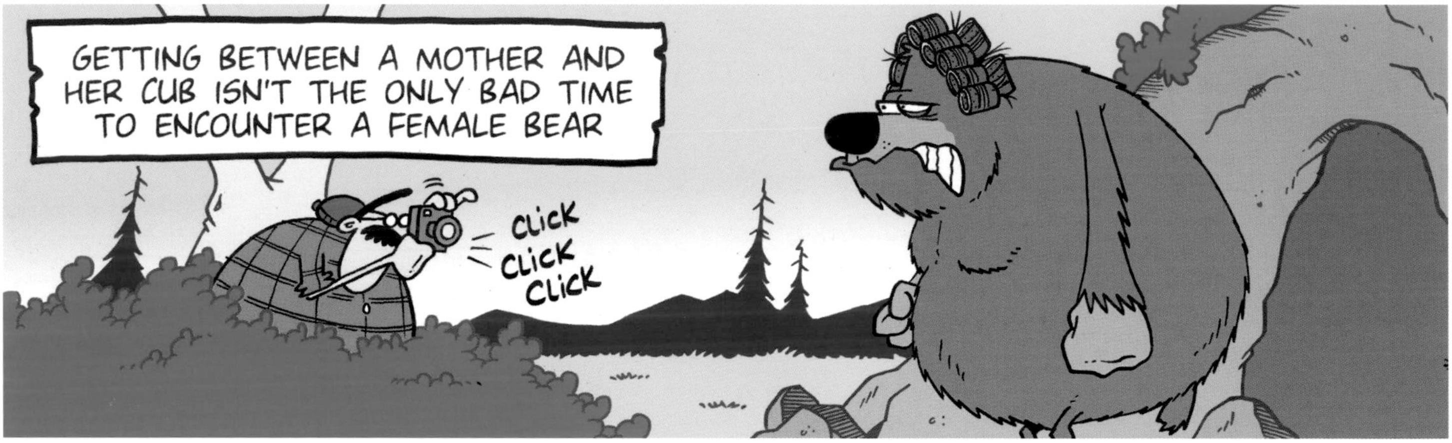
GETTING BETWEEN A MOTHER AND HER CUB ISN'T THE ONLY BAD TIME TO ENCOUNTER A FEMALE BEAR
CLICK
CLICK
CLICK

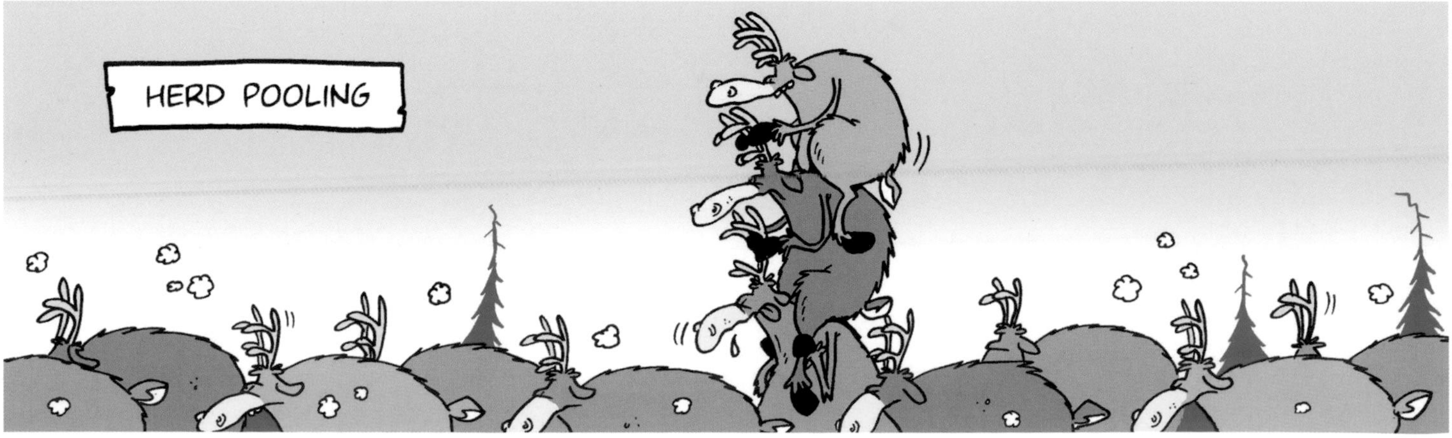
HERD POOLING

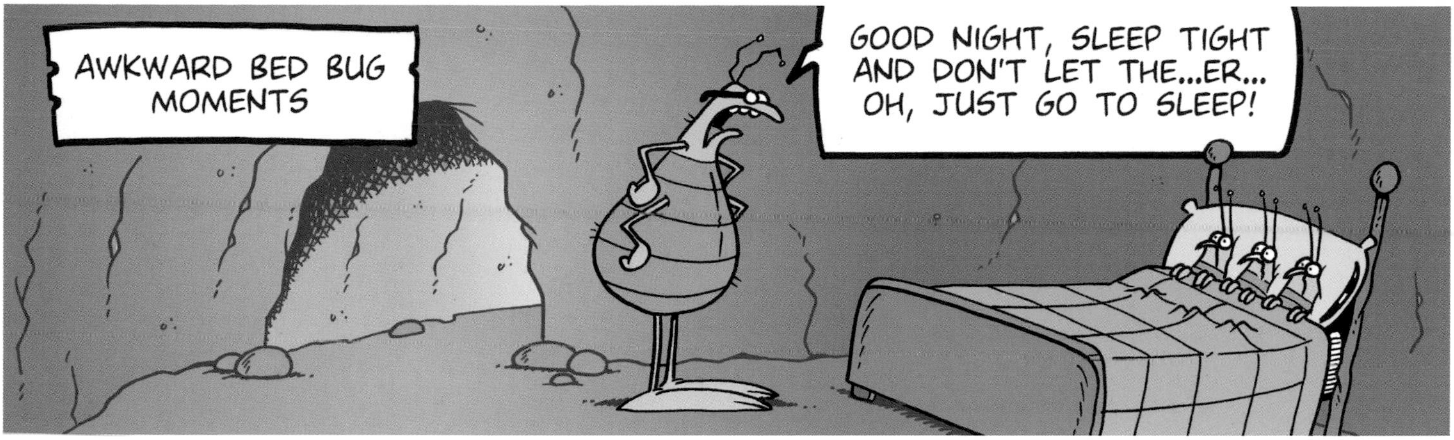
AWKWARD BED BUG MOMENTS
GOOD NIGHT, SLEEP TIGHT AND DON'T LET THE...ER... OH, JUST GO TO SLEEP!

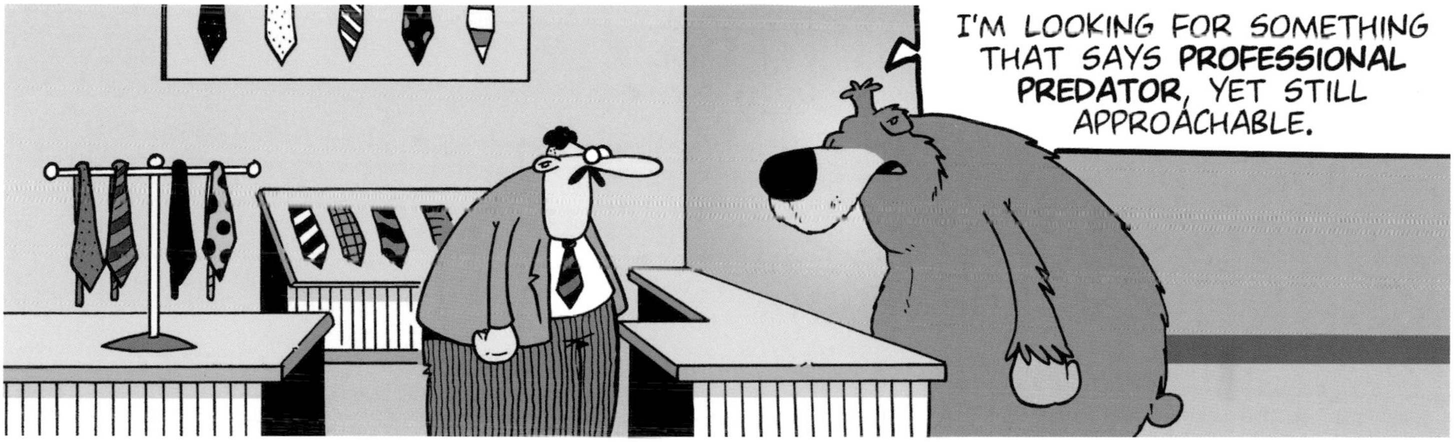
I'M LOOKING FOR SOMETHING THAT SAYS PROFESSIONAL PREDATOR, YET STILL APPROACHABLE.

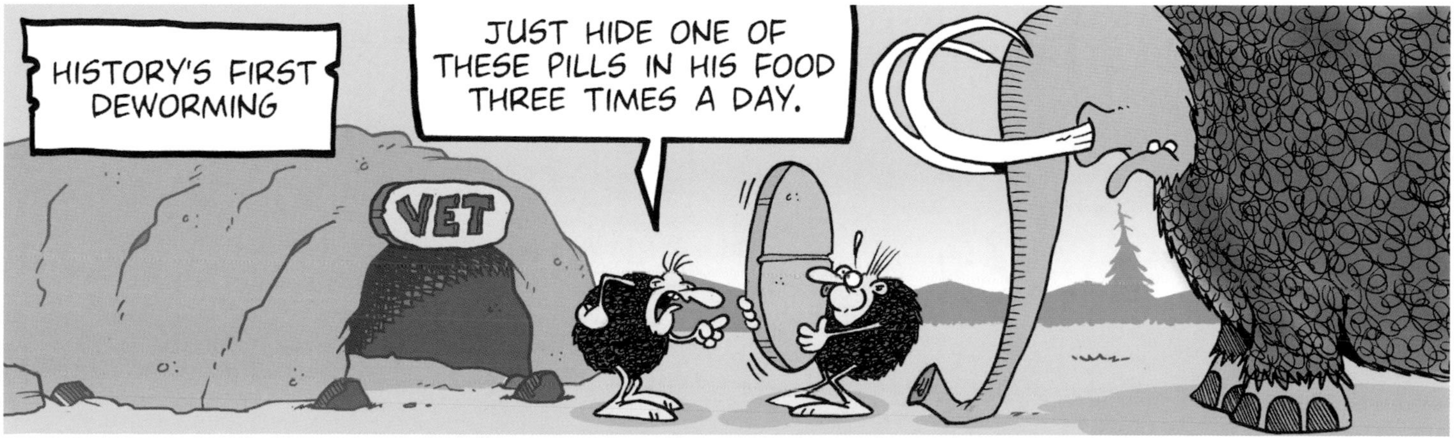
HISTORY'S FIRST DEWORMING
JUST HIDE ONE OF THESE PILLS IN HIS FOOD THREE TIMES A DAY.
VET

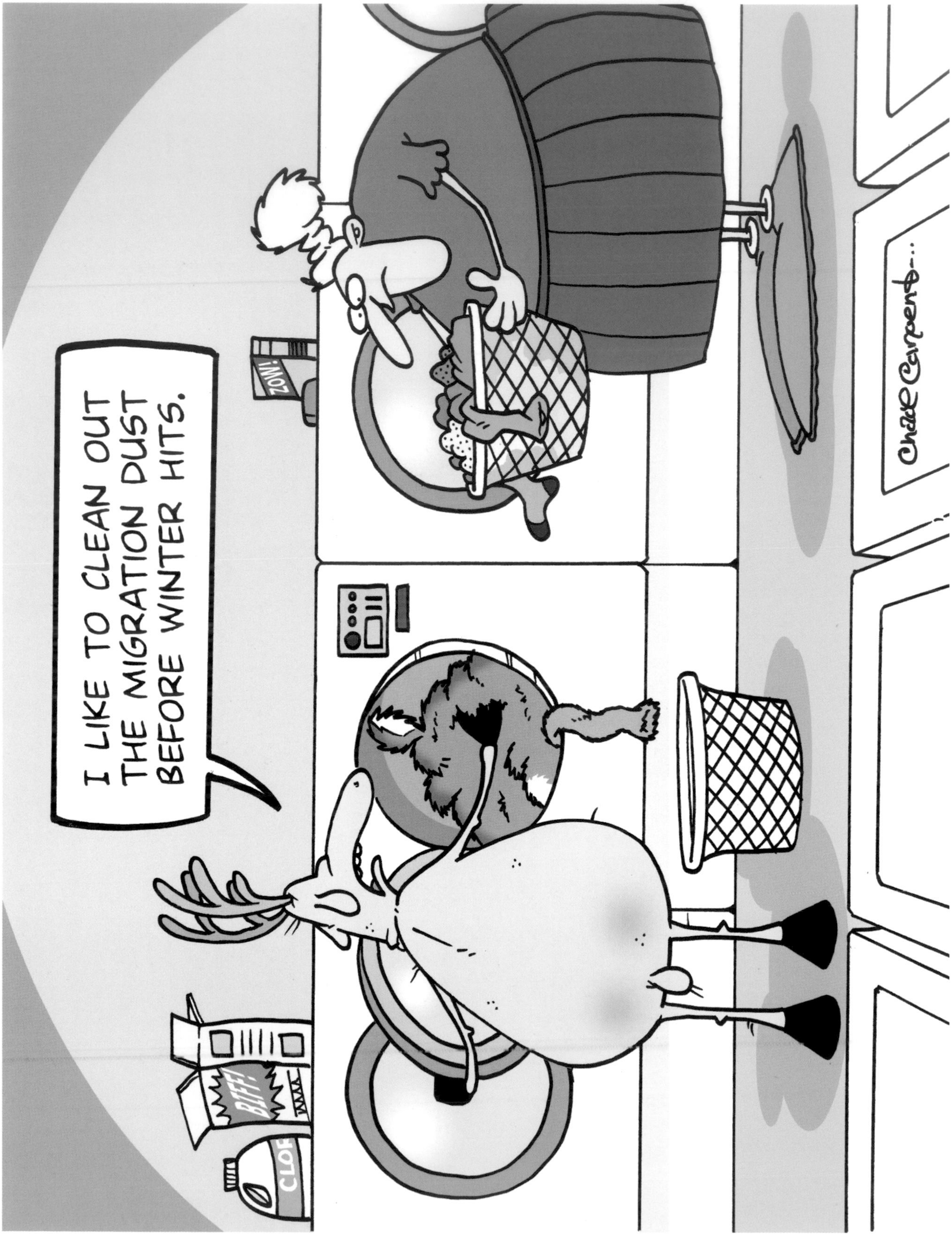
I LIKE TO CLEAN OUT THE MIGRATION DUST BEFORE WINTER HITS.
BIFF!
ZOW!
CLOR
Chad Carpenter

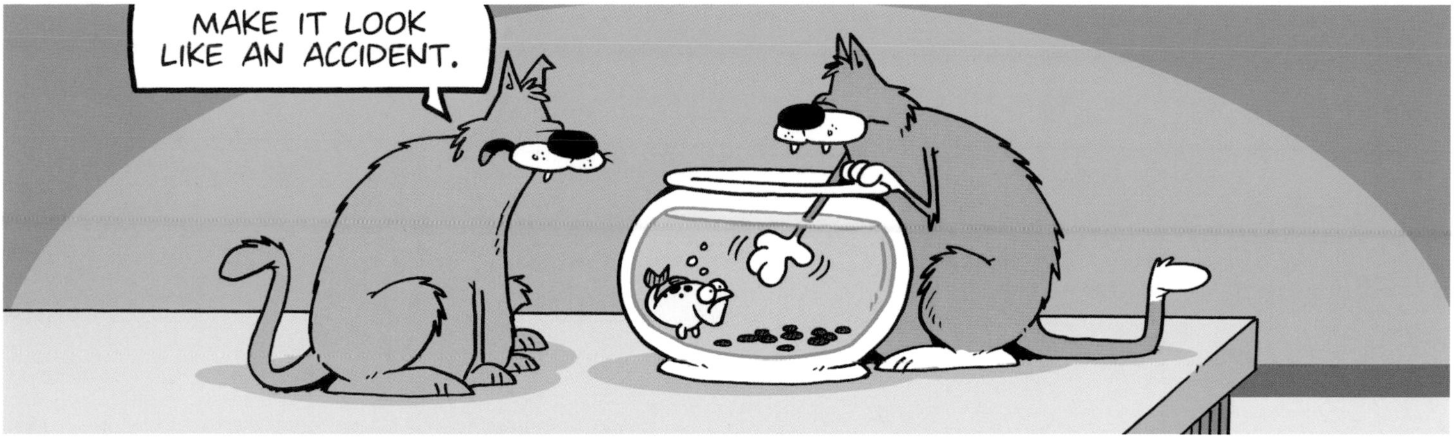
MAKE IT LOOK LIKE AN ACCIDENT.

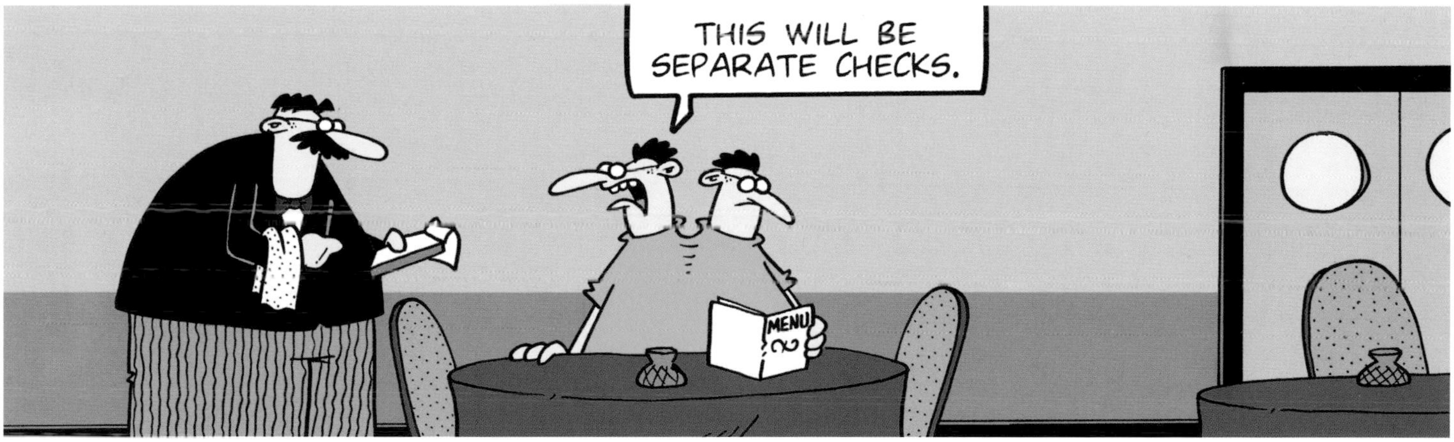
THIS WILL BE SEPARATE CHECKS.
MENU

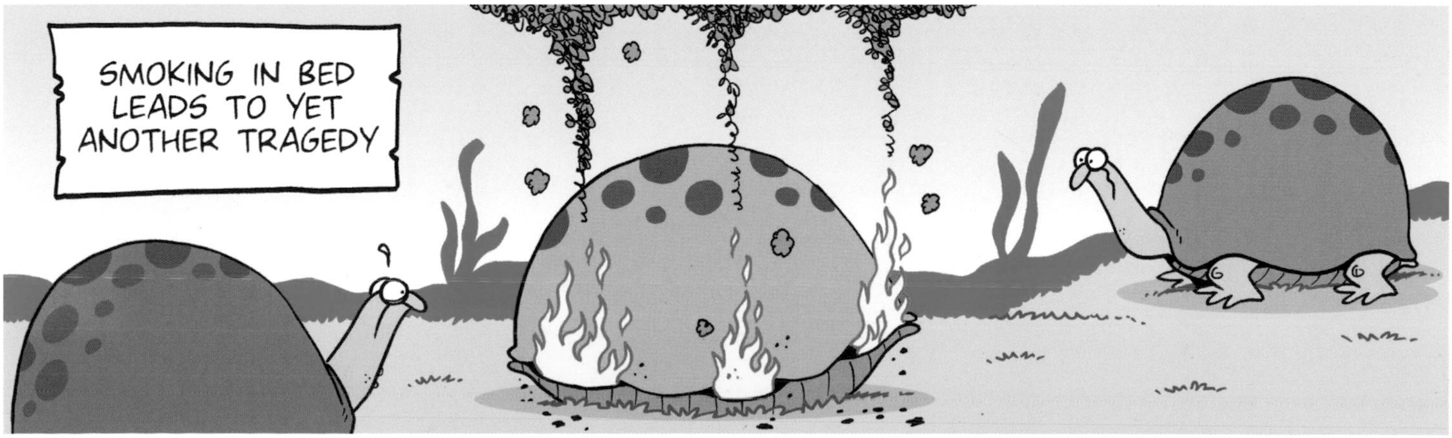
SMOKING IN BED LEADS TO YET ANOTHER TRAGEDY

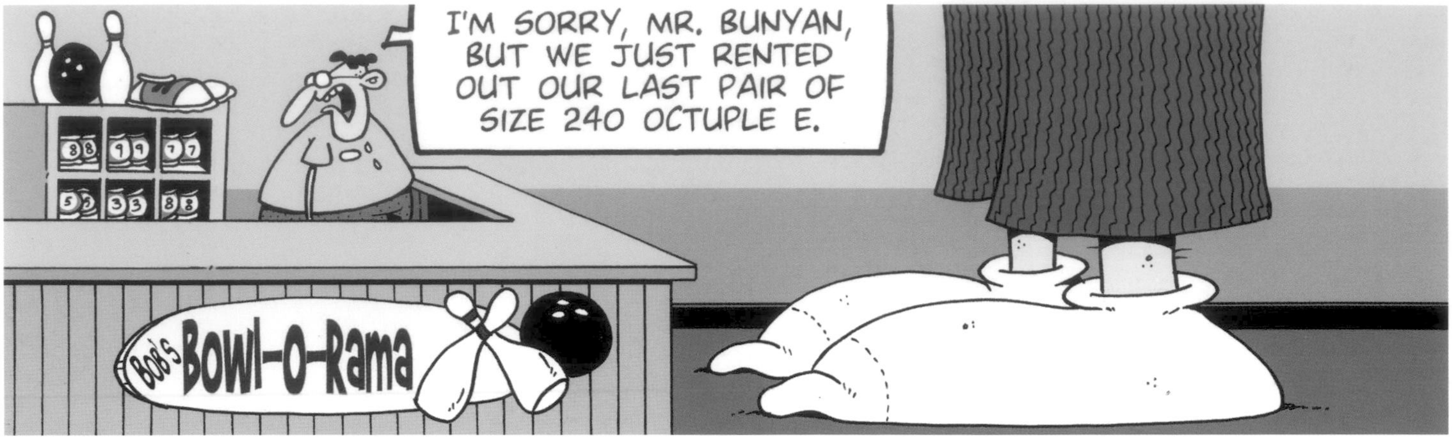
I'M SORRY, MR. BUNYAN, BUT WE JUST RENTED OUT OUR LAST PAIR OF SIZE 240 OCTUPLE E.
Bob's Bowl-O-Rama

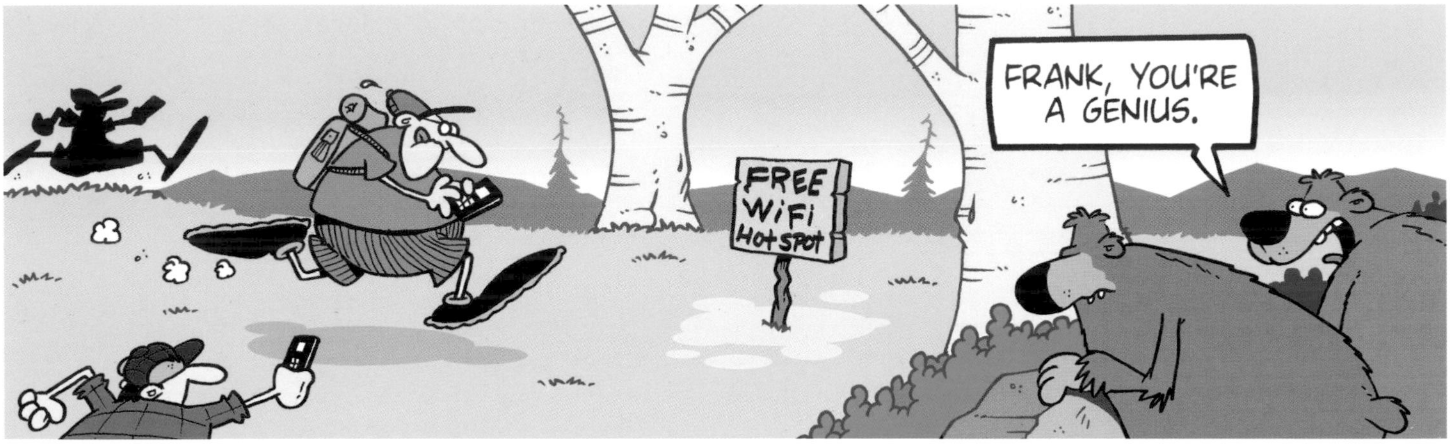
FREE WiFi Hot SPOT
FRANK, YOU'RE A GENIUS.

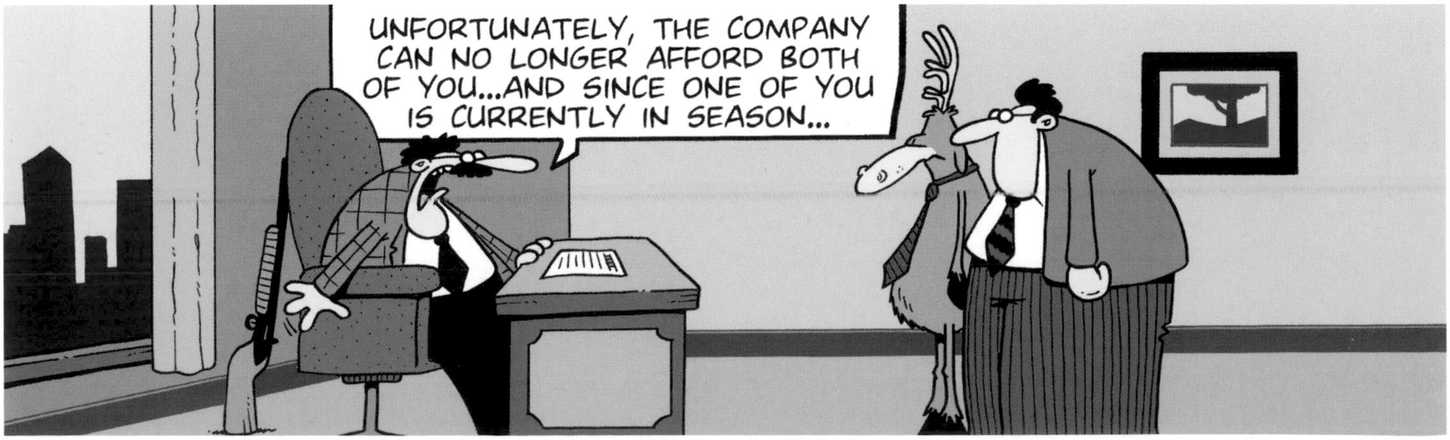
UNFORTUNATELY, THE COMPANY CAN NO LONGER AFFORD BOTH OF YOU...AND SINCE ONE OF YOU IS CURRENTLY IN SEASON...

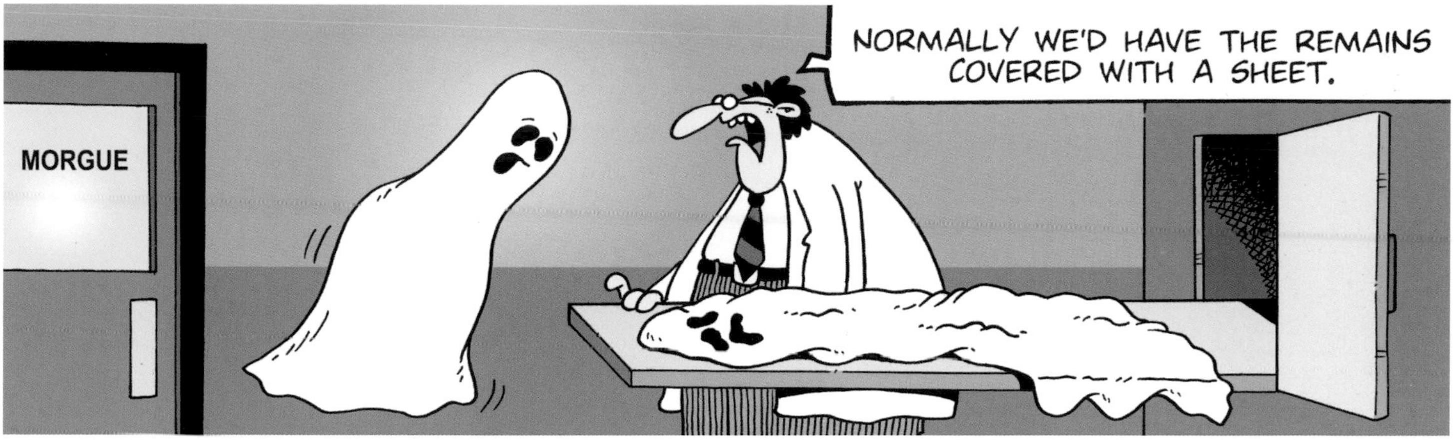
MORGUE
NORMALLY WE'D HAVE THE REMAINS COVERED WITH A SHEET.

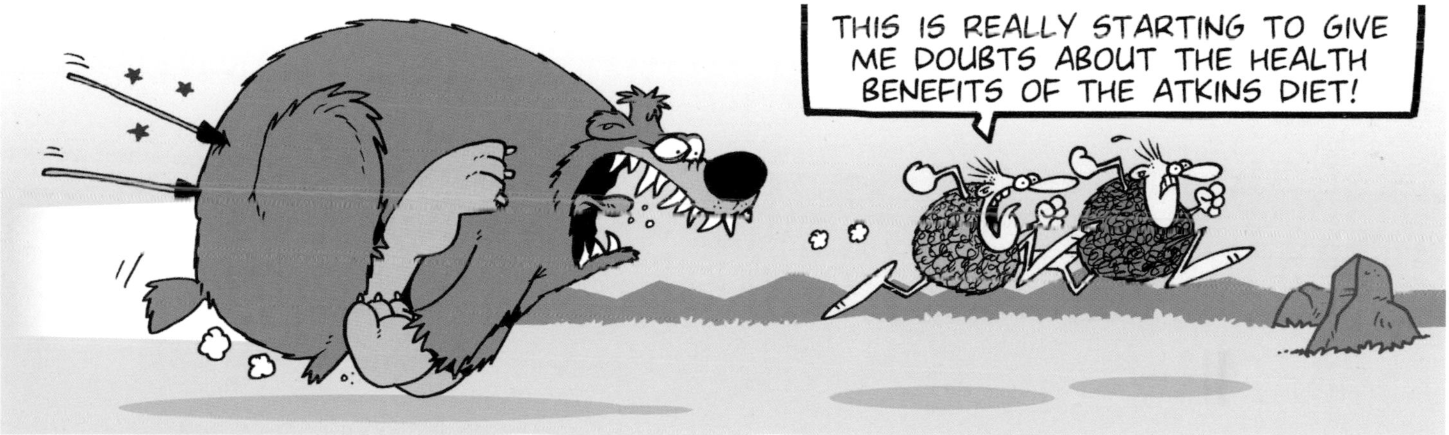
THIS IS REALLY STARTING TO GIVE ME DOUBTS ABOUT THE HEALTH BENEFITS OF THE ATKINS DIET!

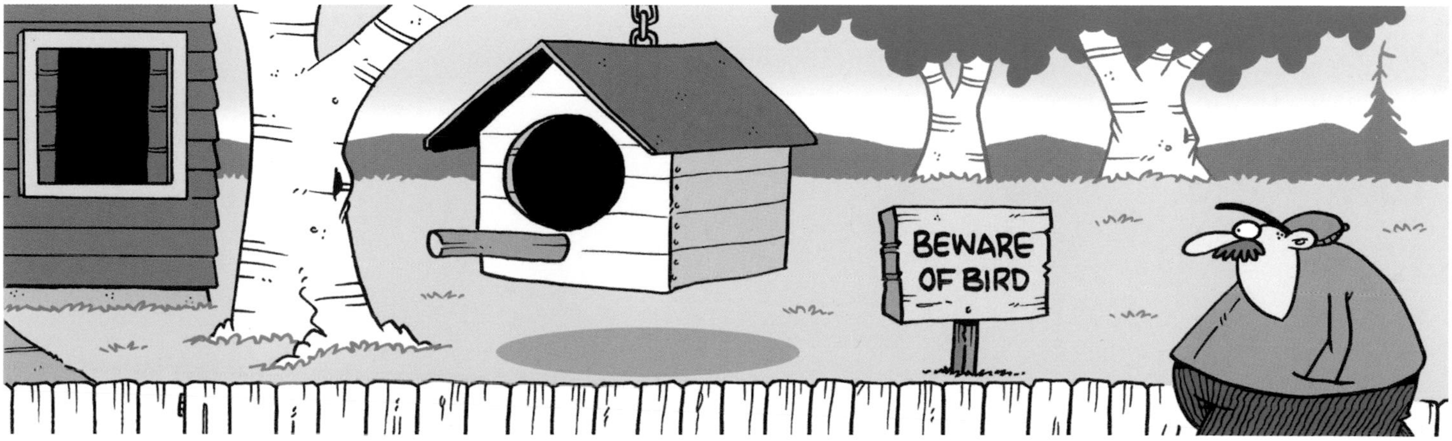
BEWARE OF BIRD

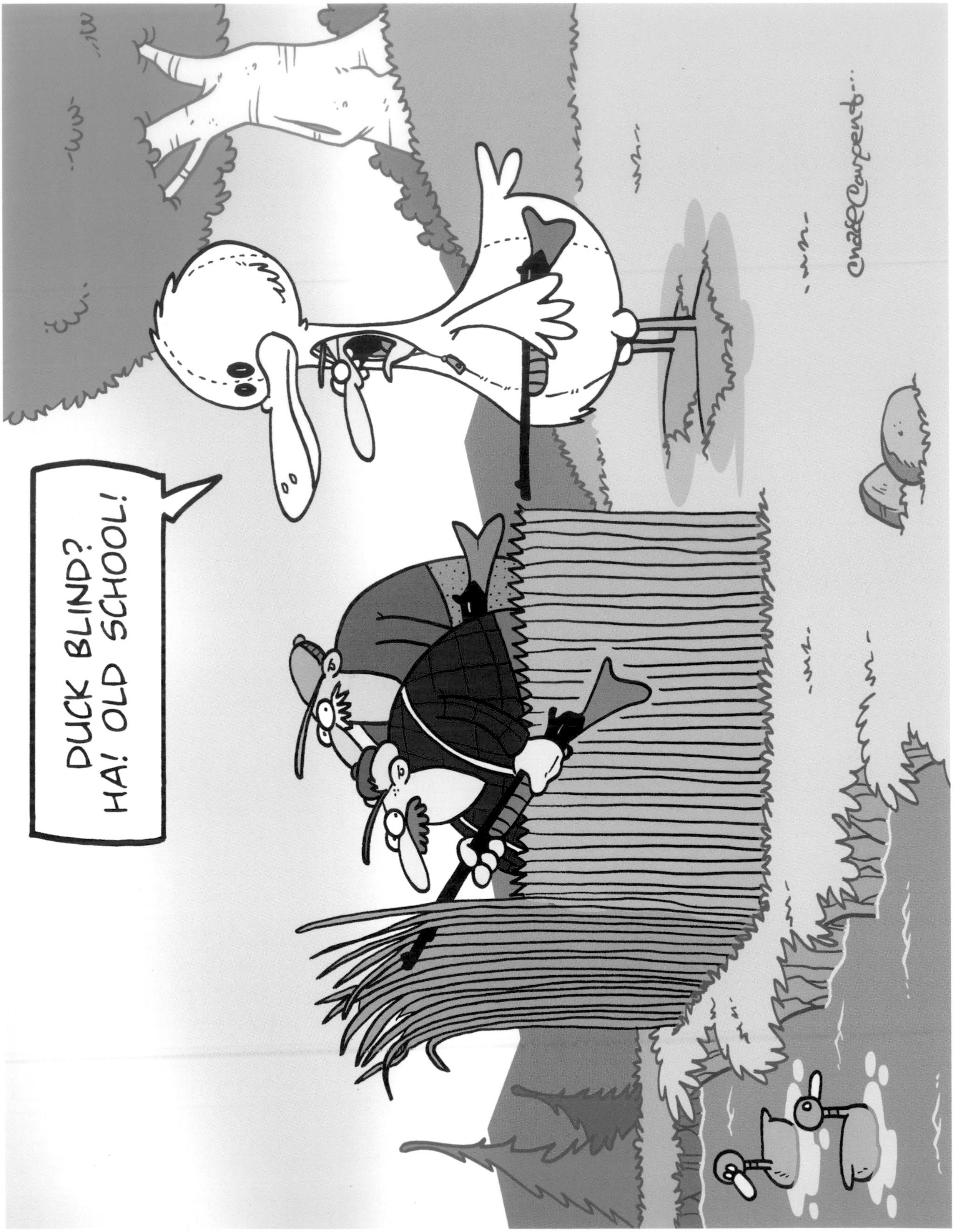
DUCK BLIND?
HA! OLD SCHOOL!

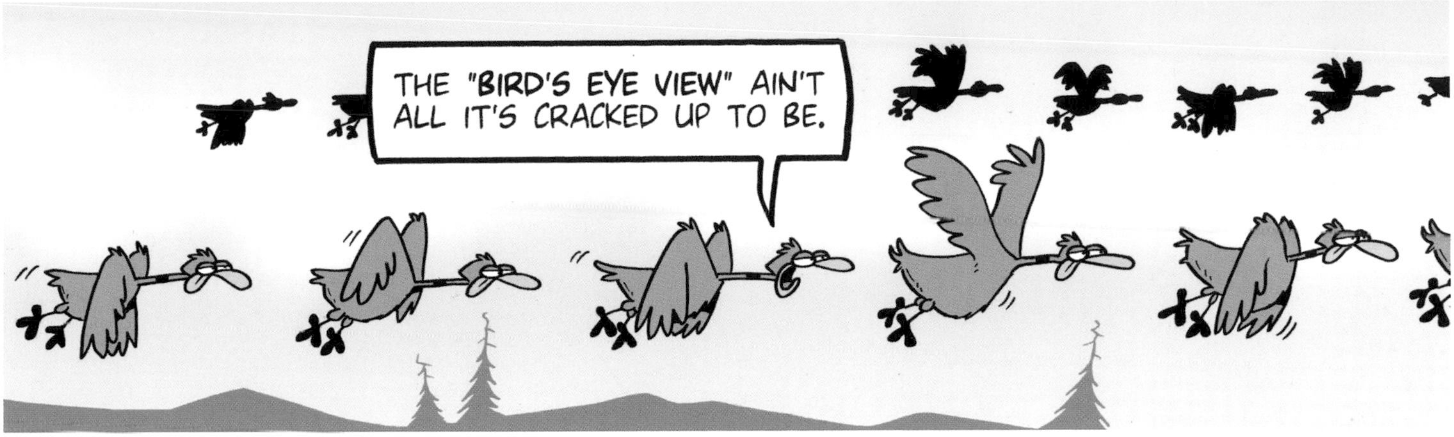
THE "BIRD'S EYE VIEW" AIN'T ALL IT'S CRACKED UP TO BE.

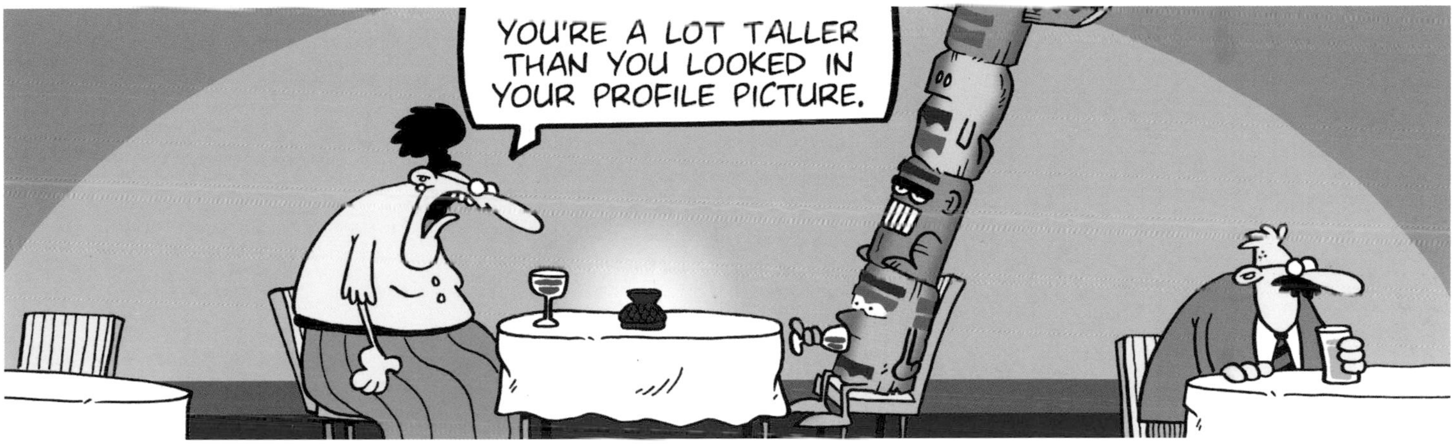
YOU'RE A LOT TALLER THAN YOU LOOKED IN YOUR PROFILE PICTURE.

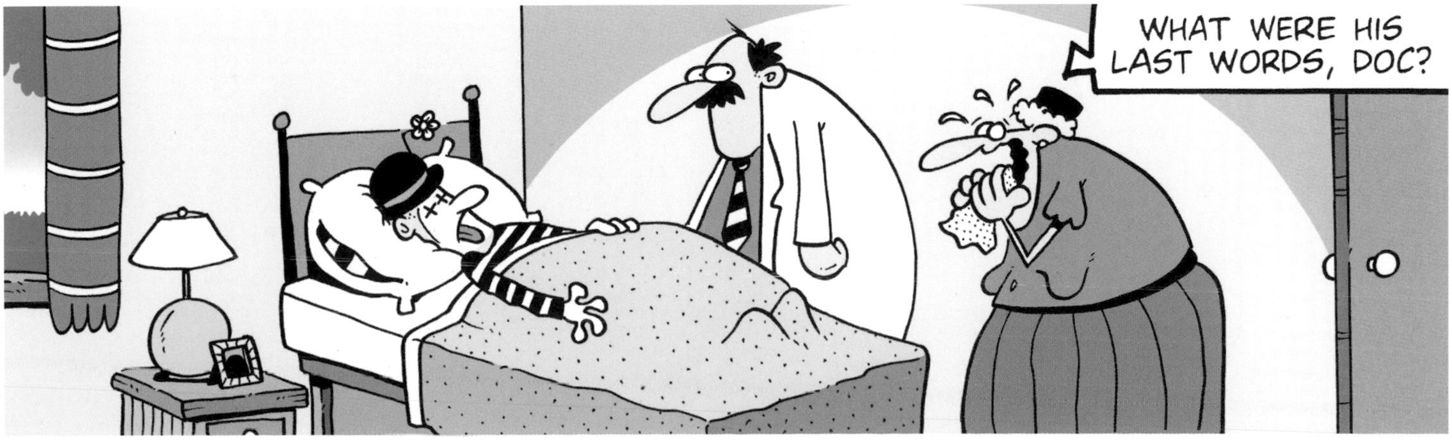
WHAT WERE HIS LAST WORDS, DOC?

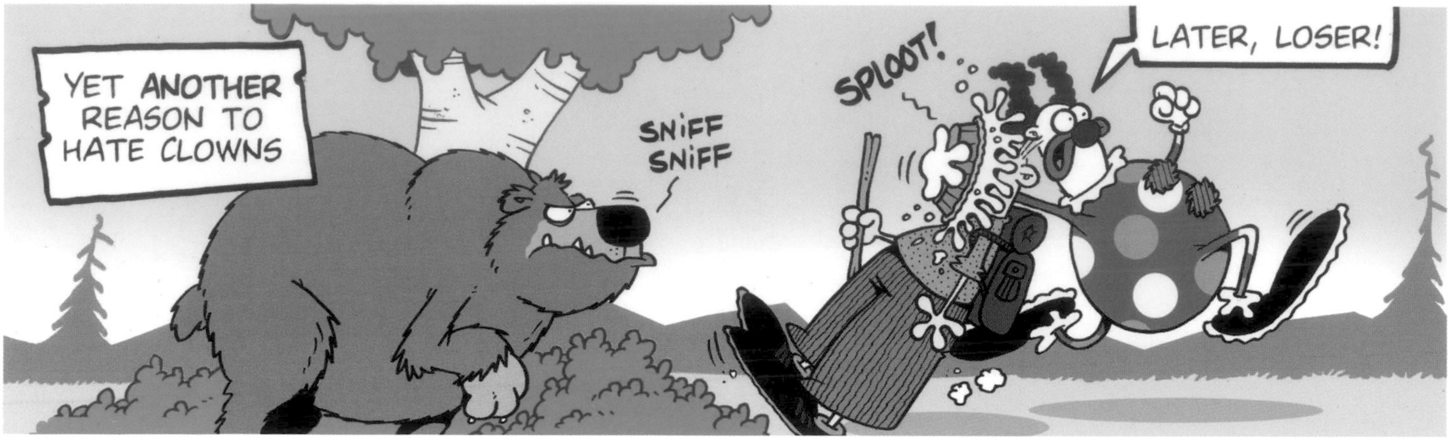
YET ANOTHER REASON TO HATE CLOWNS
SNIFF SNIFF
SPLOOT!
LATER, LOSER!

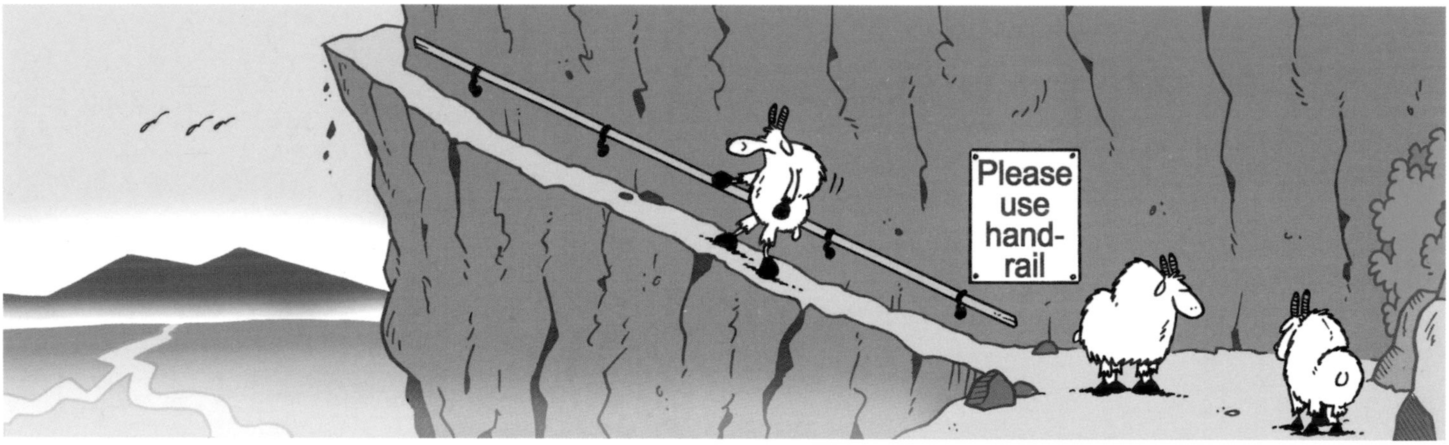
Please use hand-rail

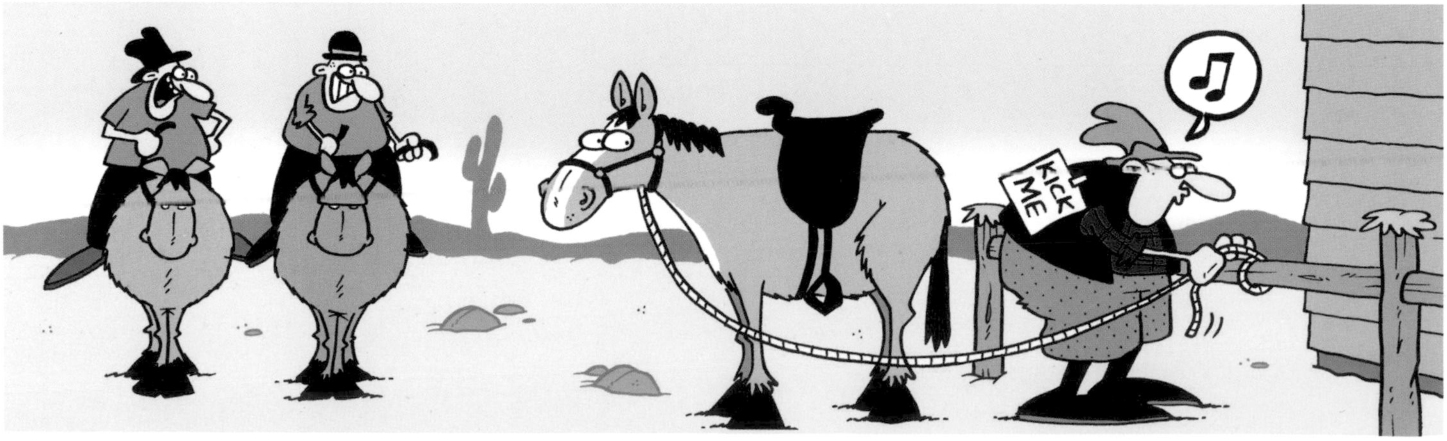
KICK ME

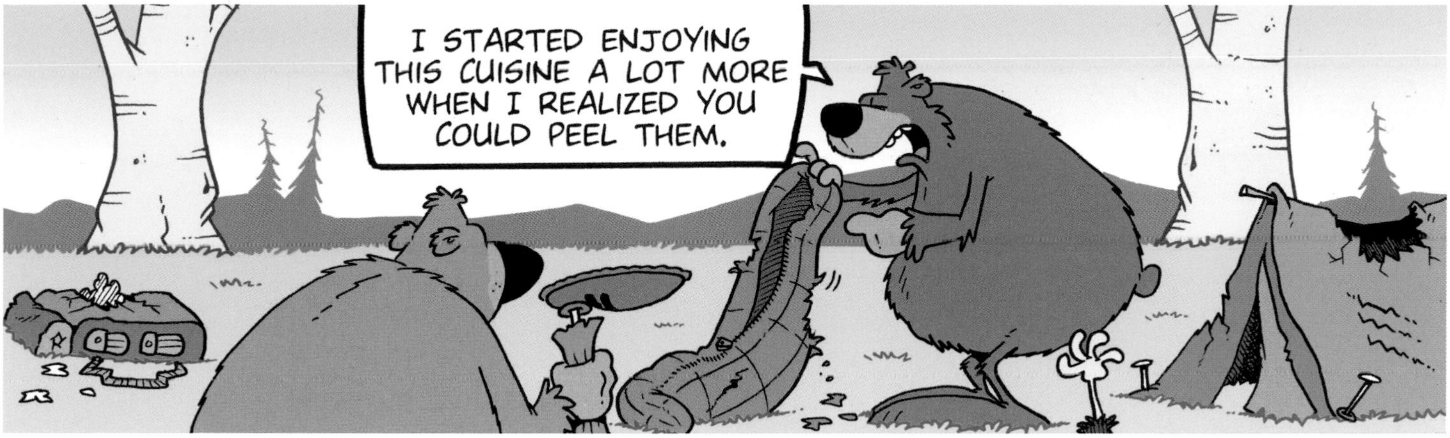
I STARTED ENJOYING THIS CUISINE A LOT MORE WHEN I REALIZED YOU COULD PEEL THEM.

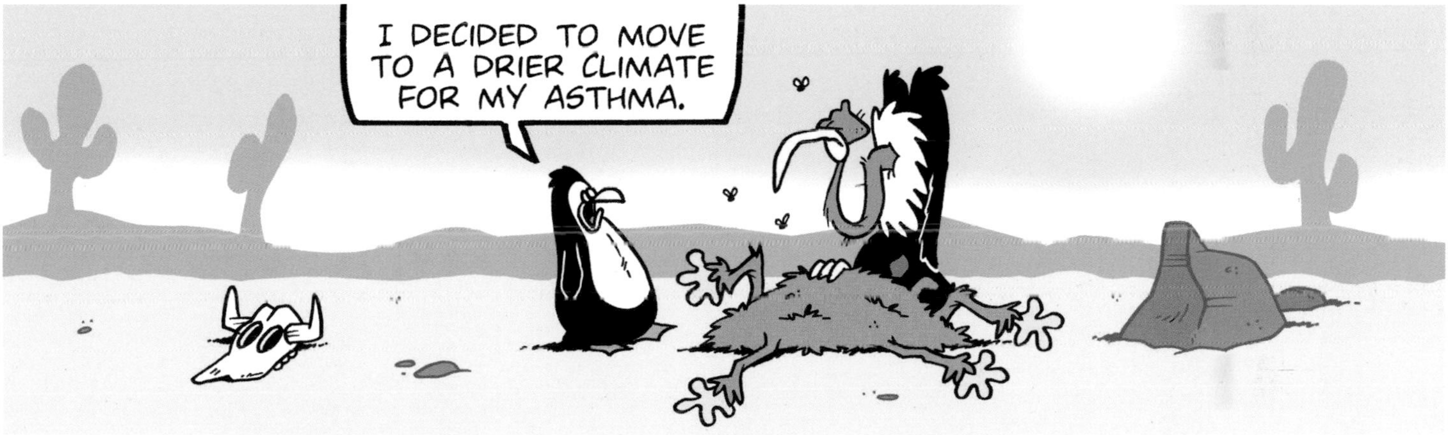
I DECIDED TO MOVE TO A DRIER CLIMATE FOR MY ASTHMA.

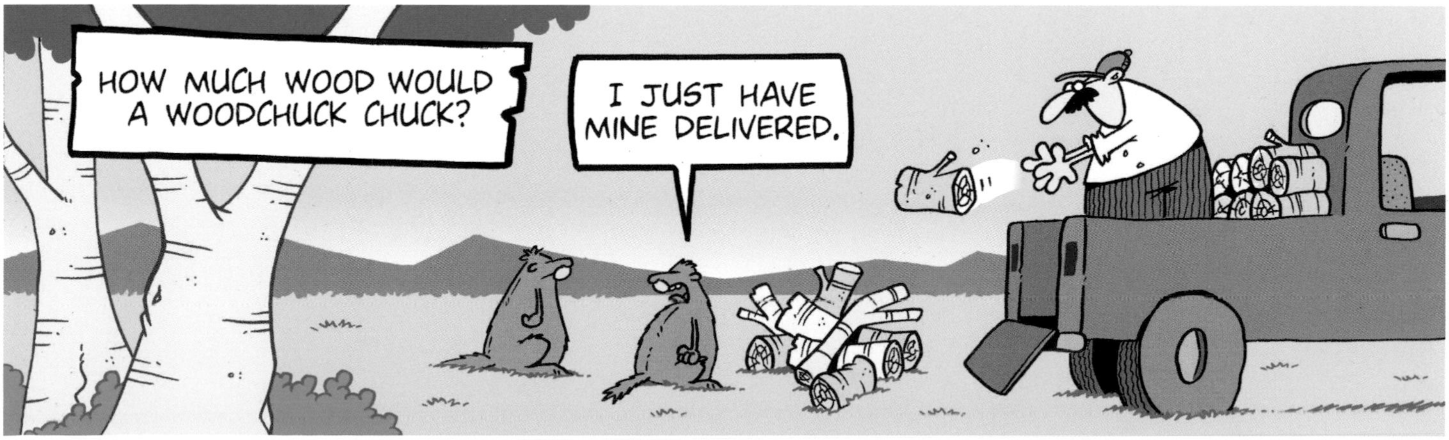
HOW MUCH WOOD WOULD A WOODCHUCK CHUCK?
I JUST HAVE MINE DELIVERED.

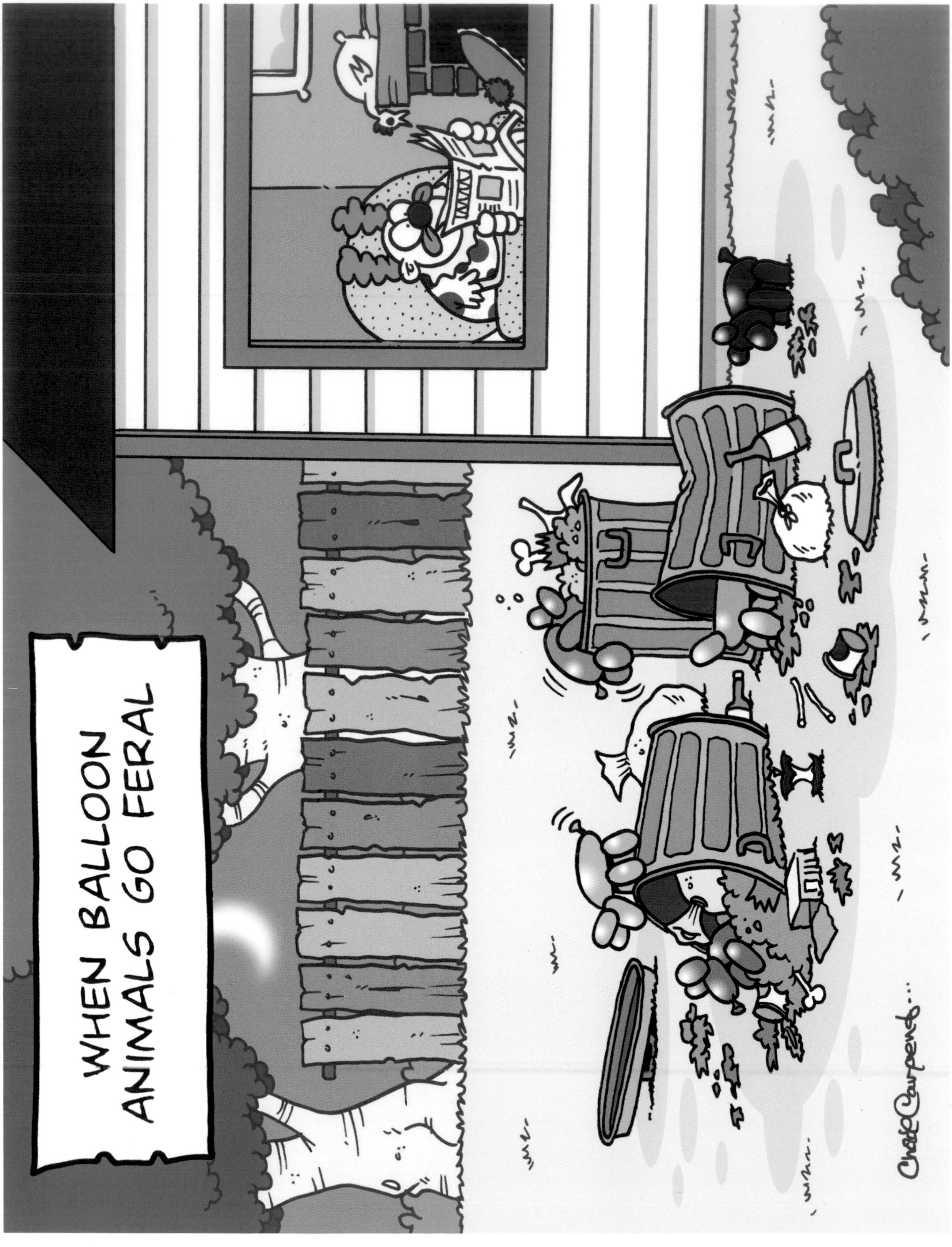
WHEN BALLOON ANIMALS GO FERAL
Chad Carpenter

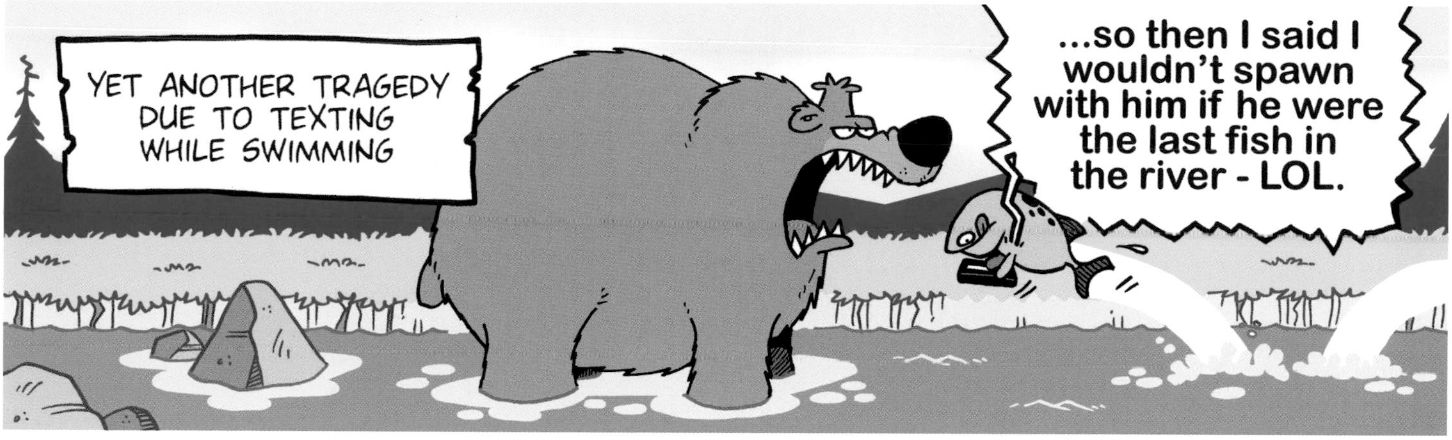
YET ANOTHER TRAGEDY DUE TO TEXTING WHILE SWIMMING
...so then I said I wouldn't spawn with him if he were the last fish in the river - LOL.

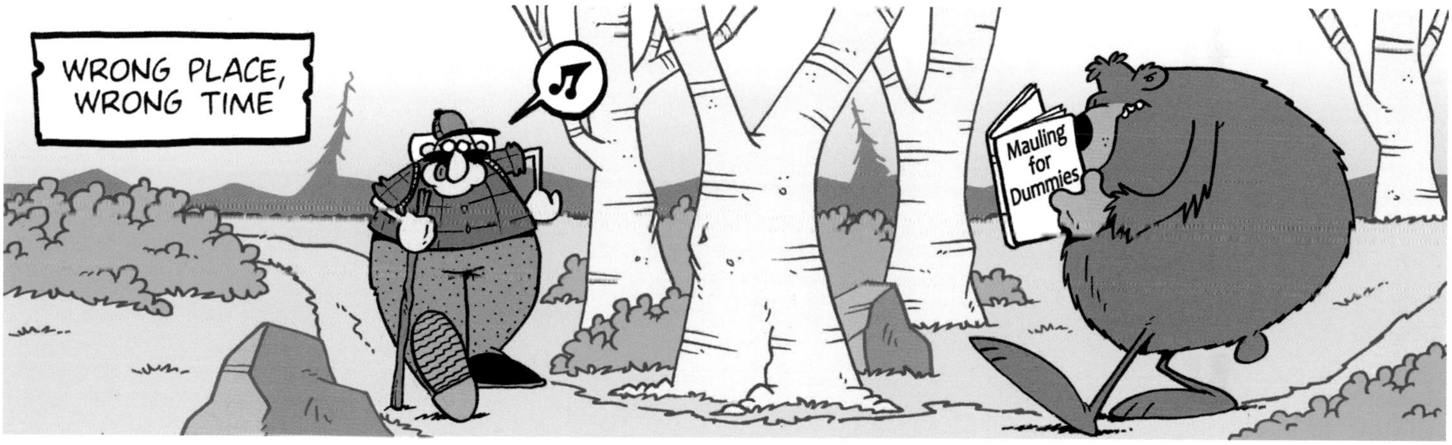
WRONG PLACE, WRONG TIME
Mauling for Dummies

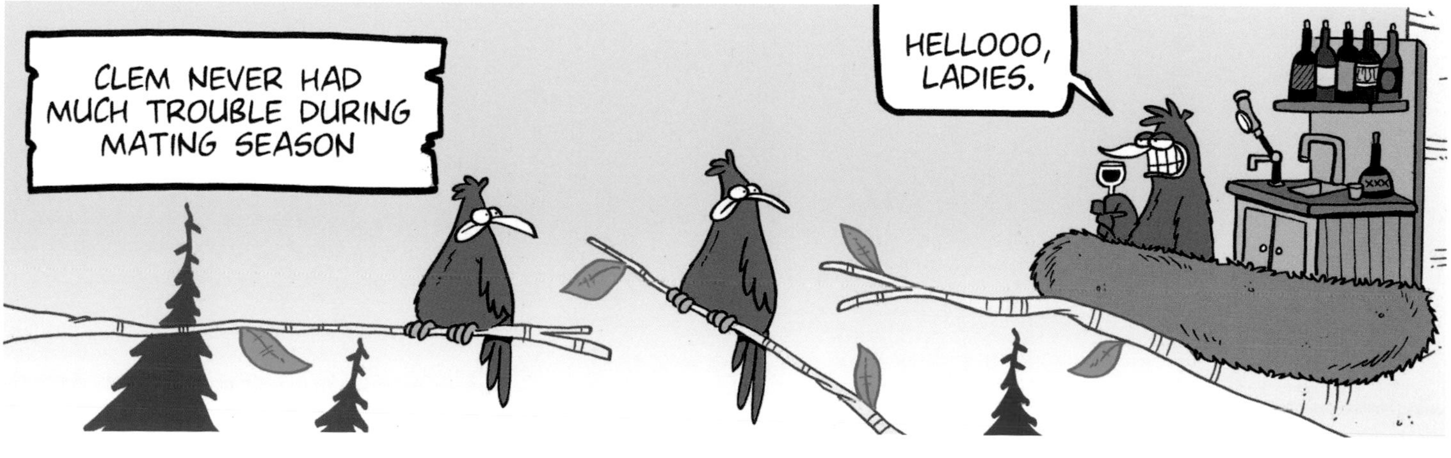
CLEM NEVER HAD MUCH TROUBLE DURING MATING SEASON
HELLOOO, LADIES.

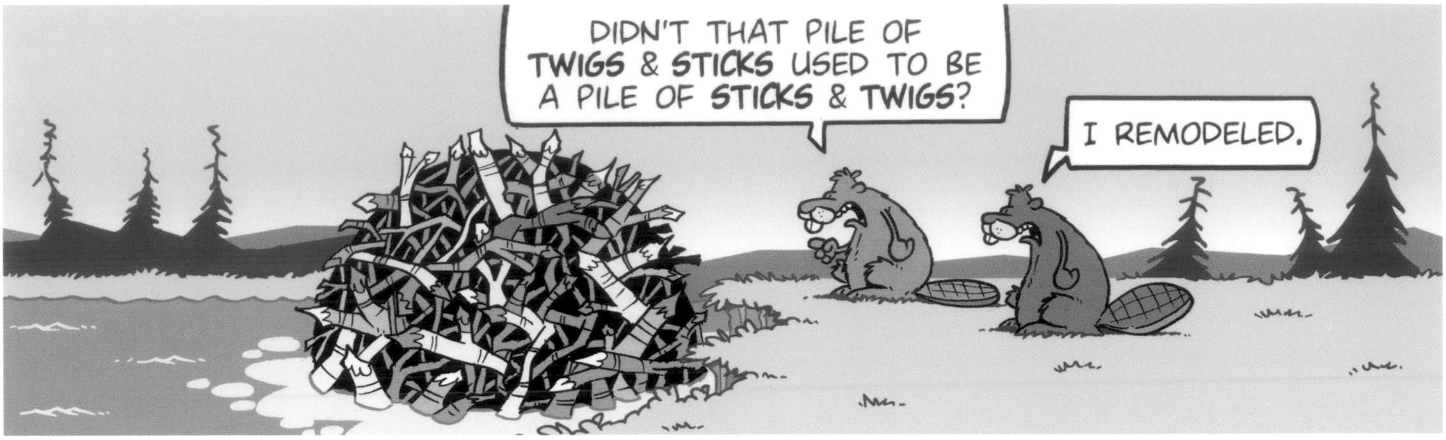
DIDN'T THAT PILE OF TWIGS & STICKS USED TO BE A PILE OF STICKS & TWIGS?
I REMODELED.

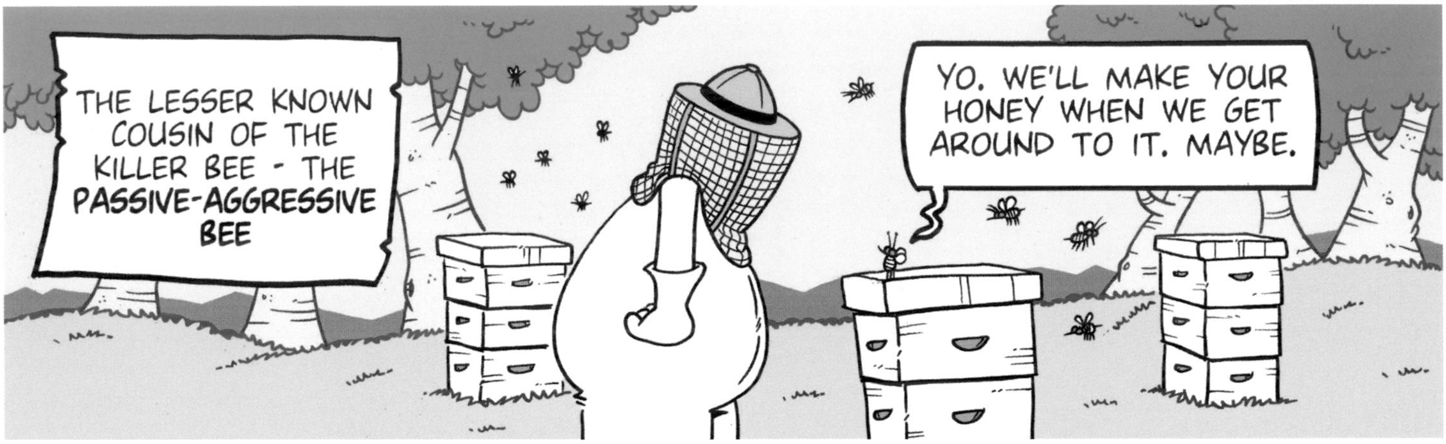
THE LESSER KNOWN COUSIN OF THE KILLER BEE - THE PASSIVE-AGGRESSIVE BEE
YO. WE'LL MAKE YOUR HONEY WHEN WE GET AROUND TO IT. MAYBE.

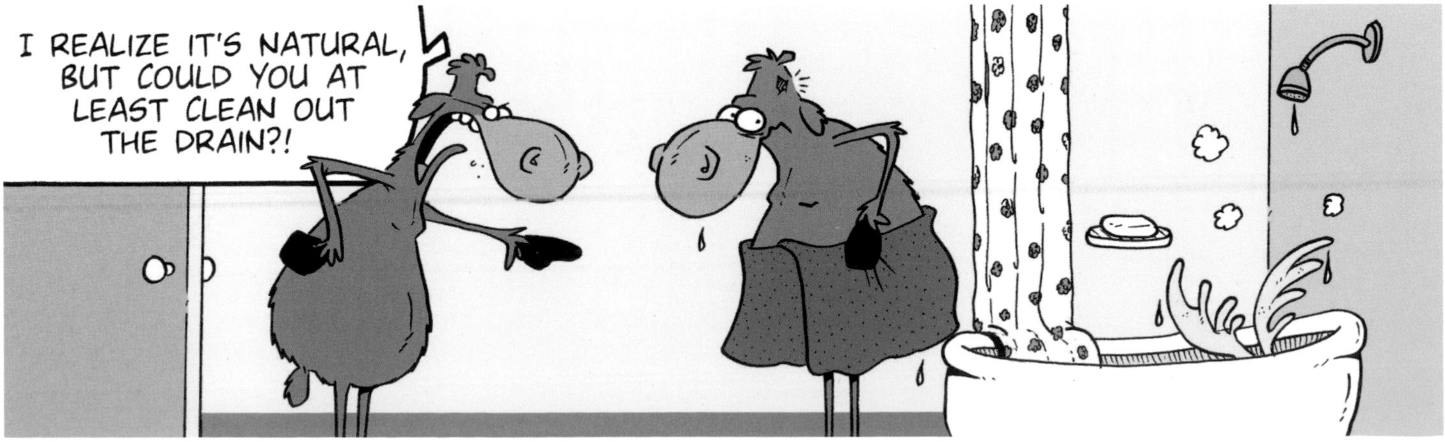
I REALIZE IT'S NATURAL, BUT COULD YOU AT LEAST CLEAN OUT THE DRAIN?!

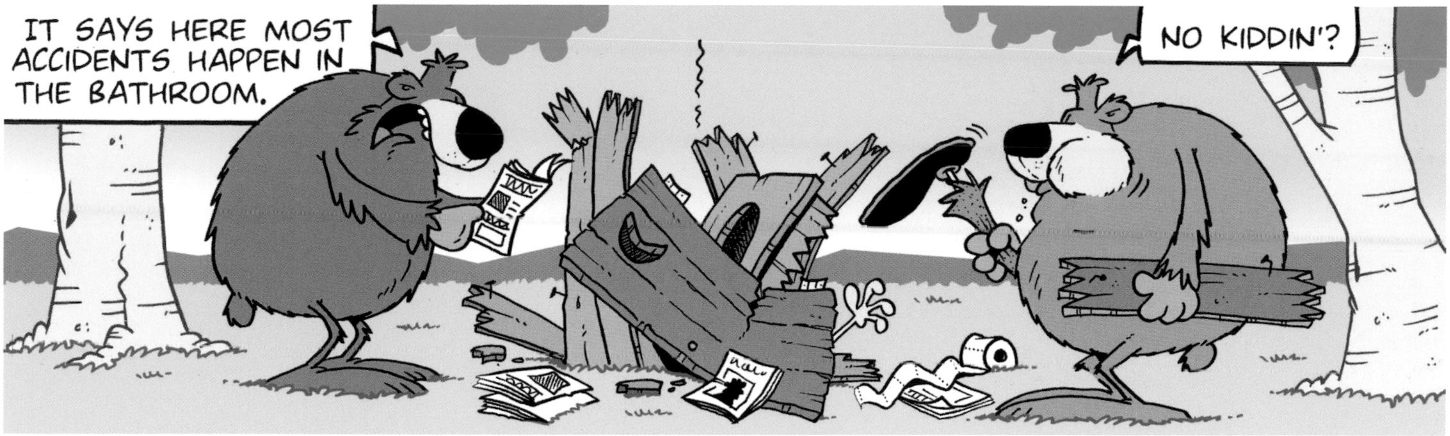
IT SAYS HERE MOST ACCIDENTS HAPPEN IN THE BATHROOM.
NO KIDDIN'?

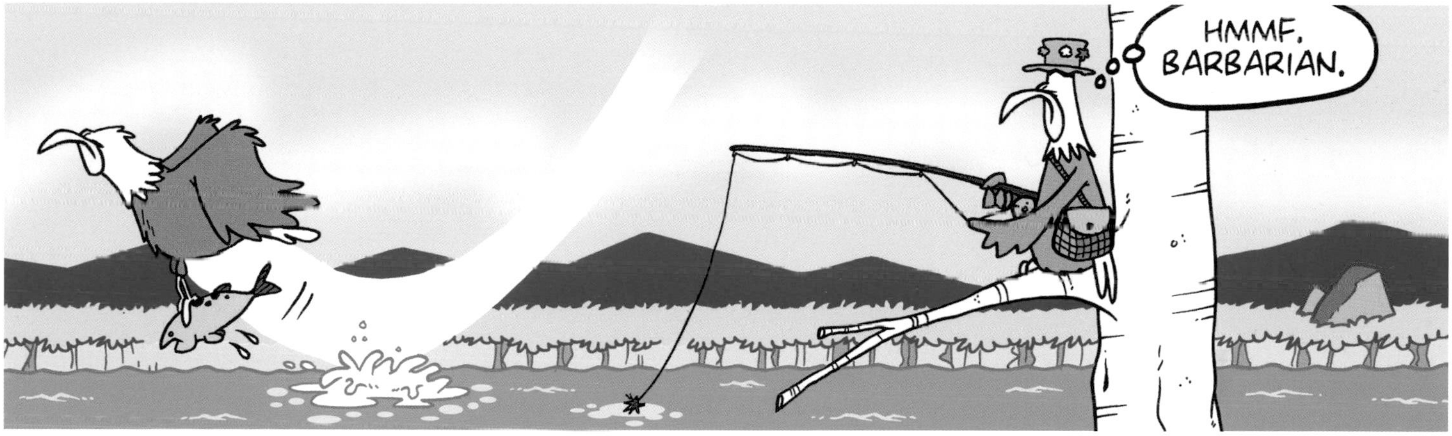
HMMF. BARBARIAN.

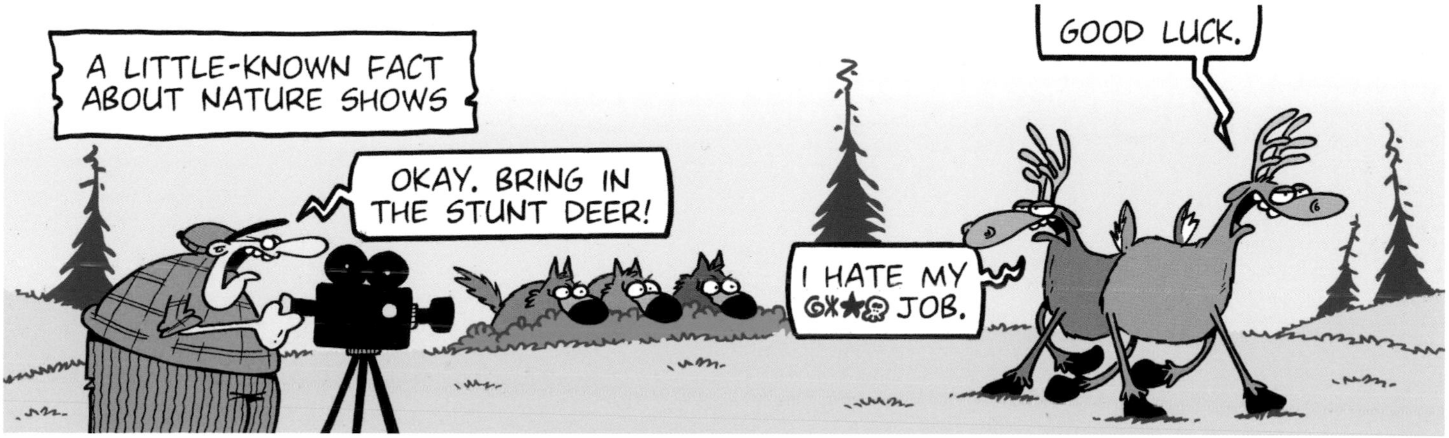
A LITTLE-KNOWN FACT ABOUT NATURE SHOWS
OKAY. BRING IN THE STUNT DEER!
I HATE MY JOB.
GOOD LUCK.

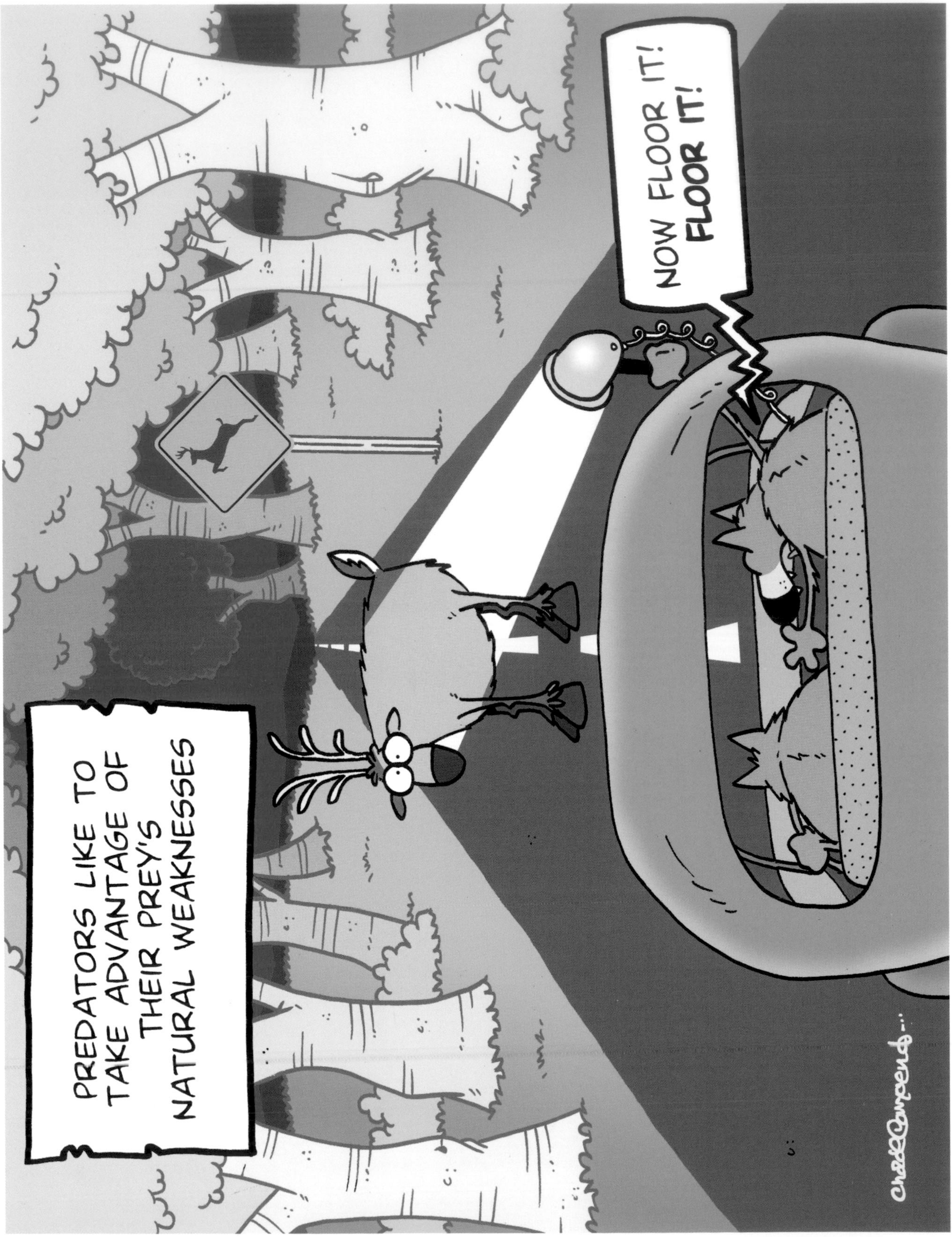
PREDATORS LIKE TO TAKE ADVANTAGE OF THEIR PREY'S NATURAL WEAKNESSES
NOW FLOOR IT! **FLOOR IT!**

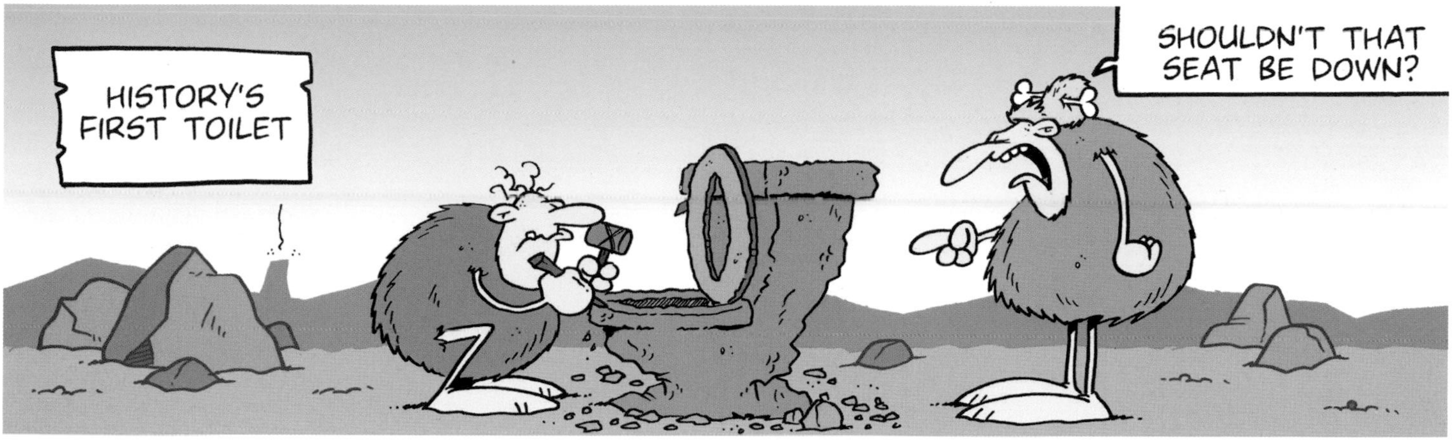
HISTORY'S FIRST TOILET
SHOULDN'T THAT SEAT BE DOWN?

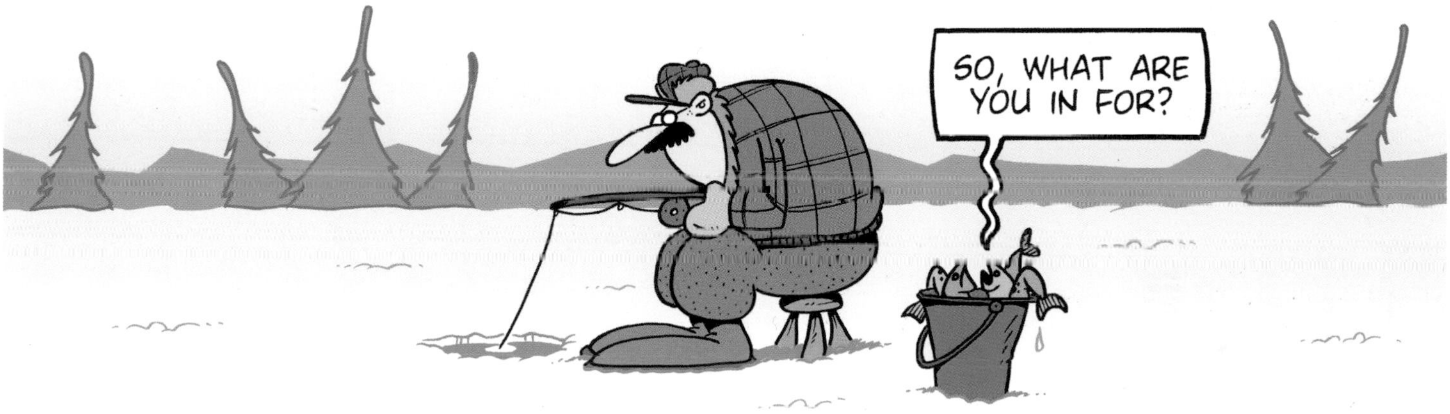
SO, WHAT ARE YOU IN FOR?

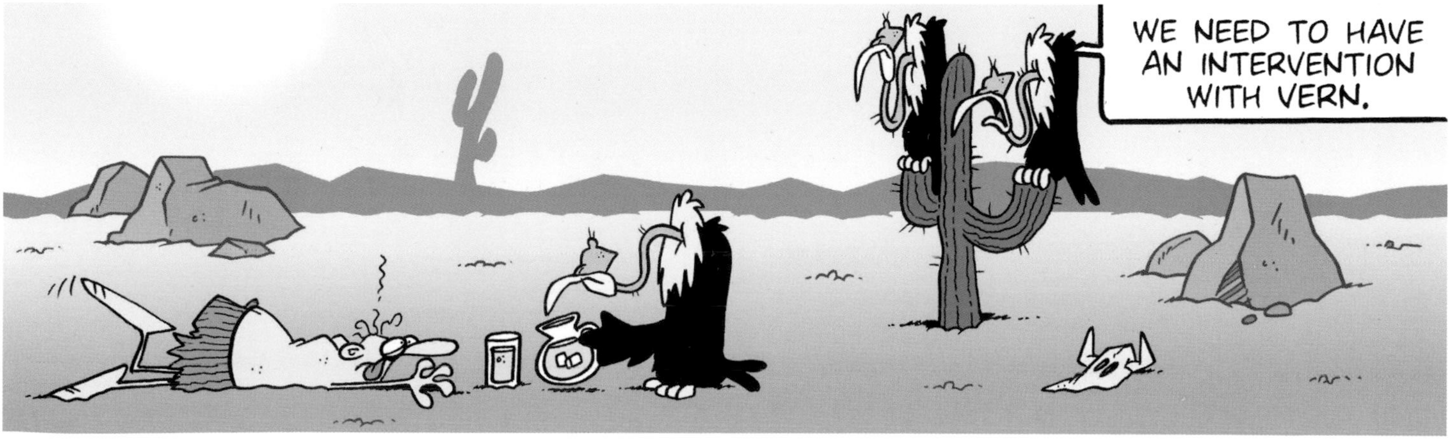
WE NEED TO HAVE AN INTERVENTION WITH VERN.

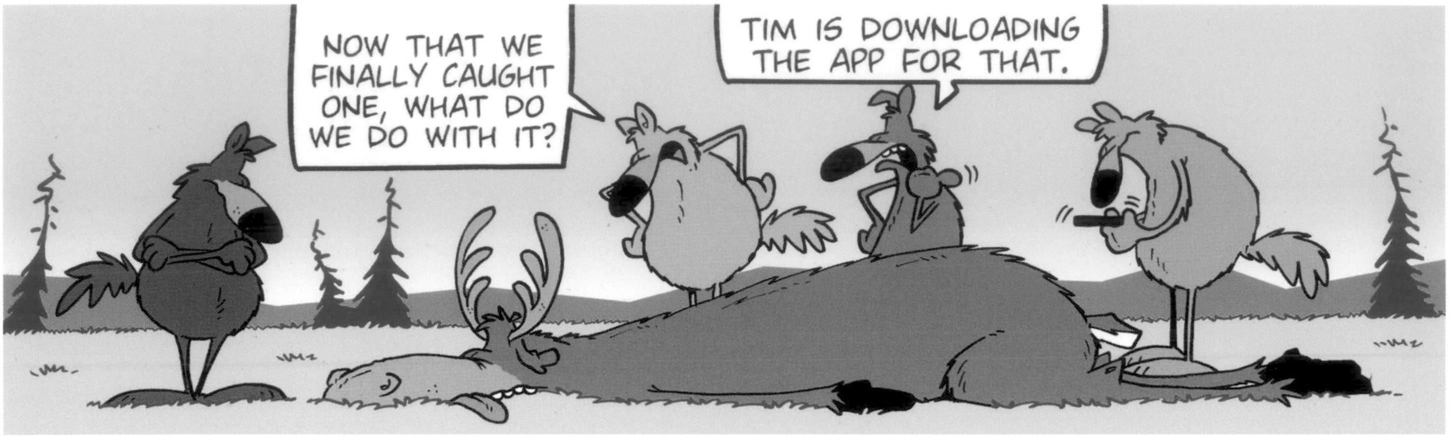
NOW THAT WE FINALLY CAUGHT ONE, WHAT DO WE DO WITH IT?
TIM IS DOWNLOADING THE APP FOR THAT.

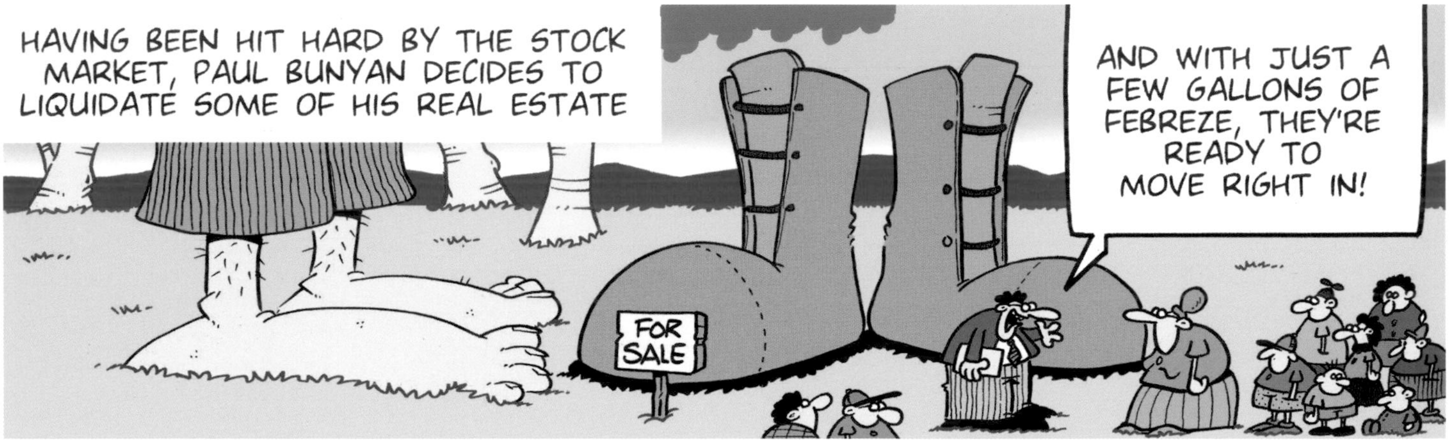
HAVING BEEN HIT HARD BY THE STOCK MARKET, PAUL BUNYAN DECIDES TO LIQUIDATE SOME OF HIS REAL ESTATE
AND WITH JUST A FEW GALLONS OF FEBREZE, THEY'RE READY TO MOVE RIGHT IN!
FOR SALE

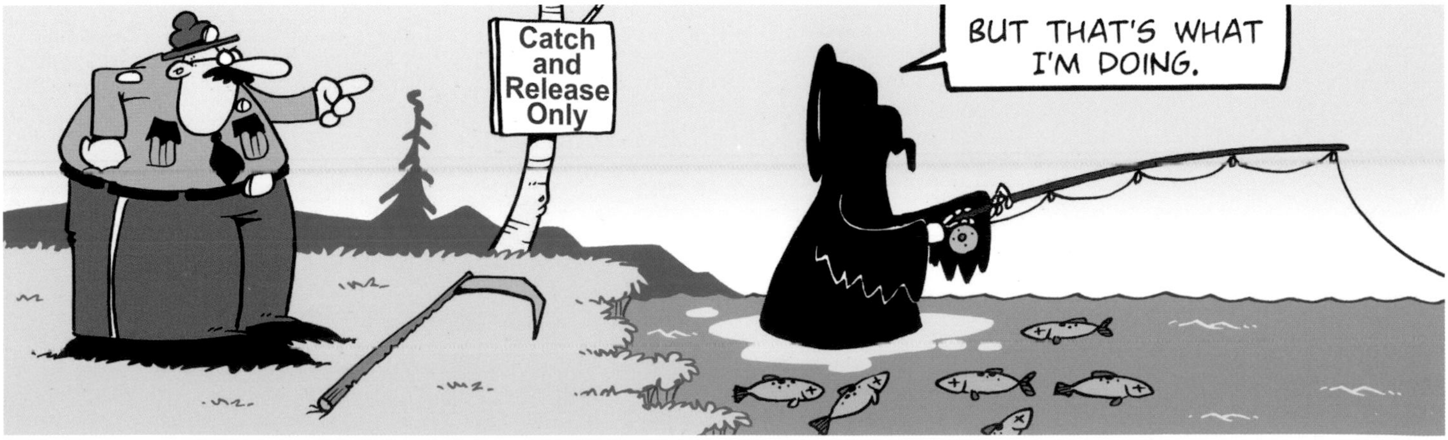
Catch and Release Only
BUT THAT'S WHAT I'M DOING.

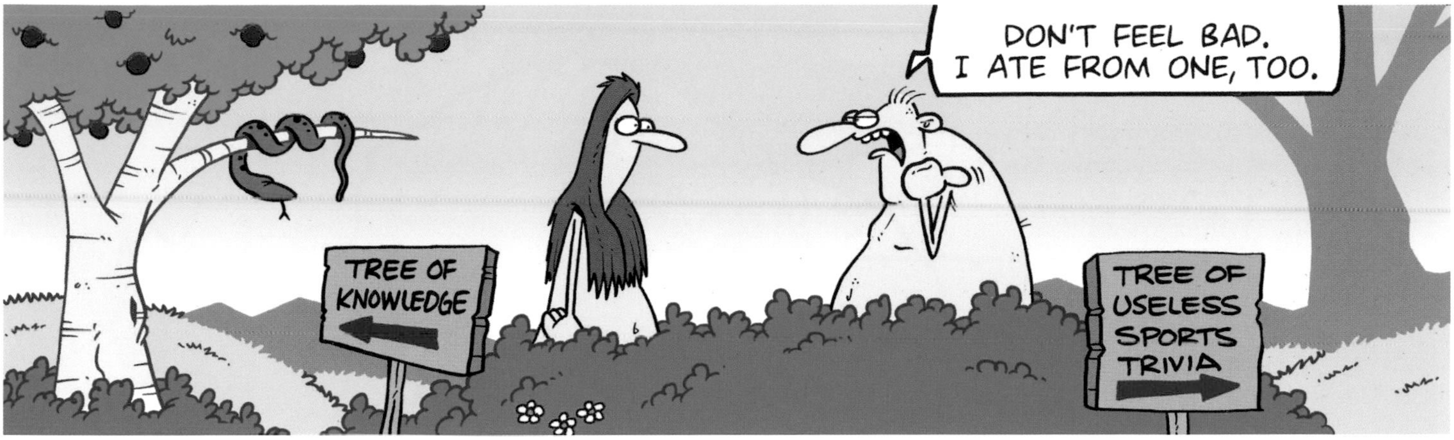
DON'T FEEL BAD. I ATE FROM ONE, TOO.
TREE OF KNOWLEDGE
TREE OF USELESS SPORTS TRIVIA

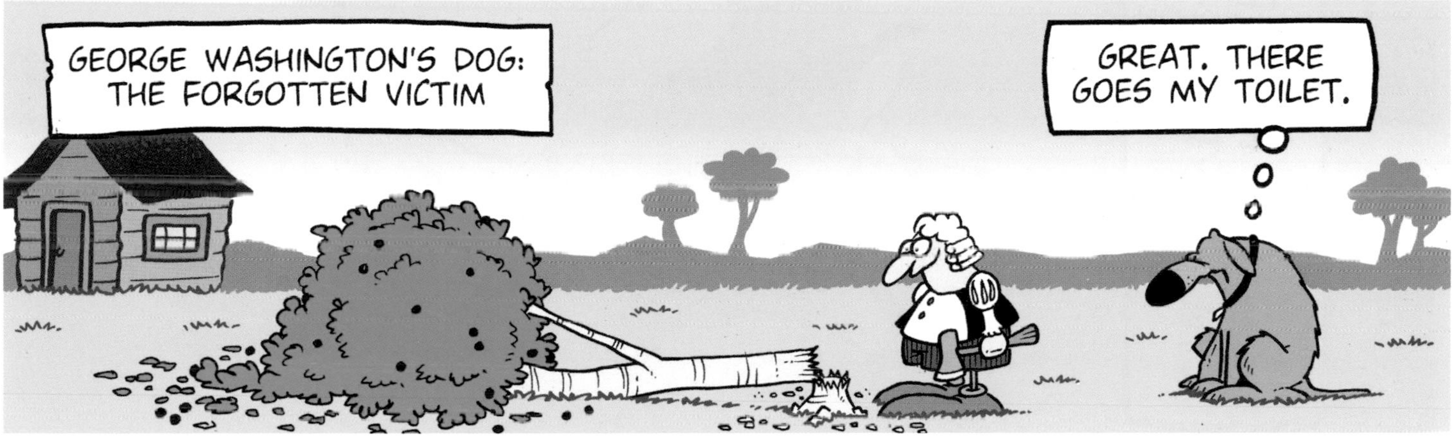
GEORGE WASHINGTON'S DOG: THE FORGOTTEN VICTIM
GREAT. THERE GOES MY TOILET.

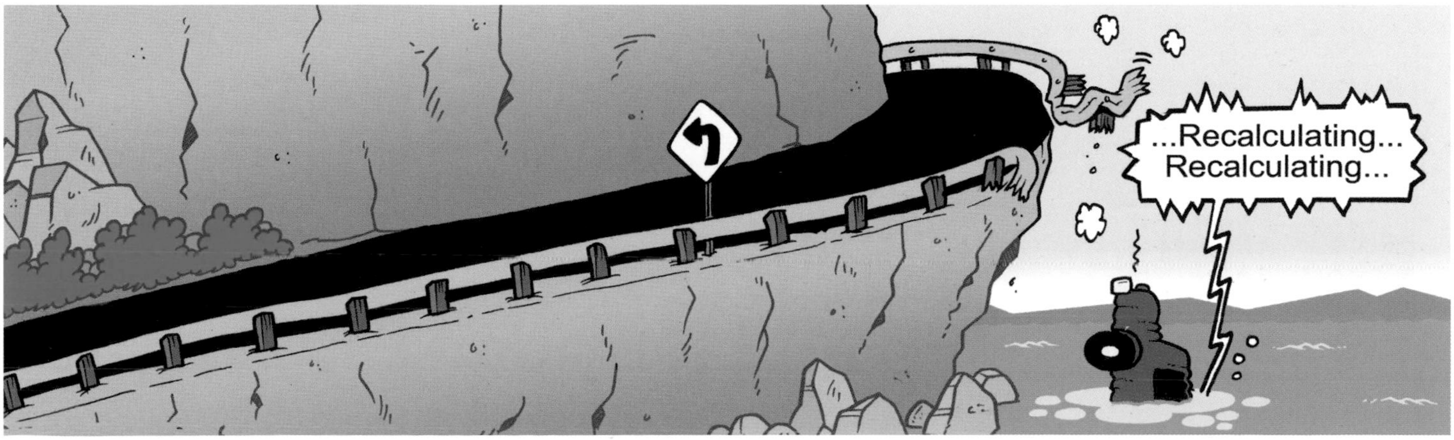
...Recalculating...
Recalculating...

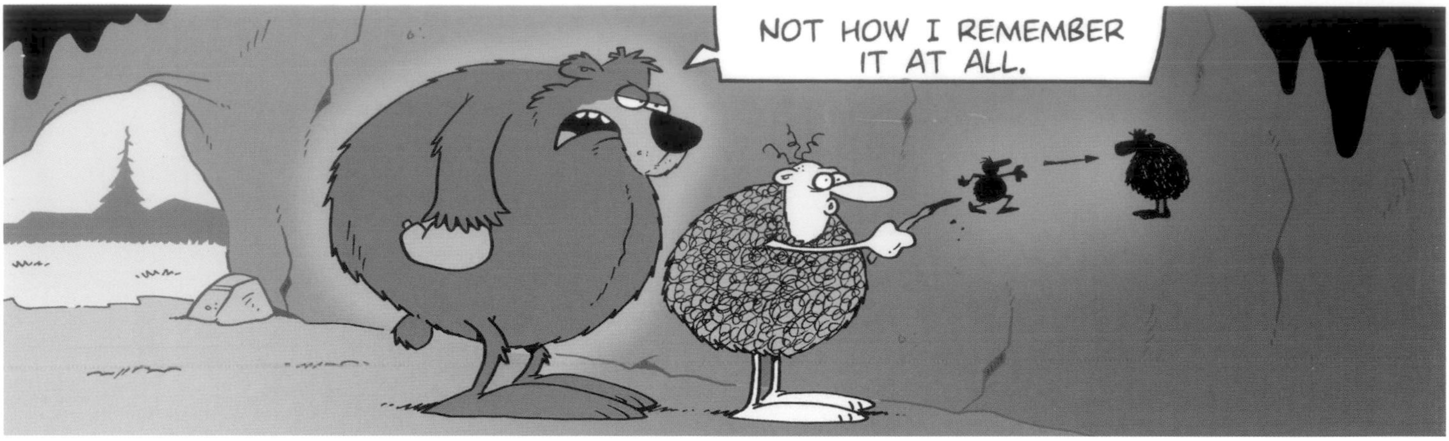
NOT HOW I REMEMBER IT AT ALL.

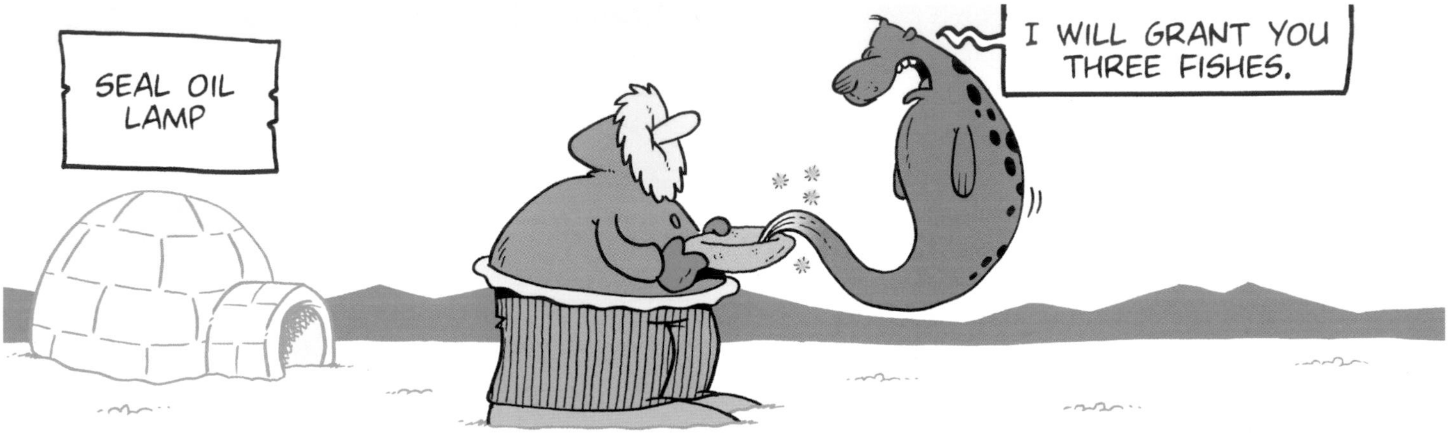
SEAL OIL LAMP
I WILL GRANT YOU THREE FISHES.

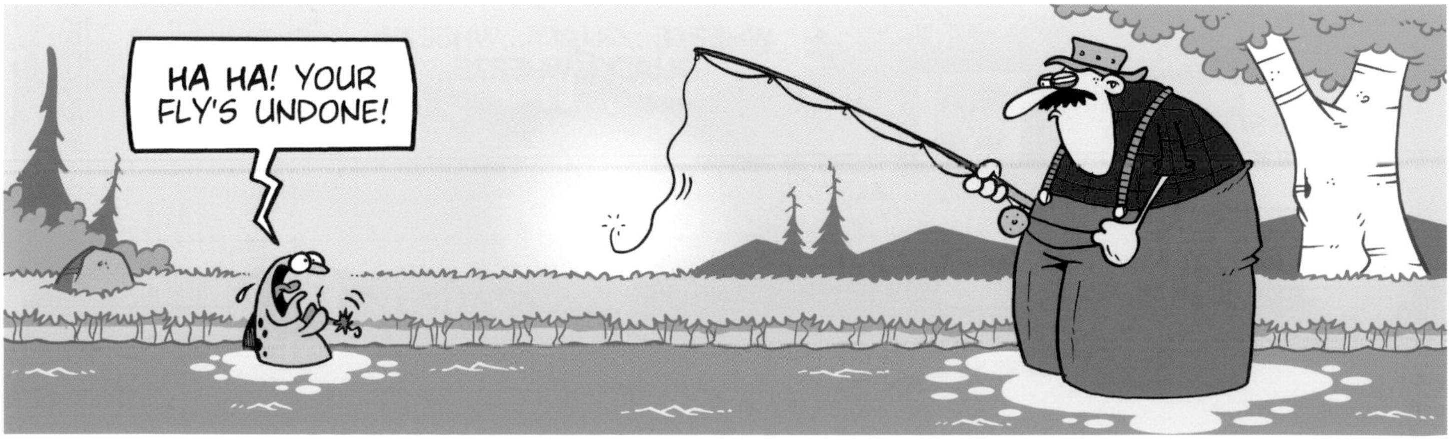
HA HA! YOUR FLY'S UNDONE!

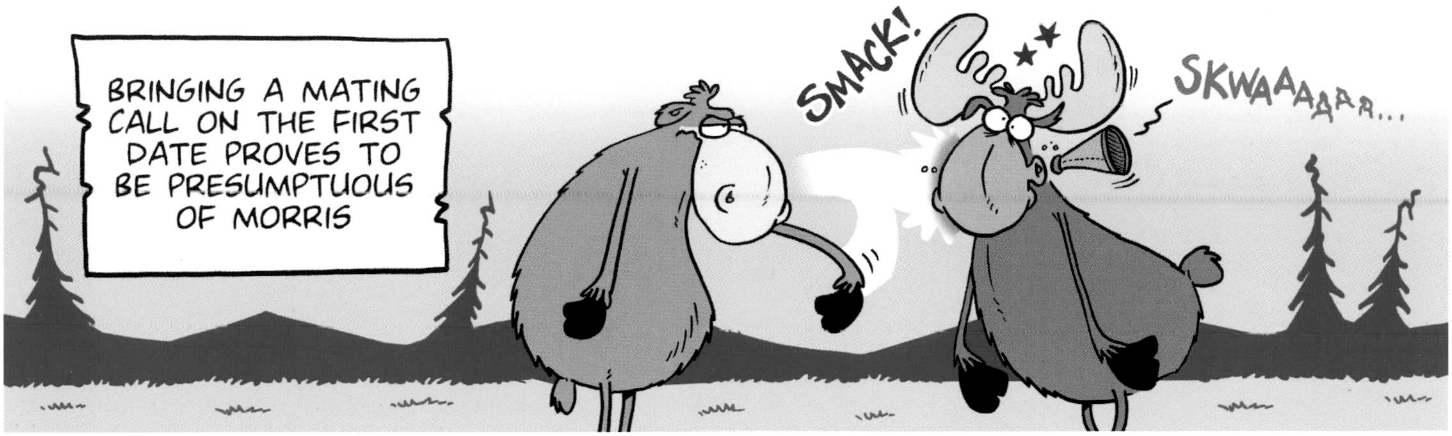
BRINGING A MATING CALL ON THE FIRST DATE PROVES TO BE PRESUMPTUOUS OF MORRIS
SMACK!
SKWAAAAAAA...

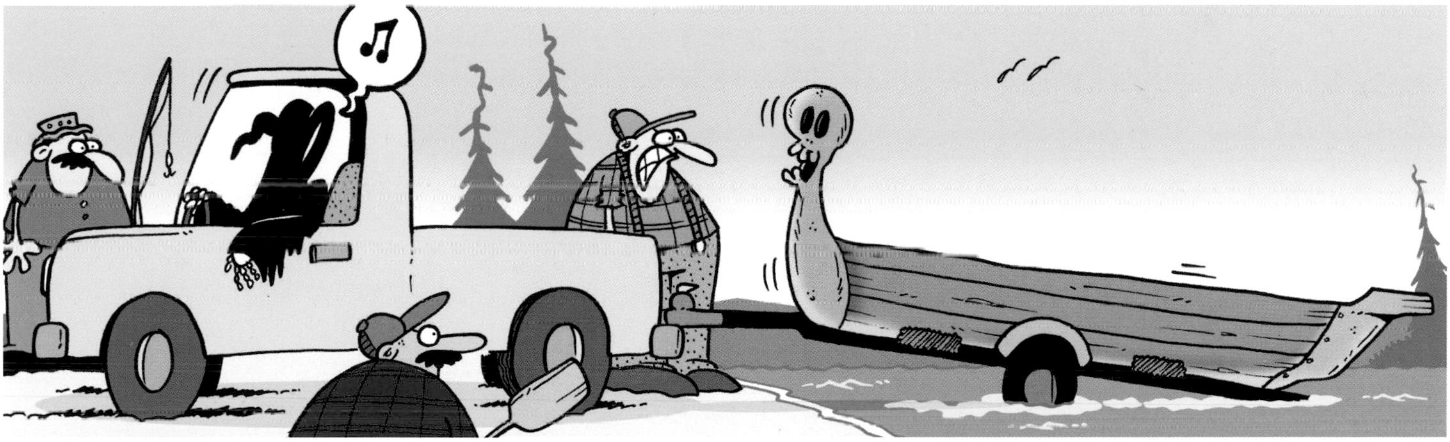

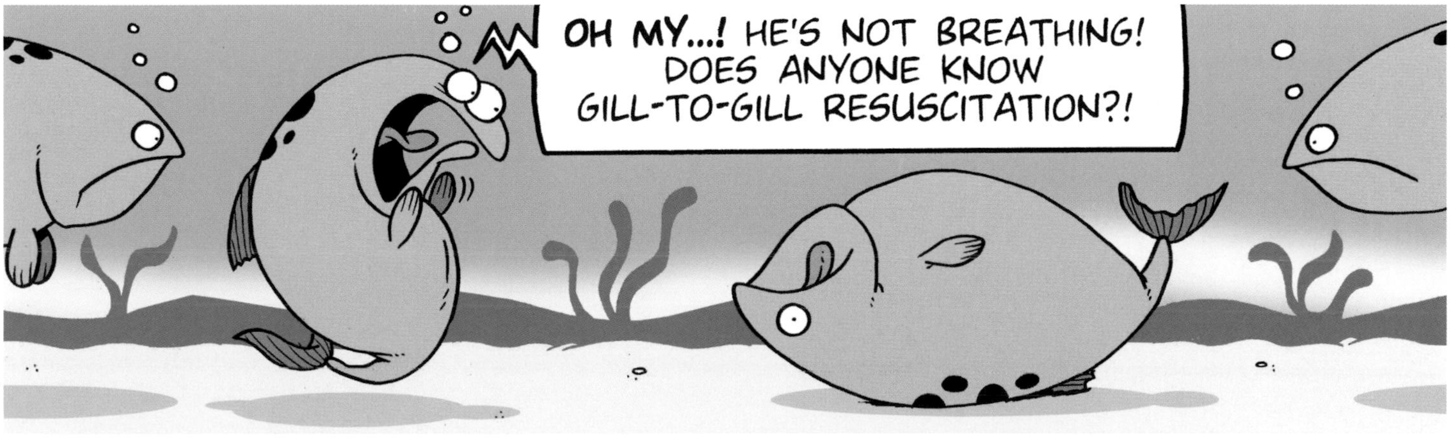
OH MY...! HE'S NOT BREATHING! DOES ANYONE KNOW GILL-TO-GILL RESUSCITATION?!

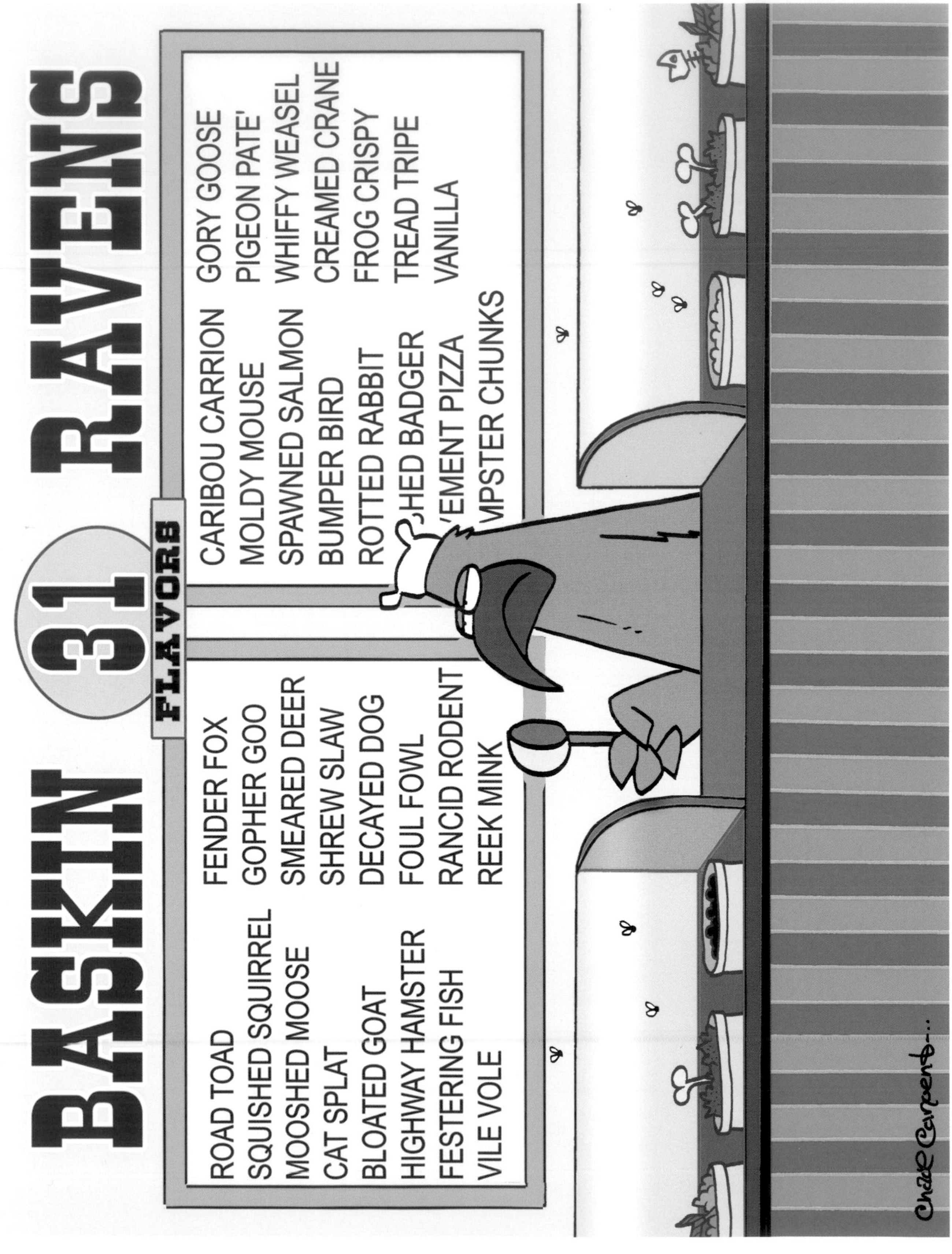
BASKIN 31 RAVENS
FLAVORS
ROAD TOAD
SQUISHED SQUIRREL
MOOSHED MOOSE
CAT SPLAT
BLOATED GOAT
HIGHWAY HAMSTER
FESTERING FISH
VILE VOLE
FENDER FOX
GOPHER GOO
SMEARED DEER
SHREW SLAW
DECAYED DOG
FOUL FOWL
RANCID RODENT
REEK MINK
CARIBOU CARRION
MOLDY MOUSE
SPAWNED SALMON
BUMPER BIRD
ROTTED RABBIT
HED BADGER
EMENT PIZZA
MPSTER CHUNKS
GORY GOOSE
PIGEON PATE'
WHIFFY WEASEL
CREAMED CRANE
FROG CRISPY
TREAD TRIPE
VANILLA
Chad Carpenter...

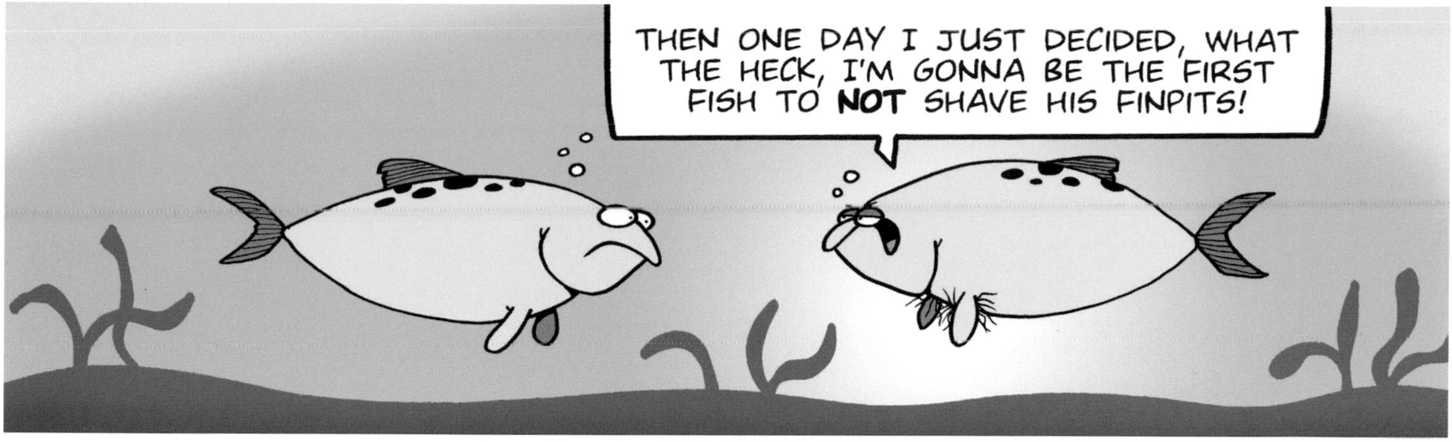
THEN ONE DAY I JUST DECIDED, WHAT THE HECK, I'M GONNA BE THE FIRST FISH TO **NOT** SHAVE HIS FINPITS!

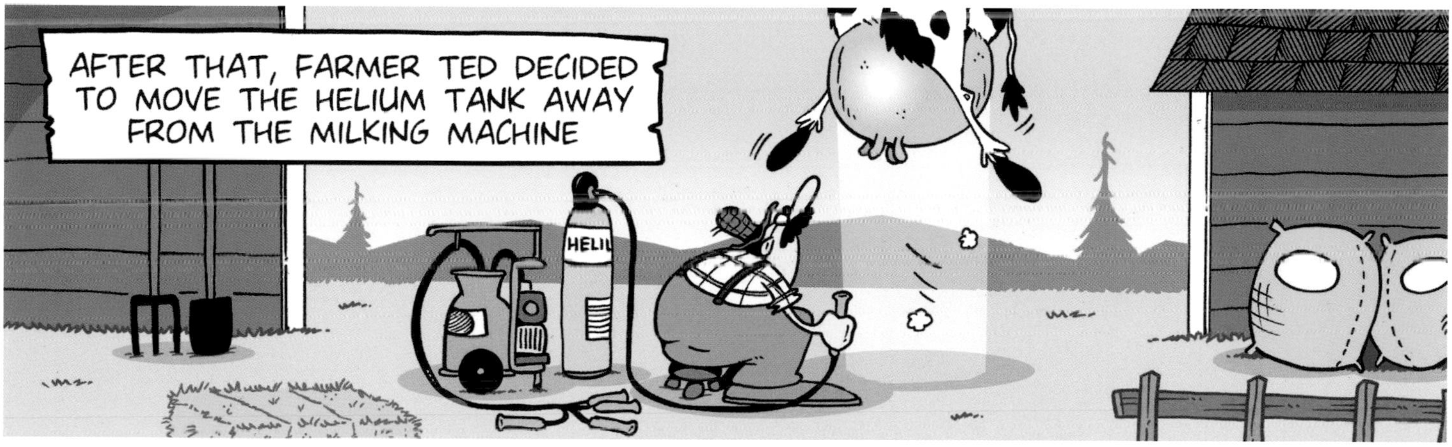
AFTER THAT, FARMER TED DECIDED TO MOVE THE HELIUM TANK AWAY FROM THE MILKING MACHINE
HELI

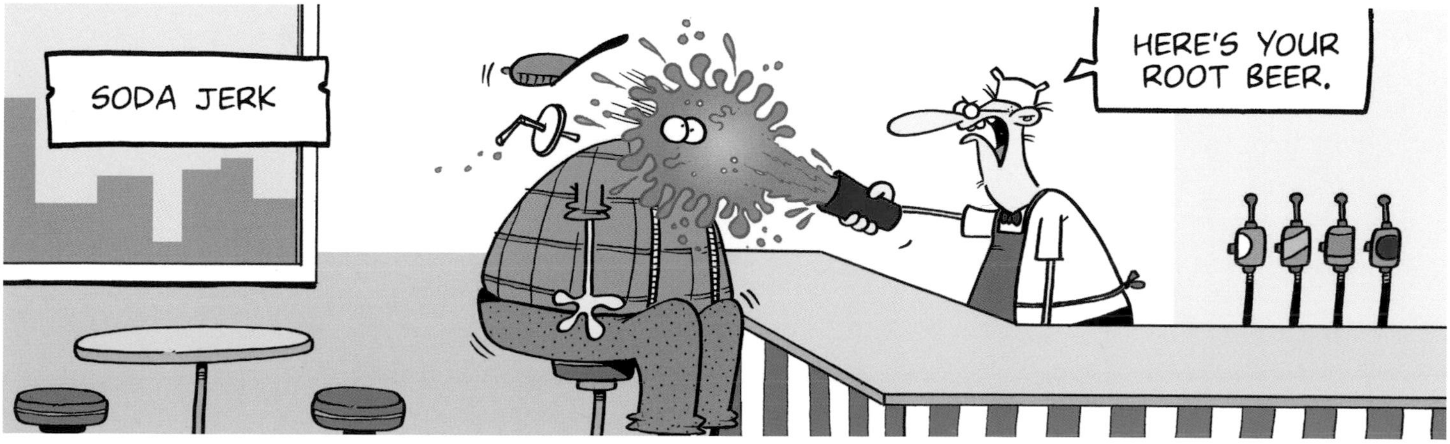
SODA JERK
HERE'S YOUR ROOT BEER.

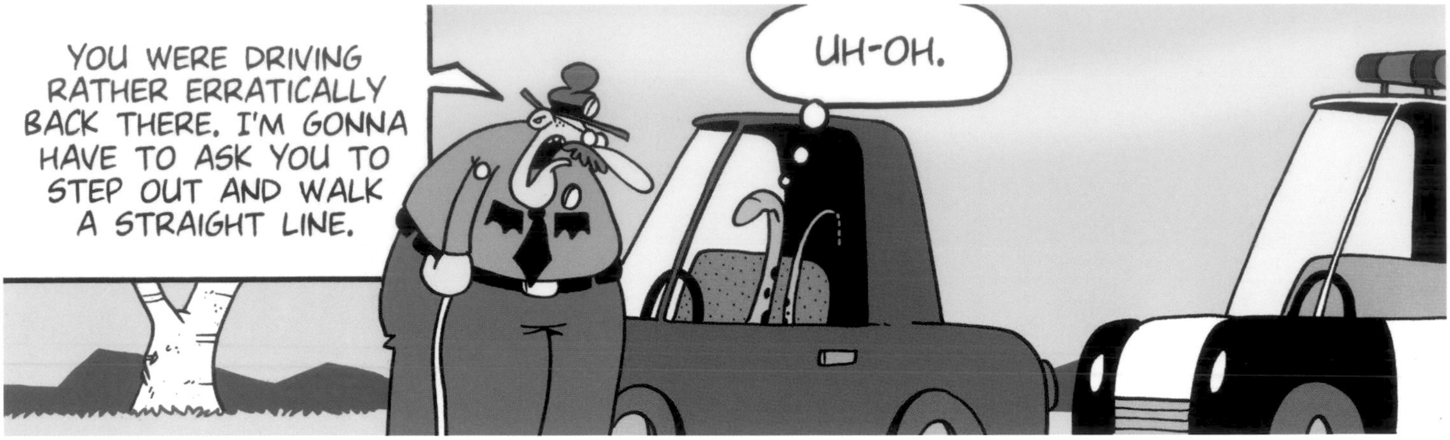
YOU WERE DRIVING RATHER ERRATICALLY BACK THERE. I'M GONNA HAVE TO ASK YOU TO STEP OUT AND WALK A STRAIGHT LINE.
UH-OH.

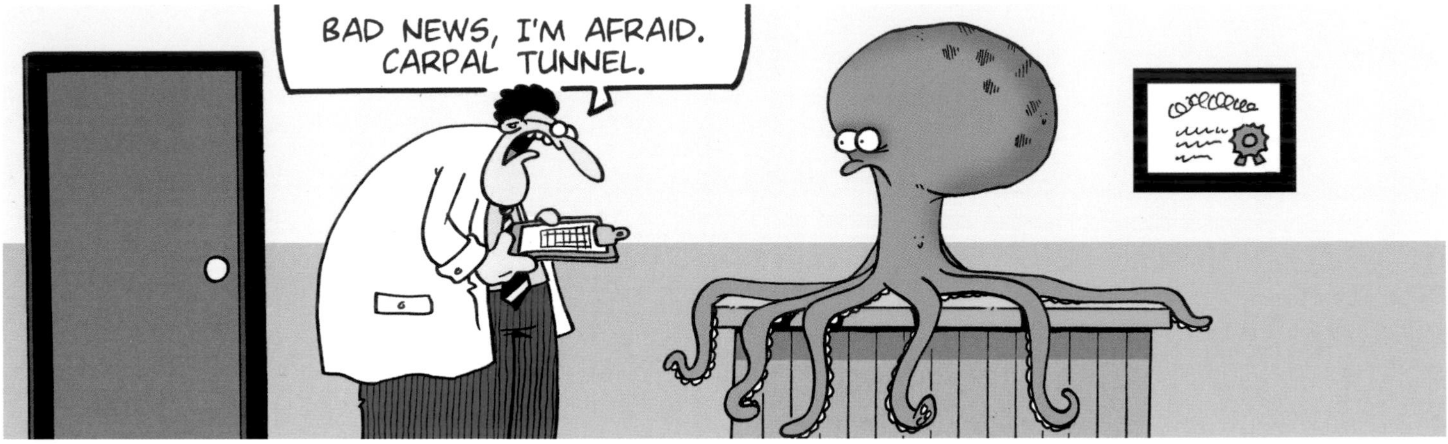
BAD NEWS, I'M AFRAID. CARPAL TUNNEL.

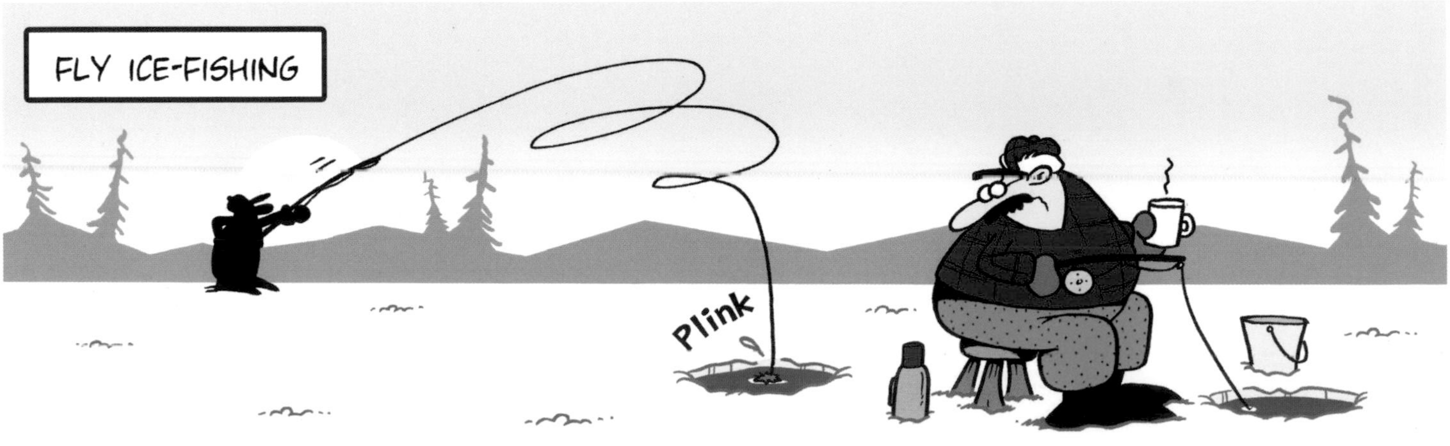
FLY ICE-FISHING
Plink

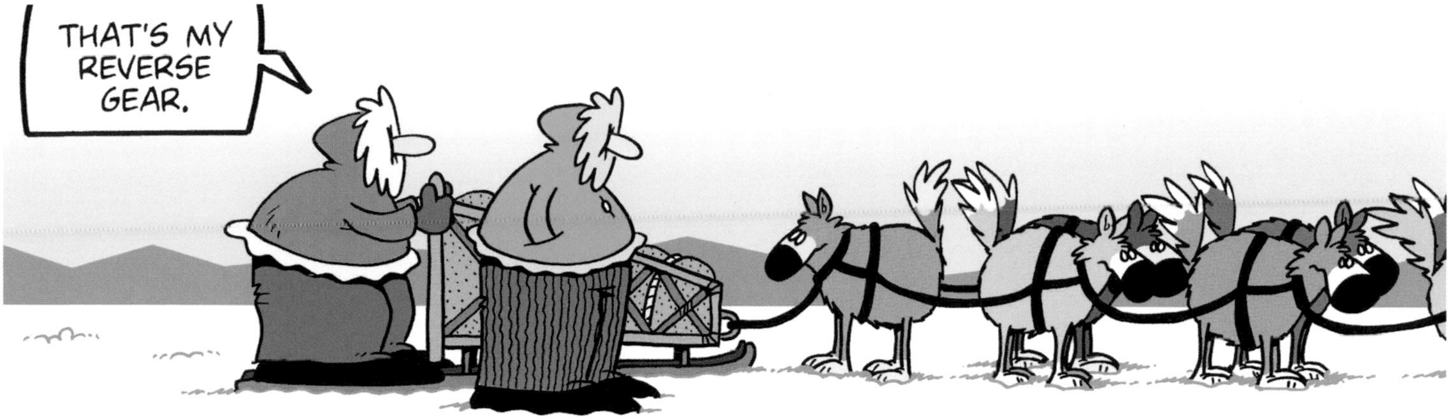
THAT'S MY REVERSE GEAR.

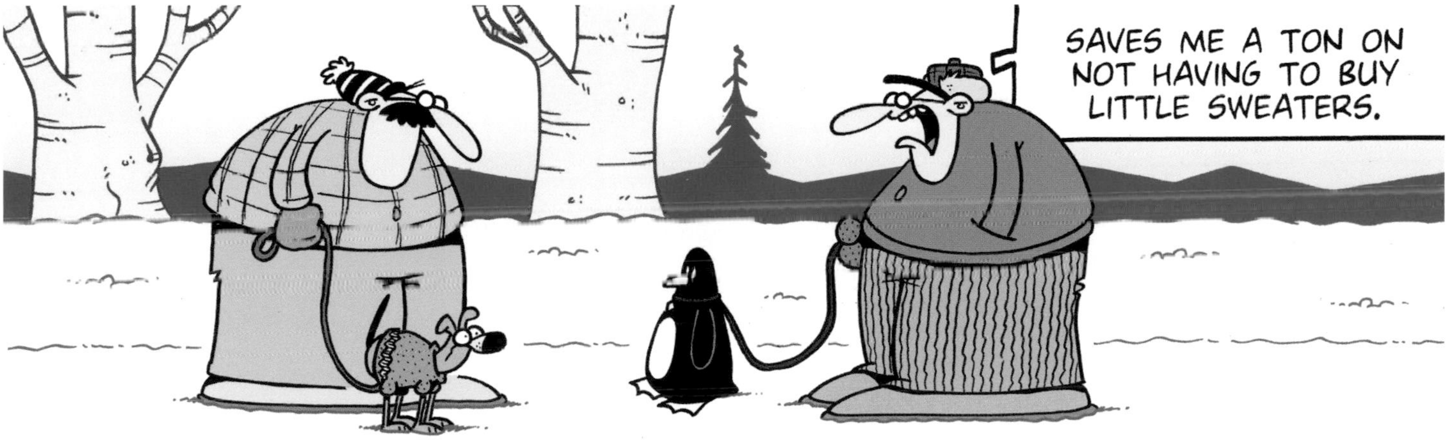
SAVES ME A TON ON NOT HAVING TO BUY LITTLE SWEATERS.

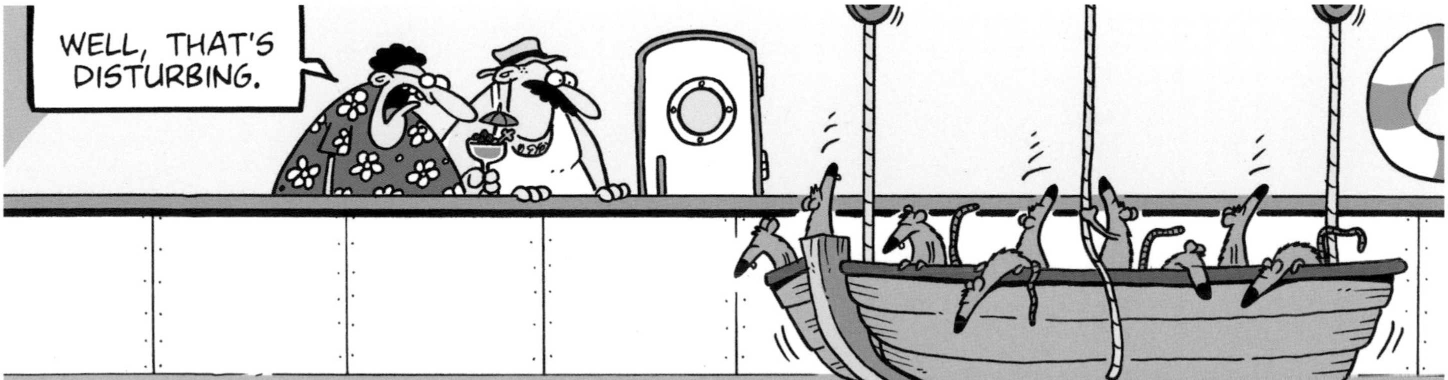
WELL, THAT'S DISTURBING.

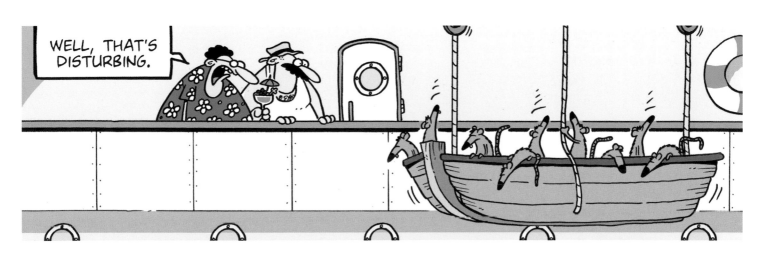

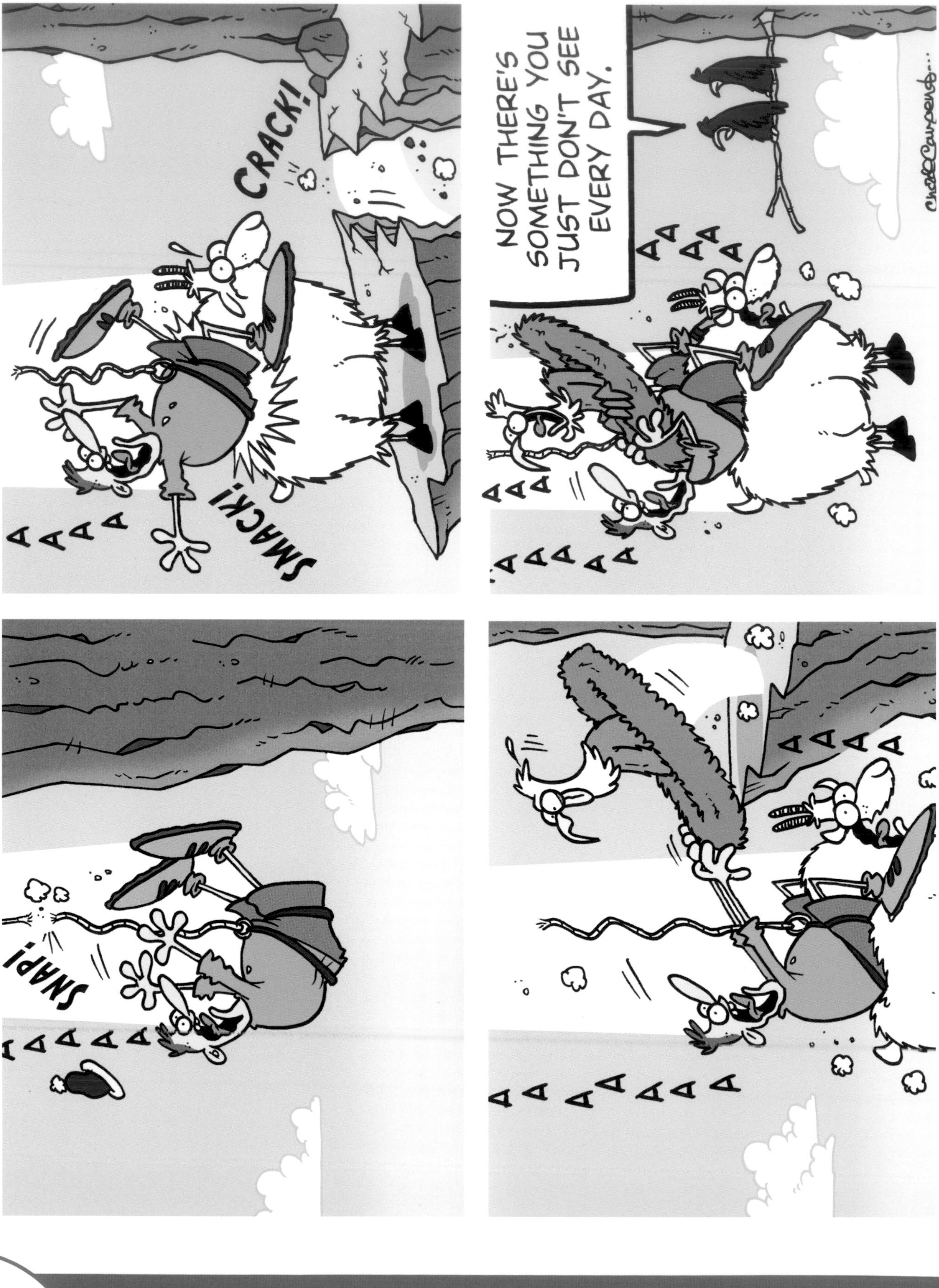
AAAAAA
SNAP!
AAAA
SMACK!
CRACK!
AAAAAAA
AAAAAA
NOW THERE'S SOMETHING YOU JUST DON'T SEE EVERY DAY.

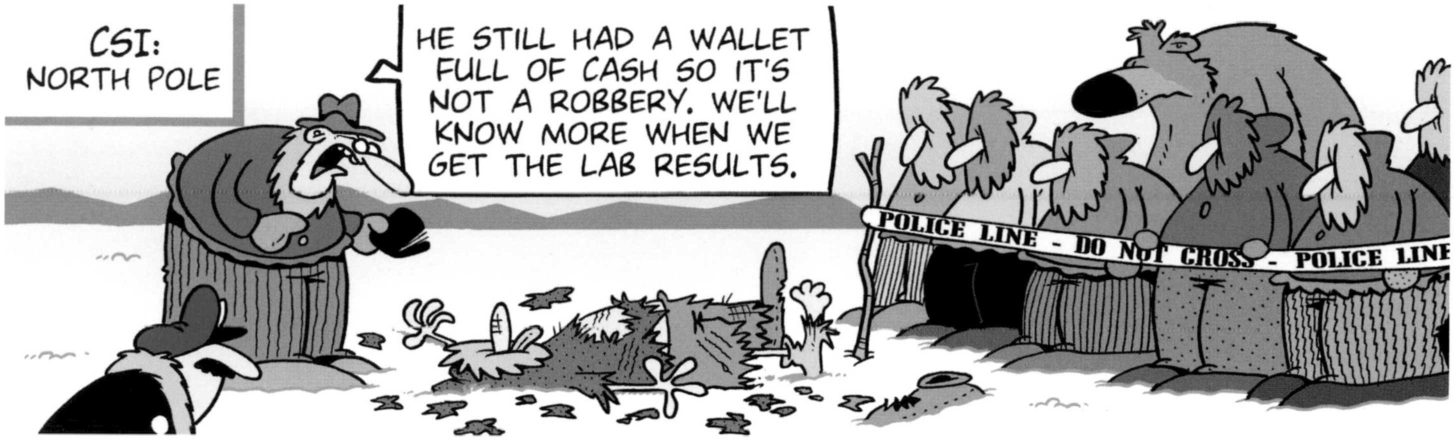
CSI: NORTH POLE
HE STILL HAD A WALLET FULL OF CASH SO IT'S NOT A ROBBERY. WE'LL KNOW MORE WHEN WE GET THE LAB RESULTS.
POLICE LINE - DO NOT CROSS - POLICE LINE

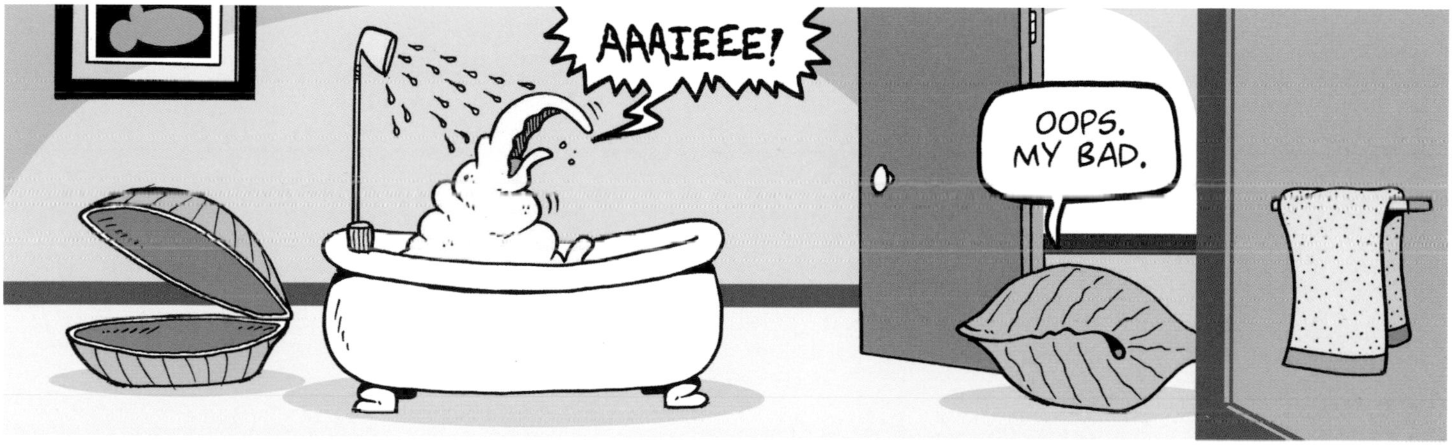
AAAIEEE!
OOPS. MY BAD.

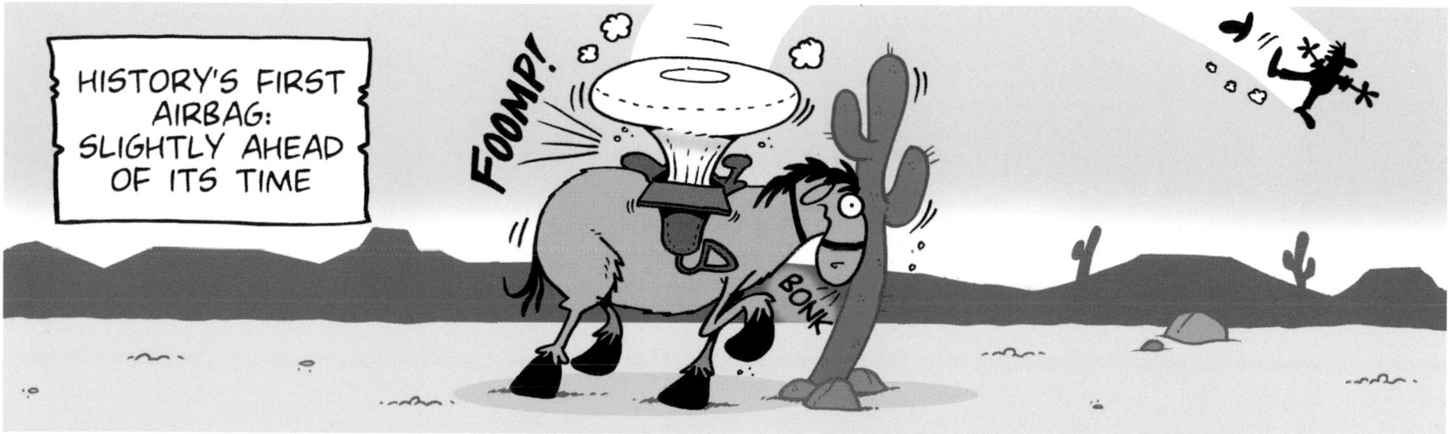
HISTORY'S FIRST AIRBAG: SLIGHTLY AHEAD OF ITS TIME
FOOMP!
BONK

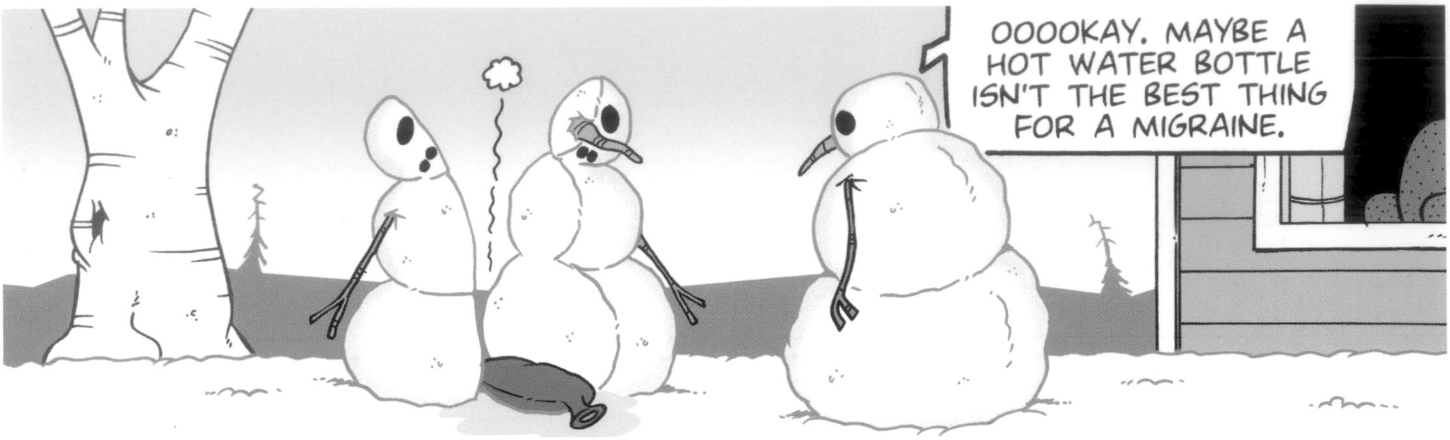
OOOOKAY. MAYBE A HOT WATER BOTTLE ISN'T THE BEST THING FOR A MIGRAINE.

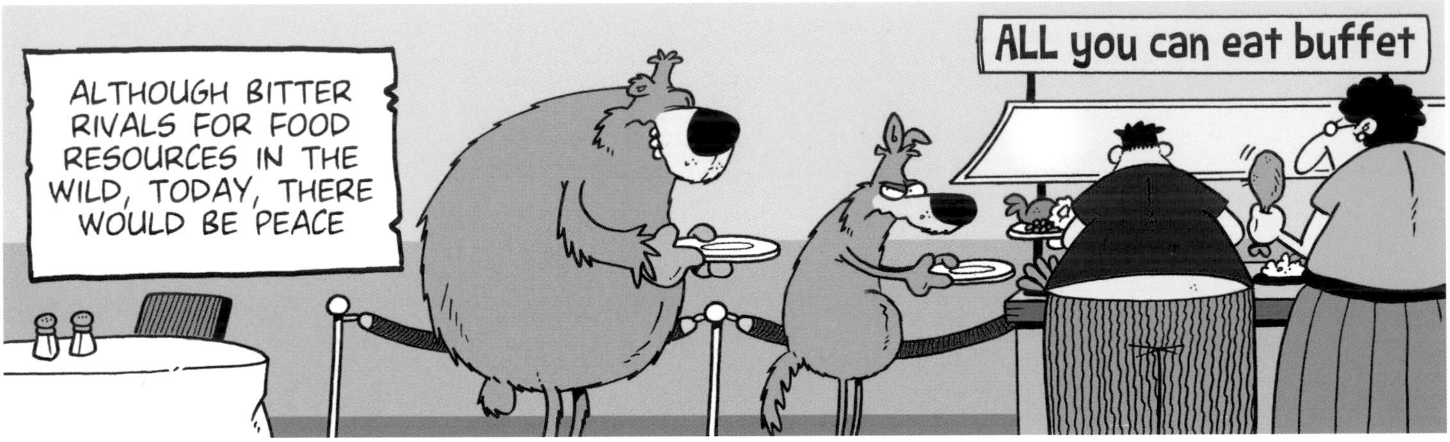
ALTHOUGH BITTER RIVALS FOR FOOD RESOURCES IN THE WILD, TODAY, THERE WOULD BE PEACE
ALL you can eat buffet

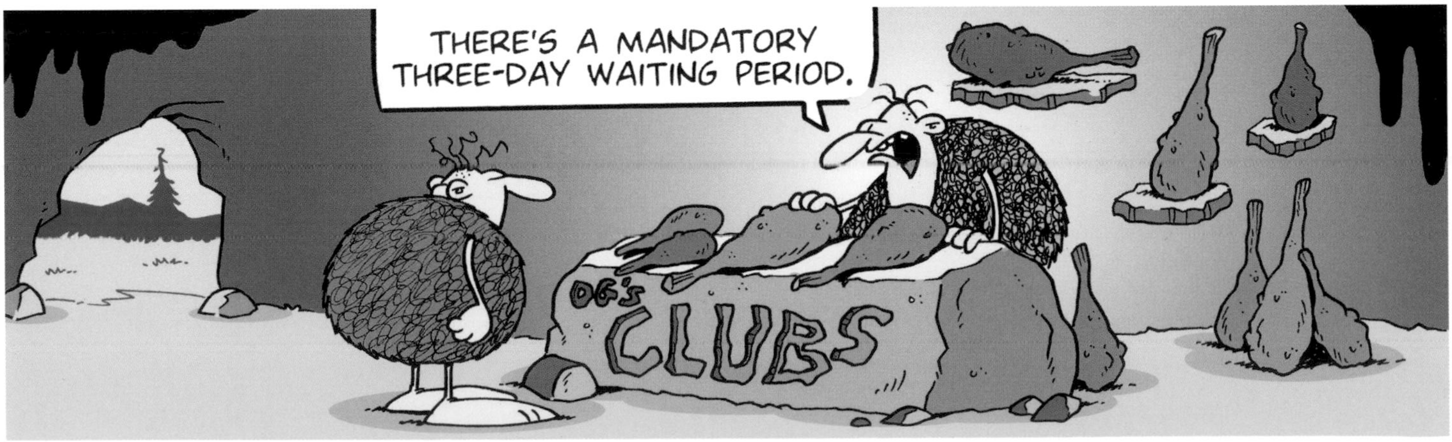
THERE'S A MANDATORY THREE-DAY WAITING PERIOD.
OG's CLUBS

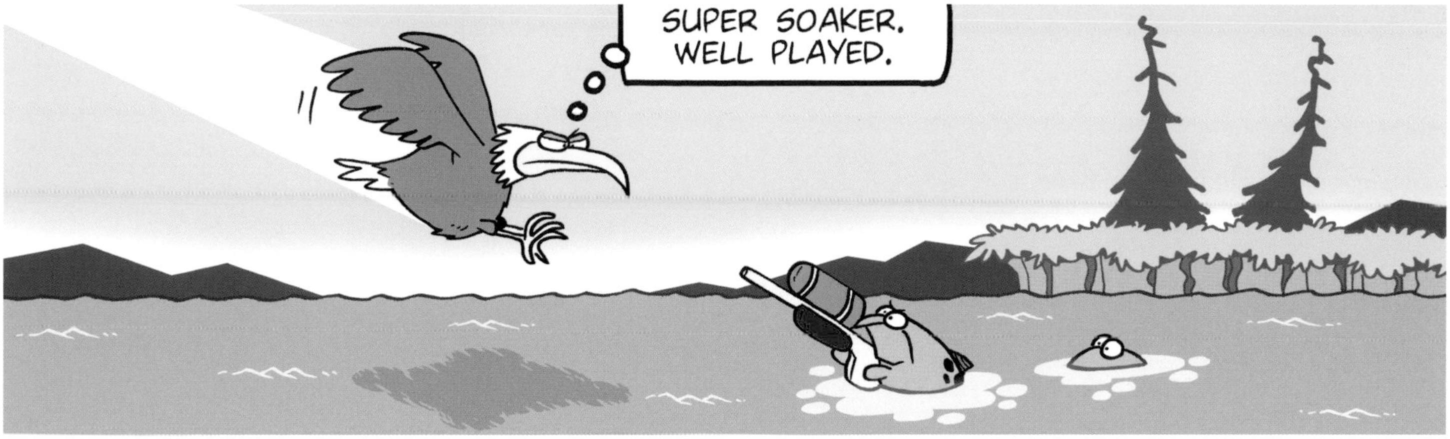
SUPER SOAKER.
WELL PLAYED.

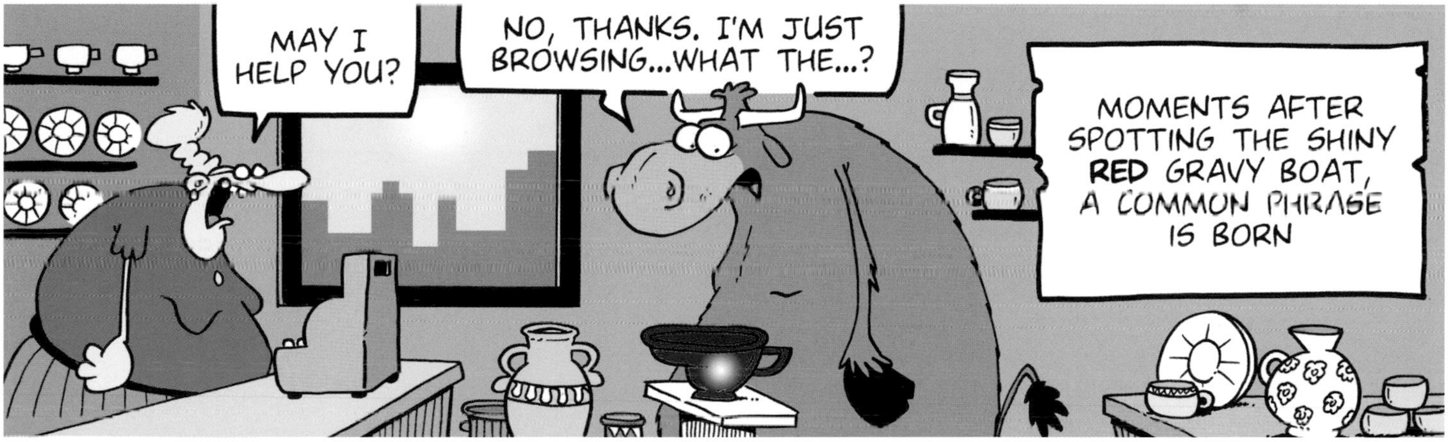
MAY I
HELP YOU?
NO, THANKS. I'M JUST
BROWSING...WHAT THE...?
MOMENTS AFTER
SPOTTING THE SHINY
RED GRAVY BOAT,
A COMMON PHRASE
IS BORN

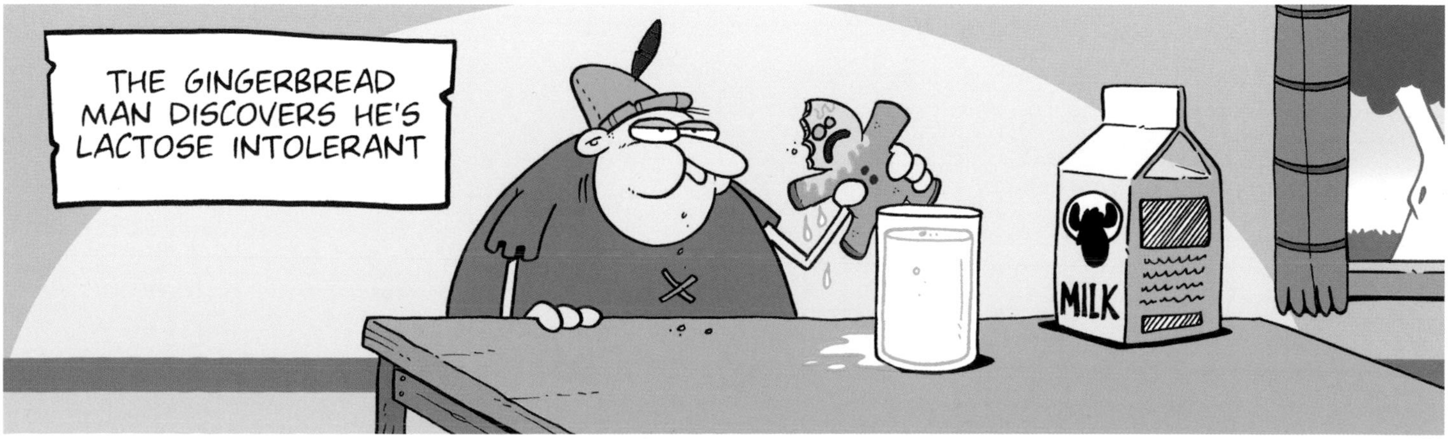
THE GINGERBREAD
MAN DISCOVERS HE'S
LACTOSE INTOLERANT
MILK

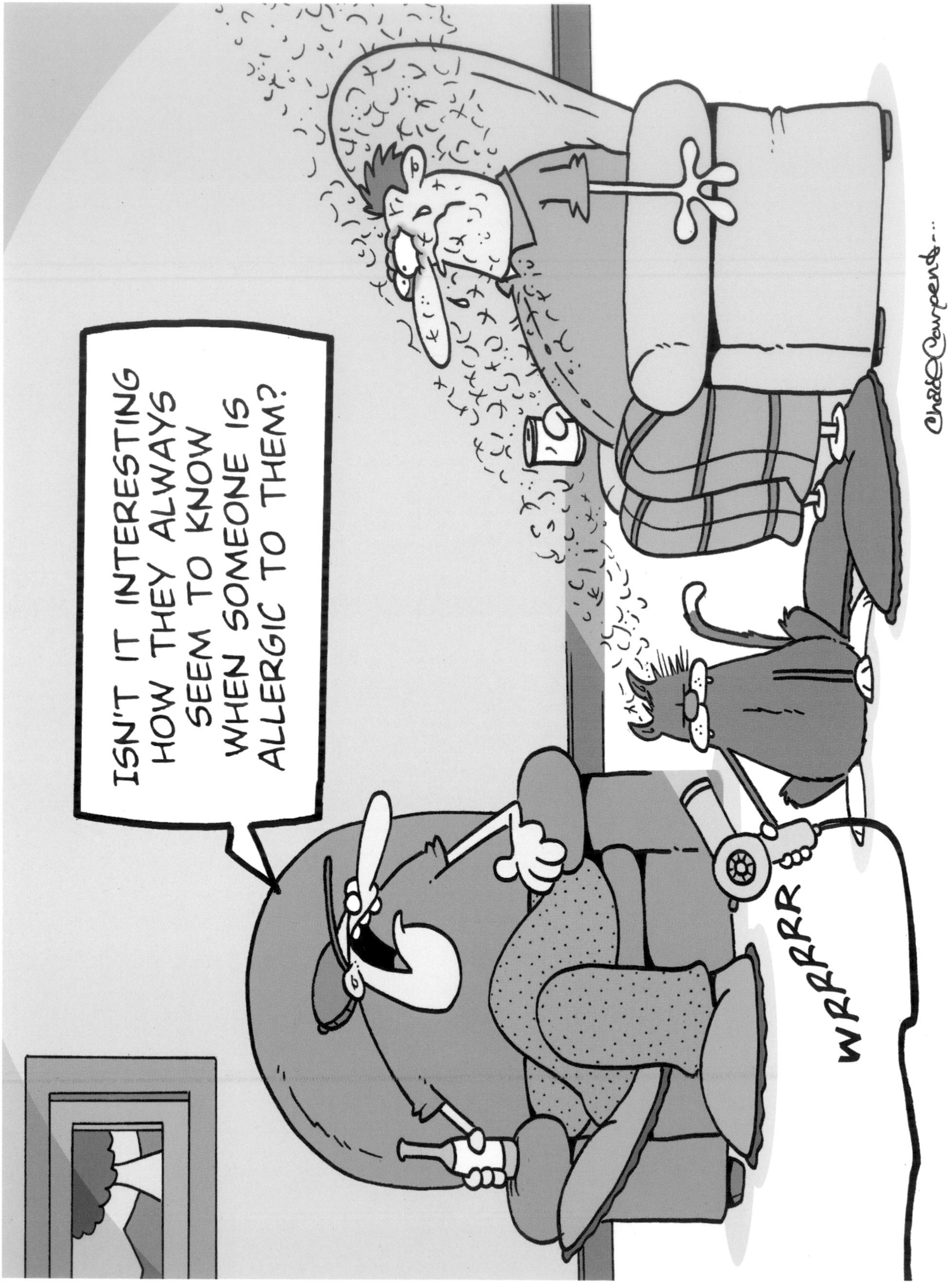
ISN'T IT INTERESTING HOW THEY ALWAYS SEEM TO KNOW WHEN SOMEONE IS ALLERGIC TO THEM?
WRRRRRR

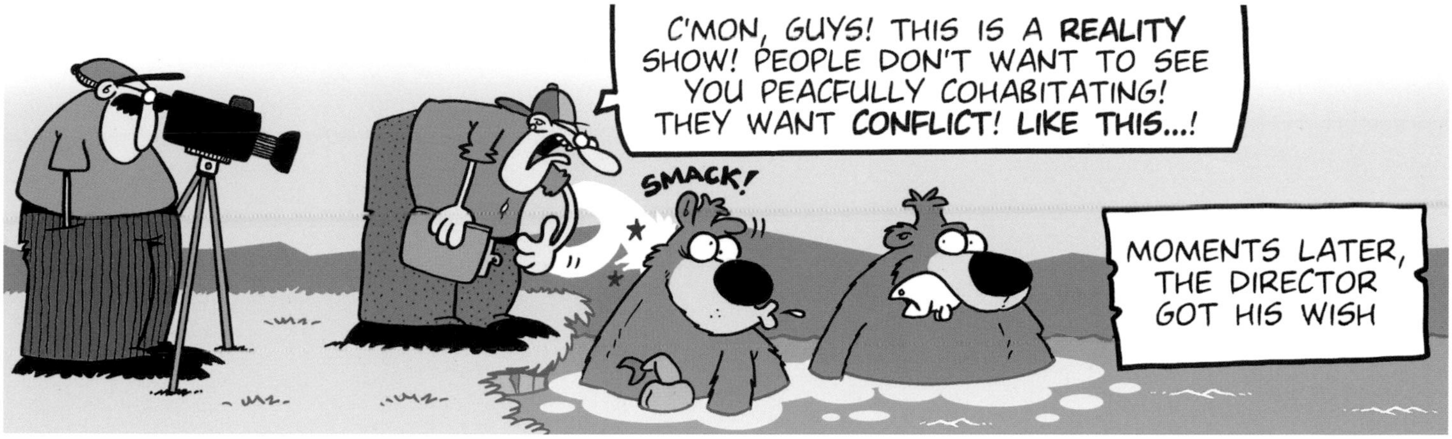
C'MON, GUYS! THIS IS A **REALITY** SHOW! PEOPLE DON'T WANT TO SEE YOU PEACFULLY COHABITATING! THEY WANT **CONFLICT**! **LIKE THIS...!**
SMACK!
MOMENTS LATER, THE DIRECTOR GOT HIS WISH

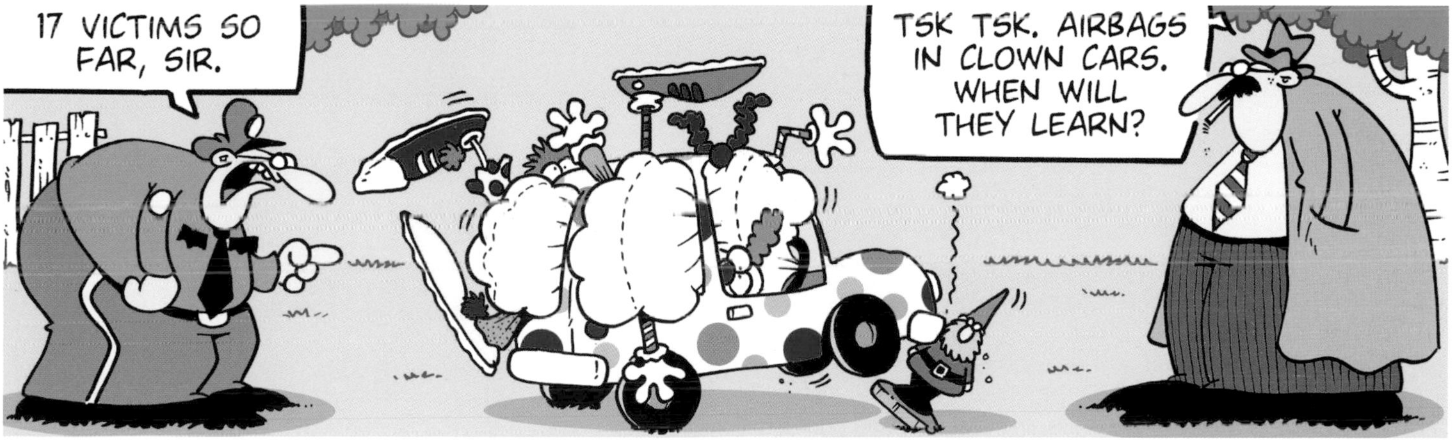
17 VICTIMS SO FAR, SIR.
TSK TSK. AIRBAGS IN CLOWN CARS. WHEN WILL THEY LEARN?

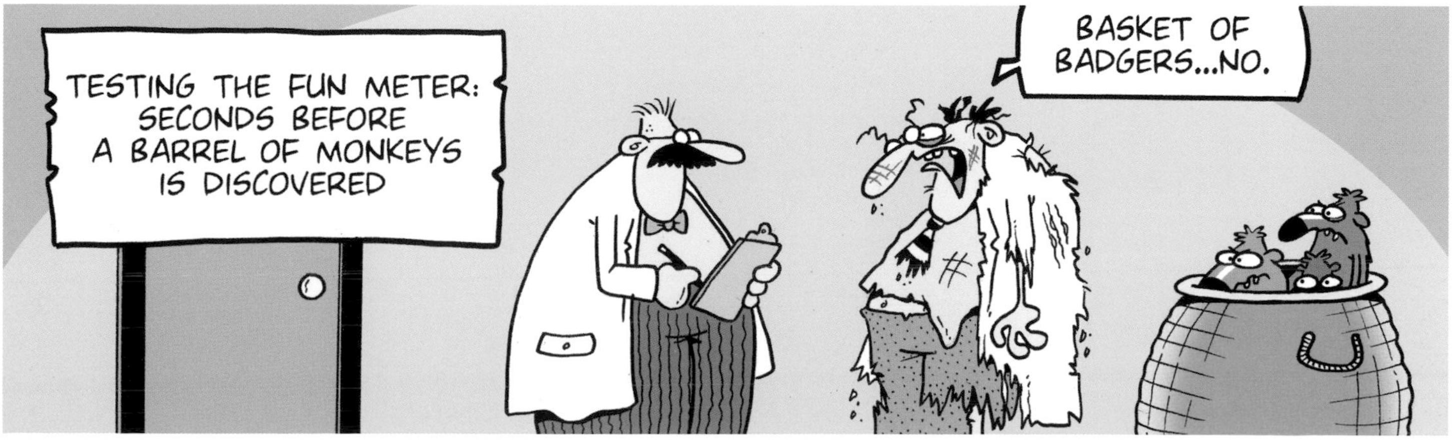
TESTING THE FUN METER: SECONDS BEFORE A BARREL OF MONKEYS IS DISCOVERED
BASKET OF BADGERS...NO.

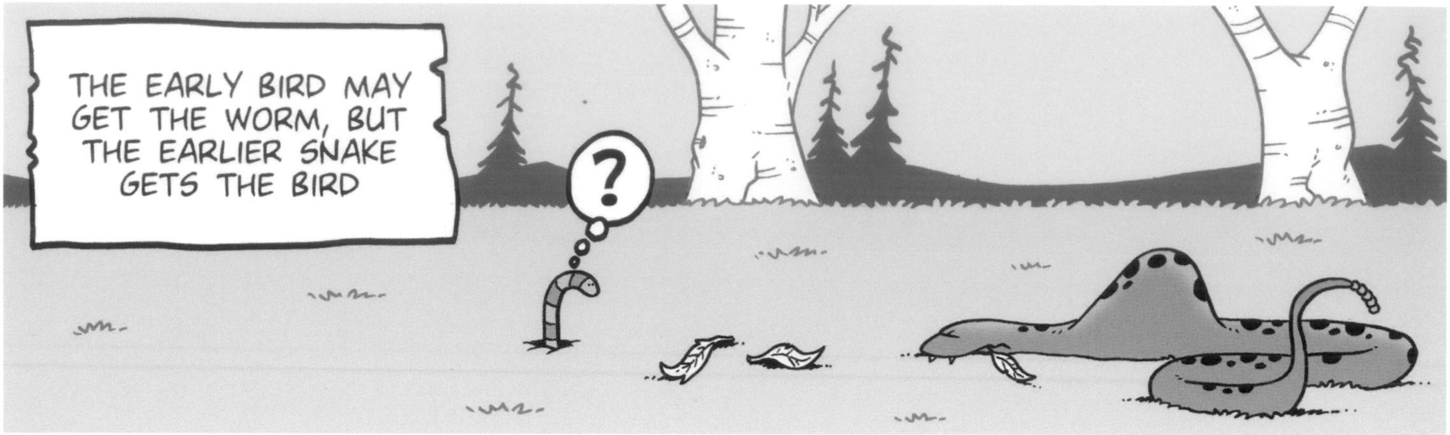
THE EARLY BIRD MAY GET THE WORM, BUT THE EARLIER SNAKE GETS THE BIRD
?

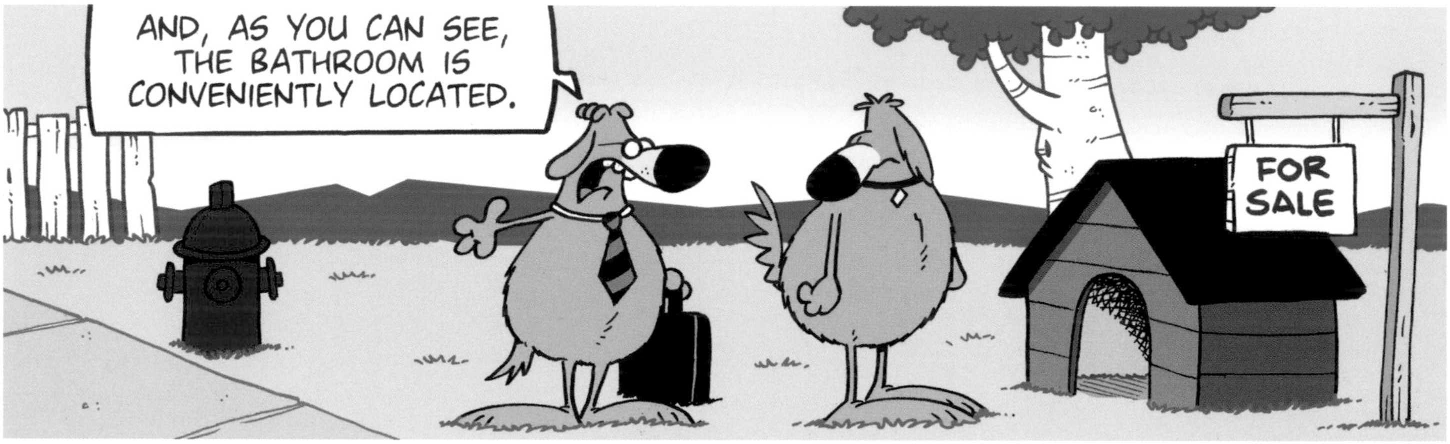
AND, AS YOU CAN SEE, THE BATHROOM IS CONVENIENTLY LOCATED.
FOR SALE

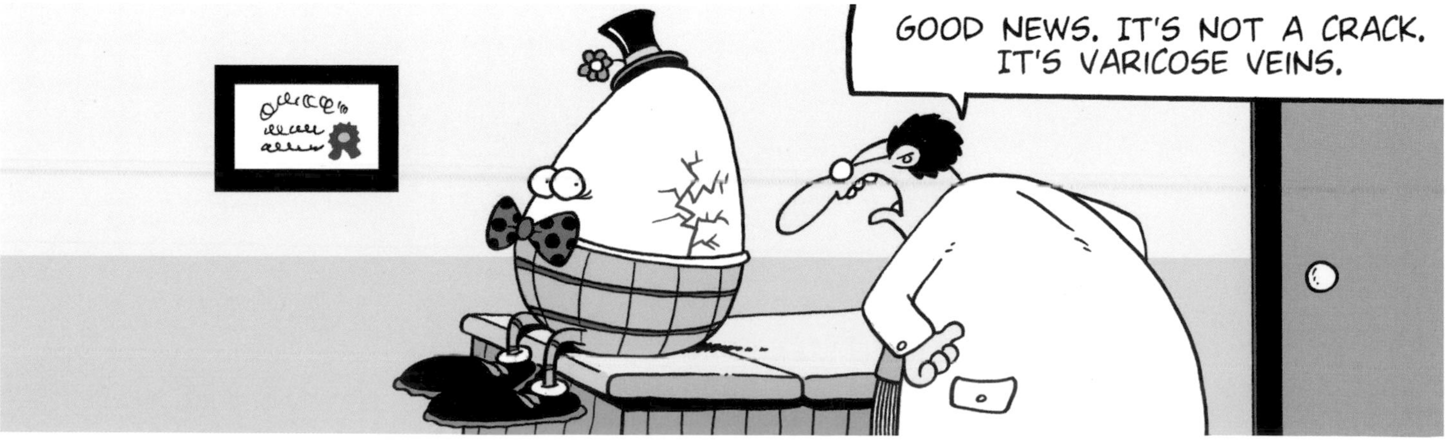
GOOD NEWS. IT'S NOT A CRACK. IT'S VARICOSE VEINS.

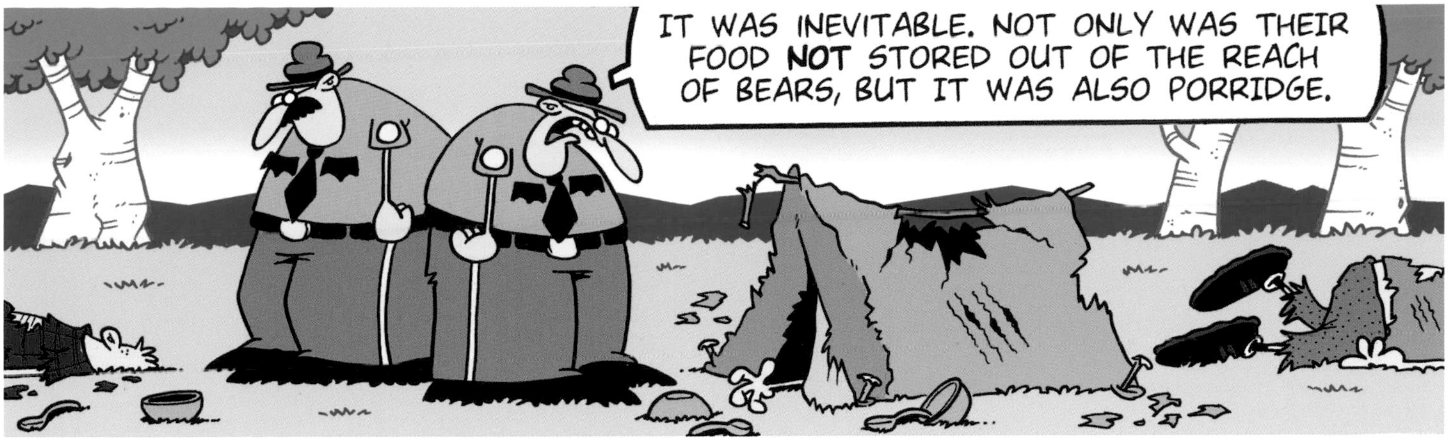
IT WAS INEVITABLE. NOT ONLY WAS THEIR FOOD **NOT** STORED OUT OF THE REACH OF BEARS, BUT IT WAS ALSO PORRIDGE.

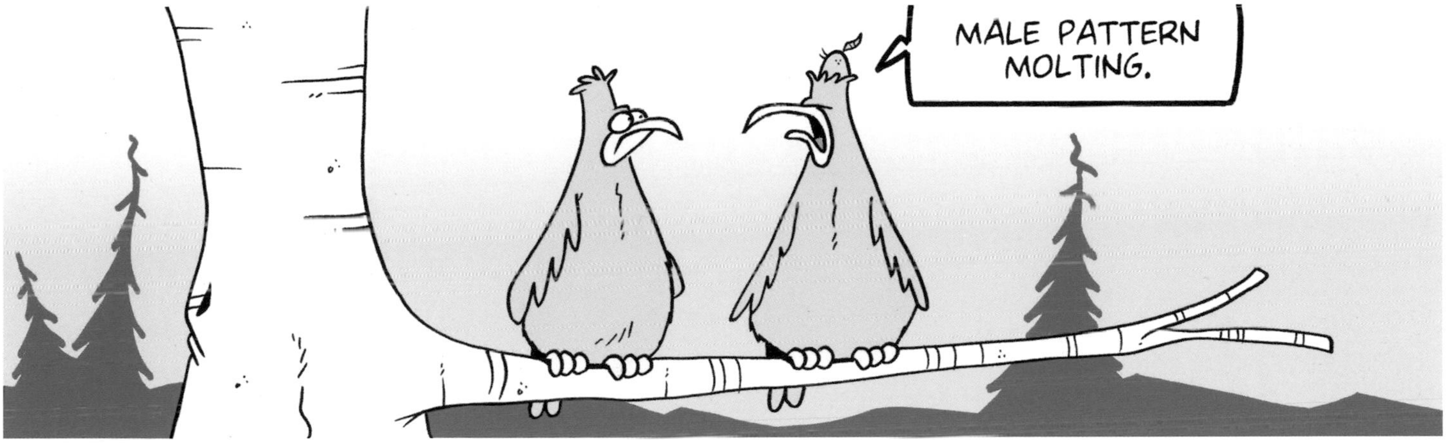
MALE PATTERN MOLTING.

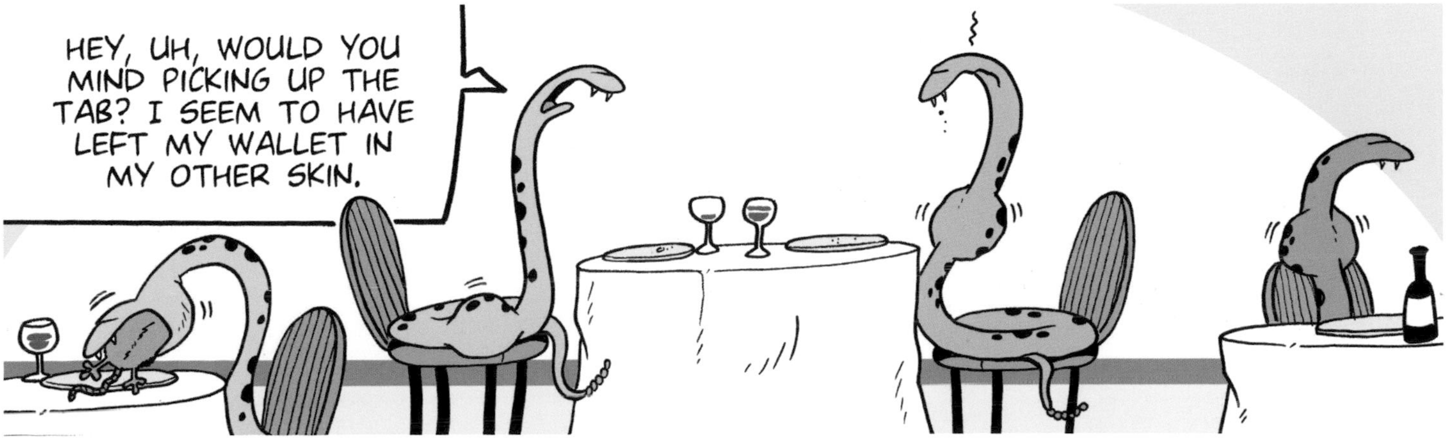
HEY, UH, WOULD YOU MIND PICKING UP THE TAB? I SEEM TO HAVE LEFT MY WALLET IN MY OTHER SKIN.

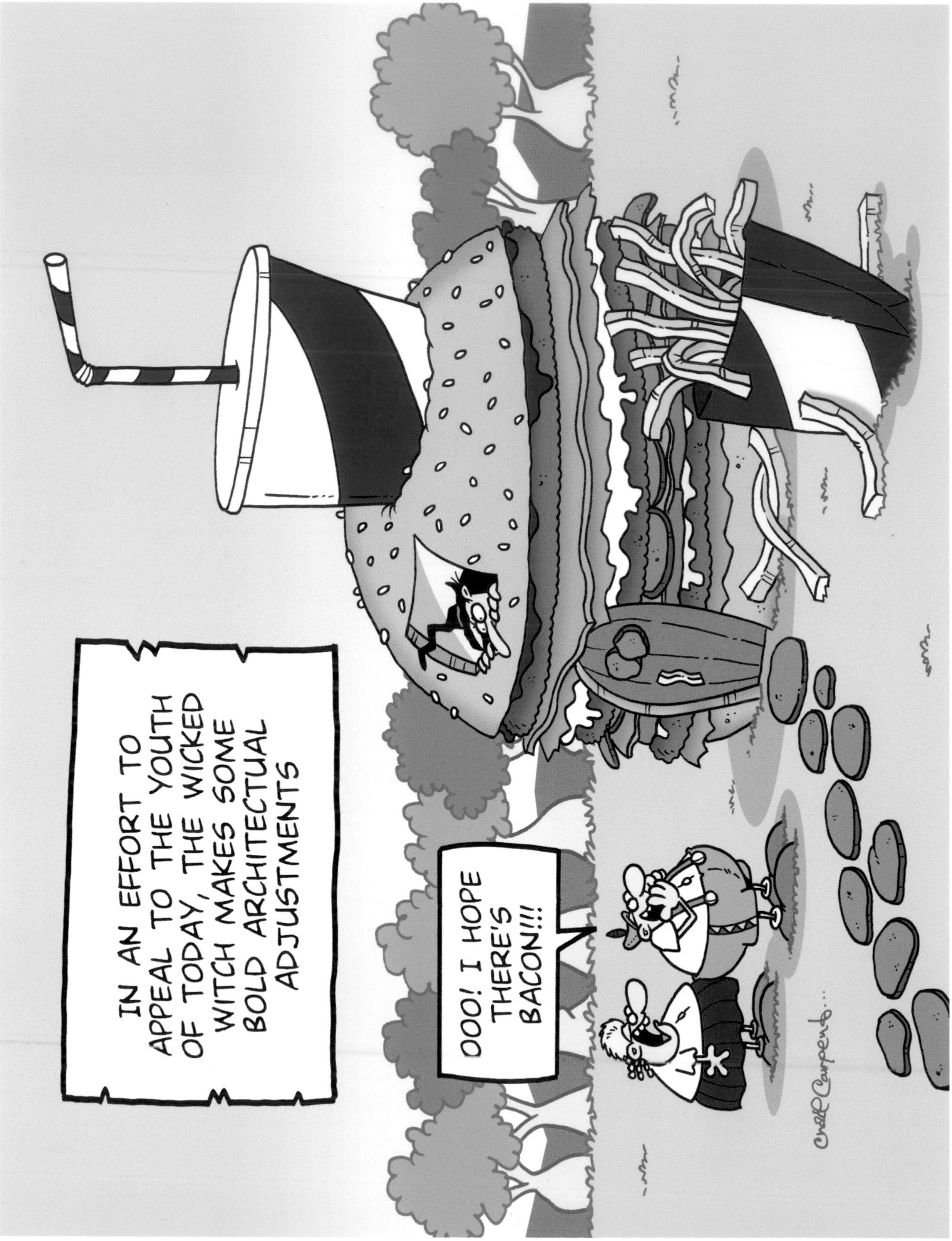
IN AN EFFORT TO APPEAL TO THE YOUTH OF TODAY, THE WICKED WITCH MAKES SOME BOLD ARCHITECTUAL ADJUSTMENTS
OOO! I HOPE THERE'S BACON!!!

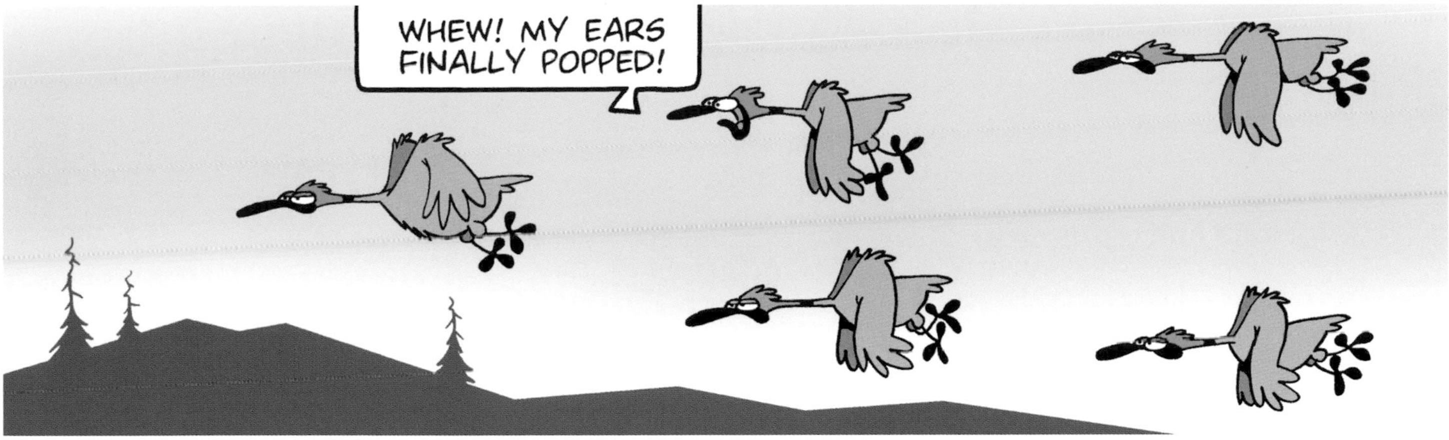
WHEW! MY EARS FINALLY POPPED!

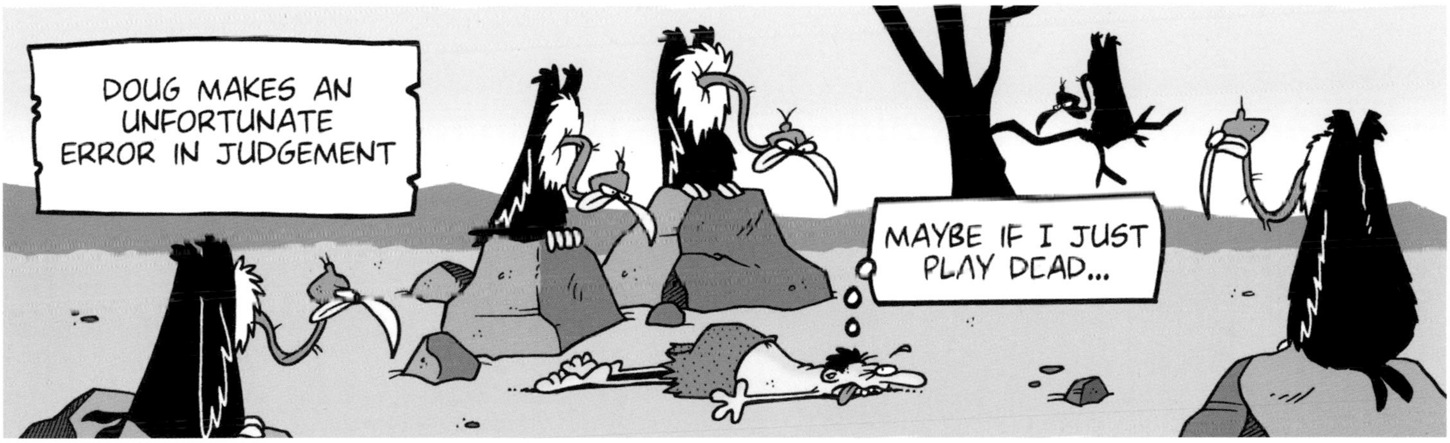
DOUG MAKES AN UNFORTUNATE ERROR IN JUDGEMENT
MAYBE IF I JUST PLAY DEAD...

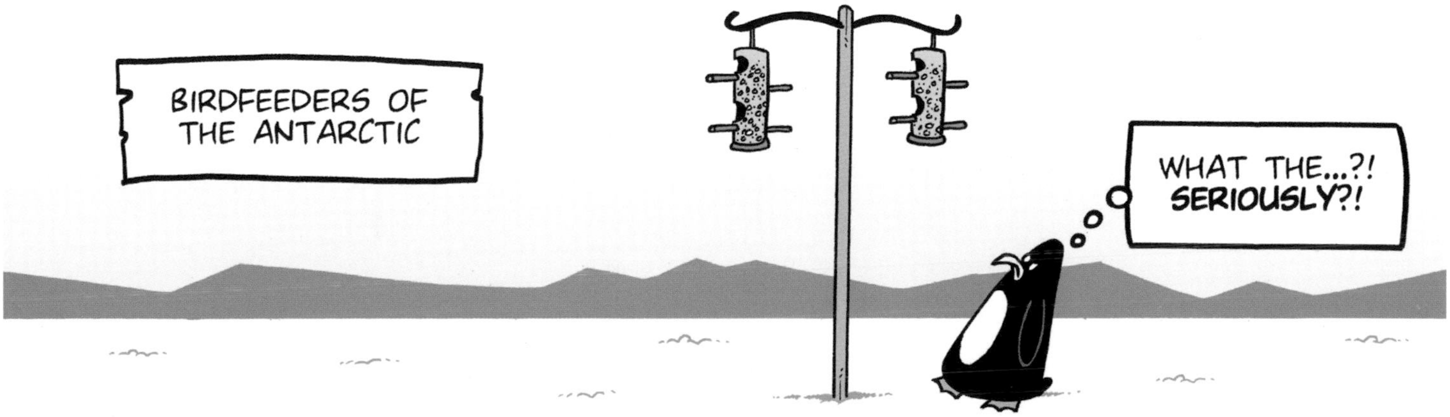
BIRDFEEDERS OF THE ANTARCTIC
WHAT THE...?! **SERIOUSLY?!**

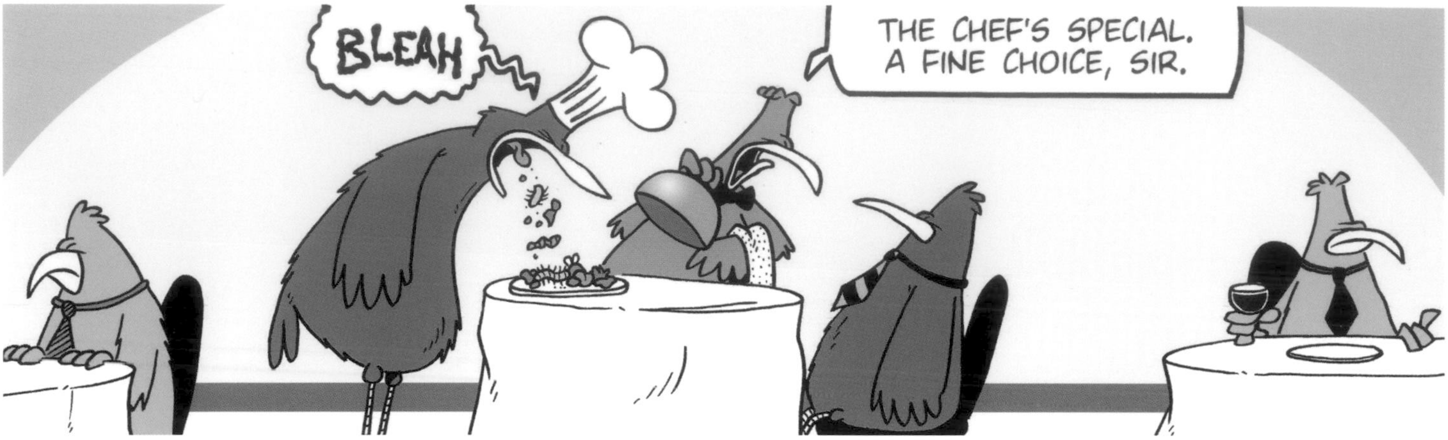
BLEAH
THE CHEF'S SPECIAL. A FINE CHOICE, SIR.

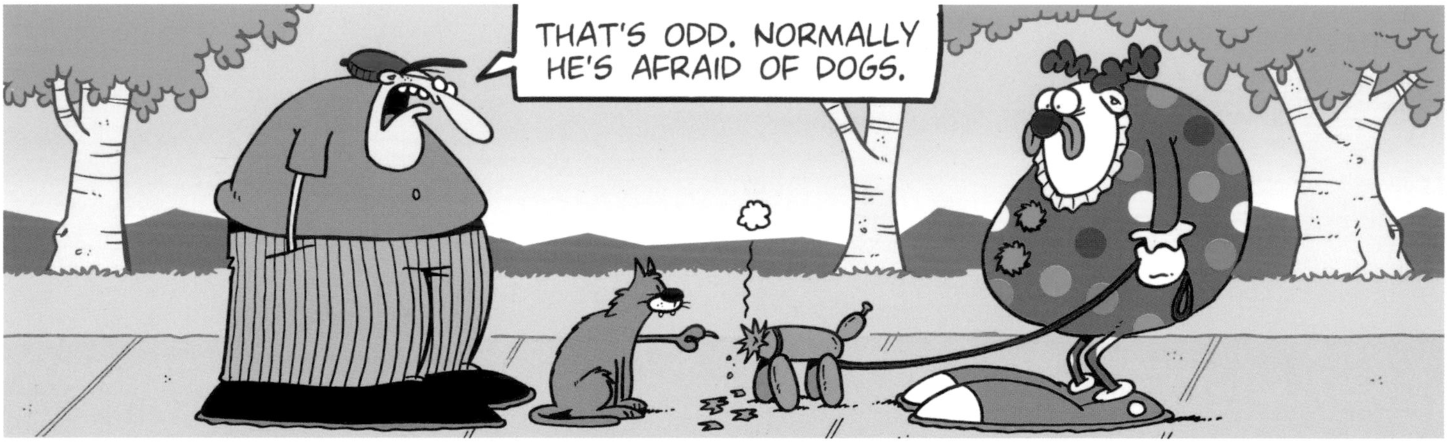
THAT'S ODD. NORMALLY HE'S AFRAID OF DOGS.

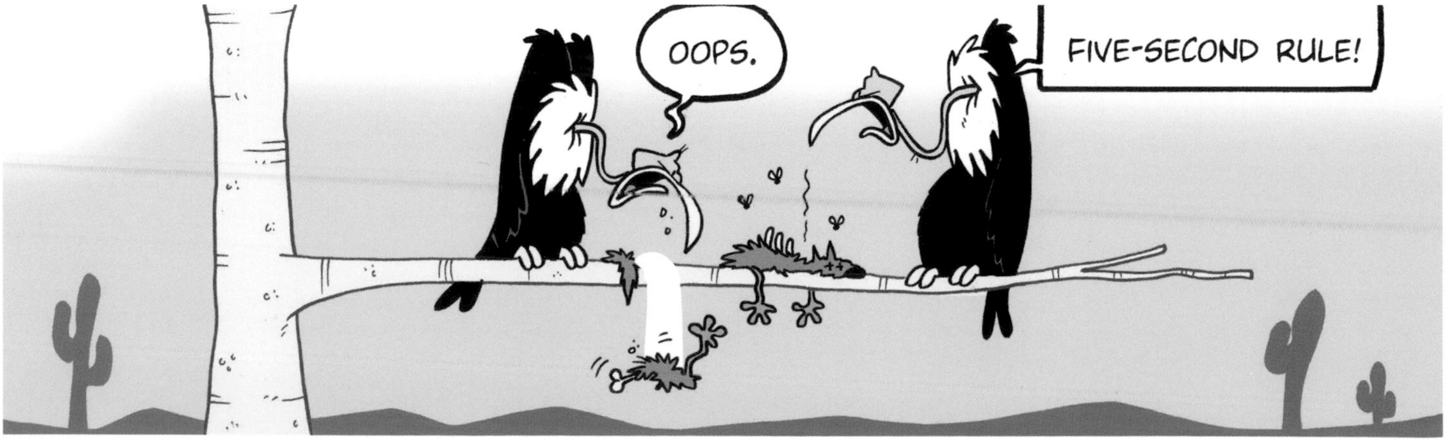
OOPS.
FIVE-SECOND RULE!

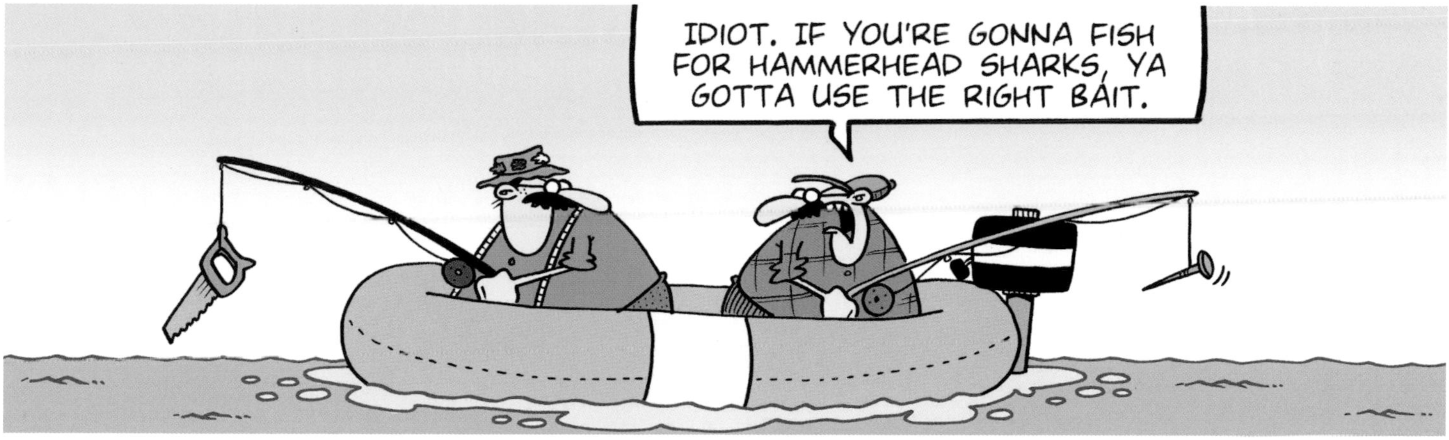
IDIOT. IF YOU'RE GONNA FISH FOR HAMMERHEAD SHARKS, YA GOTTA USE THE RIGHT BAIT.

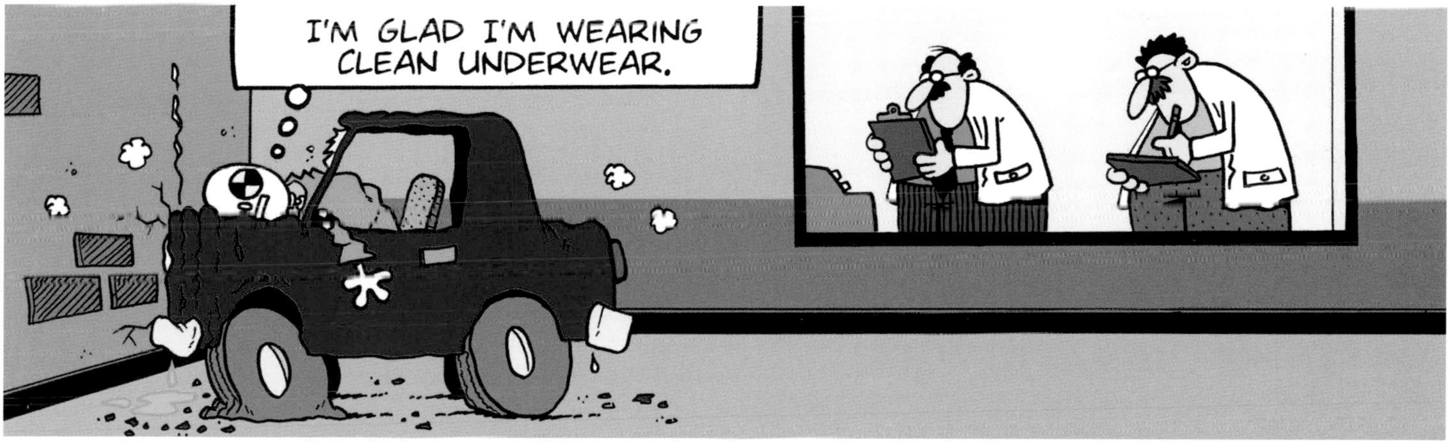
I'M GLAD I'M WEARING CLEAN UNDERWEAR.

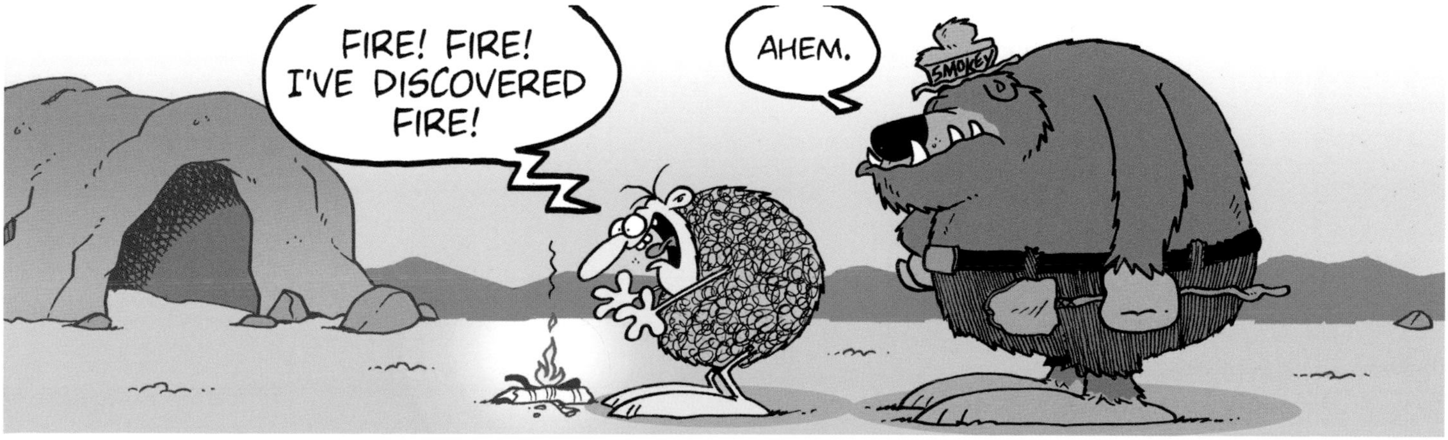
FIRE! FIRE! I'VE DISCOVERED FIRE!
AHEM.
SMOKEY

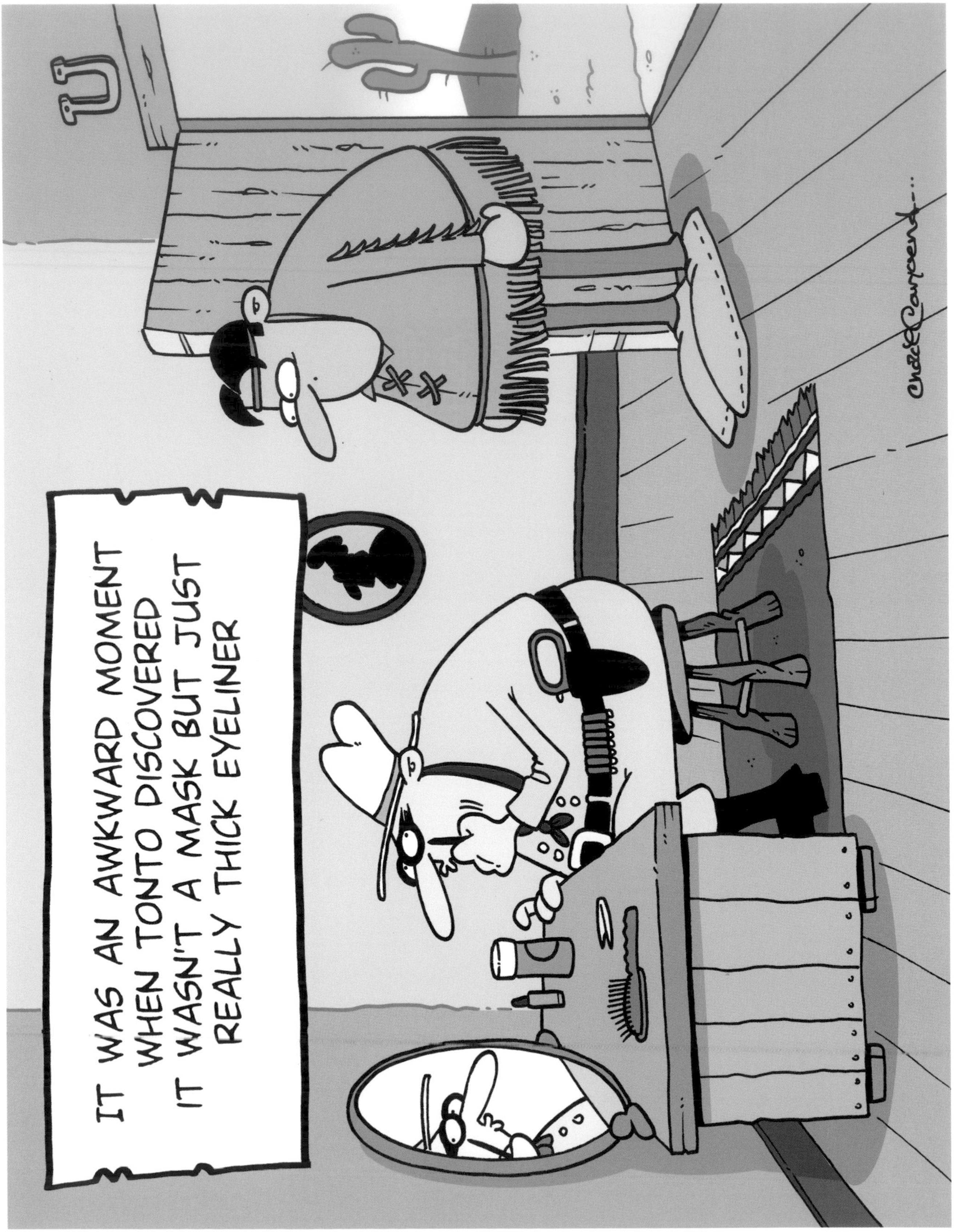
IT WAS AN AWKWARD MOMENT WHEN TONTO DISCOVERED IT WASN'T A MASK BUT JUST REALLY THICK EYELINER

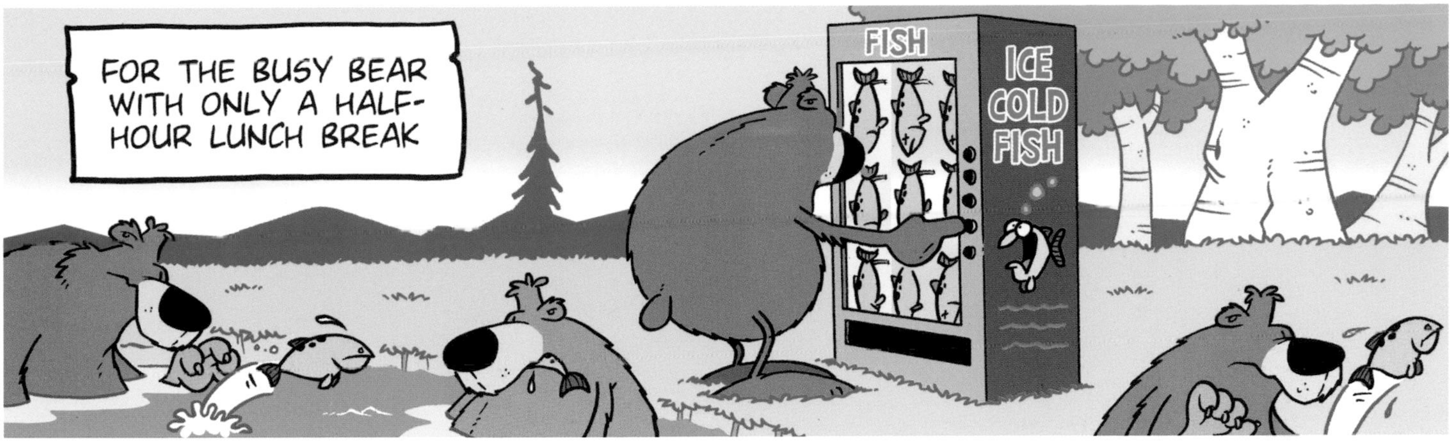
FOR THE BUSY BEAR WITH ONLY A HALF-HOUR LUNCH BREAK
FISH
ICE COLD FISH

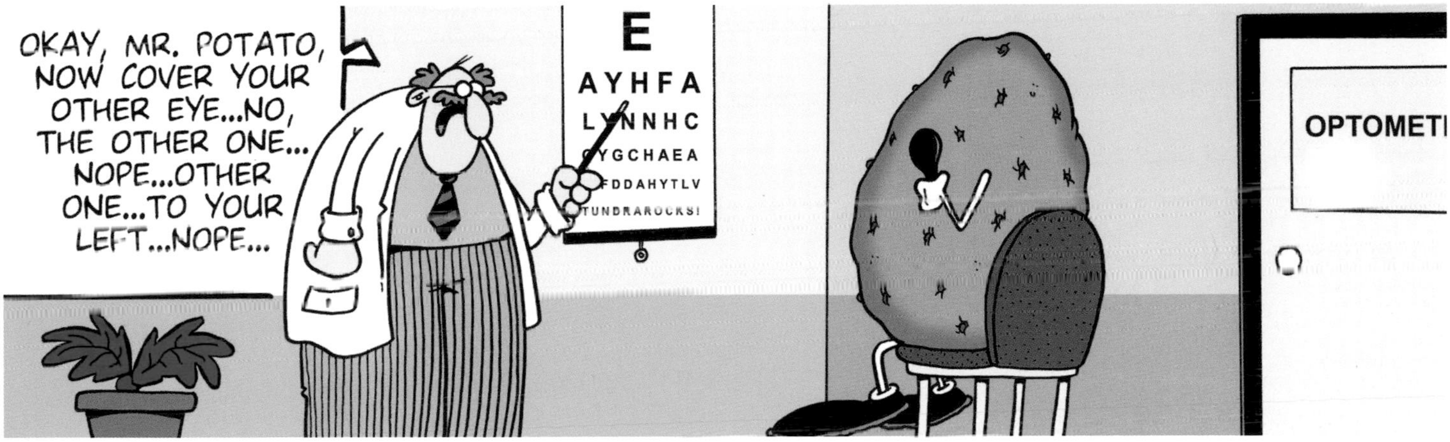
OKAY, MR. POTATO, NOW COVER YOUR OTHER EYE...NO, THE OTHER ONE... NOPE...OTHER ONE...TO YOUR LEFT...NOPE...
E
AYHFA
TUNDRAROCKS!

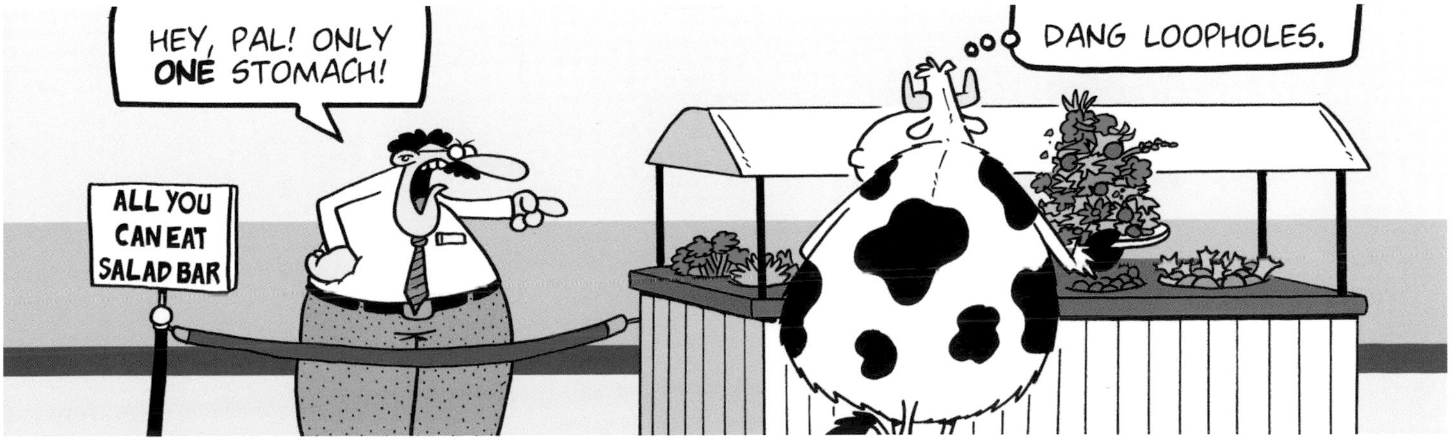
HEY, PAL! ONLY **ONE** STOMACH!
DANG LOOPHOLES.
ALL YOU CAN EAT SALAD BAR

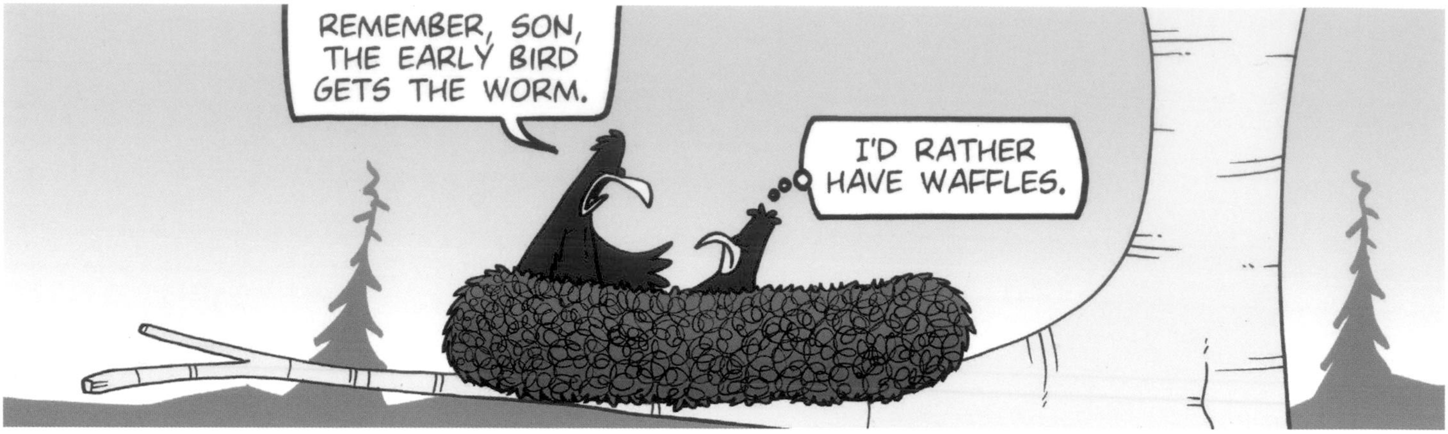
REMEMBER, SON, THE EARLY BIRD GETS THE WORM.
I'D RATHER HAVE WAFFLES.

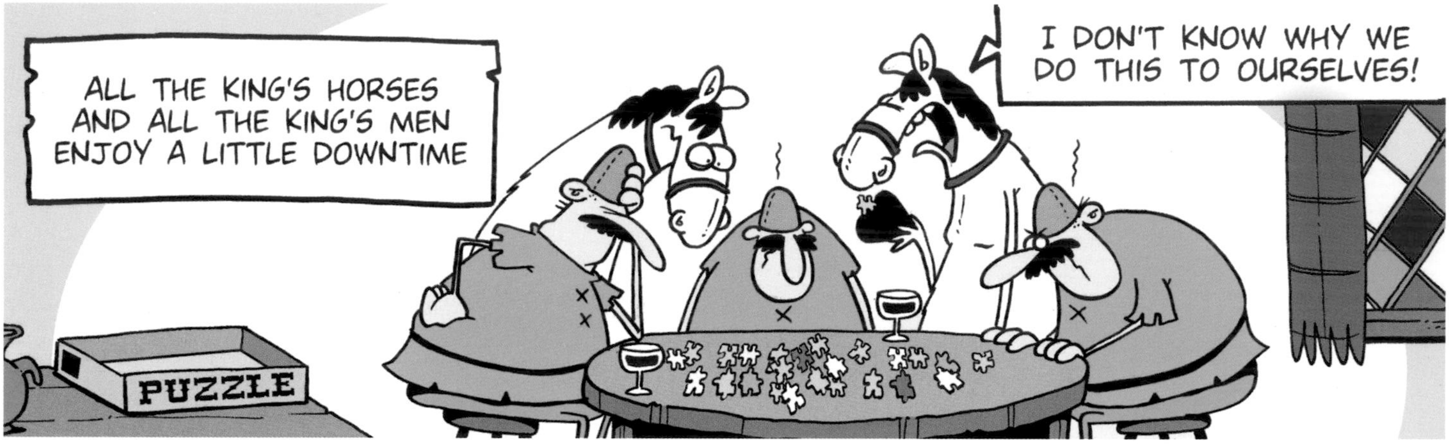
ALL THE KING'S HORSES AND ALL THE KING'S MEN ENJOY A LITTLE DOWNTIME
I DON'T KNOW WHY WE DO THIS TO OURSELVES!
PUZZLE

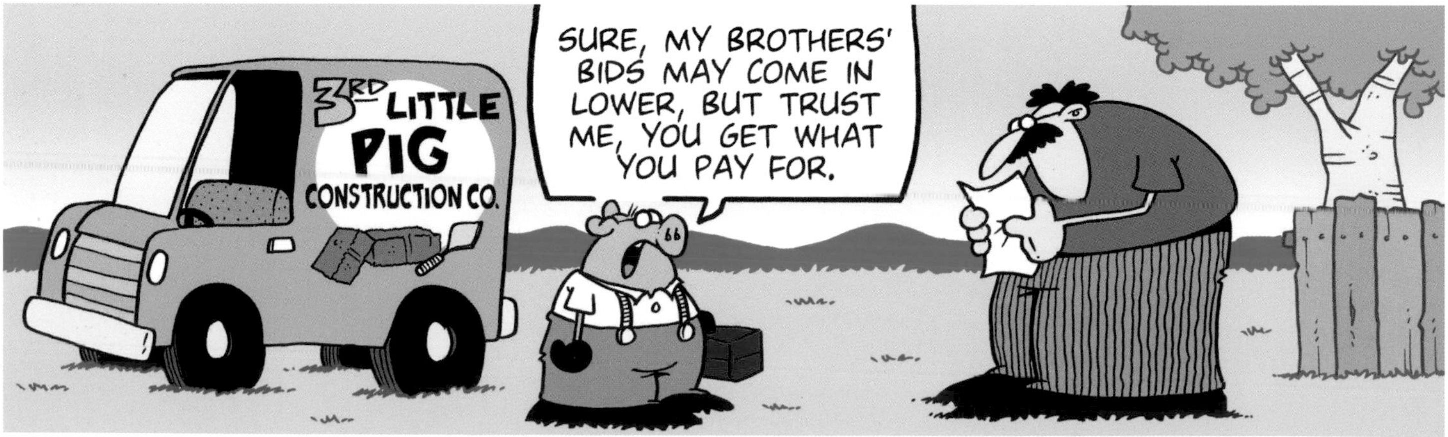
3RD LITTLE PIG CONSTRUCTION CO.
SURE, MY BROTHERS' BIDS MAY COME IN LOWER, BUT TRUST ME, YOU GET WHAT YOU PAY FOR.

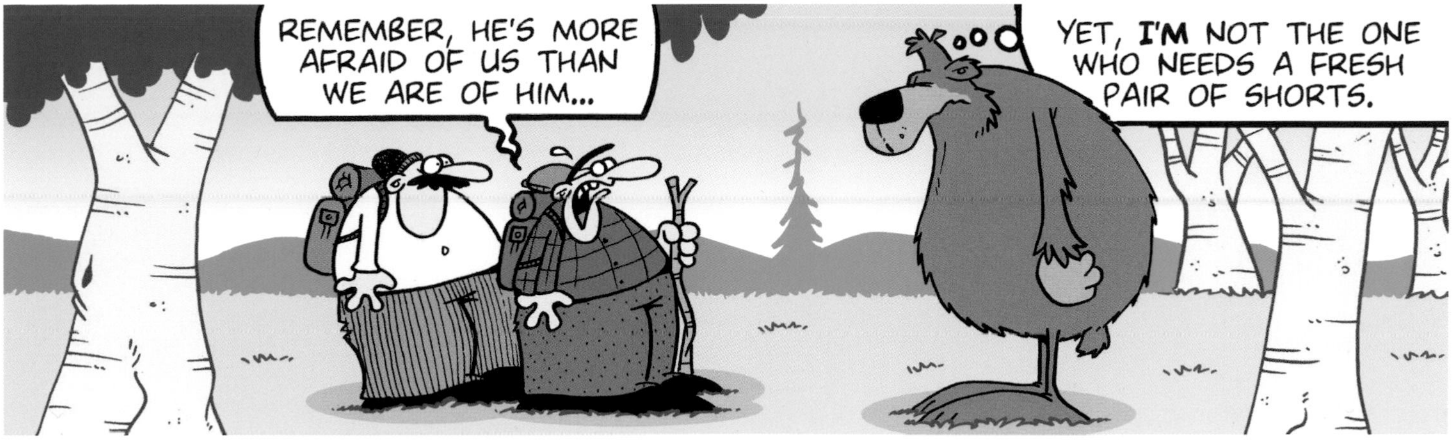
REMEMBER, HE'S MORE AFRAID OF US THAN WE ARE OF HIM...
YET, **I'M** NOT THE ONE WHO NEEDS A FRESH PAIR OF SHORTS.

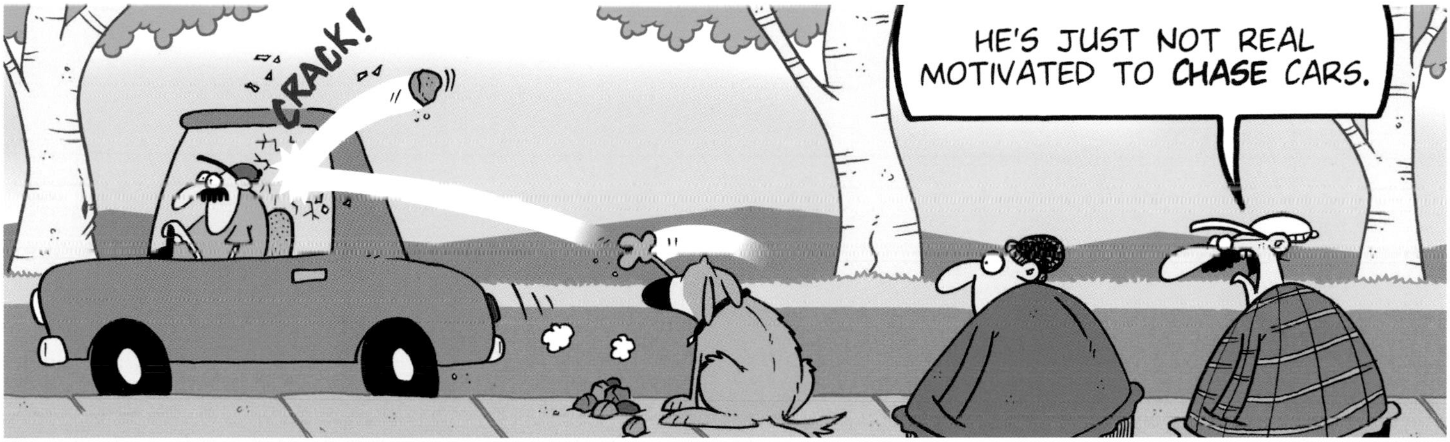
CRACK!
HE'S JUST NOT REAL MOTIVATED TO **CHASE** CARS.

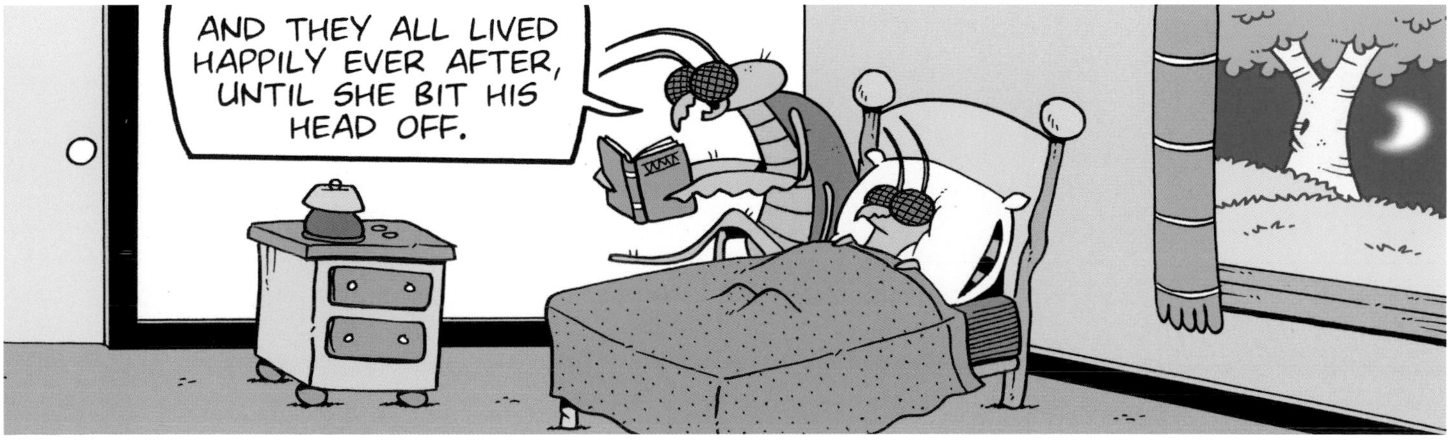
AND THEY ALL LIVED HAPPILY EVER AFTER, UNTIL SHE BIT HIS HEAD OFF.

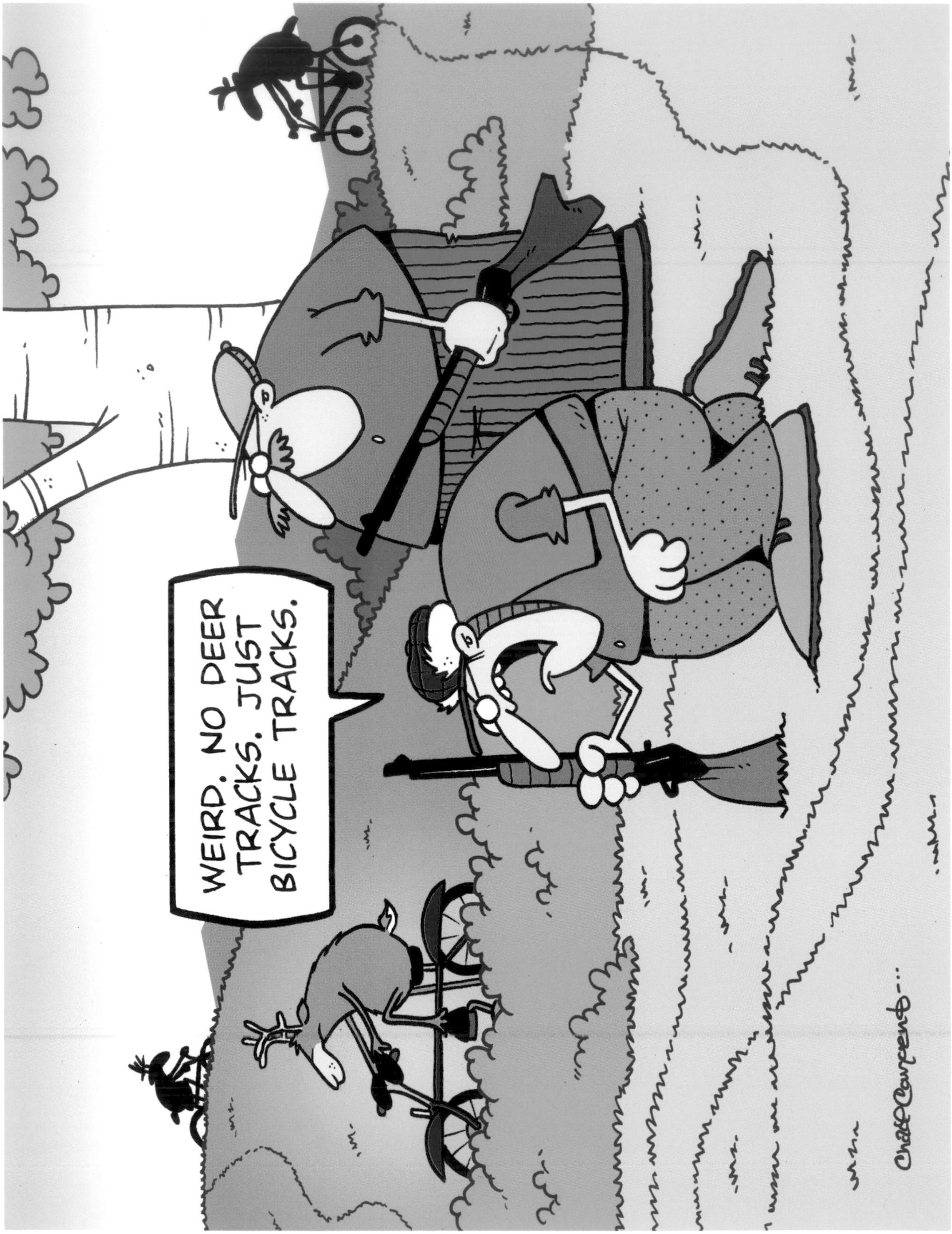
WEIRD. NO DEER TRACKS. JUST BICYCLE TRACKS.

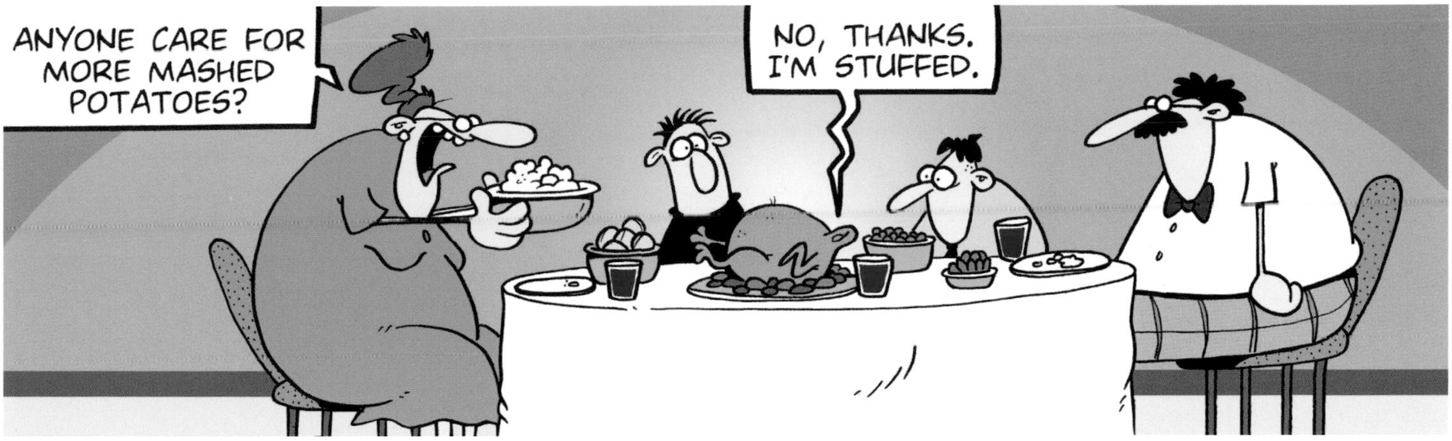
ANYONE CARE FOR MORE MASHED POTATOES?
NO, THANKS. I'M STUFFED.

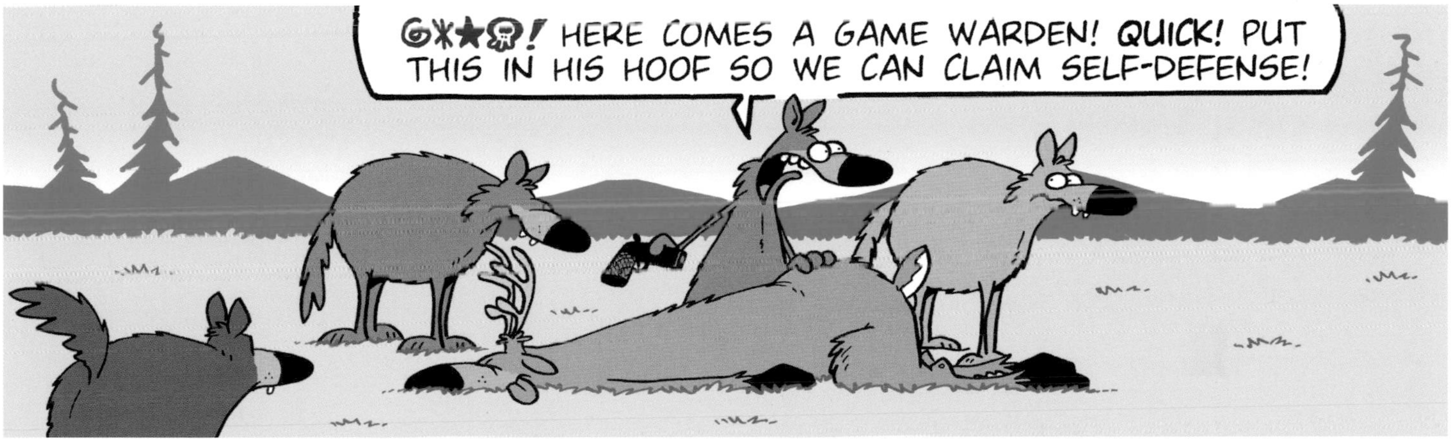
G✱★@! HERE COMES A GAME WARDEN! **QUICK!** PUT THIS IN HIS HOOF SO WE CAN CLAIM SELF-DEFENSE!

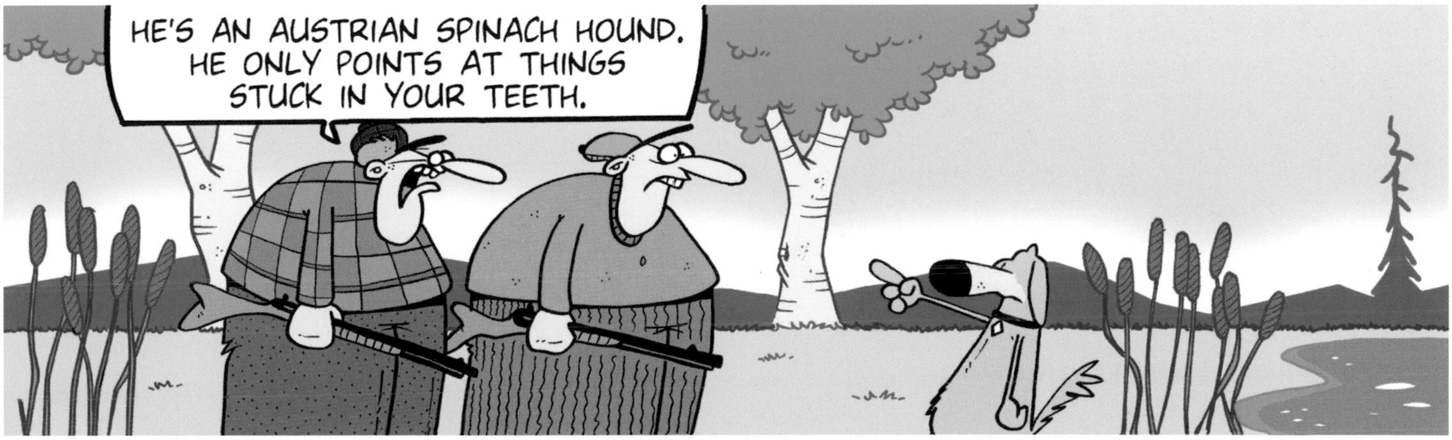
HE'S AN AUSTRIAN SPINACH HOUND. HE ONLY POINTS AT THINGS STUCK IN YOUR TEETH.

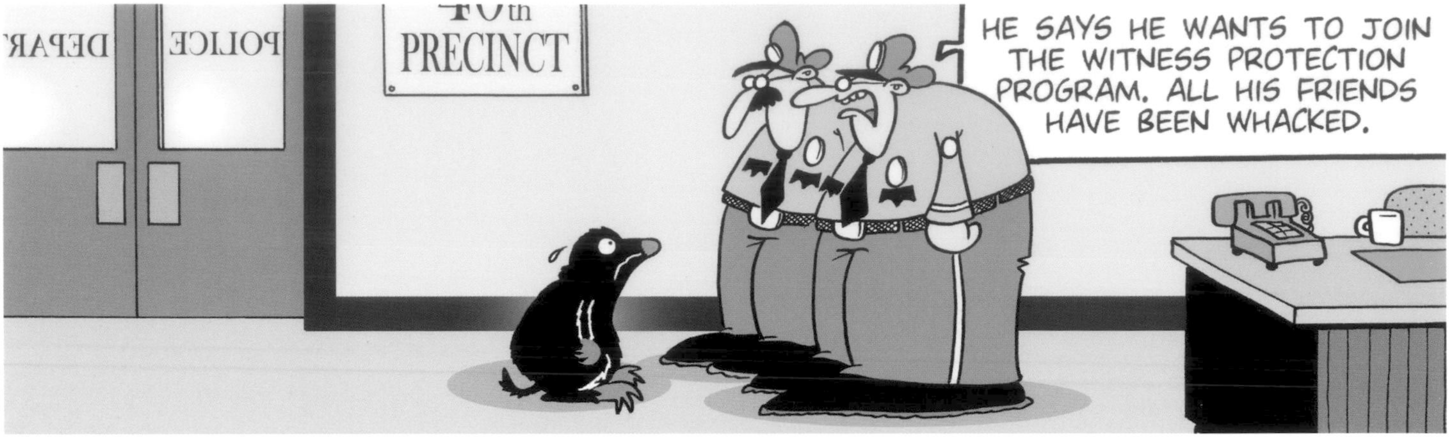
PRECINCT
HE SAYS HE WANTS TO JOIN THE WITNESS PROTECTION PROGRAM. ALL HIS FRIENDS HAVE BEEN WHACKED.

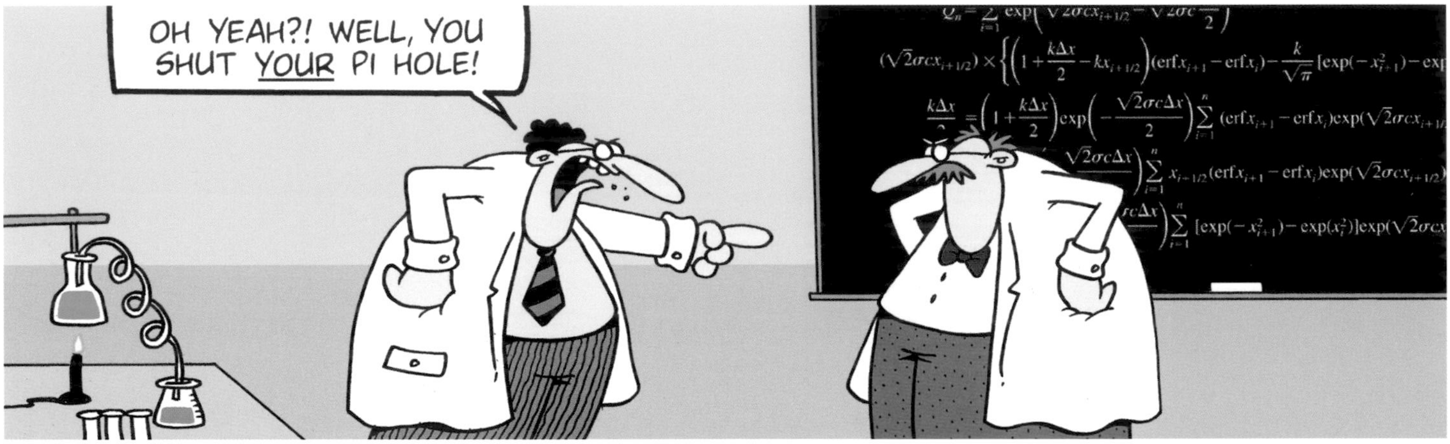
OH YEAH?! WELL, YOU SHUT YOUR PI HOLE!

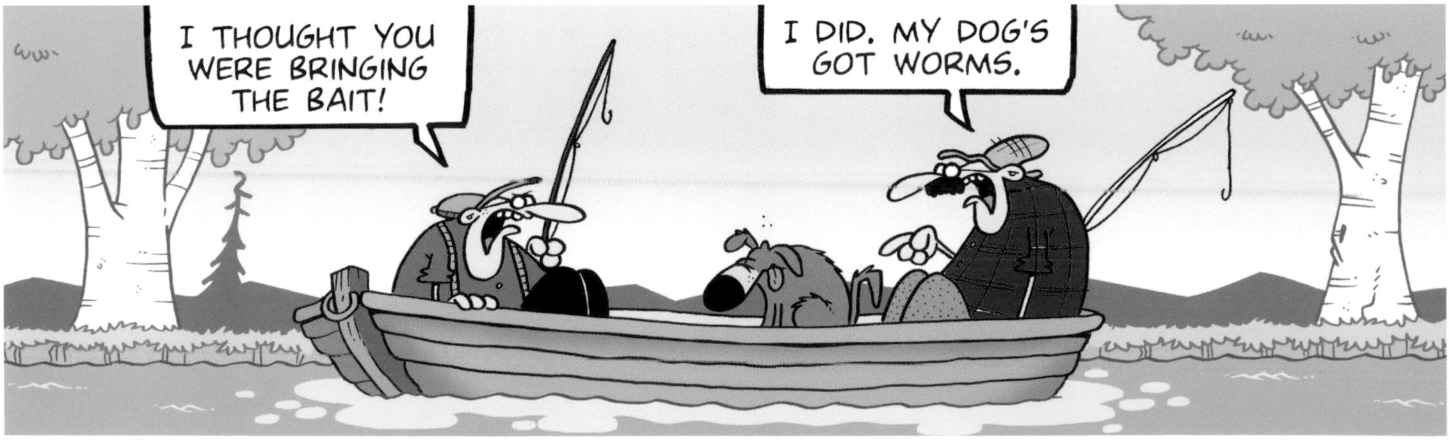
I THOUGHT YOU WERE BRINGING THE BAIT!
I DID. MY DOG'S GOT WORMS.

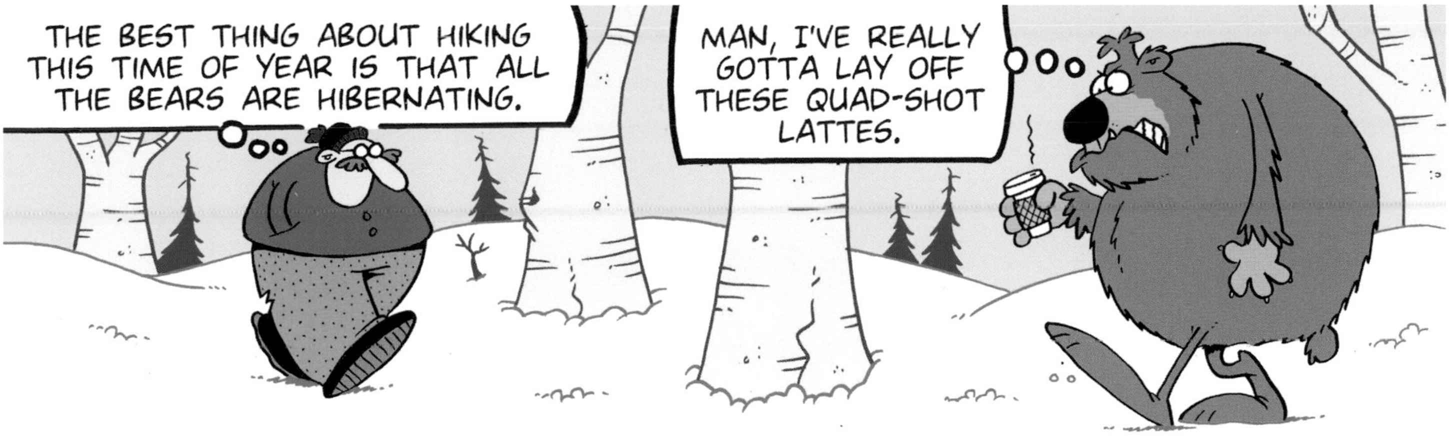

THE BEST THING ABOUT HIKING THIS TIME OF YEAR IS THAT ALL THE BEARS ARE HIBERNATING.
MAN, I'VE REALLY GOTTA LAY OFF THESE QUAD-SHOT LATTES.

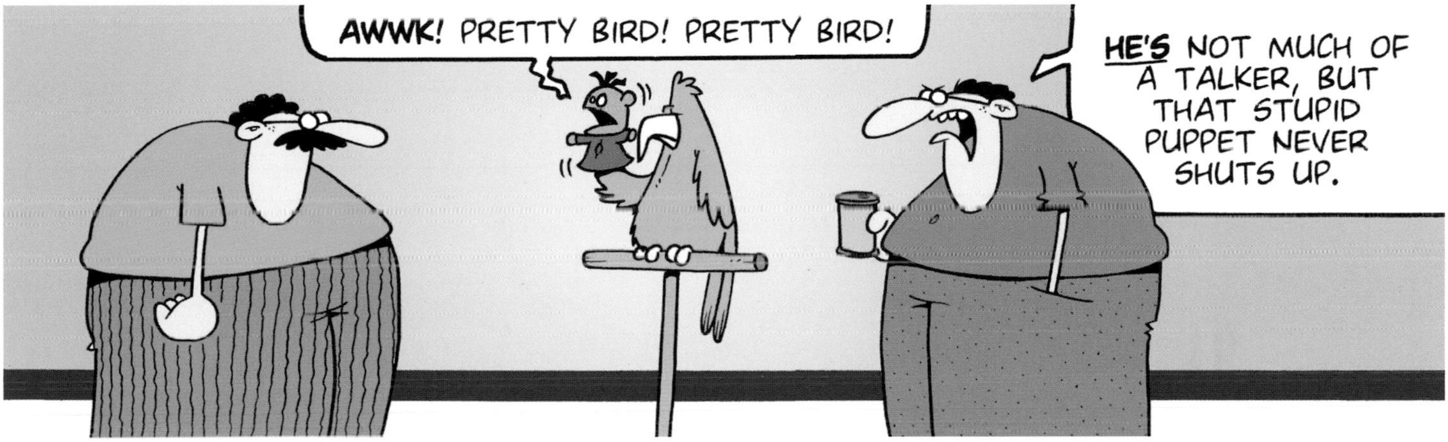

AWWK! PRETTY BIRD! PRETTY BIRD!
HE'S NOT MUCH OF A TALKER, BUT THAT STUPID PUPPET NEVER SHUTS UP.

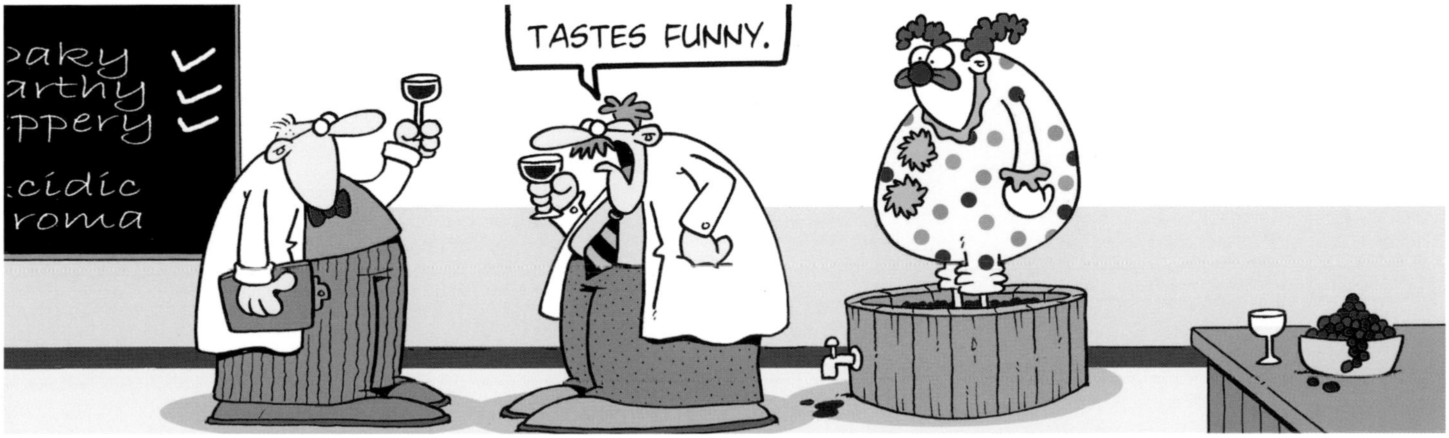

oaky
arthy
ppery
cidic
roma
TASTES FUNNY.

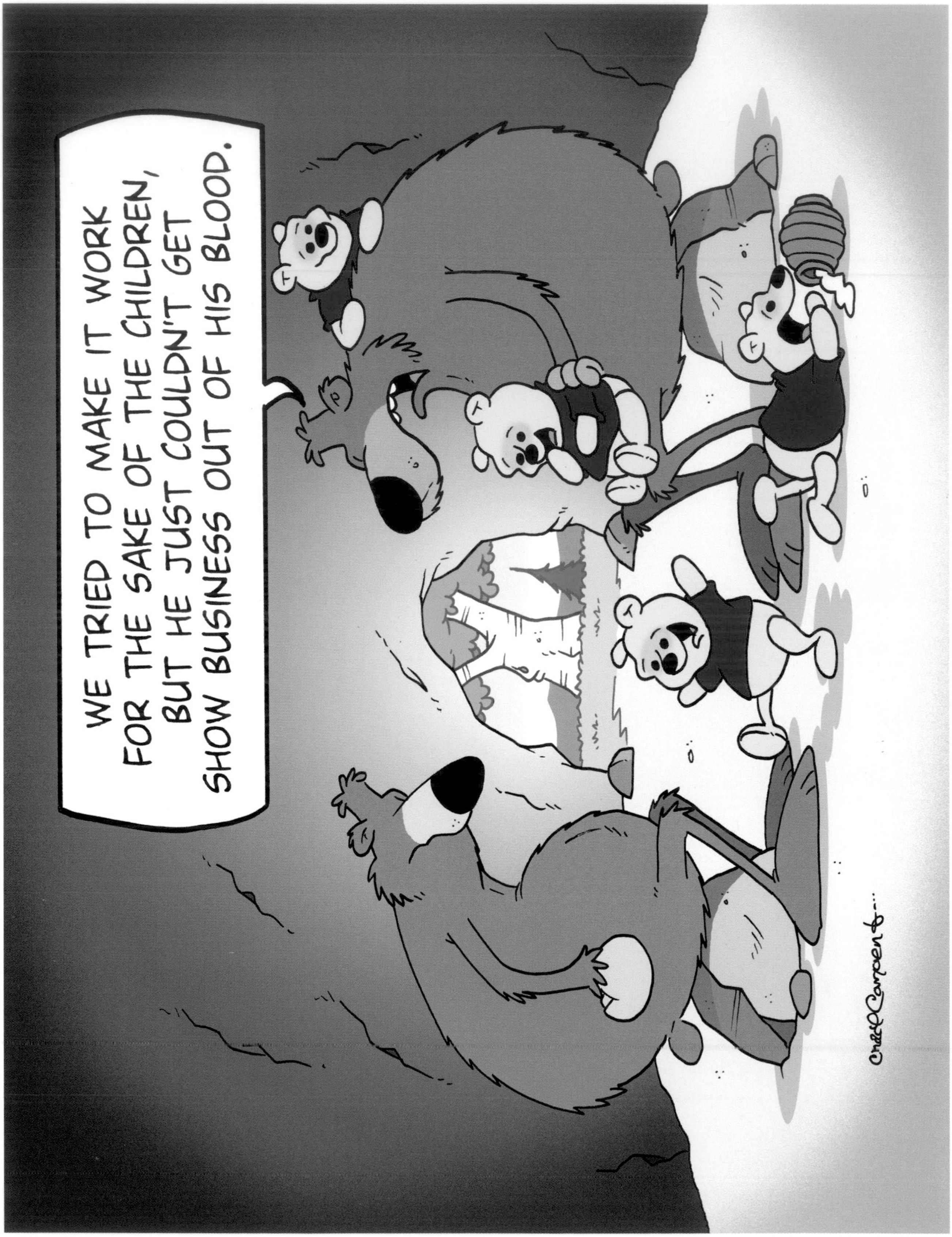
WE TRIED TO MAKE IT WORK FOR THE SAKE OF THE CHILDREN, BUT HE JUST COULDN'T GET SHOW BUSINESS OUT OF HIS BLOOD.

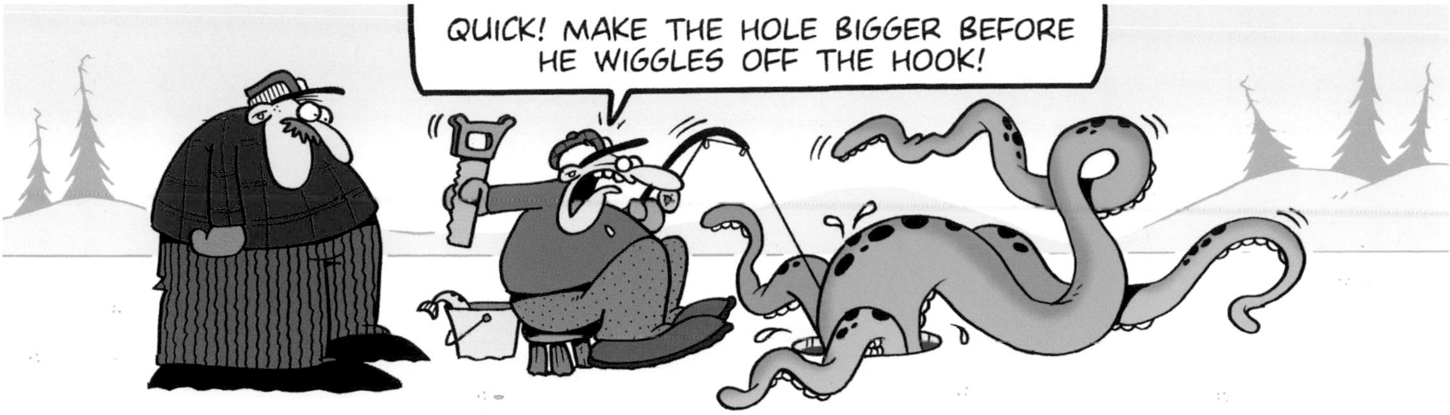
QUICK! MAKE THE HOLE BIGGER BEFORE HE WIGGLES OFF THE HOOK!

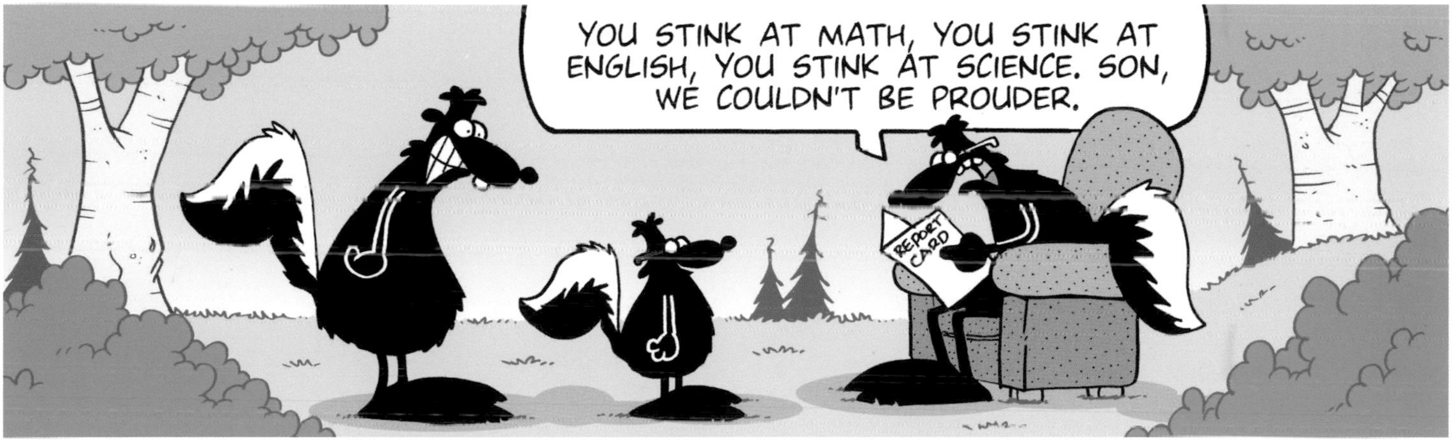
YOU STINK AT MATH, YOU STINK AT ENGLISH, YOU STINK AT SCIENCE. SON, WE COULDN'T BE PROUDER.
REPORT CARD

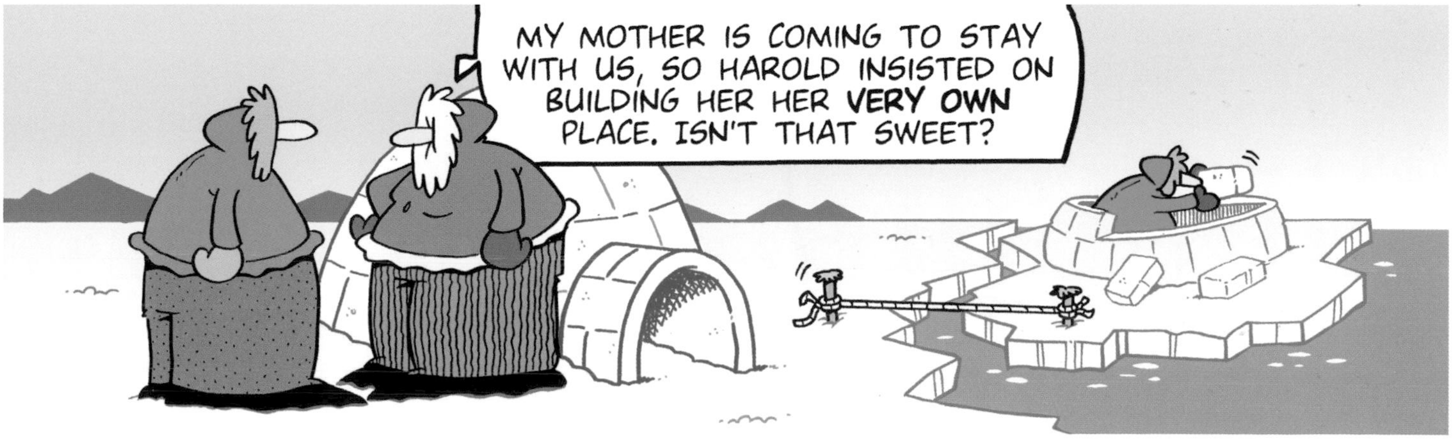
MY MOTHER IS COMING TO STAY WITH US, SO HAROLD INSISTED ON BUILDING HER HER **VERY OWN** PLACE. ISN'T THAT SWEET?

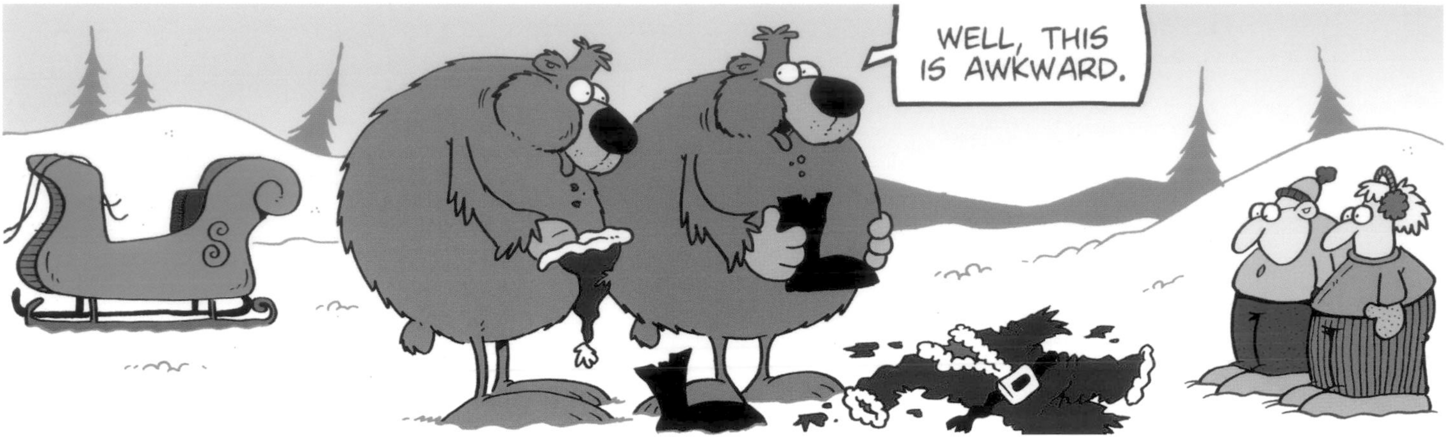
WELL, THIS IS AWKWARD.

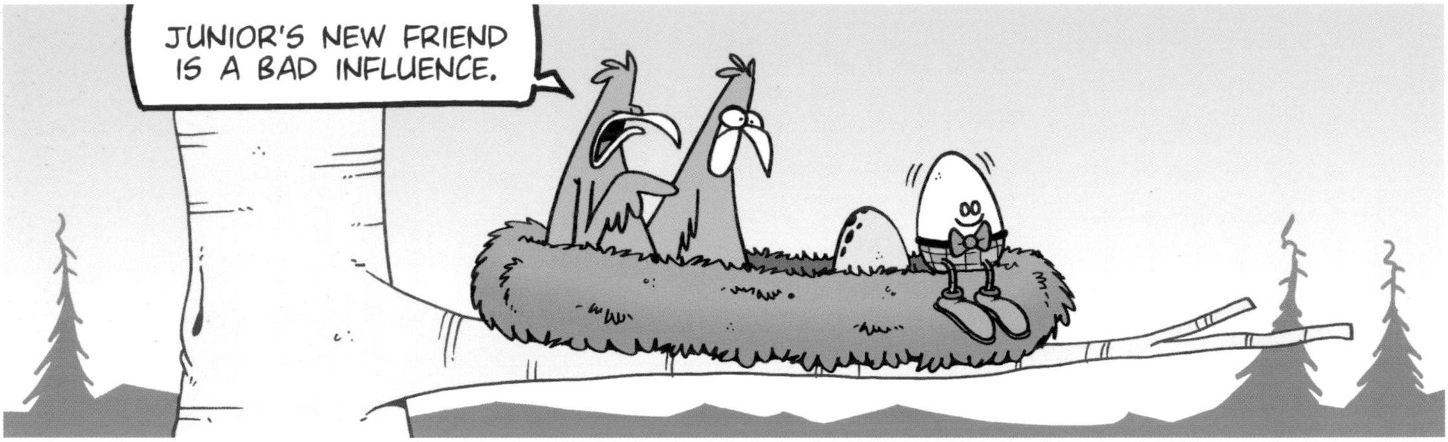
JUNIOR'S NEW FRIEND IS A BAD INFLUENCE.

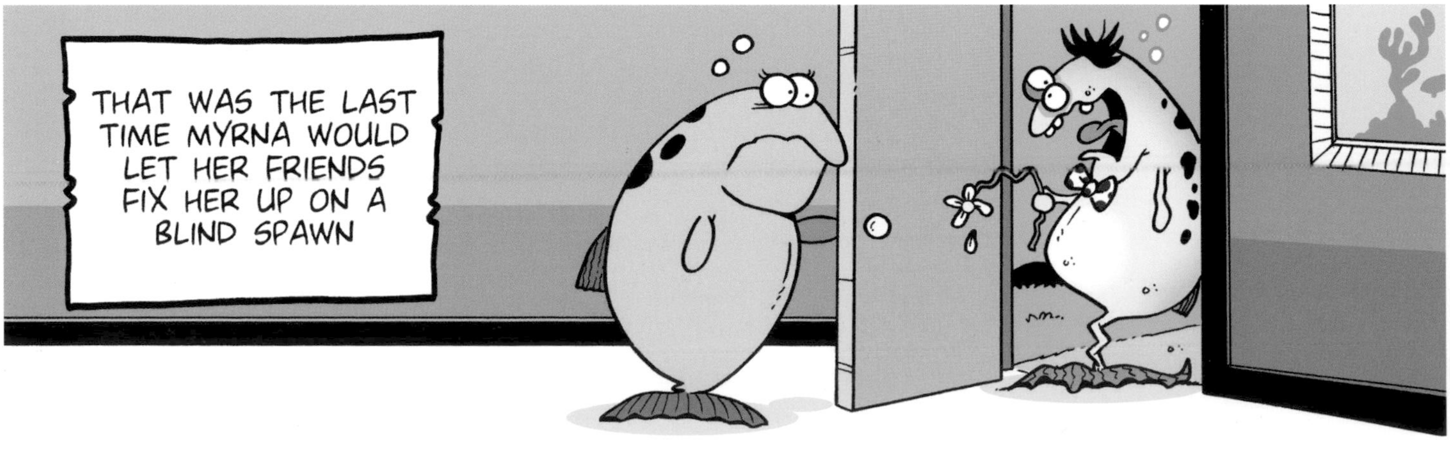
THAT WAS THE LAST TIME MYRNA WOULD LET HER FRIENDS FIX HER UP ON A BLIND SPAWN

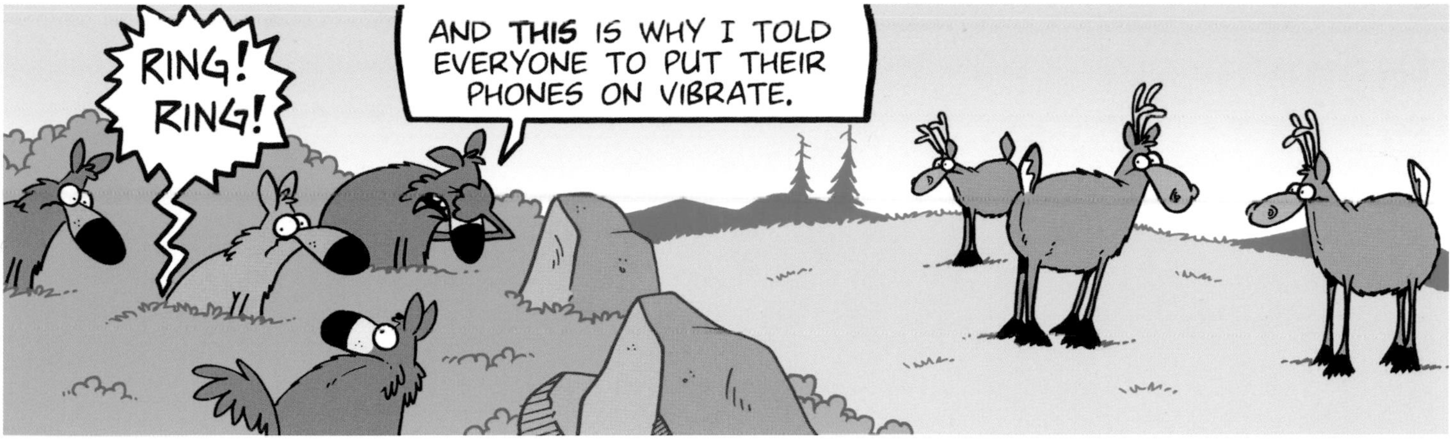
RING! RING!
AND THIS IS WHY I TOLD EVERYONE TO PUT THEIR PHONES ON VIBRATE.

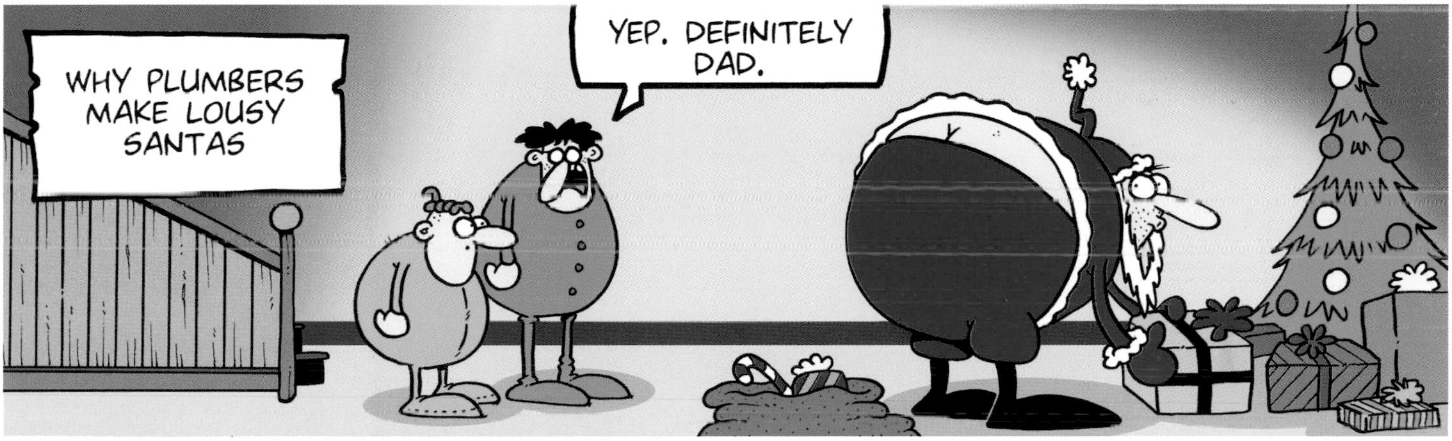
WHY PLUMBERS MAKE LOUSY SANTAS
YEP. DEFINITELY DAD.

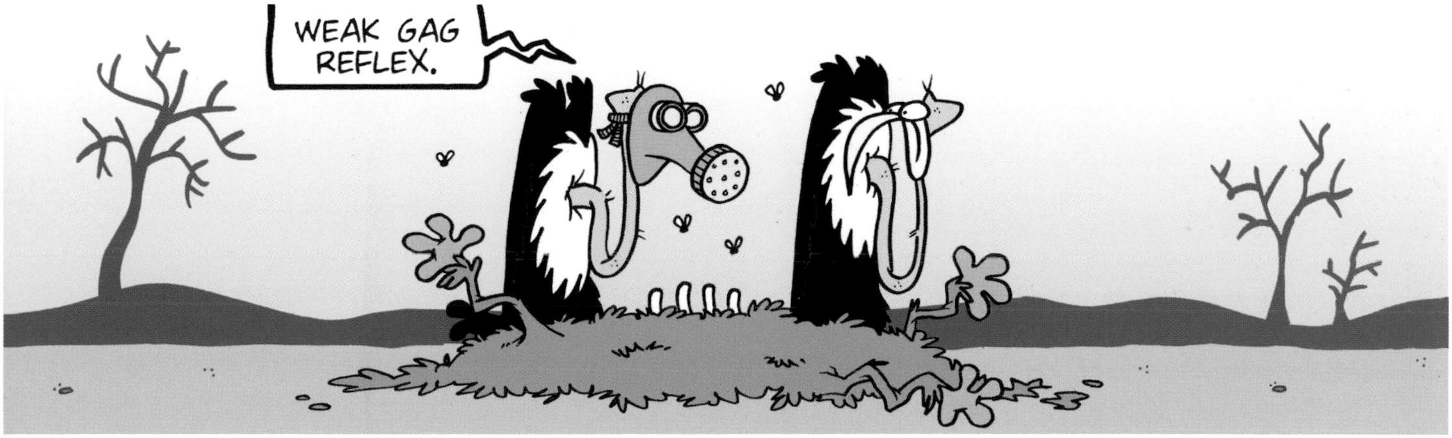
WEAK GAG REFLEX.

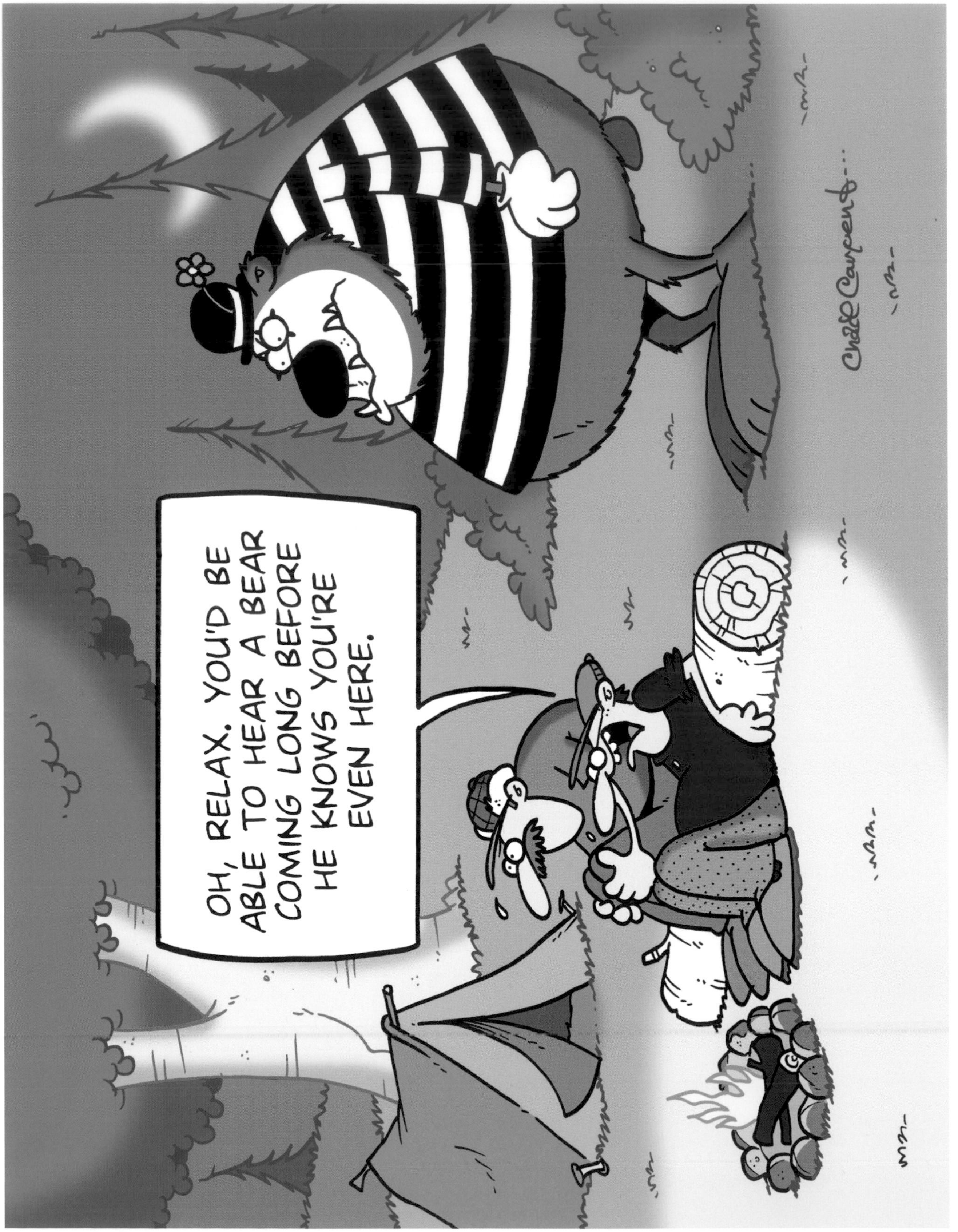
OH, RELAX. YOU'D BE ABLE TO HEAR A BEAR COMING LONG BEFORE HE KNOWS YOU'RE EVEN HERE.

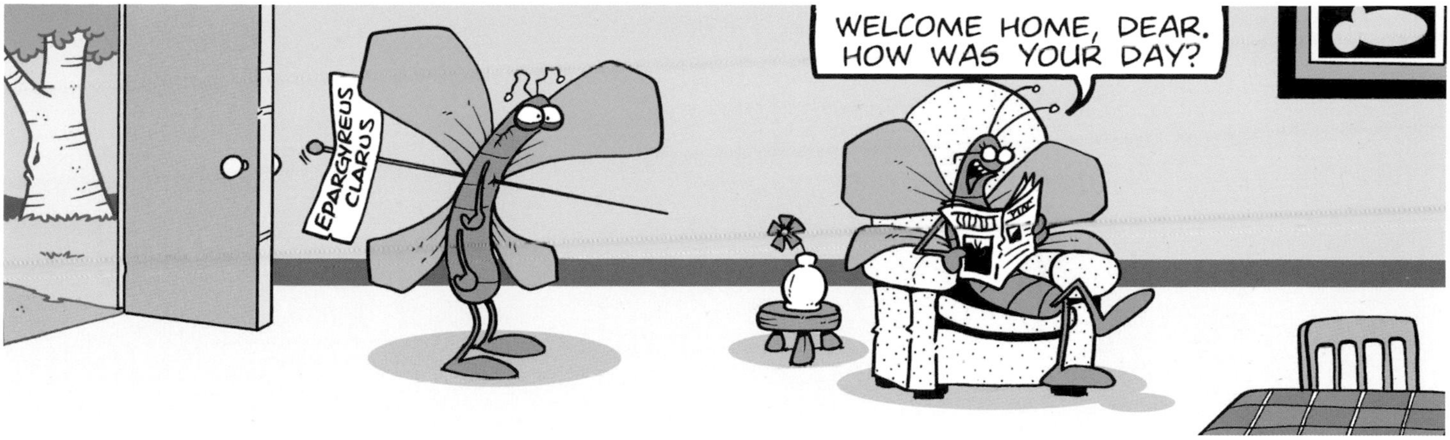
EPARGYREUS CLARUS
WELCOME HOME, DEAR. HOW WAS YOUR DAY?

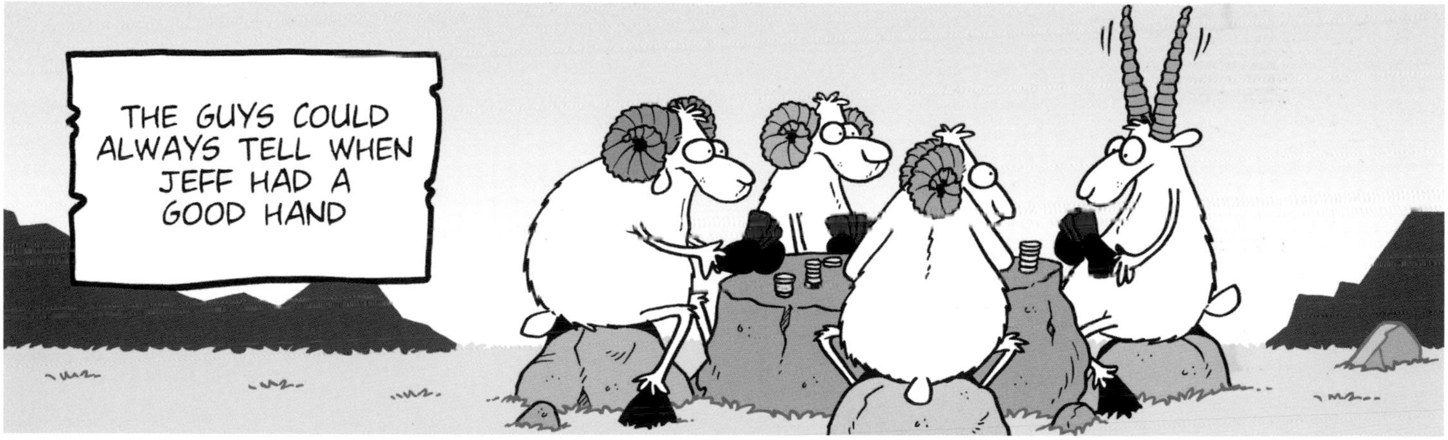
THE GUYS COULD ALWAYS TELL WHEN JEFF HAD A GOOD HAND

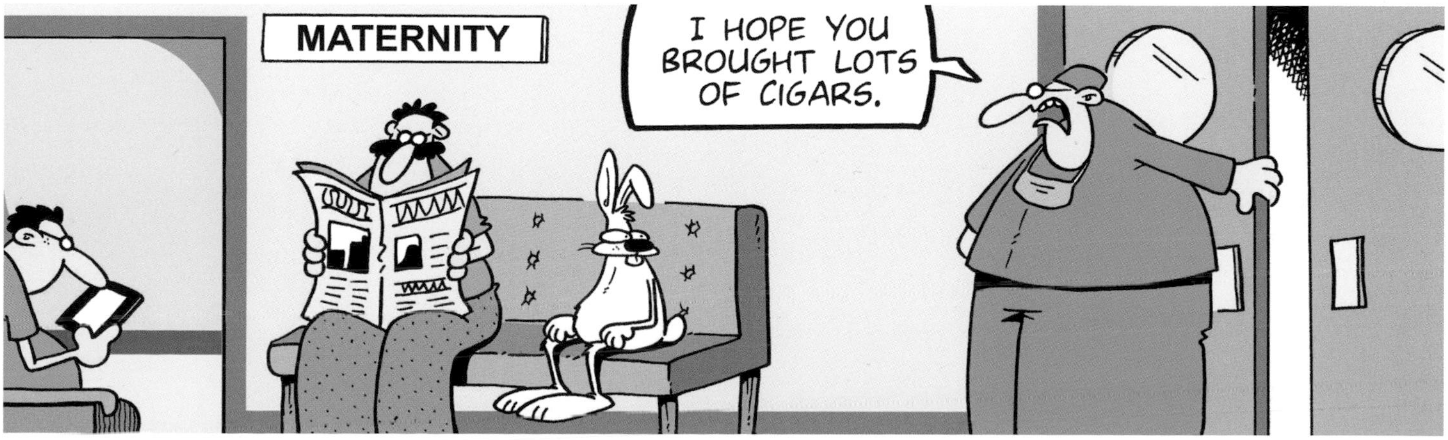
MATERNITY
I HOPE YOU BROUGHT LOTS OF CIGARS.

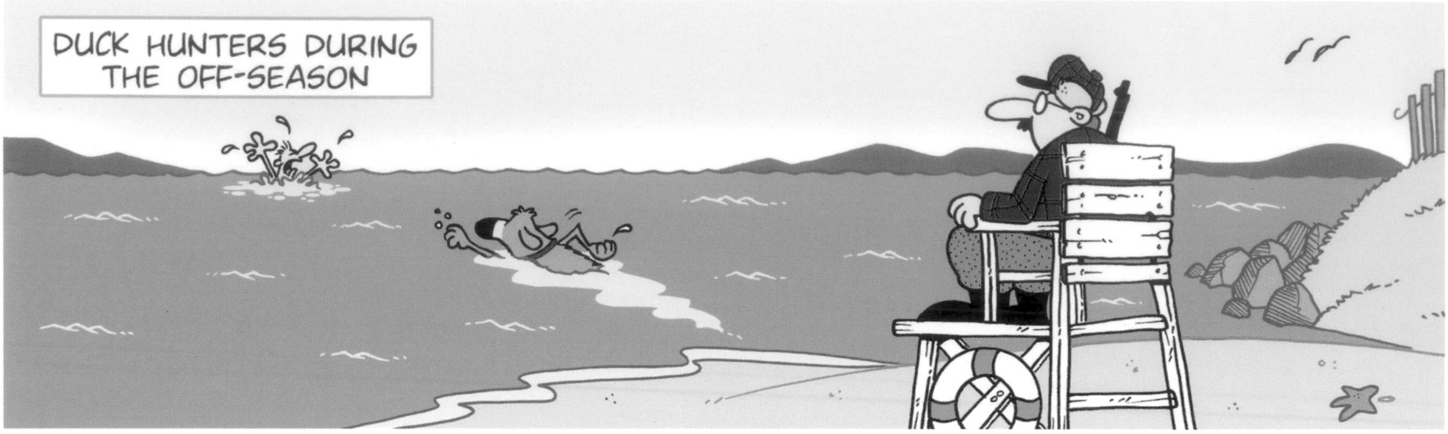
DUCK HUNTERS DURING THE OFF-SEASON

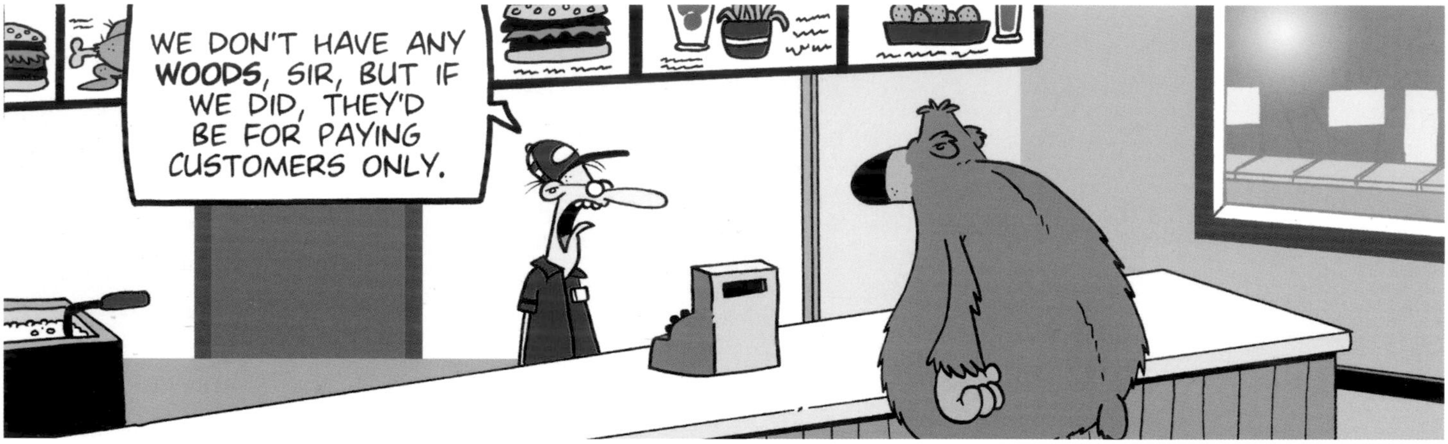
WE DON'T HAVE ANY **WOODS**, SIR, BUT IF WE DID, THEY'D BE FOR PAYING CUSTOMERS ONLY.

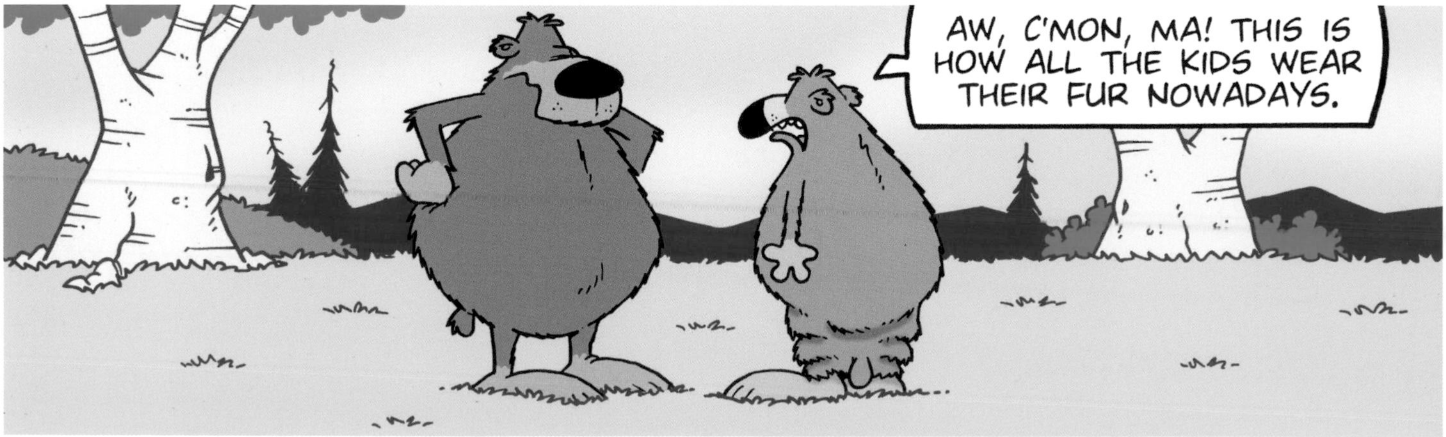
AW, C'MON, MA! THIS IS HOW ALL THE KIDS WEAR THEIR FUR NOWADAYS.

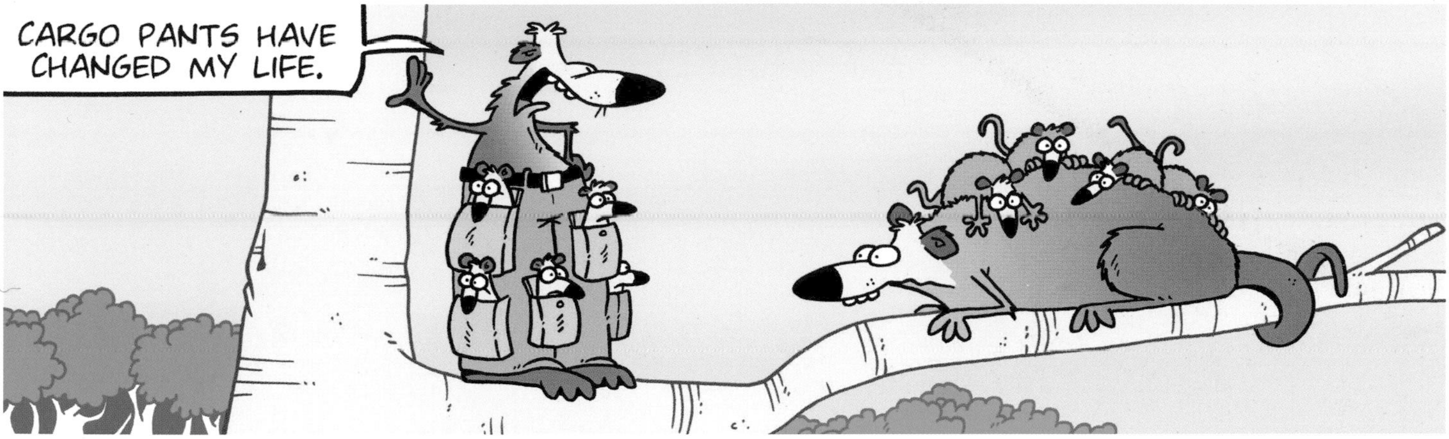
CARGO PANTS HAVE CHANGED MY LIFE.

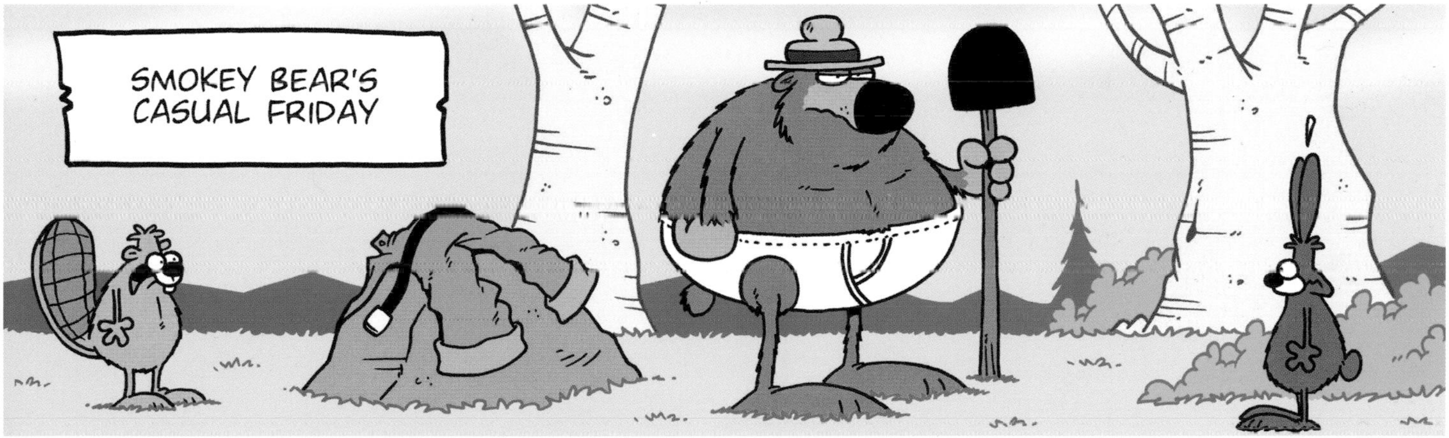
SMOKEY BEAR'S CASUAL FRIDAY

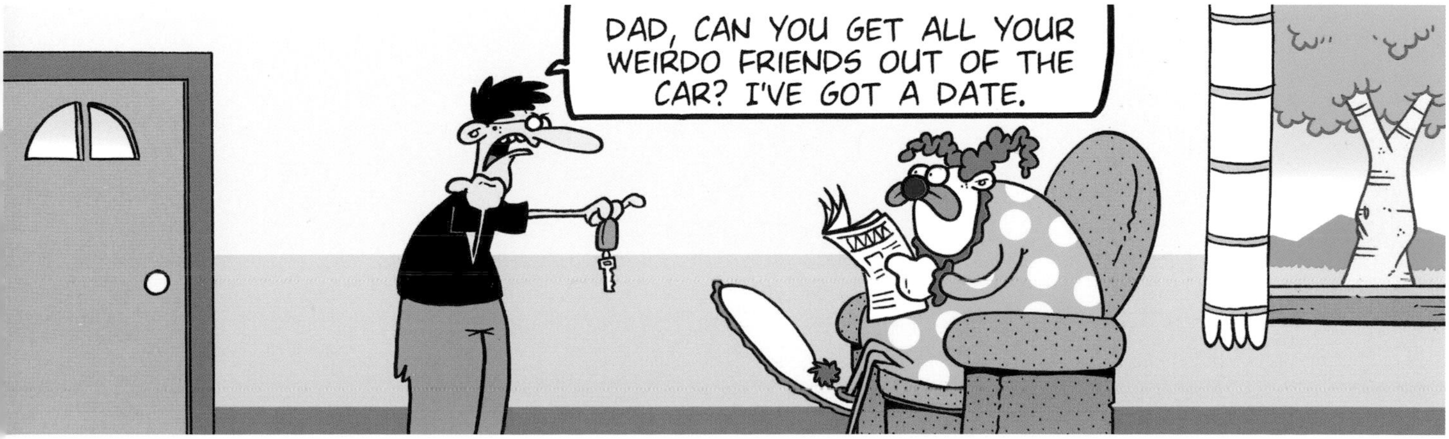
DAD, CAN YOU GET ALL YOUR WEIRDO FRIENDS OUT OF THE CAR? I'VE GOT A DATE.

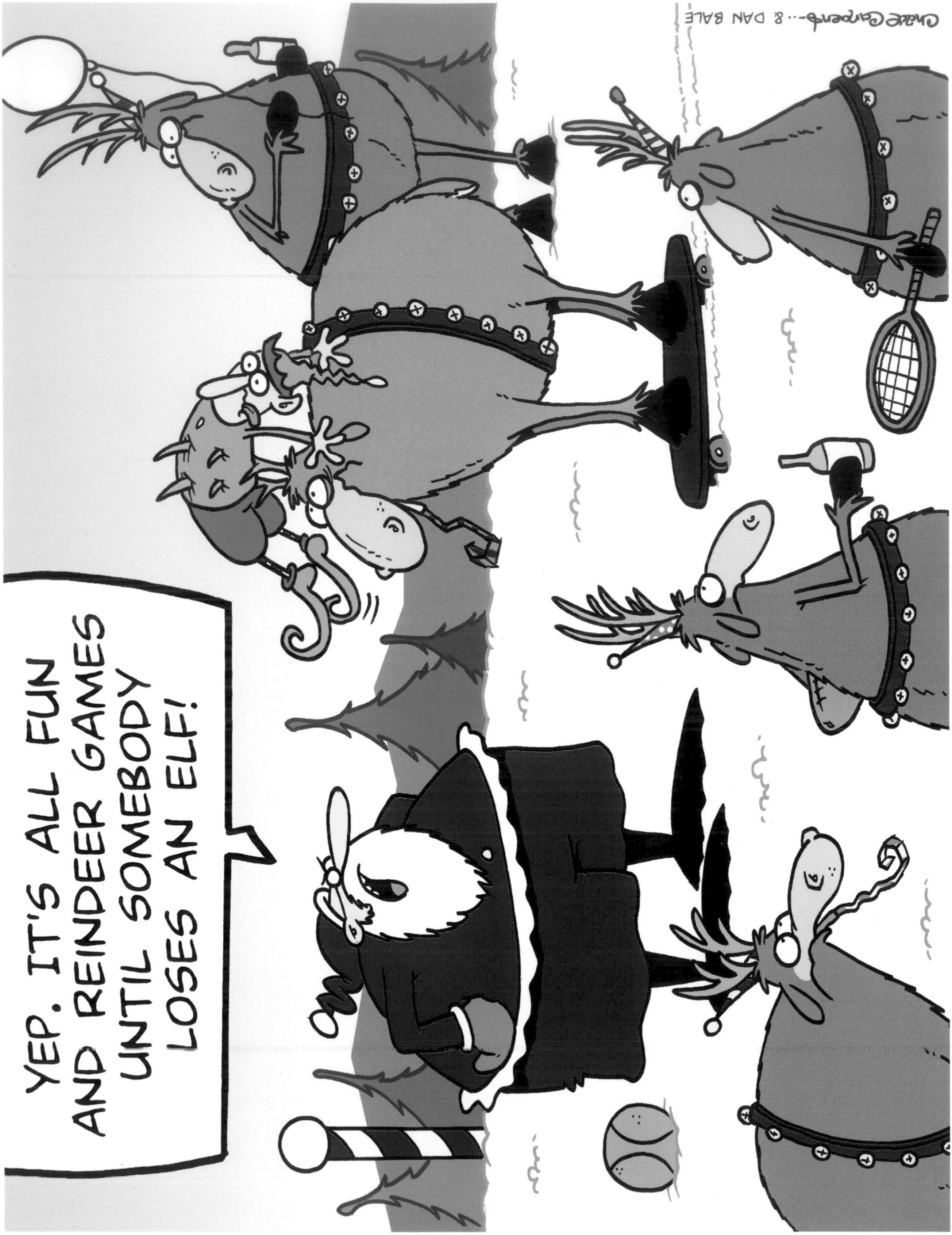
YEP. IT'S ALL FUN AND REINDEER GAMES UNTIL SOMEBODY LOSES AN ELF!

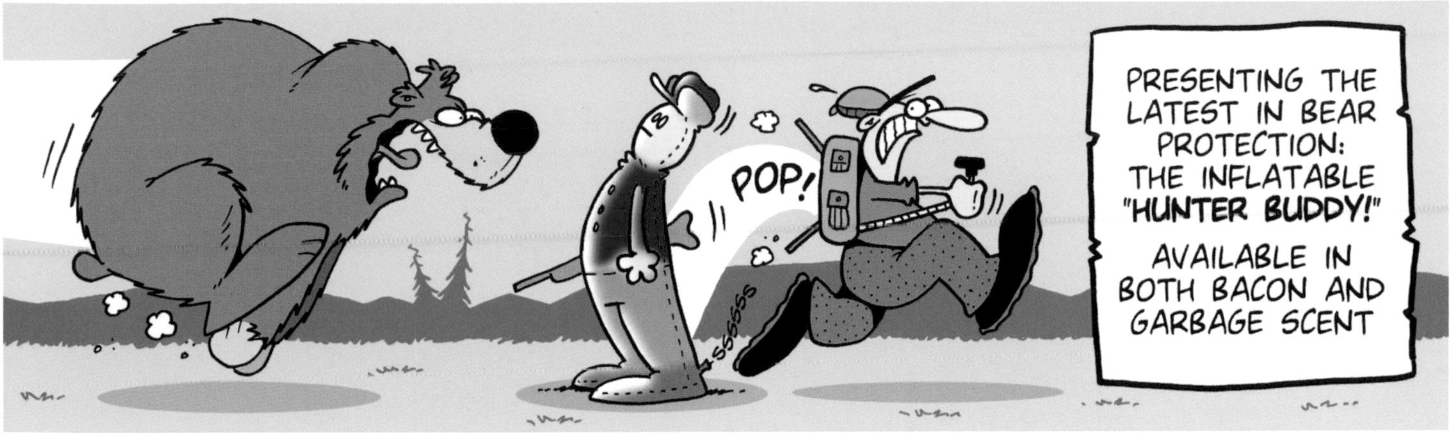
POP!
SSSSSS
PRESENTING THE LATEST IN BEAR PROTECTION: THE INFLATABLE "HUNTER BUDDY!"
AVAILABLE IN BOTH BACON AND GARBAGE SCENT

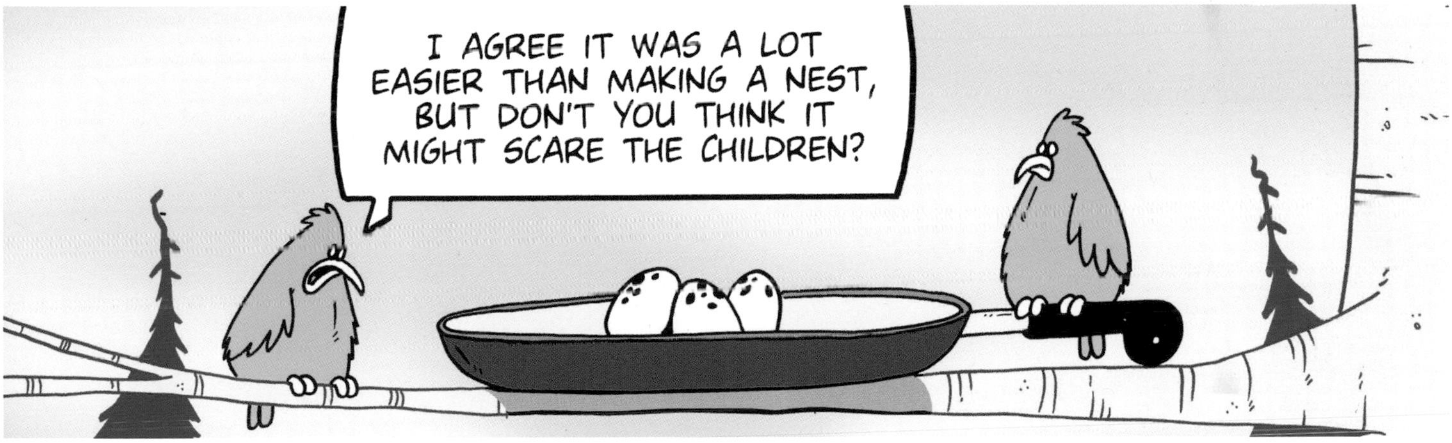
I AGREE IT WAS A LOT EASIER THAN MAKING A NEST, BUT DON'T YOU THINK IT MIGHT SCARE THE CHILDREN?

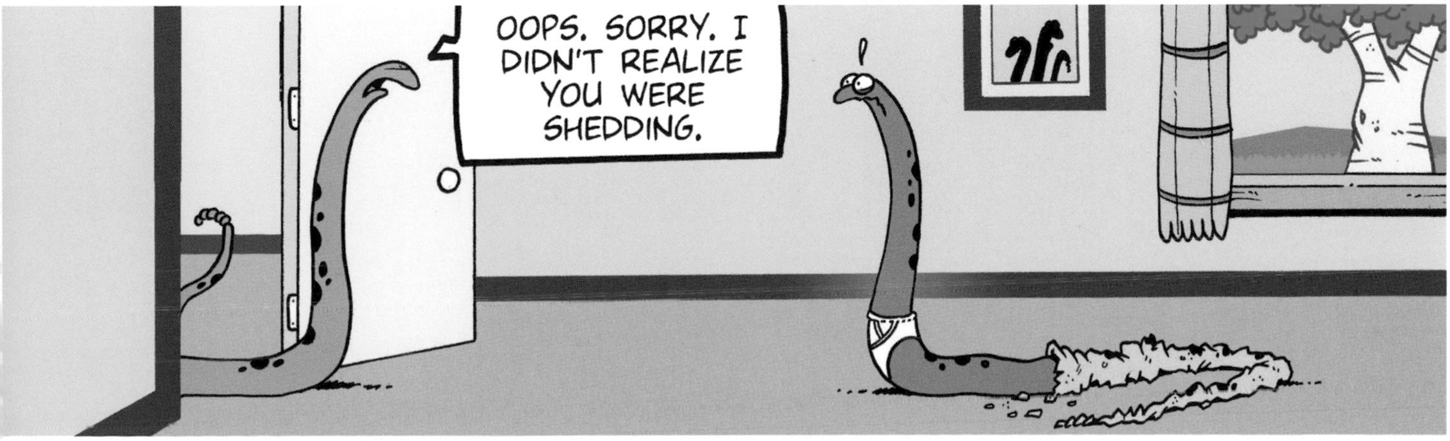
OOPS. SORRY. I DIDN'T REALIZE YOU WERE SHEDDING.

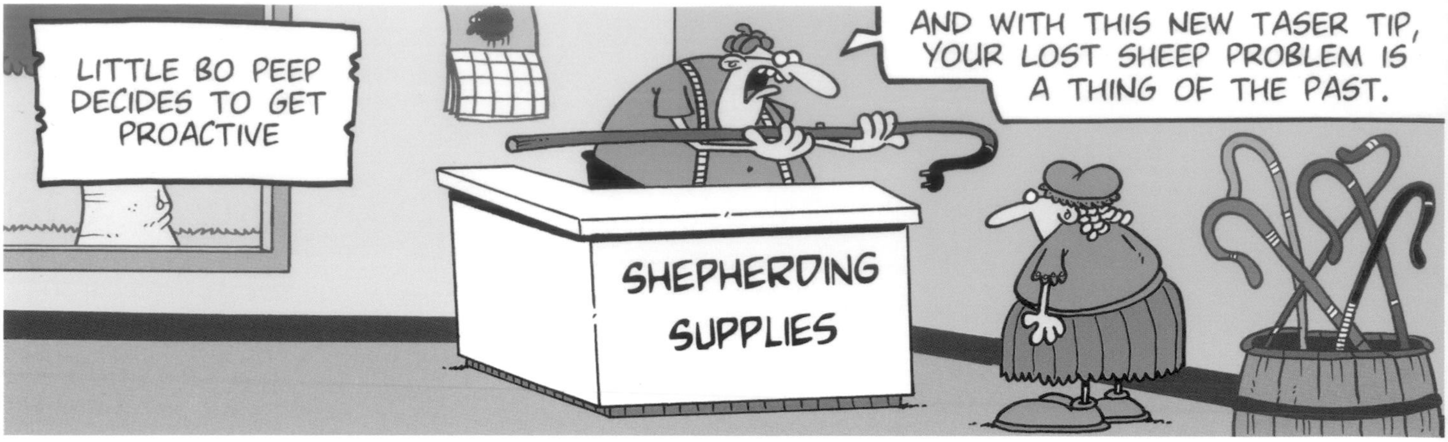
LITTLE BO PEEP DECIDES TO GET PROACTIVE
AND WITH THIS NEW TASER TIP, YOUR LOST SHEEP PROBLEM IS A THING OF THE PAST.
SHEPHERDING SUPPLIES

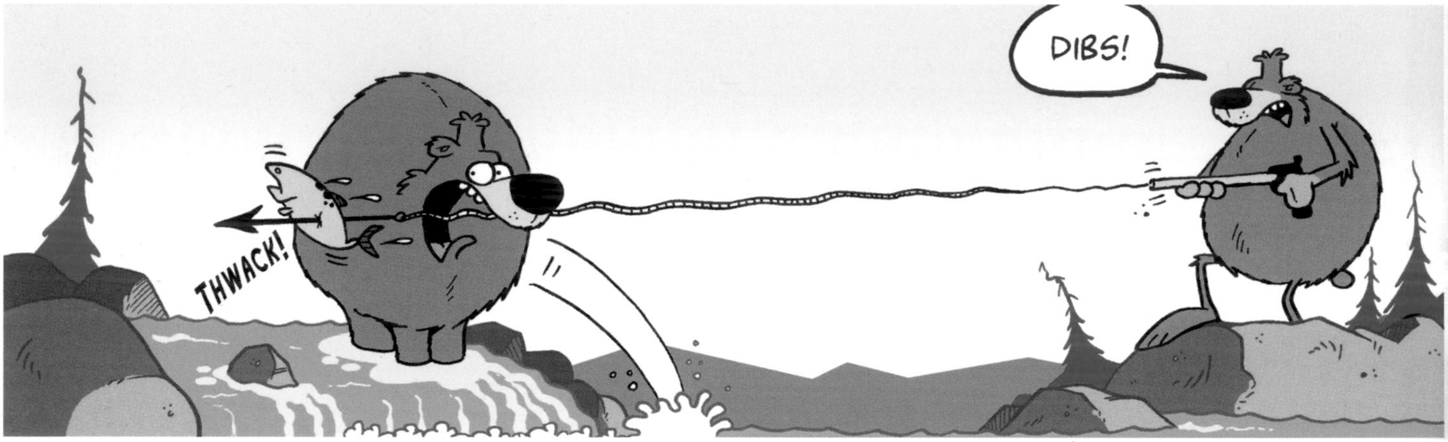
DIBS!
THWACK!

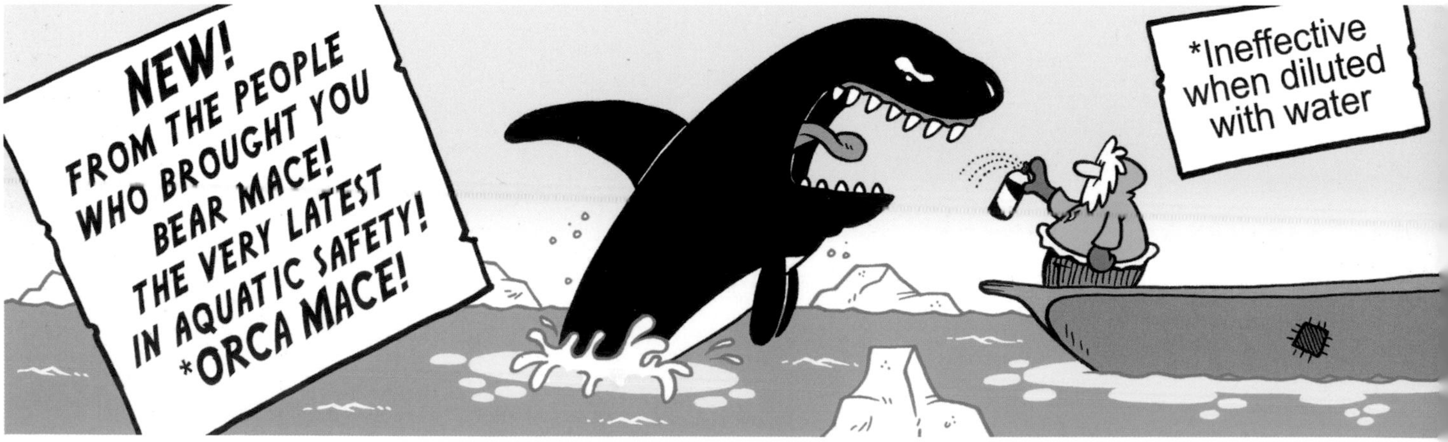
NEW! FROM THE PEOPLE WHO BROUGHT YOU BEAR MACE! THE VERY LATEST IN AQUATIC SAFETY! *ORCA MACE!
*Ineffective when diluted with water

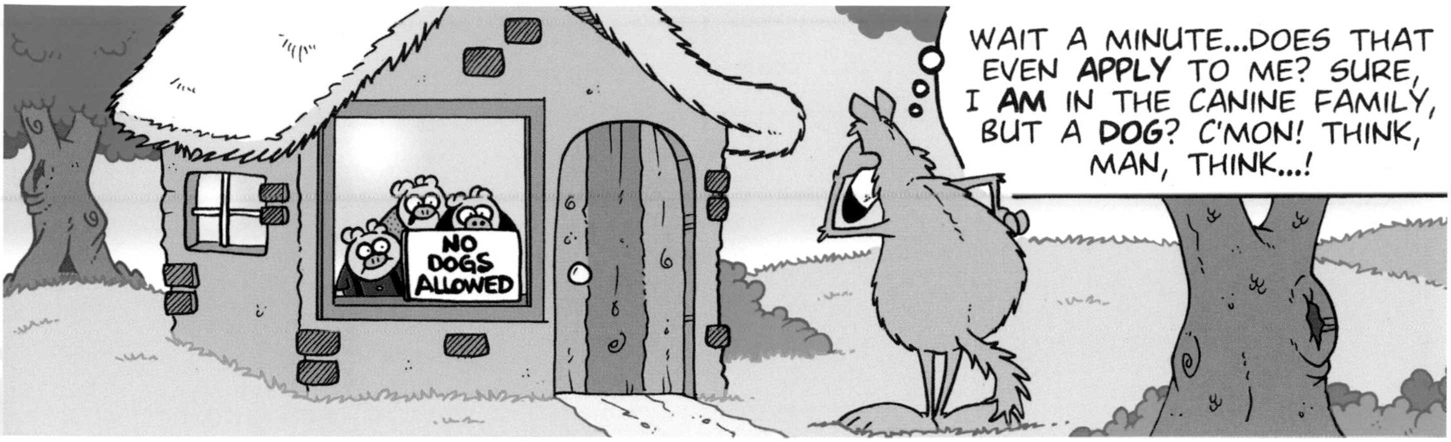
NO DOGS ALLOWED
WAIT A MINUTE...DOES THAT EVEN APPLY TO ME? SURE, I AM IN THE CANINE FAMILY, BUT A DOG? C'MON! THINK, MAN, THINK...!

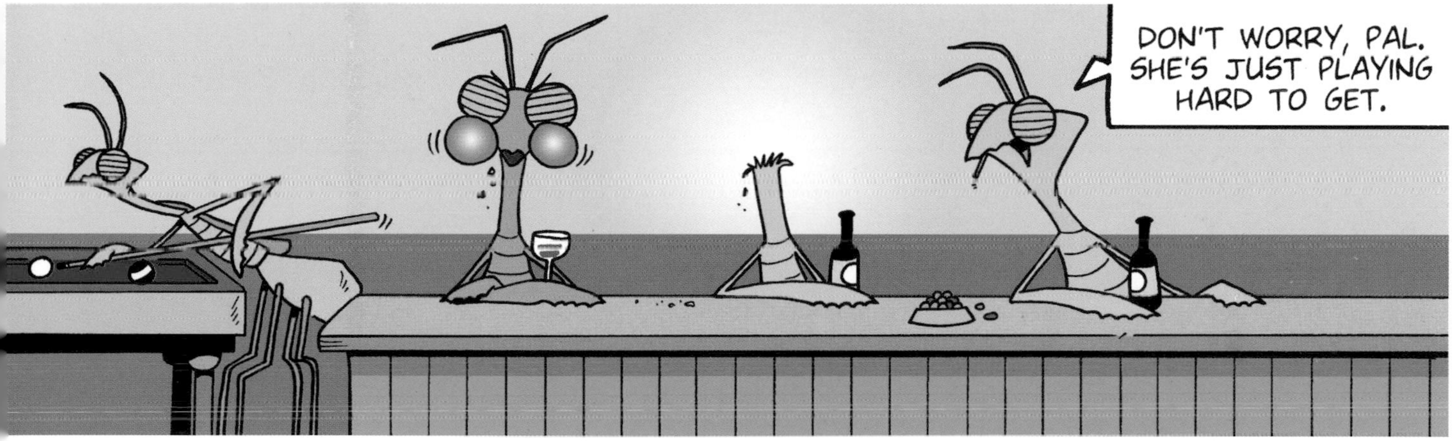
DON'T WORRY, PAL. SHE'S JUST PLAYING HARD TO GET.

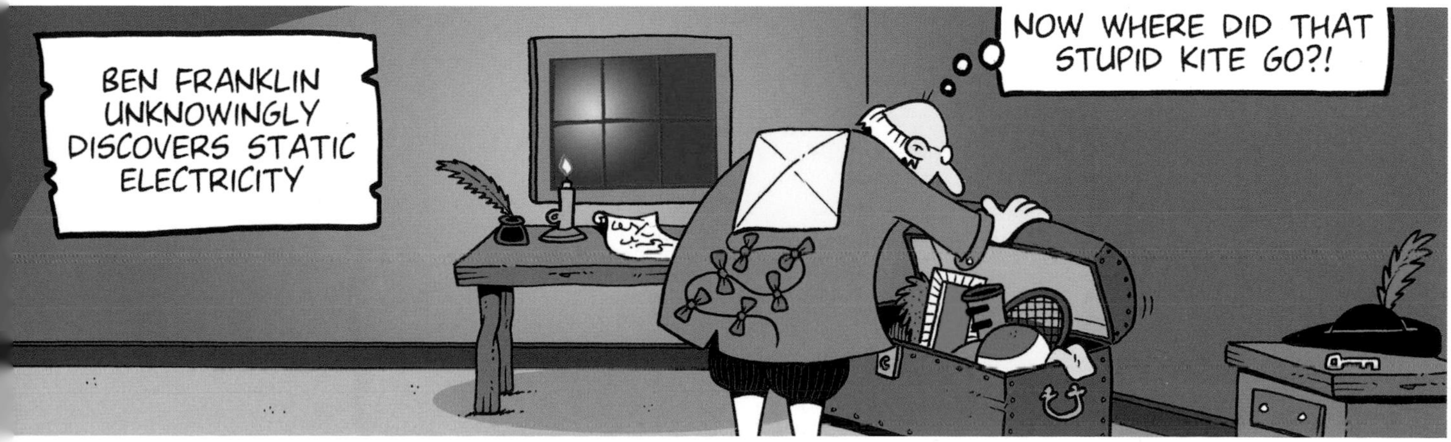
BEN FRANKLIN UNKNOWINGLY DISCOVERS STATIC ELECTRICITY
NOW WHERE DID THAT STUPID KITE GO?!

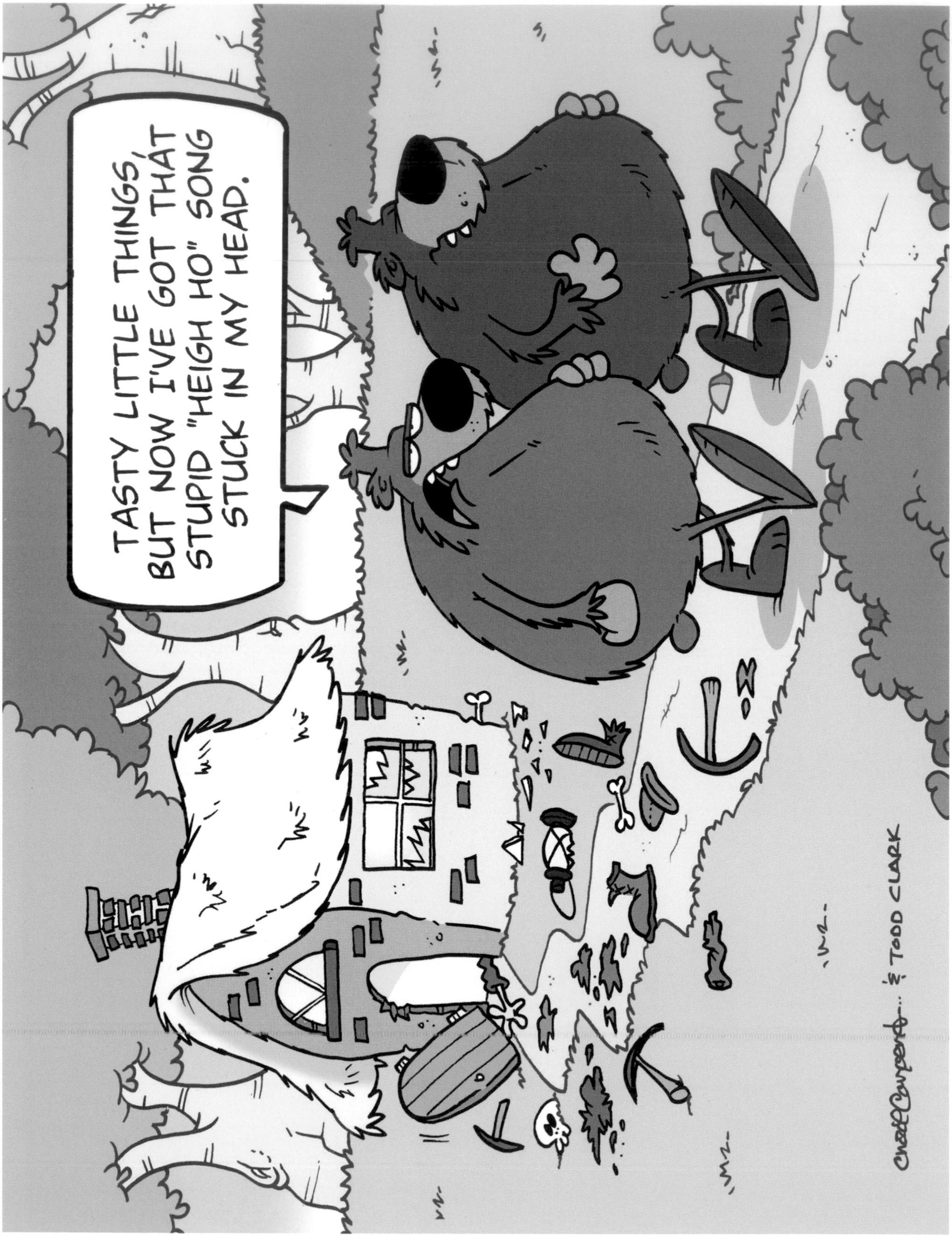
TASTY LITTLE THINGS, BUT NOW I'VE GOT THAT STUPID "HEIGH HO" SONG STUCK IN MY HEAD.
TODD CLARK

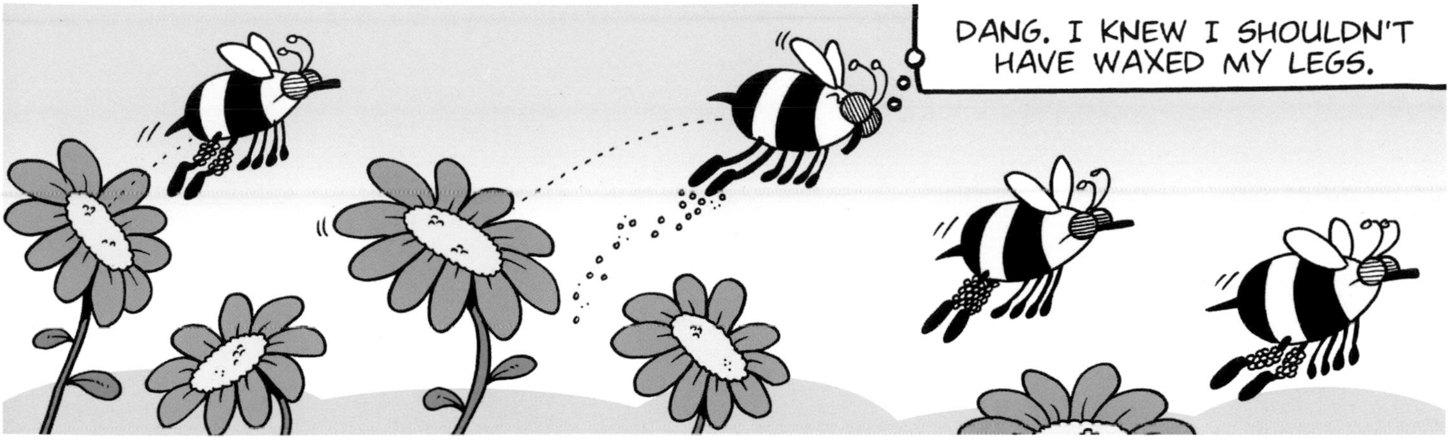
DANG. I KNEW I SHOULDN'T HAVE WAXED MY LEGS.

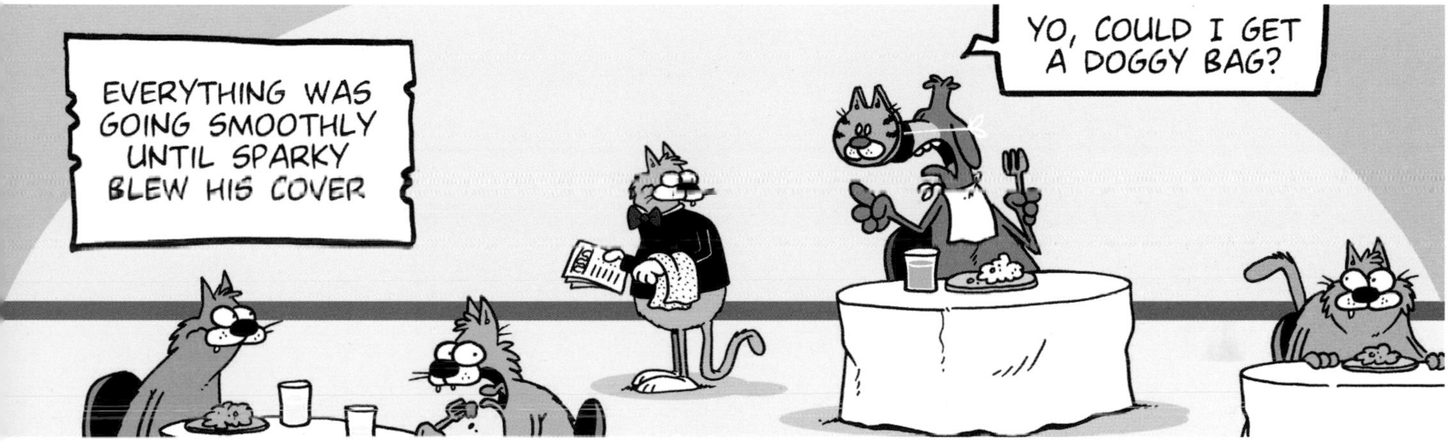
EVERYTHING WAS GOING SMOOTHLY UNTIL SPARKY BLEW HIS COVER
YO, COULD I GET A DOGGY BAG?

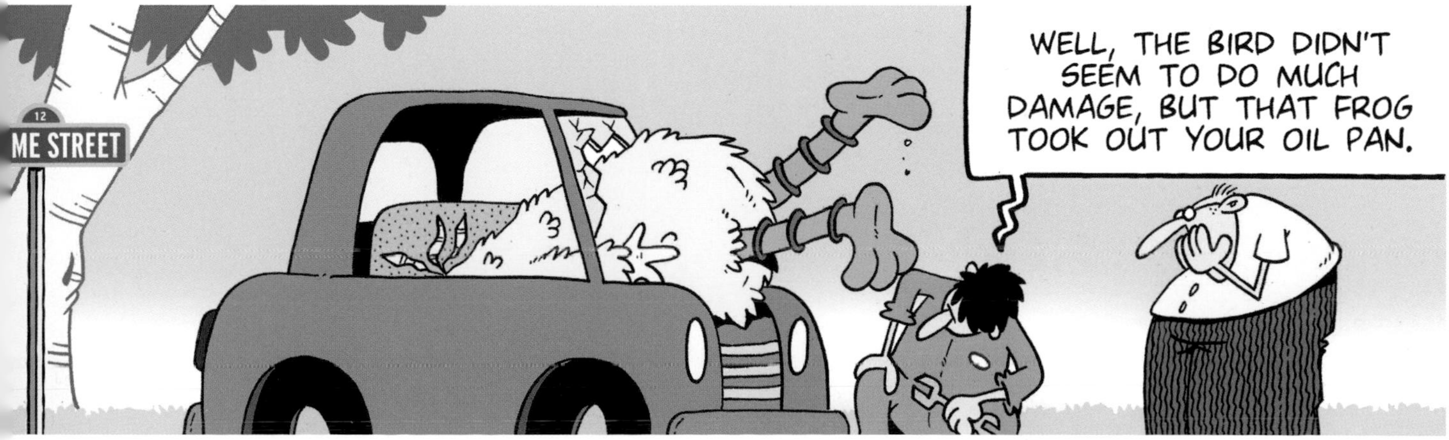
ME STREET
WELL, THE BIRD DIDN'T SEEM TO DO MUCH DAMAGE, BUT THAT FROG TOOK OUT YOUR OIL PAN.

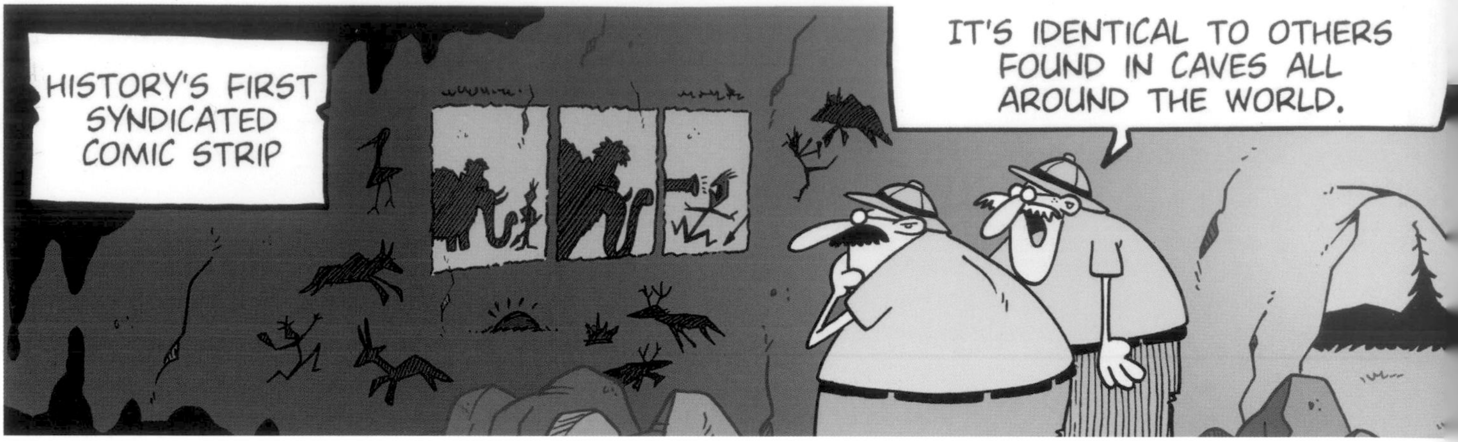
HISTORY'S FIRST SYNDICATED COMIC STRIP
IT'S IDENTICAL TO OTHERS FOUND IN CAVES ALL AROUND THE WORLD.

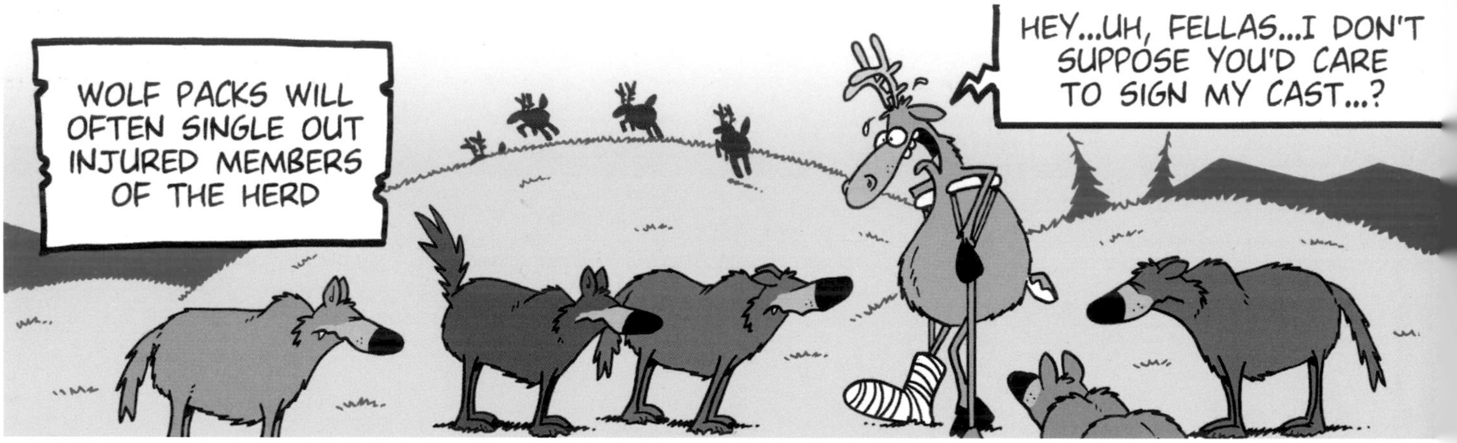
WOLF PACKS WILL OFTEN SINGLE OUT INJURED MEMBERS OF THE HERD
HEY...UH, FELLAS...I DON'T SUPPOSE YOU'D CARE TO SIGN MY CAST...?

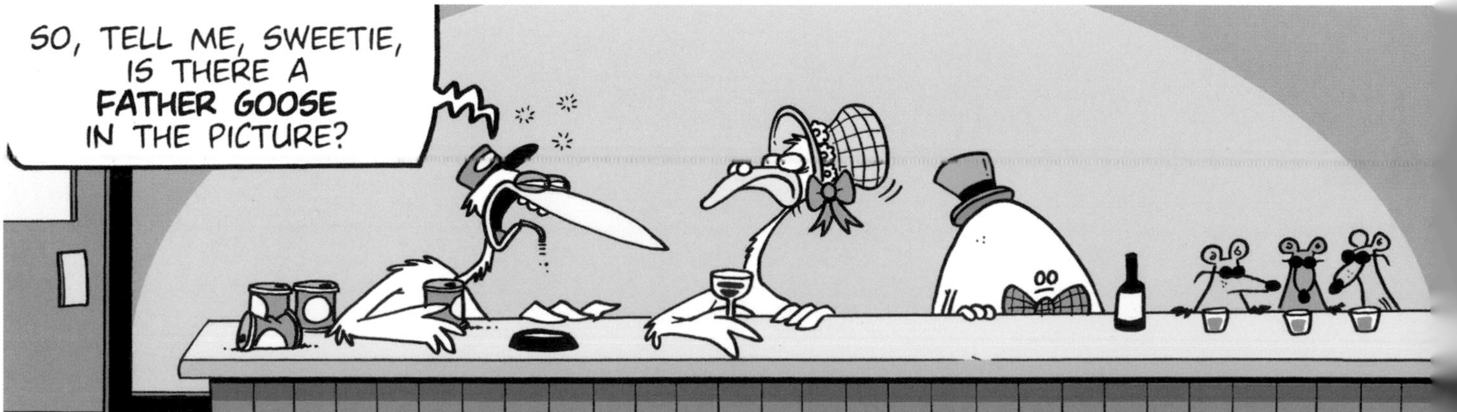
SO, TELL ME, SWEETIE, IS THERE A FATHER GOOSE IN THE PICTURE?

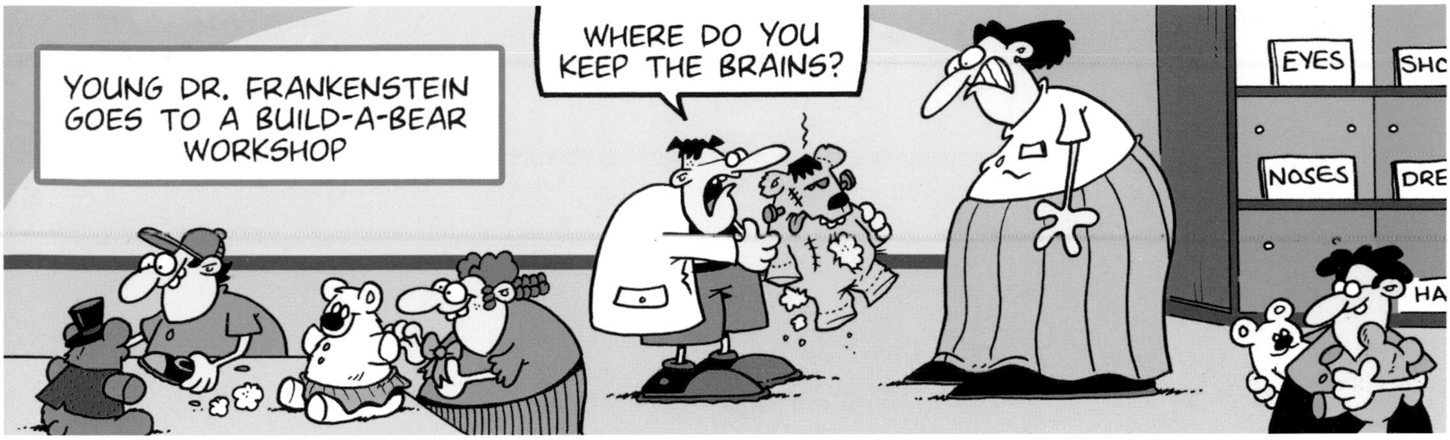
YOUNG DR. FRANKENSTEIN GOES TO A BUILD-A-BEAR WORKSHOP
WHERE DO YOU KEEP THE BRAINS?
EYES
NOSES

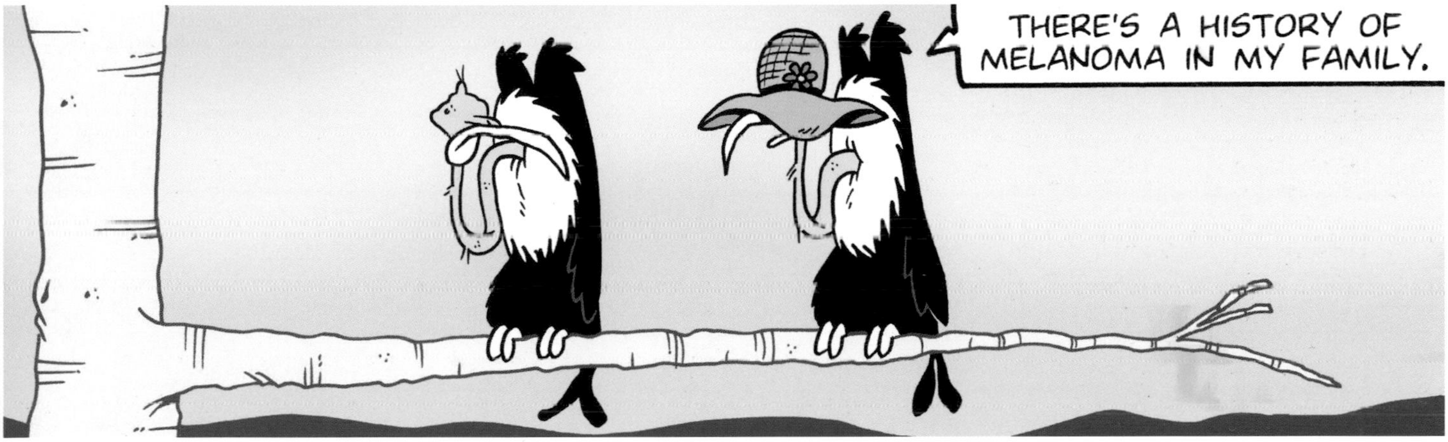
THERE'S A HISTORY OF MELANOMA IN MY FAMILY.

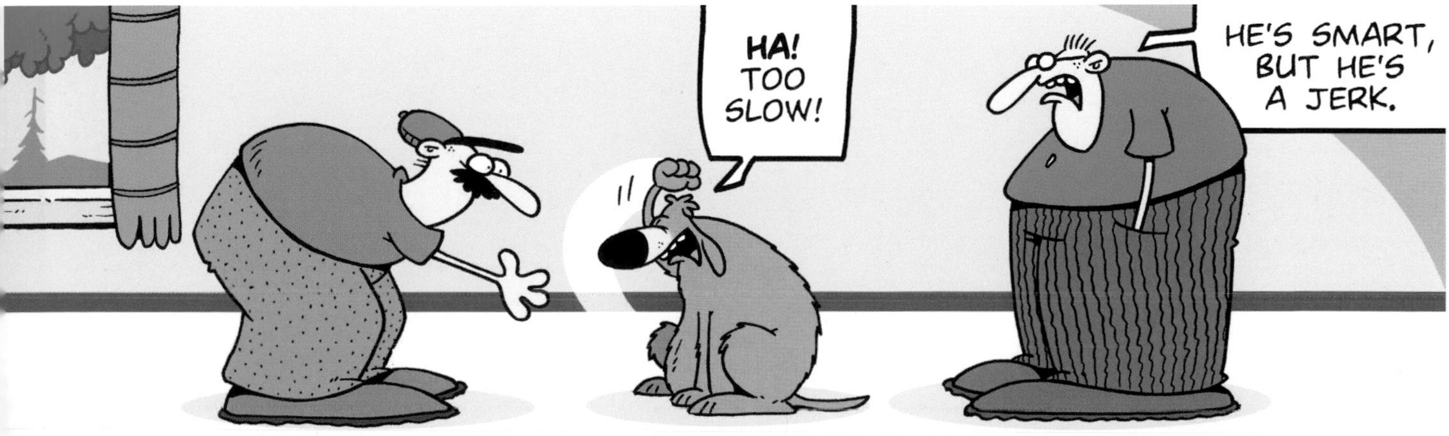
HA! TOO SLOW!
HE'S SMART, BUT HE'S A JERK.

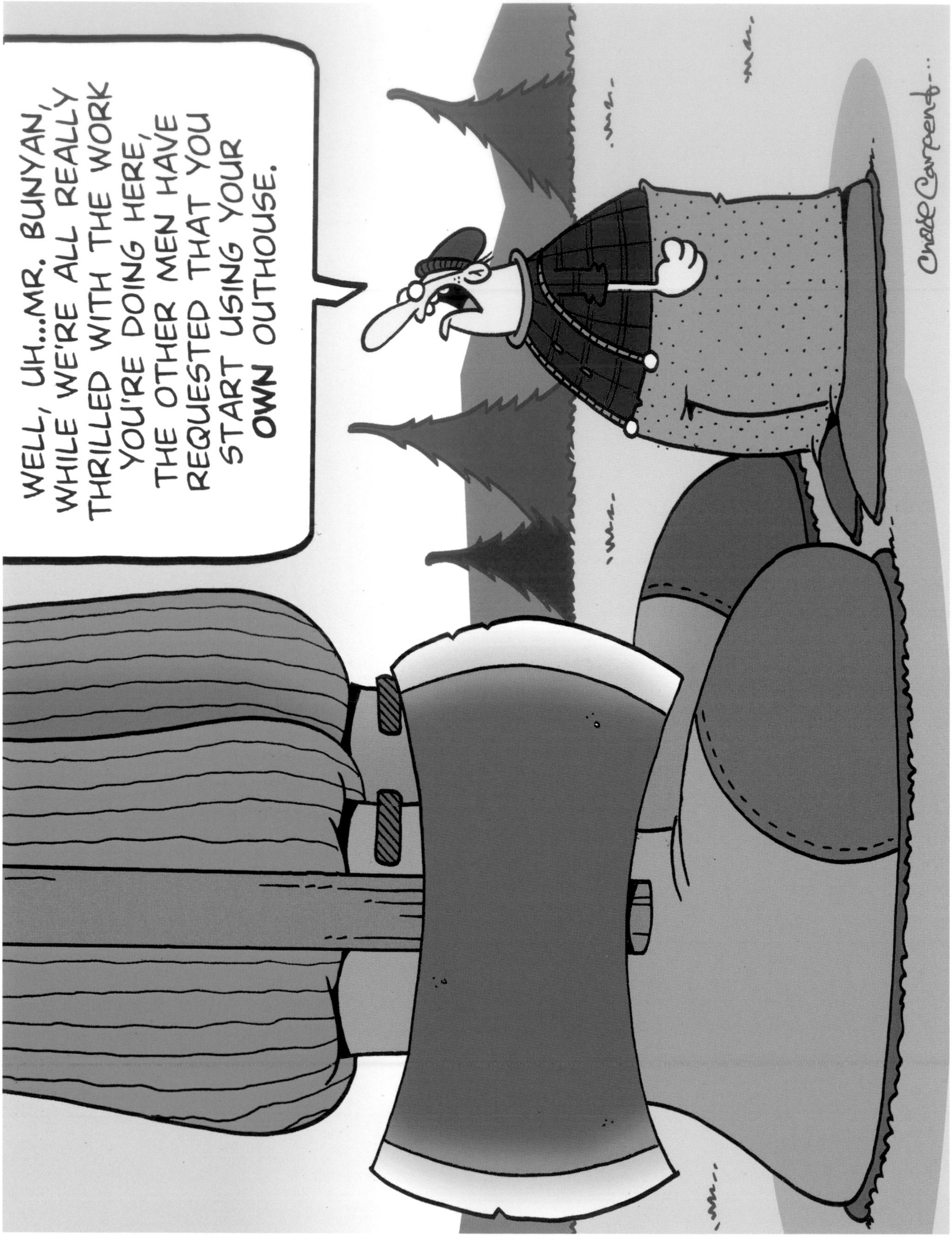
WELL, UH...MR. BUNYAN, WHILE WE'RE ALL REALLY THRILLED WITH THE WORK YOU'RE DOING HERE, THE OTHER MEN HAVE REQUESTED THAT YOU START USING YOUR **OWN** OUTHOUSE.
Chad Carpenter

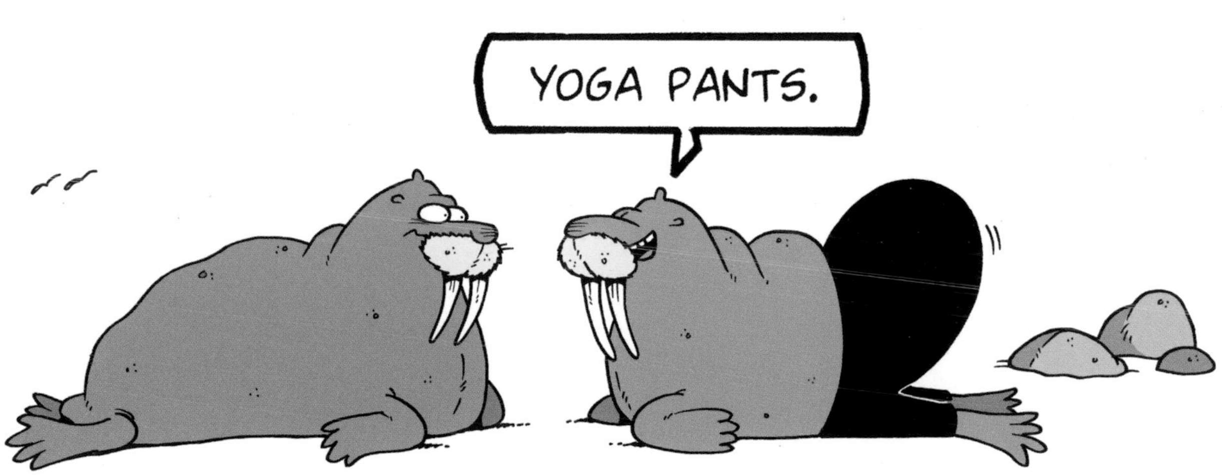
YOGA PANTS.

This space for rent.